P9-BBQ-965

INTERNATIONAL COLLEGE
LIBRARY – FT. MYERS
DEMCO

# FREEDOM
## IN THE FAMILY

# FREEDOM IN THE FAMILY

## A Mother-Daughter Memoir of the Fight for Civil Rights

TANANARIVE DUE
AND
PATRICIA STEPHENS DUE

ONE WORLD
Ballantine Books
New York

A One World Book
Published by The Ballantine Publishing Group



Grateful acknowledgment is made to the following for permission to reprint previously published material:
*GRM Associates, Inc.*: "Incident" from *Color* by Countee Cullen. Copyright © 1925 by Harper & Brothers; copyright renewed 1953 by Ida M. Cullen. Reprinted by permission of GRM Associates, Inc., Agents for the Estate of Ida M. Cullen.
*Alfred A. Knopf, a division of Random House, Inc.*: excerpt from "Merry Go Round" from *The Collected Poems of Langston Hughes* by Langston Hughes, copyright © 1994 by The Estate of Langston Hughes. Used by permission of Alfred A. Knopf, a division of Random House, Inc.



www.ballantinebooks.com/one/

The Cataloging-in-Publication Data for this title is available from the Library of Congress.

ISBN 0-345-44733-6

Book Design by Susan Turner

Manufactured in the United States of America

First Edition: January 2003

10 9 8 7 6 5 4 3 2 1

# Dedication

To Mother and Daddy Marion, without whom this story would never have been.

Not all warriors fight on foreign soil. This book is also dedicated to the foot soldiers who told us their stories, but who died before this book was published:

*George Calvin Bess II*
*Judy Benninger Brown*
*Rev. Witt Campbell*
*Mary Ola Gaines*
*Marion M. Hamilton*
*Lottie Sears Houston*
*Kwame Turé (Stokely Carmichael)*
*Daisy O. Young*
*Shirley Zoloth*

And to the foot soldiers who died before they could tell us their stories:

*Neal Adams*
*Nancy Adams*
*Rev. Herbert Alexander*
*Susan Ausley*
*George Calvin Bess III*
*Father David Brooks*
*Gwendolyn Sawyer Cherry*
*James Farmer*
*Father Theodore Gibson*
*Rev. R. N. Goodon*
*Rev. Edward Graham*
*Grattan E. Graves Jr.*
*Richard Haley*
*James Harmeling*
*Dr. William Howard*
*Rev. James Hudson*
*Odell Johns*
*Steve Jones*
*William Larkins*
*George Lewis II*
*William Miles*
*James Parrott*
*Carrie Patterson*
*Jackie Robinson*
*James Shaw*
*Earl Shinnhoster*
*Tobias Simon*
*Rev. Charles Kenzie Steele*
*Rev. Charles Kenzie Steele Jr.*
*Lois Steele*
*Leroy Thompson*
*Probyn Thompson*
*James Van Matre*

And to those foot soldiers whose names are not included, but who also have stories to be told. Stories can live forever, but storytellers do not. Ask, and they will tell. But ask soon.

# FREEDOM
## IN THE FAMILY

# One

# Patricia Stephens Due

**"The American Negro must remake his past in order to make his future."**
***—Arthur A. Schomburg***

There are so many misconceptions today about the civil rights movement. People think blacks were a unified front in the "old days," with everyone marching and holding hands. Well, that's not true. If only it had been that easy! Just like today, in cities and towns across the South, there were always a select few who lit the fires and went to the meetings—and, eventually, others followed. Dr. Martin Luther King wasn't the only one lighting the fires. He had a lot of influence, but he was only one man. It concerns me when I hear people say *If only we had Martin Luther King today,* as if we are helpless without him.

I wish we had Dr. King today, too. But Dr. King did not create the Movement. There were hundreds and thousands of ordinary people who did extraordinary things. Daily heroism went unrewarded and unrecorded. Some heroes were children, and some were retired. They were maids, ministers, students, teachers, housewives.

And they suffered! Their families suffered. Their jobs suffered. I know people who never recovered from the Movement. I know people who today cannot bring themselves to talk about what happened to them during that era. I know people who had to spend time in mental institutions. I knew people who committed suicide. I knew people who died. And they were all ordinary people.

I remember sitting on a textbook committee for schoolchildren in Miami–Dade County a few years ago, and when I asked why the social studies books under consideration mentioned nothing about Tallahassee's civil rights struggle, school officials tried to tell me that nothing of note had happened in Florida. "I was *there!*" I protested, but they looked at me as if I were speaking a foreign language. A living witness didn't matter to them. Without written documentation, I was told, the forty-nine days my sister and I spent in jail, the tear gas that burned my eyes, and the people I knew could not be included. As if we had never existed.

There's a saying I believe in: *History belongs to those who write it.*

I have to write ours.

Two

# Tananarive Due

**"I could not be sure whether for the rest of my life**
**I would be able to tell when it was really my mother**
**or when it was her shadow**
**standing between me and the rest of the world."**
***—Jamaica Kincaid***

By the time I was thirteen or fourteen, I was already taller than my mother, but my height was irrelevant to the way I saw our proportions. She might be short physically, but she seemed like a giant. All children believe their parents are larger than life, but that feeling was much more pronounced for me and my two sisters because of the things our mother and father had done. They were civil rights activists. To us, that meant our lives were filled with opportunities no previous generation of blacks who lived in the South had ever known. *Ever.*

In our home—where only my father could claim a reliable singing voice, a silky, soothing baritone—freedom songs were every bit as much of the family sing-along repertoire as nursery songs. In fact, we knew the choruses and refrains of 1960s standards like "This Little Light of Freedom," "We Shall Overcome," and "Oh, Freedom" better than we knew most Christmas carols. Freedom songs were always the background music of long car trips and annual family celebrations of Dr. Martin Luther King Jr.'s birthday. I can still hear our voices blending together, with my mother's deep, rolling timbre underneath: *And before I'll be a slave . . . I'll be buried in my grave . . . and go home to my Lord . . . and be free.*

And, of course, we knew the stories. Like the children of refugees, the children of immigrants, the children of veterans—the children of any survivors who are willing to speak of what they have seen and experienced—my sisters and I were raised on stories at our parents' knees. We knew that my mother wore dark glasses even indoors and that her eyes had never been right since she was teargassed during a peaceful march in

1960. We knew that she and her sister were part of the student sit-in movement's landmark first "jail-in," where they spent forty-nine days in jail rather than pay their bail for the "crime" of sitting at a Woolworth lunch counter. We knew that my father once worked with Dr. Martin Luther King Jr. as a civil rights attorney in St. Augustine, Florida, where Dr. King and hundreds of protestors were arrested.

That was how we learned who our parents were and, by extension, who *we* were. My parents were more than parents to me, they were living monuments. As far as we were concerned, they had helped change the world.

When my parents were concerned about an issue—and they were *always* concerned about an issue—their telephone calls were returned by everyone from the mayor to then–Dade State Attorney Janet Reno to the school superintendent to legislators. Once, when my mother was upset after black candidates had been passed over in the search for a replacement for a school board member, she put in a call to the state capital and left a message for the governor's office. That same afternoon, I answered the telephone to hear a man's voice: "Hi, is Patricia Due there? This is Governor Bob Graham."

He called right away. The governor!

But the excitement was often offset by the price. Once, soon after a Southern federal judge had been killed with a letter bomb, the FBI called my father. The agent told Dad that because of his activism, and particularly his role representing black parents in a long-lasting federal desegregation suit against Miami–Dade County schools, the FBI feared he might be a target for the bomber, a homegrown terrorist. *Please,* the agent said, *be careful about opening unfamiliar mail—just in case.*

The past was not yet past. Not quite.

And yet, it seems that so few people remember. So few of the storytellers remain.

That point became all the more poignant to me when I visited the Holocaust Memorial on Miami Beach one afternoon in the summer of 1996, soon after I had taken a long-awaited leave of absence from my job as a reporter at the *Miami Herald* to write and research this book.

The memorial is an arresting bronze monolith fashioned in the shape of one reaching, tattooed hand made up of myriad Holocaust victims struggling to climb up from its base. I walked past groups of schoolchildren gathered there, some with lighted candles, as they learned painful portions of their people's history the way I was being forced that summer to learn details about the more painful portions of mine. My path led to a group of boys younger than ten squatting to listen to tales from an old woman with a thick accent, a woman I knew right away must be a Holocaust survivor. I immediately recognized the fervor of a survivor's voice.

I have heard a similar fervor in my mother's voice many, many times.

The old woman was telling her story. She told the restless boys, who wore yarmulkes and baseball caps to cover their heads, about how naive she'd been when she'd first been taken to camp, how she hadn't been hungry and she'd thrown a piece of bread across a fence to feed another hungry man. "Don't do that," she was warned, because the time would come when she would learn that food was precious. She learned that soon enough, she said.

She spoke of being marched across the frozen ground for two weeks when the Russians got closer to their camp. She spoke of being surrounded by bodies of people who had died of disease. She spoke of how frightened everyone was every time they walked in lines at Auschwitz, because they were being led toward the crematorium, and how, when they passed it, one person and then the next would whisper down the line, "We have passed the place," so they would no longer have to be afraid—*that time.*

She talked on, even when the children, distracted, squirmed and turned away. She talked on, despite the midafternoon Miami heat, a perspiration-making heat in the 90s that made all of us long to go inside somewhere cool. She talked on.

I watched her show the children the green-colored tattoo on her arm, and for the first time she had the children's undivided interest as they crowded around her for a closer look. "You see?" said the man leading the boys' group, hoping to seize their interest, to make a lasting impression. "To the Nazis, you weren't human. To the Nazis, you were an animal, so they put a tattoo on you to identify you, like an animal."

Anything to help the children understand. To help them remember.

*She is such an old woman,* I thought. *Soon, she will be gone, and all of her stories will go with her.* I'd had the same thought many times while my mother and I researched the civil rights movement, going through the names of activists she'd known in the 1960s, noting who had already died, and who was dying, their stories vanishing.

I was very young when I read *The Diary of Anne Frank,* and that book helped me understand the importance of simply telling a personal story.

Because of her diary, Anne Frank was a real person, not a nameless statistic, and her plight was real. Her simple diary is a reminder of a time in history no one wants to repeat. Her diary—and other remarkable stories from Holocaust literature, written by witnesses and survivors—gives voice to those who suffered.

I had tears in my eyes as I heard the woman's stories, fixing my gaze on the hollow-eyed, anguished faces and the gaunt, bony figures in the memorial's sculpture. But I didn't see any tears in the children's eyes that day.

I wondered: Did those children believe that events from sixty years ago do not touch them? Certainly, black children don't remember a time when they could be lynched in the American South for learning to read, or for whistling at a white woman. Or how, forty years ago, children their own age and people like my parents were forced to risk their lives so the United States Constitution could live up to its own ideals. How they had to fight for even the simplest dignities. How they lived in times when injustice was not only rampant, but it was proud of itself. It was proclaimed on signs. It was upheld in courts.

Is it all just too awesome, too remote, for children to imagine?

I felt deeply inspired by the Auschwitz survivor at the memorial that day, but as I drove away, a nagging question came to me: Where are *our* storytellers? How many of *us* are standing in the hot sun to make sure the children of strangers—and even our own—will never, ever forget?

# Three

# Patricia Stephens Due

**"A man's character always takes its hue, more or less, from the form and color of things around him."**
***—Frederick Douglass***

I've been a serious person all my life, always the sensible and responsible one. I can't explain why I'm that way. It's just my personality. Biologically, I became a woman when I was only nine, when my menstrual period began early. Maybe that made me feel older than most other children. Sometimes it's a real burden, having to be the one who's toeing the line when others around me are carefree. Even when I was a child, the people close to me tended to rely on me, to expect me to be strong and self-sufficient. In the end, maybe I became what I was expected to be.

I like music so much that I have a CD player in almost every room of my house so I can listen to Roy Hamilton, B. B. King, Tina Turner, James Brown, Harry Belafonte, Al Green, Aretha Franklin, Beethoven, and others. I like to laugh and enjoy myself as much as anyone—but there's a switch in my head that won't allow me to ignore injustice when I see it. There are many times I've wished I could turn that switch off, but that's not the way it works. It's on. It always has been, and it always will be. I've learned to accept that.

I was born in 1939 to Lottie Mae Powell and Horace Walter Stephens, although I have very little memory of my parents being married. My father was a local entrepreneur who, I have been told, was running his own restaurant business even while he was in high school. At one time, Daddy was run out of town because many whites, as well as Negroes, frequented his nightclub, and the local white powers threatened him because they wouldn't tolerate "mixing." In addition to being a chef, he was also a talented tap dancer. My mother told me many times he was so accomplished that he no doubt would have been famous if he had been white. It's true there were famous Negro dancers in the 1920s and 1930s, but skin color was, of course, still an obstacle for most Negroes—as it always has been. Discrimination has cost the dreams of many generations of black people in this country, and I believe it was no different for my father.

I was the middle child. My older sister, Priscilla, is fourteen months older than I am, and I have a brother—named Horace Walter for my father (although we call him Walter)—who is two years and nine months younger than I. My parents were married as teenagers and could not handle the responsibilities of marriage, especially my father. They divorced when I was about four, and as a teenager I saw him from time to time when we visited him in Miami, where he had moved when I was older.

My mother adored her own father, a successful carpenter and farmer named Richard Allen Powell. (He was named for Richard Allen, the founder of the African Methodist Episcopal Church. Although Mother was raised as an only child by her father, she had three half siblings: a sister, Corrie Jackson, and two brothers, Guy Lee Barnes and Leland Barnes, who were raised by her mother.) Mother was a real "Daddy's girl," and I think she wanted us to feel the same way about our father, so she made a fuss about reminding us to call him and give him cards at holiday time. But I thought that was hypocritical, even when I was young. He seldom came to see about us, so why should I care about him? The bottom line is, even though I always called him "Daddy," I never had a real relationship with my biological father.

We lived outside of Quincy, Florida, in an area called St. Hebron, which was a very small rural farming community. Today, some long-standing black families there own land tracts and have streets named for them. A lot of Negro residents back then were in tobacco, priming it for the big growers, pulling the leaves from the tall stalks. The leaves were about twelve inches wide, eighteen to twenty inches long. You'd use cord to string eighteen or twenty leaves together to hang in the large tobacco barns. Even the schedule of the black schools was set around the time the tobacco was to be picked; they closed a month earlier and opened a month earlier than any other schools in the state so students would be available for harvest. Once, when we were about twelve or thirteen, my sister and I came to visit Quincy and tried to get a job in the tobacco fields so we could renew friendships with children we had known before we moved away, but the supervisor sent us home. "Those jobs are for people who really need them, and we don't need you here socializing and distracting the workers," he said. My sister and I never had a knack for farm work, as my grandfather also discovered when we visited him. He tried to put us to work in his cotton fields in the early-morning hours, but I enjoyed riding horses and playing in the huge, dizzying tobacco barns.

Of course, Florida being in the South, all of the schools and facilities were segregated. But when my sister and I attended the so-called "colored" or "Negro" school each day, my mind didn't flood with questions about why there were no white children there. I didn't even wonder where the white children went to school. Come to think of it, I'm not sure I *knew* any whites. My mother had white relatives in her family who had occasionally visited her childhood home, so she'd grown up with more familiarity with whites than I did. I just accepted segregation for what it was, just as my mother had a generation earlier.

I had lighthearted moments as a child, especially when I was very young. My favorite pastime was fishing, and every day after school I walked down a hill from my house to Mr. Jerry Brown's creek. I caught pails full of catfish and brim. I guess I was too young to be afraid of the snakes hanging from the trees overhead. Priscilla and I once dragged a dead snake a long way down the red clay road near my house—a snake that was five feet long, according to shocked onlookers. Children aren't as aware of the world around them, and those were my years of blissful ignorance.

When my mother left her husband, she decided to find work in Miami. She was caring for her own mother then, as she had been since 1942, because Grandmother had lost her hearing as a young woman and was completely deaf. Mother took us all on a segregated train when we moved—but again, because I was so young, I didn't pay special attention to the "White Only" and "Colored" signs on the trains. All I noticed were the uniformed Negro soldiers who were riding the train with us. My mother found a job in Miami Beach as a customer attendant and window trimmer in a very exclusive dress shop for whites only. There were no other Negro women working in the shop, and she probably only got that job because she was so fair-skinned. I started school in Miami, at Anderson's Kindergarten in Overtown, then I went to Phillis Wheatley Elementary School. After a time, Mother found it too difficult to take care of all of us in a city atmosphere, so she rented a house back in St. Hebron and asked Grandmother to care for us while she returned to Miami to get herself in a better position to bring us all back together again. We spent several years with Grandmother.

Of course, being children, we found ways to take advantage of my grandmother's inability to hear. After bedtime, when Grandmother thought we were sleeping, Priscilla and I used to climb out of the bedroom window to engage in our little card-playing games. We'd set up a table and chairs, the neighbors' children would come over, and we'd sit outside in the moonlit backyard playing bid whist and other card games, laughing and carrying on because we knew Grandmother would never hear a sound. Thinking back on that, it seems like a lost era, because it would not be safe for young children to do that now.

Mother came back to retrieve us when I was about nine, and that was probably a good thing. It was time for us to have more supervision. But Mother didn't come for us alone; she had remarried a very tall, refined man named Marion M. Hamilton, of the Atlanta Hamiltons (who, it was said, were direct descendants of statesman Alexander Hamilton, one of the framers of the U.S. Constitution, which might be one reason my stepfather was so fair-skinned, even more so than my mother). All of the Hamilton offspring were highly educated. Marion Hamilton had a master's degree, and his brother, Henry Cooke Hamilton, whom we later learned to call "Uncle Cookie," would later become the registrar and head of the psychology and education departments at Morehouse College in Atlanta. Uncle Cookie was married to Grace Towns Hamilton, who, in 1965, would herself be the first Negro woman elected to the Georgia House of Representatives.[1]

This new man in Mother's life had an impressive pedigree, but he did not impress me. Not at first. I know now that my mother remarried because she wanted to provide a father for us—but to me, he was just a stranger who'd driven up to our house in a shiny black car I later learned was a Cadillac. His shoes were as shiny as his car, so shiny you could see your face reflected back when you stared at them. And I don't think I had ever seen a man so tall! He must have been at least six-foot-six. The more he tried to reach out to me and encourage me to call him "Daddy Marion," the more I retreated from him. I have never opened up to people immediately. It took me six or eight months just to call him "Daddy Marion." As for building up my trust, that would take years.

Whether I liked it or not, we were a family now, and we moved to a South Florida town called Belle Glade. Belle Glade was in Palm Beach County, but it was nothing like the affluent areas of Palm Beach most people think of. Ours was a community of migrant workers and struggling people who lived in tin shelters that looked like barracks, but there were also professionals with their own homes. Housing was provided for teachers who, for the most part, came from West Palm Beach. Belle Glade was situated on dark black soil everyone called "The Muck." The soil was called "Black Gold" because it was so fertile, but I had asthma and very sensitive skin as a child and was highly allergic to it. My stepfather taught in the local colored high school, Everglades Vocational High School, so this became our new home. He was also a minister, and he preached in the local AME church with a style that I enjoyed.

The thing I grew to appreciate most about Daddy Marion, however, was that he was a very talented musician, and he shared his love of music with all of us. He had played with jazz great Lionel Hampton. Every Christmas Eve we sat around the piano as he played Christmas carols, and my entire family would join in; my brother and mother shaking maracas, my sister playing the flute, and me playing my trumpet. We played until midnight, then went to bed eager to open our gifts later in the morning.

In Belle Glade, I became aware of the racial differences around us.

On the one hand, many of my new observations of whites had led me to have positive feelings about them. My mother was a Democratic committeewoman, and Belle Glade had an interracial council even in the 1950s, so my mother brought me around whites who addressed her respectfully as "Mrs. Hamilton," which was rare in those days even though I didn't realize it.

But there were also things I *didn't* like, and I learned to rebel early.

The Dairy Queen, for example. When I was in junior high school and probably twelve or thirteen, my sister Priscilla and I liked to walk up to the Dairy Queen window to order ice cream, but there were two windows: one marked WHITE in front and one marked COLORED in the rear. Well, most of the customers were standing at the WHITE window, and Priscilla and I saw no reason that we shouldn't stand there to be served, too. We sensed that the COLORED window would not receive the same care and attention as the window for whites, and we figured we were as good as any other paying customers. We went to the WHITE window every time. And the man would say, "The colored side is back there," pointing it out to us as if he thought we were too stupid to know how to read. When he realized we *did* know the difference and we were there just flashing our sweetest smiles with no intention of moving, he got irritated. But he served us. If we had been adults, it probably would have been a different story. Someone might have called the police.

In my brother's case, he had an incident where someone *did* call the police. I only found out very recently from Walter that when he was fifteen, after I'd already left home for college, he and some of his friends went to that same Dairy Queen and were told to go to the COLORED side. They were shocked, he told me later. "We didn't know about it, because we were sheltered in a black neighborhood," he said. He and his friends left in a rage.

They were so angry, in fact, that when they were driving in his friend's car and encountered a lone white boy walking by the side of the road, they all shouted "Cracker!" at him as they passed. Walter had never done anything like that before.

"We took out our frustrations on him," Walter says. "When we got home, the sheriff came to the house and told Daddy Marion we had done this. We tried to act like we didn't do it. The sheriff reprimanded us, and Daddy Marion acted very Uncle Tomish and said, 'Yes, sir' and 'No, sir' and 'It won't happen again.' At that point, I didn't understand it—but that was part of survival. The sheriff was the one in charge."[2]

An incident in high school really left an imprint on me, too.

When I was about fifteen, I was on the student council. As student council members, we were assigned to welcome guests to the high school during our free periods. I remember very vividly that I was wearing my favorite red corduroy suit as I sat in the breezeway one day, and suddenly I heard a man's voice say behind me, "How 'bout a little bit?" There was a white postman standing there smirking, and I was absolutely shocked. You have to remember—this was the 1950s, and for an adult to say something like that to a child was outlandish. I challenged him, to make sure I hadn't heard wrong. I said, "*What* did you say?"

He had the nerve to repeat it. "How 'bout a little bit?" Then he walked away laughing, without a care in the world. And why not? I was just a Negro girl. During those days, white men could *rape* Negro girls and never see justice in the South, so why should he expect any kind of penalty? When my mother was growing up, she routinely heard about Negro girls who were forced to climb into white men's cars so the men could have their way with them, and that sort of practice had been going on in the South since the days of slavery.

Oh, but I was mad! I marched right into that school and went to find Daddy Marion, who by that time was the dean of students. This was when I first began to notice the volatility of the white versus Negro question, because Daddy Marion hesitated. I know that if a Negro man had made a comment like that to me, Daddy Marion would have reacted with the same kind of outrage I felt. But we were discussing the actions of a *white* postal worker, a government employee, and I could see the doubt and nervousness pass across his face like a shadow. By then, I'd developed a lot of respect for Daddy Marion. After all, he had been my civics teacher, and had taught me about my rights and responsibilities as a citizen. But I lost some of my respect that day. I didn't want to wait for him to make up his mind about what to do. Instead, I went straight home and told my mother about it.

Let me tell you a little bit more about Mother. As a young woman, Lottie Mae Powell had no stomach for the indignities she watched Negroes subjected to. When my sister, brother, and I were very young, according to my mother, a controversial trial involving a Negro defendant took place in Quincy. Negroes were told to shut their businesses for the day and keep clear of the streets, but my mother was expecting a money order from her brother, and no racist decree was going to prevent her from marching downtown to Western Union to take care of her business. My mother was a very small-boned woman, with delicate features, and she remembered how the whites sat chewing tobacco and watching her from shaded porches downtown. There she was, a lone Negro woman, walking forbidden streets. No one said a word to her.

To her, however, what was even worse than the attitudes of the whites was the compliance of the Negroes. She was disgusted to see men she had admired and respected cowering in hidden corners "like rats," she recalled. She went home and packed a bag to leave town that same night. She later learned there was nowhere to run, really, but since she had ended her relationship with her husband, she fled to Miami with us in tow.

Years later, after we moved to Belle Glade, my mother took us out with her at night as she taught Negroes to register to vote. As a Democratic committeewoman, she brought new voters to churches to demonstrate how to fill out the ballots, and we helped her. I grew up with a very strong sense of civic duty.

So when my mother heard about the sexual advance a white postman had made toward me, she was just as shocked and angry as I'd been. She didn't hesitate to pick up the telephone and begin making the necessary calls to report the man's actions and to file a formal report. She hoped the complaint would make it all the way to Washington, D.C., but I don't think either of us expected it would. Looking back on it now, I think Daddy Marion was afraid we would be visited by misfortune if we stirred up trouble—and men, of course, usually had to bear the brunt of retribution in the South, so I understand why he hesitated. But for my mother, fear of repercussions was the last thing on her mind.

It was a year before anything at all happened. But the report *did* make its way to Washington. Apparently, this postman had made similar comments to white females, too, so our complaint was lumped in with the others. When the white investigator showed up on our front porch, though, he made it clear he was trying to blame *me* for what had happened. First, he seemed skeptical because I was sixteen by then, and he pointed out that I'd claimed to be *fifteen* when we filed the report, as if that made all the difference in the world. Patiently, we explained that I *had* been fifteen when it happened. Then he used a different tactic: "Well, how do you *know* what he meant when he said, 'How 'bout a little bit?' " I think he wanted to intimidate us, since so many Negroes could be very easily intimidated by white men of authority. My mother and I were very angry, but we answered his questions as patiently as we could. My mother didn't scratch her head foolishly or let herself get confused. She said curtly, "Well, *she* knew what he meant and *he* knew what he meant." And that was that.

Eventually, that postman disappeared, and we heard he was fired. I never fooled myself into thinking he lost his job because I spoke out—it was because whites had spoken out, too—but I was proud that I had stood my ground. It was a lesson I would draw upon again and again as I became a young woman. I didn't know it then, but refusing to back down would become a trademark in my life.

Unfortunately, however, sometimes racial discrimination was much closer to home. Of Mother's three children, Priscilla and Walter were both brown-skinned, and I was lighter, closer to Mother's complexion. Priscilla always called me "dirty yellow" or "dingy yellow," which I found very hurtful. When I was about eleven years old, an incident took place that left a strong impression on Priscilla: Daddy Marion's mother died, and I was the only one of my siblings allowed to accompany Mother and Daddy Marion to the funeral in Atlanta. At the time, I had no idea why I was the one who went while Priscilla and Walter stayed at home. When we got there, all of Daddy Marion's relatives were hugging me, and I found myself wondering, "Who are all these white people?" Although everyone there was considered Negro, the church pianist and I were the two darkest people at the funeral! Mother had arranged for me to spend time with another girl who was my age, but some of those present objected right away, and I felt my face burning as I realized they didn't like her because of her *color.* Mother was very angry about it. That was how I slowly came to realize that Priscilla and Walter had been left at home because Mother didn't want to subject them to rejection by these fair-skinned Negroes. Years later, I learned that Priscilla had been very hurt and resentful about being left behind. The issue seemed to fester between us. I was nominated to serve at the prom in the tenth grade, and when Priscilla heard my name called, she raised her hand and asked the teacher, "Why just the *yellow* girls?" Priscilla hadn't objected to any of the other girls. The teacher called Mother to tell her about it, because she thought it indicated sibling rivalry at home. Obviously, Priscilla believed color separated us. Society had created the barrier.

When I was in high school, changes in those barriers seemed imminent. In 1954, the Supreme Court handed down its *Brown v. Board of Education* ruling, and the news of that antisegregation measure rocketed through the Negro community. Finally, after so many years of being forced to attend separate schools with less adequate facilities and supplies, the Supreme Court struck down the "separate but equal" lie that had been the law of the land, particularly in the South, ever since the racist *Plessy v. Ferguson* decision of 1896. The *Brown v. Board of Education of Topeka* case was actually five combined cases, all of them spearheaded by the respected National Association for the Advancement of Colored People (NAACP) Legal Defense Fund. Attorney Thurgood Marshall—who later became the first black U.S. Supreme Court Justice—argued the case before the high court, pointing out sociological and psychological research showing that segregation led to feelings of inferiority in Negroes.

I was so excited about the *Brown* decision, it's almost too difficult to describe in words. I was in the ninth grade at the time, and I immediately had a grand vision of Negroes and whites sitting side by side, building a future *together.* The way I saw it, there would no longer be a world of limitless possibilities for whites and a second-class citizenship for Negroes—for the first time, this nation would belong to all of us equally! I thought the *Brown* decision would bring sweeping changes. As young as I was, I realized it would not eliminate all the problems we had in education, but I envisioned Negroes and whites working together to solve our common problems, and I wanted to be ready.

Of course, my reaction was fueled by naivete. It was May 17 when the decision was handed down, and I expected that we would all be going to school together by September. I had no idea what kind of delaying impact the phrase "with all deliberate speed" would mean in terms of bringing about desegregation. I also didn't have the wisdom or experience to ask myself what *negative* changes might take place in the black community as a result of *Brown*—for example, that a Negro principal at a Negro school could not hope for such a prime assignment at a white school because he would be an outsider, subject to the prejudices of his superiors. (As it happened, in the state of Florida, all Negro high school principals were eventually demoted and made elementary school and junior high school principals[3]—including Daddy Marion, who had become a high school principal a few years after the *Brown* decision, but instead found his school designated for students in grades five through seven.) Or that the burden of "busing" students from one neighborhood to another would so often fall on Negro children, since white parents would not want to send their children to Negro neighborhoods.

None of this, of course, occurred to me in high school. All I knew was that I was excited by the prospect of all things implied by "integration"—better science equipment, up-to-date books, modern school buildings, and all of the other benefits I knew white children received. I wanted *all* Negro students to benefit from integration, and to me that meant we could not afford to be ill-prepared.

There were many fine instructors at my high school in Belle Glade, and Daddy Marion was a top-notch instructor who taught social studies as well as band. He had our little school playing sophisticated orchestra and marching band pieces while I was there. Somehow, he convinced the school to buy a bassoon, a very expensive, beautiful, and uncommon instrument he believed should be part of our school's ensemble. Our school was in such a poor area that many of the students couldn't even afford their uniforms, so we regularly held fund-raising drives to buy uniforms, but Daddy Marion never lowered his sights simply because most of the students were disadvantaged. He had grown up in affluence, in a home that had a music room and a library, and he thought it was critical to expose his music students to everything he could.

I wish I could say that all of the teachers at my high school were as dedicated.

This was "The Muck," after all, a community of mostly poor blacks and migrants from the Caribbean who picked beans and other vegetables to earn a living, and my school was far from a coveted teaching assignment. Some of the teachers, like Daddy Marion, lived in Belle Glade and had a stake in the area—participating in church, taking part in the social fabric—but many lived during the school week in cottages owned by the Belle Glade Housing Authority, then on weekends drove forty miles to their homes in West Palm Beach. Some of those commuters were remarkably devoted to their students, but for many it was not a choice assignment. Sometimes, I felt I could see them watching the clock on

Friday afternoons, eager to jump into their cars and drive away from Belle Glade as fast as they could. In my eyes, some of those teachers were not invested in the welfare of their students. Their attitude seemed to be "Well, this is just a bunch of migrant children. What good will it do to teach them anything?"

Since promises of integration were now in the air, I couldn't tolerate the idea that we weren't getting the best possible education. The person accountable for that, I decided, was our principal. Don't get me wrong. My high school principal was a very nice man, very well-liked. He always had a smile on his face as he walked through the halls, and he knew how to make people feel good. But when it came to setting tough guidelines and enforcing them, he just did not measure up. He was not an assertive man, so I had the impression, even as a student, that some of his teachers were getting away with doing less than they should. They weren't prepared, they weren't following curriculum guidelines, and they weren't putting nearly as much of themselves into teaching as Daddy Marion and the other dedicated teachers.

So what did I do? I started a petition drive to get the principal removed. Since Daddy Marion had also been my civics teacher, and I had watched my mother registering people to vote and conducting petition drives throughout the town, I had a good understanding of the procedure. I explained what I was doing to my classmates, and slowly they began to sign. First a dozen signatures, then two dozen, and before I knew it, hundreds of students had signed. I was a good motivator, even then.

Word of my petition got out, and it frightened some teachers. One day, a math teacher I respected began discussing my petition in his class—and he told the students that if any of them had signed it, they could be arrested and thrown in jail. To me, because I had not yet seen what this black teacher had probably seen in his lifetime, this was the most ridiculous thing I had ever heard. We lived in the United States of America! He probably just didn't want to upset the administration at the school. Whatever his reason, he spread that lie, and it spread fast. That same day, students began approaching me, desperately asking to have their signatures removed. I tried to explain that there was no way they could be sent to jail for signing a petition, but they wouldn't believe my word over a teacher's. I felt sad and disillusioned.

I wasn't going to give up. The way I saw it, they had given me their signatures, so those signatures now belonged to *me,* and I refused to let anyone remove his or her name on the basis of false information. The students were very anxious, though. At one point, their demands got so heated that I figured I should make a run for it and put my petition in a safe place—suddenly I was being chased out of the school yard by thirty or forty students!

I didn't know it then, but my future as a freedom fighter had already begun. In the years to come, I would have experiences I never would have dreamed of as a fifteen-year-old high school student. Once I got to college, other instructors—teachers I truly admired—would continue to criticize any actions they deemed as radical. Students would be afraid to participate in activities that would make valuable changes. I would learn that one could, indeed, be jailed for the simplest of actions.

I graduated from high school in 1957, three years after *Brown v. Board of Education*. By that time, the excitement over the ruling had died down and reality had set in. I never attended an integrated school, and even today some schools have never been truly integrated.

Our principal was removed by the school board the term after I circulated the petition against him, but later I would wonder if maybe that math teacher had been sincere in trying to protect the students from unjust retribution. He knew something I had not fully learned back then: He knew that, as Negroes, the rules we had learned in our student lessons about the blessings of freedom in the United States of America surely did not apply to us.

I would learn that for myself very soon.

# Four

## Tananarive Due

**"Sometimes, I feel discriminated against,**
**but it does not make me angry.**
**It merely astonishes me. How can anyone**
**deny themselves the pleasure of my company?**
**It's beyond me."**
***—Zora Neale Hurston***

I tried to change my skin color right away, almost from the first time I noticed it.

My parents decided to move to Miami from Quincy when I was three years old, convinced I would receive a better education in a big city than I would in the quiet, rustic area of my mother's birth. There were no schools in Quincy that could take me. Mom loved living in Quincy, with its moss-draped trees and red clay roads steeped in family history, but Mom and Dad already had two children by 1968, and they considered us their first priority. My grandmother, whom I called Mother, had also moved back to Miami by then, and she would be invaluable in giving our growing family added support. So we moved.

Because I needed to be at least five to enroll in kindergarten in Dade County's public school system, my mother began to apply to Montessori and other private schools. My grandmother was working, so Mom had to take me with her when she visited several schools by driving around town in the family station wagon. I watched curiously as the white children played on the school jungle gyms, wondering if I would be joining them soon. But at each school, we got the same answer from administrators with pinched, pale faces: *Whites only.*

I already had a solution in mind. Once we were back home, I found a bottle of Johnson & Johnson baby powder, poured the powder into my hand, and began to pat it on my face. Then my neck. Then, stretching my arms out one by one, I patted the powder onto each of them until they were covered. I took off all my clothes and dusted myself from head to toe.

I was proud of myself. "Mommy!" I called, excited, from the crib I still slept in because my mother—never one to follow convention for its own sake—had never seen a need to replace it. "Will they let me go to school *now?"*

I'm sure I didn't understand why my mother suddenly looked so stricken. I was her first child, only three years old, and I'd already been infected by the racism she'd spent her entire adult life trying to fight, as if racism were a stranger who'd entered our home despite all the locks on the doors. I already wanted to change who I was so the outside world would be willing to accept me. Okay, so I had to be white to go to school. That was easy enough to fix!

As far as I was concerned, my mother and grandmother were white, anyway. I was richly brown-skinned like my father, but my mother was a golden peanut color, and her mother was even lighter, the color of a peanut shell. Even my baby sister, Johnita, had coloring closer to my mother's than my own. These variances in shading had not meant anything in particular to me until the day I covered myself with powder. Suddenly, I saw my complexion with a more critical eye. I needed to be white like Mommy and Mother, and everything would be fine.

My sisters and I were the children of integration. My mother and grandmother's generations had grown up in a very segregated setting, as had nearly all Southern blacks since we first arrived on this nation's shores, but my sisters and I were born after the Civil Rights Act, after the Voting Rights Act, the first generation of so-called "Freedom." In many ways, we were the testing ground for the ideals my parents had been sacrificing their time and lives for.

While my parents didn't set out on purpose to raise us in a nearly all-white setting when we were very young, that was the end result. We lived in three mostly black neighborhoods in Miami for a time—we rented homes in Liberty City and Opa-locka, and later we rented a house from relatives in middle-class, black Richmond Heights, closer to my grandmother—but eventually my parents were ready to buy a house, and they found themselves stymied. Black families have always cherished property because it was denied us for so long, and my parents were unable to find families willing to sell their homes in the mostly black neighborhoods that appealed to them. Instead, they took their home search to suburbia, and we ended up in the land of whites.

We did not feel welcome there. My parents shielded us from the direct threats some of our neighbors made—like one in particular who dumped his garbage in our backyard and vowed to shoot me or my sisters if he saw us walking on his grass, and was, ironically, father to one of my favorite playmates—but we felt the unspoken effects of intimidation. We knew when tomatoes or eggs had been thrown against our house. Or when someone had put rocks in my father's gas tank overnight. Or when stones were thrown against our house, making me wonder if one would shatter a window and come flying into my bedroom. More than my sisters, I was also subjected to the pain of the word "nigger," for which I never had a comeback. That was a word that had been used by slaveholders and murderous mobs. *Nigger* was not a word I took lightly.

We were even surrounded by whites at church. Both Mom and Dad had African Methodist Episcopal backgrounds, but in the 1960s my father had been intrigued by the Unitarian Universalists—a more informal version of Christianity once supported by Thomas Jefferson, among others. Unitarian churches accept members of all faiths; the religious aspect is left much more to individual rumination, and sermons tend to reflect broad ideas such as peace and social activism. Unitarians in Tallahassee had been very supportive of civil rights, since many of them were politically active white liberals, I had been dedicated at the Unitarian Church, and there was a Unitarian Universalist church in Miami. At our church altar were large paintings of a Christian cross, a Jewish Star of David, and a Yin and Yang, all side-by-side, showing the church's sense of inclusion. But this was not a traditional church, and most of the members, many of whom wore shorts and sandals to services, were white. I can think of only one other black family at our church, and they, like most Unitarians we knew, attended Sunday services only sporadically.

Quite by accident, I had also ended up at a mostly white private school in Miami. A woman named Nancy Adams, a dear friend of my mother's from the civil rights movement, arranged for me and Johnita to receive scholarships to the Horizon School for Gifted Children. Horizon was run by Dr. Benjamin Fine, a progressive thinker in gifted education. Nancy was convinced that the three of us were truly special children, although my youngest sister, Lydia, was not old enough to attend the school. Nancy paid for our first year out of her own pocket, which at the time was more than $1,000 each. Because our parents had done so much for others, she wanted to make sure their children would have advantages in life. The curriculum specialized in bright children, and Mom thought it would give me and my sister the best start. I have no recollection of any other black children at the Horizon School except my sister—although my mother reminds me that a *Miami Herald* newspaper reporter, Bea Hines, had a son there, and my godmother, Florida Rep. Gwendolyn S. Cherry, had a niece there—although they were much older than we were.

When I was in the second or third grade, a boy in my class asked me, "What color is black people's blood?" It was the most ridiculous question I could imagine. "It's green," I lied, completely straight-faced. I think he believed me.

Despite my realization that many whites were apparently ignorant about black people, I could not help constantly noticing our differences and comparing myself unfavorably to whites. I remember draping a bath towel across my head and swinging it back and forth as if the towel represented my long tresses of hair, imitating the white women I saw on television and the long-haired white girls at my school. I might have forgotten all about this fantasy except for Whoopi Goldberg, who, reliving her own childhood during her one-woman show on Broadway many years ago, put a towel on her head and did the exact same thing. It brought the memory back like a thunderclap.

I hated my wiry, unmanageable hair. I hated getting my hair combed and greased. I hated driving into West Perrine, a nearby black neighborhood where some of the homes were unsettling to me in their shabbiness, to go to the beauty shop. The beauty shop didn't have air-conditioning, so it was always hot and filled with sour-faced strangers, and the radio was always preaching about Jesus instead of playing music. "You better stop being so tenderheaded," my hairdresser said when I cried out in pain, either from a sharp yank or, sometimes, a burn from her pressing comb. On a few occasions, my mother sat me on a kitchen stool at home and tried to straighten my hair herself, heating up the big burner until it was a glowing red coil, filling the house with the sweet scent of hair oil and the sour scent of singed hair. Once, she burned the top of my earlobe so badly that the dark crust of a scab was visible for days, though usually the burns weren't so obvious. "Oh, darling, I'm so sorry!" Mom always exclaimed. I was thankful that my sisters and I only had our hair straightened for special occasions, such as Easter. Then, of course, once the hair was straight, it had to be treated oh-so gingerly, which meant that if my school took a field trip to a public pool, I had to wear a swimming cap and keep my head above the surface because I could not get my hair wet. It was hard to enjoy the pool at all, I was so worried about my hair. I couldn't stand having kinky hair, and I couldn't stand having it straightened. I couldn't stand my hair hardly at all.

I combed my Barbie dolls' hair with a burning sense of envy. Almost all of my dolls were black, including my Barbies—to her immense credit, Mom saw to that, even if she had to travel far and wide to find them—but while Barbie's skin may have been the some color as mine, her features and hair looked more like a white woman's. Her hair was so *soft,* so *silky.* And, best of all, it was so *lonnng,* hanging down as far as her waist. Barbie didn't need a towel on her head. Barbie's hair blew in the breeze.

My mother did her best to combat my hair envy. "White people's hair is very thin, and it tangles easily," she told me once. Another time she said, "Well, white children are more liable to get hair lice. The oil black people put in their hair keeps the lice away." I took small comfort in those bits of information. But in a world full of girls with long, soft hair, where even my Barbie dolls were traitors, sometimes it was very little comfort.

Of course, I noticed other differences, too. Sometimes my father took me with him when he went to his meetings in Miami's black neighborhoods, like Liberty City and Overtown, and I noticed the stark contrast between those neighborhoods and the ones where my more affluent friends from the Horizon School lived. I saw black children playing barefoot in the street, and it troubled me. "Are all black people poor?" I asked my parents. They assured me that this was not the case, but that because of discrimination there has always been more poverty in the black community. In fact, I remember my parents specifically taking me to black neighborhoods in disrepair to show me how many blacks live ("The *real* Miami," my mother always called it), so I would know how fortunate we were. We were not rich, we were told, but we were lucky.

I also noticed social differences between blacks and whites. Sometimes, I actually saw my white friends and classmates *yelling* at their parents, which would have been a catastrophe in my home. My sisters and I were not beaten, but my parents were very strict and, if we were especially bad, we could expect to be instructed to find a leather belt and bring it to my mother. Her little slaps with a belt against our palms were intended much more for symbolic ritual than actual pain, but my sisters and I lived in fear of it. We did not yell at our parents. Not once.

I had a good friend named Paul, a blond-haired stick figure of a boy with a sweet smile who, with the exception of my best friend Dorothy, was my favorite person at the Horizon School. I think we were fourth-graders together. When he invited me to his birthday party at his home, I was amazed to learn that he addressed his parents by their first names. "Thanks, Bill. Thanks, Sue." My jaw nearly fell to the floor. Paul seemed to have much higher standing in his home than I had in mine; instead of being parents and a child, they all appeared to be buddies just hanging out. Inspired, I went home and asked my parents if I could call them "Patricia" and "John."

This was the first of many times I would receive my parents' lecture on the differences between white culture and black culture, which were probably more stark than ever in the aftermath of the hippie generation. Some whites, especially liberals, were much more informal than most blacks, my parents explained. Their ideas on discipline were different. Their ideas on child rearing were different. That was why the dress code at our Unitarian church was so different from when we attended Mother's AME church in Richmond Heights, where the black worshipers wore pretty dresses, hats, and suits and ties, and why the AME services were so emotional while the Unitarian services were so sedate.

Needless to say, I never called my parents "Patricia" and "John."

It may sound as if my parents set me and my sisters out upon the sea of whiteness without any kind of cultural life raft, but that's actually far from true. They were well aware of the nutrients we were not receiving from our outside experiences, and I know they agonized over it, so my mother in particular made it her mission to teach us *who we were.* In a sense, although we attended school, we were also homeschooled.

Our home bookshelves were always full of books. Like many children, I started on the Golden Books and *Grimm's Fairy Tales* and then moved up to *Little House on the Prairie* and Nancy Drew mysteries, but my mother also searched very carefully for the kind of books she thought would educate and enrich us culturally. She bought us Ezra Jack Keats's books illustrated with brown-faced children, like *A Snowy Day, Whistle for Willie,* and *John Henry: An American Legend.* We had a wonderful coloring book filled with black historical figures called *Color Me Brown,* published by *Ebony* magazine, and we subscribed to a now-defunct magazine designed for black children, called *Ebony Jr!* We had comic books about Nat Love and other black cowboys, and on Sojourner Truth and the amazing Harriet Tubman, who had sometimes held slaves she was leading to freedom at gunpoint rather than allow them to turn back and jeopardize everyone in her party. We had illustrated books on different Native American tribes (including the Cherokees, who, our father told us, shared our bloodline on his side). And we had children's history books on Mexican-American activist Cesar Chávez, John F. Kennedy, and, my very favorite, Dr. Martin Luther King Jr.

Because there was no national holiday commemorating Dr. Martin Luther King's birthday, on that day my parents let us stay out of school in the morning and we drove a long forty-five minutes to go to downtown Miami's Torch of Friendship, a memorial originally built to honor John F. Kennedy. There, standing in a circle beneath the torch that burned perpetually skyward, we sang "We Shall Overcome" and talked about why Dr. King and others like him had been so important. We also rededicated ourselves to another year of trying to make the world a better place. Then my parents held an open house so that people could come talk, hear the freedom songs, listen to the "I Have a Dream" speech, or watch documentaries on TV. I remember loving Dr. King as if he had been a fallen member of our family.

Yet it was not enough.

I don't remember the incident, but my mother says I came home from school one day and said, "Martin Luther King was just a troublemaker. He caused a lot of problems." Obviously, I had overheard one of my classmates saying that, the classmate having overheard it from a parent.

That was the last straw. Although my mother liked the academic program at the Horizon School, she decided the isolation was unacceptable for us. The summer between my fourth- and fifth-grade years in school—when we moved into yet another white neighborhood—I attended summer school for the first time at a public school, Colonial Drive Elementary. I noticed the difference right away, since there were several other black students at the school that summer. I felt like I was under a magnifying glass: The way I spoke, the way I dressed, the way I could read passages from books above my grade level—everything was noted by both classmates and teachers. I remember black students at my table staring at me while I put mustard on my chicken sandwich in the cafeteria. I felt like an oddity.

In my family's new neighborhood, I felt worse—like a pariah.

In 1975, when I was nine, my family moved to a waterfront home in a peaceful suburb named Point Royal, at the southern end of Dade County. Everything was fresh and untried: a new room, a wonderful new backyard on the bank of a wide canal, my very own bedroom—with carpeting! We were the only black family there, in the beginning, but that had been true in our last neighborhood, and I'd made friends. I'd played football with white neighborhood boys, breaking my glasses more than once in my scramble to catch a pass or avoid a tackle. True, some nights white members of the Unitarian church our family attended sat in their cars to patrol our home because of threats against our family, but my parents never told us this. I would make friends again, I figured.

Walking down my new street not far from home, one day I encountered an older boy, a teenager, ambling in my direction. I did not look at him or speak to him, in the way younger children expect to be invisible to older children. "If there's one thing I can't stand," the boy said as he passed, almost as if he were speaking to himself, "it's a four-eyed nigger."

He was looking at me, and his words stabbed me to my soul. I had heard the word "nigger" before, but it had never been leveled at me in that way, and the boy was so much older, he might as well have been a grown man. I felt exposed, stripped of all essence save my skin color. To me, "nigger" was a word used by lynch mobs and Ku Klux Klan members, a relic I'd never expected to break the peace of one of my first days strolling happily on my family's new street. Recalling that encounter brings to mind a poem by Harlem Renaissance poet Countee Cullen, "Incident," about the devastating effect of the word "nigger" on a black child.

*Once riding in old Baltimore,*
*Heart-filled, head-filled with glee,*
*I saw a Baltimorean*
*Keep looking straight at me.*

*Now I was eight and very small,*
*And he was no whit bigger,*
*And so I smiled, but he poked out*
*His tongue, and called me, "Nigger."*

*I saw the whole of Baltimore*
*From May until December;*
*Of all the things that happened there*
*That's all that I remember.*

"Nigger!" a five-year-old boy teased another day, horrifying me not for myself, but for him. What kind of parents would teach such superiority and hate? "I wish niggers were still slaves!" another boy, this one my age, called at me once while I was walking our dog. I began to expect outbursts from every white child, and braced for them.

There was also vandalism. I tried not to be bothered too much when one night someone threw slimy tomatoes against the new white wall of our house. Or when, another time, someone slipped rocks into the gas tank of our station wagon. Still, I couldn't help internalizing the notion of being unwelcome, that it was safer to play indoors with my sisters than to venture outside, that we were under attack.

My parents' explanation made it a little better. "People who are prejudiced are just ignorant. They don't know any better," they said, which made me feel sorry for bigots, but it wasn't long before I didn't like my new neighborhood much at all. I learned to dread public encounters, to dread being noticed.

For years afterward, when I left the safety of my yard, I walked with my eyes cast down.

---

When the school year began, I was bused with the white students in my neighborhood to West Perrine, a black neighborhood, to attend R. R. Moton Elementary School. By now, desegregation had been achieved in many neighborhoods through busing, and the very young black children from West Perrine were bused to Bel-Aire Elementary School, where my sisters attended school, until the fifth grade. Fifth and sixth grades belonged to R. R. Moton.

The poverty surrounding R. R. Moton was stark and depressing to me. Through no fault of their own, the residents had very little, and that was clear in the appearance of some of their homes. The neighborhood looked a little foreign to me, but I loved the school, and my mother noticed the change in me right away. R. R. Moton had a black principal, a very caring and supportive woman named Maedon S. Bullard. R. R. Moton also had some black teachers—the first I'd ever seen—one of whom was my fifth-grade teacher, Janelle Harris. I delighted in seeing people who looked like me in positions of authority at my school. Suddenly, the same girl who had criticized Dr. Martin Luther King Jr. as a troublemaker was writing poems like "The Struggle for Equality," which I wrote when I was about eleven:

*It started in Africa, in the days of old,*
*When liberty and freedom were better than gold.*
*Then great ships came across the sea,*
*Taking away in chains the ancestors of you and me.*
*For many, many years the tired slaves worked,*
*Until at Lincoln's speech, their ears really perked.*

*Between the States anger arose.*
*Some said, "Lincoln's a great man!"*

*Others, "I ought to punch him in the nose!"*
*Anger turned to hate, hatred turned into war,*
*Until many men lay dead upon the ground*
*And on the floor.*
*The bloody war went on—men died by the ton.*
*It went on for about four years,*
*Until supposedly freedom for Blacks was won.*

*"Slavery is dead," the big signs read.*
*Yet, it still seemed harder for Blacks to get*
*Their daily bread.*
*The law said that they could vote, but many armed men*
*Kept them away from the polls.*
*How long could this bad treatment hold?*

*Then it came into realization—*
*They had to change that civilization.*
*"We must rise, let us waste no more time.*
*Discrimination is a terrible crime.*
*Down with the Ku Klux Klan! Up with the NAACP!*
*We'll show them how really tough we can be!"*

*Marches, sit-ins, jail-ins—they did everything—*
*Like listen to the speeches of Malcolm X and M. L. King.*
*They had peaceful demonstrations, yet they still got arrested.*
*The courage of these people had really been tested.*

*We struggled then, and will still struggle now;*
*And we are going to keep on struggling until victory is won.*
*And, as said in the words of Frederick Douglass, "There is*
*No progress without struggle. This struggle may be a moral*
*One, or it may be a physical one, or it may be both moral*
*And physical; but it must be a struggle. Power concedes*
*Nothing without a demand. It never did and it never will."*

I had become politicized, feeling a stronger sense of identity and belonging. I began reciting my poem in oratorical contests sponsored by black organizations in Miami; at one, the Theodore R. Gibson Oratorical Contest, I won year after year. (Father Gibson was a former Miami

NAACP president and a very influential minister, civil rights activist, and Miami City Commissioner. When Florida's McCarthyism-inspired "Johns Committee" tried to subpoena his NAACP membership list in 1959, Father Gibson refused to comply and was arrested as a result).[1] My sisters and I were also attending NAACP meetings and annual national conventions, and as I got older, I was able to absorb more of the meaning of the rhetoric of civil rights.

Yet at school my classmates mocked the way I spoke in clear, grammatical English, calling me "Oreo." Even a *teacher* mocked my accent in the cafeteria one day. I was hurt, but the irony was not lost on me: Many of these same students probably had never heard of the NAACP, nor could they say what the initials stood for. They did not consider me "black enough," yet I knew more about black history than they did, and I had more of a sense of being a link in a chain that stretched back to the days of slavery. I longed for close black friends at Moton, but I did not allow my classmates' attitudes toward me to sour my feelings about blacks. To me, other black children simply remained a mystery: brash, sometimes intimidating, streetwise, always awakening a sense of longing in me. One thing that puzzled me about the black students at Moton was why they always seemed to be wearing the latest fashions—whereas my mother was dressing me and my sisters from department-store bargain racks, her cousin Joyce's bags of hand-me-downs, and thrift stores like Goodwill. The black students also tended to wear flashy jewelry. My sisters and I looked neat, but we were far from fashionable, and we wore very little jewelry. Why could poorer families afford better clothes and gold chains?

Again, I received a cross-cultural lesson: Poor families, my mother said, often attach more significance to designer labels and fashion trends because of damaged self-esteem. Parents couldn't afford higher education for their children or move their families into bigger or nicer houses, so they spent what money they did have on clothes and jewelry for their children. Middle-class blacks, too, tended to surround themselves with material goods—bigger cars, more expensive furniture, clothes, and jewelry—to make up for being treated as second-class citizens. That was the only visible measure of wealth in a neighborhood where people have so little, she told us. (And this is certainly something that has remained true in inner city neighborhoods today, where children lose their lives over Nikes and emulate rap stars who shower themselves in gold.)

My first "boyfriends" were two classmates from Mrs. Harris's class at R. R. Moton. I really liked Cleo, the shy, soft-spoken boy who first asked me to "go with" him—which was a status in name only. He would be mine, and I would be his. When another classmate, Tommy, was absent for a few days because of a sudden illness—he recovered!—he heard I had asked about him. He wanted to go with me, too, and one day he came to my house and brought me a watch as a gift. My mother flipped when she saw it. I could not accept such a gift, she told me—and Tommy later confessed that he had stolen the watch from his sister. He thought he needed to give me an expensive gift to impress me, which was far from true. Cleo invited me to a school dance as his date, but at that time his parents couldn't afford to buy him a suit, so Mrs. Harris gave him one. That didn't matter to me, though, because I had always liked him as he was. I believe Tommy and Cleo came to blows over me once in the schoolyard. My favorite boy, though, was Darren, a sixth-grader who had a neatly combed Afro and played the trumpet in the school band like I did. (I'd inherited my mother's trumpet from high school and college.)

One day, Darren asked me to "go with" him, and I was thrilled. Then he heard a rumor that I was already going with Cleo and Tommy, and he confronted me to ask if it was true. "Well, yes, kind of," I said, squirming. It had never occurred to me that it was wrong to go with more than one person at a time, but I saw hurt and accusation in Darren's pretty brown eyes that day. Something inside of me shriveled.

Yes, I liked Cleo and Tommy, but Darren was different. His grammar was very good, and he was serious about school and his music. As a sixth-grader, he was also much more mature than Cleo or Tommy. Mom had not liked Tommy at all after the watch-stealing revelation, but I thought Mom would like Darren. Even at the tender age of ten, I could sense that Darren was a boy I had things in common with, someone who could be a true friend. After he found out I already had two "boyfriends," though, I don't remember him ever speaking to me again. In the next bone-dry years of junior high school and high school, when not a single boy I liked would ask me to go with him, I would remember Darren as the one who got away, the one I'd done wrong. I would always wish we'd met when we were older, when both of us didn't still have so much to learn about the perplexing, painful dance between boys and girls.

My sisters Johnita and Lydia and I never had boyfriends in junior high or high school. Although our schools were racially diverse—about one-third each black, white, and Hispanic—we tended to take honors and gifted classes, where there were hardly any other black students, and white boys, for the most part, weren't interested in us romantically. My glasses had thick lenses, and I tried no hairstyle more ambitious than pigtails for much of my high school career. I felt woefully unattractive. When I complained about the lack of male attention, my mother explained that I intimidated some of the boys, since I was editor of the school newspaper and on the speech and debate team, and my name was often heard on the morning announcements. "Wait until you go to college. It'll get better then," my mother promised me. "You'll meet boys you have more in common with."

The wait seemed interminable. I had "arranged" dates to both my junior and senior proms. I went to the first with the son of Miami activist and minister Anna Price, a good friend of my mother's, and to the other with the son of U.S. Rep. Alcee Hastings, a former federal judge who was later elected to Congress, and who had attended law school with my father. I met both boys for the first time on prom night. They were nice to me, especially considering the circumstances. (Hollis Price took me to a movie a couple of years later, when we were both in college, but we never stayed in touch.) I simply didn't have enough boys to choose from, and despite the best intentions of my parents, both proms were terribly awkward for me. How could I have fun with a stranger?

Even worse, I went to my senior prom with a guilty conscience. I'd had an unexpected incident with a male friend of mine, a boy I'll call J. who was in my newspaper class. J. and I spent a lot of time together, and he'd recently invited me to see a performance of the gospel musical *Your Arms Too Short to Box with God,* starring vocal powerhouse Patti LaBelle. I really thought of it as going to a musical with a friend, but when we walked inside, the first person I saw was a bearded man named Dr. William Perry, the president of the Miami branch of the NAACP. Dr. Perry's grin began to emerge when he spotted me, but as soon as J. appeared beside me, his face hardened. When I introduced J., Dr. Perry was polite, but it was obvious to me that he didn't like seeing me with a white boy. (One of J.'s parents was Cuban, but his skin was most certainly white). *Oh, Dr. Perry thinks we're on a date!* I thought, horrified. I longed to explain that J. and I were just friends, but I never had the chance.

But we weren't just friends in J.'s mind. Toward the end of the school year, while we were lingering in my front yard one afternoon after school, he asked me if I had a date to the senior prom. "No, not yet," I said, thinking he was just making conversation.

"Will you go to the prom with me?" he asked suddenly, in a nervous rush. Maybe I was just naive—my mother has a very endearing naive streak, and I've often suspected it must have rubbed off on me—but I was honestly shocked that he was asking me. "I really like you, Tanana," he said earnestly, clasping my hands. I must have stammered an *Okay,* because the next thing I knew, J. was stretching upward to kiss my lips. His hands were clammy. I tried not to show it, but I was almost repulsed, as if my own brother was suddenly kissing me on the mouth. I wasn't attracted to J. I liked his mind and his sense of humor, which was much sharper than the average high school boy's because he was so bright, but I'd never thought of him romantically.

Even if all other factors had been unchanged, I would have gone to the prom with J. if he had been black. The fact that he was shorter than I was wouldn't have mattered. His acne problem wouldn't have mattered. I would have gone simply as a friend if J. had been black, but I would not, *could* not, go to my senior prom with a white boy and subject myself to the stares of other blacks who had always thought I was an Oreo. I would have weathered anything for true love, but I wasn't in love with J. It wouldn't be worth alienating myself further from the people I had been longing for acceptance from since the days at R. R. Moton Elementary School.

I told my mother my problem. The next thing I knew, she'd called Judge Hastings and arranged a prom date for me. I lied to J., telling him it had all been set up beforehand without my knowledge, claiming I felt horrible about it. He told me I should stand up to my mother, that she was too domineering, but I only shrugged and sighed, feeling guilty about my lie. I just didn't think he would understand the truth. How could he? Maybe he didn't care what other people would think, but I did. I could just imagine what the football players and their black dates with manicured nails and sophisticated ways would say when they saw us: *Girl, look at her. I can't believe her nerve, showing up with that short li'l white boy. What's wrong with that Oreo wannabe?*

I let J. down, and I think somehow he knew I was lying all along. He had been a good friend to me at a time when I had virtually none other than my sisters; J. and I were both intellectuals and outcasts, and we had that in common. After that day, when I saw the same hurt in J.'s eyes I'd seen in Darren's seven years earlier, J. never spoke to me again. I thought he was overreacting, but it made my stomach hurt.

My senior prom date was black, tall, and acne-free, but he was bored silly. We danced very little, and we rarely made eye contact. He didn't know anyone at my high school, and he couldn't wait to leave. The hard contact lenses I was wearing for the occasion were stinging like saltwater in my eyes. After we'd spent a token amount of time feeling uncomfortable, he said he was ready to go, and we left early. I missed the awards ceremony, so I wouldn't find out until the next day of school that, although there were only a handful of students I could call friends at Miami Southridge High School, the senior class had voted me "Female Most Likely to Succeed." I think if I'd been there to hear it on prom night, I would have broken down in tears of joy and disbelief right there on the stage. I had no idea my classmates believed that of me. Prom night, one of high school's most disappointing memories, might have become one of my best.

Yet even today, after having dated men of different races and nationalities both here and abroad, I ask myself if I could have found a way to go with J. to that senior prom, and I still can't imagine it. Race loomed too large between us. I know why I felt I couldn't do it. I'm not even sure I wish I had.

But I've always been sorry for the lie. J. deserved to hear the truth. How would I have felt if our positions had been reversed, if he'd felt too embarrassed to take a black girl to his prom? I would have considered his position weak at best, racist at worst. I'd hoisted the weight of my racial insecurities and the history between the races onto J., and he'd only wanted to go to his senior prom with a girl he really liked.

## Five

# Patricia Stephens Due

**"Those who profess to favor freedom, and yet deprecate agitation, are men who want crops without plowing up the ground. They want rain without thunder and lightning. They want the ocean without the awful roar of its waters."**
***—Frederick Douglass***

I didn't go to college expecting to get swept into the civil rights movement. Like any young person, I was excited about living away from home for the first time, and I was eager to begin more serious study in music, which had become the great love of my life. I considered myself very good on the trumpet by the time I graduated from high school, and my dream was to make a life as a musician or band director. I had a new high school band director, a man named Eugene Woods, and he was very conscientious about helping his students secure music scholarships. I ended up getting several offers for scholarships, including from two Negro colleges; one from Central State College in Wilberforce, Ohio, and one from Florida Agricultural & Mechanical University (FAMU) in Tallahassee.

To show you how young I was emotionally, I made the decision to go to FAMU because I didn't want to be too far away from my family. My parents were still living in Belle Glade then, almost 500 miles from FAMU's Tallahassee campus. When I told my family I wasn't sure how to choose one of the schools, they reminded me about a summer I had spent with my mother's cousin in Haddonfield, New Jersey, while I was a junior in high school. I missed my daily conversations with Mother so much that I had called home every single day. Based on that experience, Mother told me, "You know, you don't need to go too far to school. Remember what happened when you went to New Jersey? We can't afford all those phone bills, and it's more expensive to come home from farther away." That was all the convincing I needed. I forgot any ideas I'd had about going to Ohio, and instead I registered at Florida A&M University, remaining deep in the South to begin my life as an adult. If I had not made that decision, I'm certain my life would have taken a very different course.

My naivete showed in other ways, too, giving my parents very little warning of the serious business that would soon overtake my life. The summer before I began college, I lived with my biological father in Miami and worked as a waitress at an Overtown restaurant called the Third Avenue Dining Room. In the 1960s, Overtown was a thriving Negro community. (Despite the black community's recent efforts at improvement, such as the renovation of the historic Lyric Theatre, and other proposed changes, Overtown today is one of the poorest areas in Miami–Dade County.) Because of segregation, Overtown was home to pharmacists, dentists, doctors, entrepreneurs, and lawyers, providing a full spectrum of Negro life; educated and uneducated, professional class and working class, well-to-do and struggling. They all had their skin color and discrimination in common, and they lived side by side. Overtown also boasted several renowned Negro-owned hotels, where celebrities like Billie Holiday and Dizzy Gillespie stayed and gave impromptu performances because they were not permitted to live in the segregated hotels in Miami Beach, where they were headlining. Wasn't Jim Crow something? These Negro artists were good enough to *play* at the white hotels, but not good enough to sleep there. But Overtown benefitted from segregation, because that was *the* place to be in black Miami. Overtown had its own tempo and rhythm back then, and I was excited to be part of it.

One of the people I met that summer was a piano player named Billy H., who entertained guests in the hotels. He was a good musician, and he was called "The Man with the Golden Hands." The Third Avenue Dining Room was very close to the Carver Hotel, and I met him because he came in to have quick meals between his sets. I loved hearing Billy H. tell stories about his gigs, and he was taken with me right away. I was only seventeen, but I was very interested in music, and a professional musician intrigued me. In high school, I'd had a "boyfriend" in name only—the most we'd ever done was hold hands. And here was Billy H., a worldly musician with two children from a previous marriage, who was much older than I was. He was twenty-nine, and his daughter was about nine, only eight years younger than I was. After only a few conversations about music at the Dining Room, he actually asked me to marry him. I don't remember going to so much as a movie with him, and he wanted to get engaged!

Well, I knew there was no way I was ready to marry anyone, much less a man I hardly knew, but I didn't want to hurt Billy's feelings, either. So, feeling shocked and shy, I must have murmured "Well, okay." But I told him I couldn't possibly get married without my parents' consent, and he readily agreed. At that, I exhaled a huge sigh of relief. Mother and Daddy Marion would never let me marry such an old man, especially when I was supposed to be going to college. I thought I could wiggle out of my engagement without the responsibility of rejecting Billy myself.

At his first opportunity, Billy dressed up in his Sunday finest and drove out to Belle Glade to meet my parents. I accompanied him, feeling like a bundle of nerves. I could only imagine the look my mother would give me when this musician told her we were engaged. I hoped she would let him down easy, without being too insulting. After all, he had been nice to me. My mother sat and listened, very tight-lipped, as Billy H. laid out his plans for our future as man and wife. Then, after he'd said his piece, she sat back in her chair and astounded me with her response: "Well, sure," my mother said in a chipper tone, "if that's what she really wants to do." Her eyes were on me, and I could see a twinkle of amusement there, along with her annoyance. My mouth dropped open, and I thought I was going to faint. I couldn't believe my ears! Then, I realized my mother was only trying to teach me a lesson, and I felt my face grow hot. It was one of the most embarrassing episodes of my young adult life. I don't think I ever truly had the nerve to tell Billy H. that I didn't want to get married. Once I went to college, we grew apart, and that was the end of my engagement.

*A Different World*—the *Cosby Show* spinoff about life on a black college campus—provides the perfect description of what college life felt like for me. I had done some traveling with my family as a young person, but it was refreshing to meet so many serious-minded students from all over the state of Florida, the nation, and even the world. FAMU had (and still has) a nationally recognized music program, especially its Marching 100 Band, which is known for its lively dance routines. In my earliest days, I spent most of my time in the music practice rooms preparing for my audition for the concert and symphonic bands. Regrettably, girls were not permitted at that time to play in the famous Marching 100 Band. Another female band member—Avalon Darby, a percussionist from Jacksonville—worked with me to try to break down the gender barrier in the marching band. Dr. William Foster, the band director, gave us all kinds of delaying tactics and excuses—*Oh, it's too rough for girls,* or *Well, learn the music and we'll see*—but as soon as we overcame one obstacle, he thought of something else. (Eventually, of course, I would have much larger battles than this on my hands.) But Dr. Foster did give me encouragement as a musician. Thanks to the preparation I did with Daddy Marion, I won a spot in the symphonic band as a bassoonist, and Dr. Foster had enough confidence in me to ask me to play a form of the instrument unfamiliar to me, the contrabassoon. With more trumpet players, I had a better chance to secure a spot in the symphonic band as a bassoon player. The hours I spent lost in a world of sound in the music practice rooms at FAMU, whether I was practicing the trumpet or the bassoon, are among my most precious memories from college. They are among my last memories of my days as a "normal" student.

Priscilla and I were very, very close during that time. We were roommates in the freshman dorm, McGuinn Hall, even though Priscilla had graduated high school a year earlier than I had. She had spent a year in Washington, D.C., in post-high-school courses, believing she had not been properly prepared for college in the segregated school system. Priscilla always kept her side of the room very neat, and my side left a lot to be desired—but other than that, we got along very well. In fact, we had begun to earn ourselves a bit of a reputation on campus by the time we were sophomores, but not because of civil rights.

I have no idea how we met this man—Priscilla has always said we met him on a bus, although I don't remember riding the buses very often—but one day we came across an exotically dressed Negro man who introduced himself as Mujuba Cetawayo, a prince from French West Africa. He was heir to the throne recently vacated by his father's death, he told us. Believe me, it wasn't every day that you encountered African royalty in the sleepy college town of Tallahassee, so naturally we were both very excited, and he asked us to introduce him to Dr. George W. Gore, the president of FAMU. With his genteel ways and his ability to speak several languages, this man instantly charmed everyone who met him, and Dr. Gore was no exception. Soon Dr. Gore was parading our prince around the campus, proclaiming, "Thanks to the Stephens sisters, we have Mujuba Cetawayo!" The prince was lavished with gifts and favors. Even the Florida governor was taken with him, as I recall.

The only person who wasn't charmed, however, was Mother. He offered me a sports car for my birthday, and I got on the telephone right away to ask Mother if I could accept it. "It's this prince. He says he's in love with me and he wants to give me a sports car for my birthday," I told her, excitedly. Mother said, "Are you crazy?" It was unthinkable to her that a young lady would accept a gift like that, so I told the prince no. Soon afterward, the prince moved on. Later, we read about our famous visitor in *Jet* magazine: He was a complete fraud! He wasn't a prince at all, just a Florida con man with an elementary-school education who had been traveling the region, accepting gifts and royal treatment as a "prince." Even the white folks at the University of Miami had been falling over themselves to host him, we heard. Eventually, he was arrested for fraud.

Unfortunately, this was how the "Stephens sisters" first became known to Dr. Gore and most of the FAMU community. Still, our inauspicious beginnings couldn't begin to foretell the impact we would soon have on the campus, the city, and even the nation as a whole. We went from being virtual children to inspired adults in a blink of an eye.

---

The summer of 1959 changed everything. The turning point was cloaked in normalcy, giving us no warning of what was to come.

Our biological father lived in Miami, and that year Priscilla and I spent part of our summer break living with him. While Priscilla and I did not know Daddy well and certainly did not have much of a relationship with him, Mother encouraged us to spend time with him. What I remember most about Daddy is that he was strict, strict, strict. He also had beautiful, thick, prematurely gray hair as long as I'd known him, and the contrast against his very dark skin was always striking. His nickname in Gadsden County was "Snow." Naturally, we were not allowed to have male visitors, and we lived with a very early curfew. Being typical young people, we tried to find ways to circumvent Daddy's authority. For example, he worked nights as a restaurateur and cook, and often he wouldn't return until early dawn—so Priscilla and I stayed out late and snuck over to the "colored only" beach, Virginia Key Beach, where there was a basketball court and a jukebox for evening dances. I *loved* dancing! I loved all the old favorites, like "Dance with Me" by The Drifters, "Don't Let Go" by Roy Hamilton, and "Please, Please, Please" by James Brown. Priscilla and I stayed out all hours, sometimes not getting home until three or four in the morning, always rushing to get in bed before Daddy got home from work.

Toward the end of that summer, we were strolling along Third Avenue in Overtown and ran into a family friend named Clifford "Baby" Combs. After the initial pleasantries, he started talking to us about an organization named the Congress of Racial Equality, or CORE. We learned later that CORE was a nonviolent, interracial civil rights organization that had been founded in Chicago in 1942, but at that time Priscilla and I had never heard of it. CORE did not have nearly the recognition of the much older NAACP (National Association for the Advancement of Colored People) or even the much newer SCLC (Southern Christian Leadership Conference), founded as an offshoot of the 1955–56 Montgomery bus boycott by activists including a young minister named Martin Luther King Jr.

To be honest, we weren't too interested in going to a meeting on a carefree summer's day. But then Baby Combs said, "If you come with me, I'll get you dinner at Wolfie's." That got our attention. Wolfie's was one of the few Miami Beach restaurants that served Negroes. After that, we agreed to go to the CORE workshop.

We never got our dinner, but our lives changed forever.

The workshop we'd been invited to was officially called the Miami Interracial Action Institute, a meeting designed to teach the principles of nonviolent direct action. The meeting was fairly large; including us, there were about seventy-five people there. Some were very young, like us, and others were older, up to their forties. The workshop was led by two CORE field secretaries I would later get to know very well—James T. McCain, who was Negro, and Gordon Carey, who was white. Rev. T. W. Foster, another minister, also had a leadership role. The workshop was held at Overtown's Sir John Hotel (now long gone, like so much in Overtown), which had nicknamed itself "Resort of the Stars" and was best known for its luxuries: a saltwater pool, barber shop, beauty parlor, health center, and shopping center. Now, however, serious business was at hand.

I was very struck by the fact that whites and Negroes from all over the country were talking and working together in this conference room, discussing solutions to the problem of racial discrimination. Although I had been exposed to interracial meetings with my mother when I was younger, this was still a very uncommon sight in 1959, especially in the South. There was a very warm feeling in that room.

Dr. John O. Brown, the first Negro ophthalmologist in the state of Florida, was the president and one of the founders of Miami CORE. He'd been brought to the organization by a white woman named Thalia Stern he'd met at the University of Wisconsin in Madison. Other white members included Stern's brother-in-law, a banker named Jack Gordon (who later became a Florida state senator), and his wife, Barbara; the Negro members included an important Miami activist, A. D. Moore, who later became the national CORE treasurer. As a longtime member of the

NAACP, Dr. Brown came to CORE because he wanted more action on the civil rights front.[1]

What struck Priscilla and me most was that CORE had a plan: The organization had developed techniques for direct action, such as sit-ins—where interracial groups of protesters sat in public places to protest discriminatory policies—and had a very specific protocol for how its protests should be carried out: They were to be nonviolent. They would only take place if an investigation of the facts confirmed that discrimination was practiced. Protests would only be a last resort, after talks had failed, and done without malice. CORE taught that you must try to destroy a system, not an individual, based on Gandhian principles of nonviolent protest. It all made perfect sense to us.

As we listened, Priscilla and I were mesmerized. Although we may have seemed sheltered in some ways, as Negroes we were of course aware of the ongoing problems around us, and it was a frustrating time. A Florida NAACP activist named Harry T. Moore and his wife, Harriet, had been killed when their house was bombed in 1951; we'd witnessed the nonresponsiveness to the Supreme Court's school desegregation decision in 1954. In 1955, a fourteen-year-old boy named Emmett Till had been killed for whistling at a white woman. Till had been horribly disfigured, but his mother had insisted upon an open casket so the whole world could see what whites in Mississippi had done to her son. Emmett Till's killers were acquitted, but the episode had helped spur civil rights legislation in 1957. We had read about these horrifying events, and others, in Negro newspapers like the *Pittsburgh Courier.*

One incident had hit much closer to home. In May 1959, shortly before the school term ended for the summer, a nineteen-year-old Negro woman from FAMU had been parked with her date and another couple when four white men forced her from a car with a knife and shotgun, drove away with her into a secluded area in the woods, and raped her seven times.[2] The white males ranged in age from sixteen to twenty-three, and the FAMU student was still with them in their car, hysterical, when police found them. Although the men were convicted and sentenced to life in prison[3]—a rarity in the South, where usually rapes against Negro women were dismissed—the attack had opened many festering wounds along racial lines in Tallahassee. The shock of the rape had lingered on the FAMU campus of 3,000 students, so it wasn't far from our minds. I'd been so enraged about it, in fact, that I'd written a letter to President Eisenhower. After all, the men had probably only been bold enough to carry out such a terrible act because they expected, after decades of discriminatory "justice," to simply get away with it. Many had before them. I did not know the unfortunate woman involved, but it might easily have been Priscilla or me who had been raped.

Besides, rape was an explosive issue in the South. While Negro women were often raped or coerced into sex by whites, Negro men were often *falsely* accused of raping white women. For Negroes, rape often carried a death sentence. My Uncle Bertram, Daddy Marion's brother, was falsely accused of rape in the mid-1920s after a weekend of tennis at a Negro-owned retreat in the sharecropping village of Kennesaw, Georgia. Beset by the Ku Klux Klan and the sheriff, Uncle Bertram had to sneak out of Kennesaw in the trunk of a car. The entire forty-five acre retreat—known as "King's Wigwam," featuring cabins, an outdoor dance pavilion, an artificial lake, and tennis court—was soon closed and sold at a huge loss. The owner, of course, suspected that the charge had been manufactured to rid Kennesaw of "uppity" Negroes, and it certainly would not have been the first time.[4] Mysteriously, they ceased to pursue the rape charge after the acquisition of King's Wigwam. Obviously, there had been no rape in the first place.

Yes, Priscilla and I were ready to help make a change. As we listened to the presenters describe CORE's philosophies and strategies and we saw the earnestness of the young people in that room, we felt our hearts and minds blossoming. We had never been exposed to an interracial group that included people our own age. One participant was twenty-one-year-old Zev Aelony, a young Jewish man from Minnesota who had recently spent the summer at an interracial community in southwest Georgia called Koinoinia Farm, which was similar to an Israeli *kibbutz* where he had lived earlier that year. Koinoinia had been bombed and attacked by racists. "I was in somewhat of a state of shock, frankly," Aelony says, recalling his first reaction to the treatment of Negroes in the Deep South. "The palpable level of fear and terror came as somewhat of a shock, so I went to that workshop to learn how to deal with that situation." (Zev didn't know it then, but his experiences with violence in the South were far from over.)

Suddenly, everything we had learned from Mother and Daddy Marion about civic responsibility had a concrete form we believed we could make a part of our lives. The workshop was several days long, and we decided we would like to stay. But first, because we were under twenty-one and considered "minors," we needed permission from our parents. One of the white Miami participants, a Jewish woman named Shirley Zoloth, volunteered to call Mother to ask her if we could stay. (Shirley and her husband, businessman Milton Zoloth, both Northerners, had discovered CORE about six months before that workshop. They'd both been disturbed during their drive from Philadelphia to Florida with their two young children in 1954, when they first saw the WHITE and COLORED signs at a gas station south of the Mason-Dixon line.)

Mother probably agreed to let us take part because her longtime friend Clifford "Baby" Combs was also involved, but I've wondered since what she would have said if she had known where that meeting would lead us. Once Mother's permission was granted, we became full-fledged participants. First, we were told, we would receive instruction. Then, we would be sent into Miami's community for real-life desegregation efforts.

In some ways, the CORE workshop was like an Army boot camp. After we had been taught the Gandhian principles of nonviolent protest, the organizers subjected us to verbal abuse, grabbed us, and shoved us hard—exactly what we might expect in a real-life protest situation. We set up tables and pretended to be sitting at lunch counters, and then white organizers called us "niggers" and "nigger lovers." We were expected not to respond, of course. If someone pulled out a weapon and tried to hit us, we would cover ourselves to try to avoid the blow, but we would not defend ourselves otherwise, and we could not strike back. We were even dragged from our seats, but we were told not to resist. If police tried to arrest us, we were instructed, we also would not resist.

The preparations were intense and very emotional, but I doubt I fully realized how much they would mirror the events soon to come. Neither Priscilla nor I had ever been subjected to real violence in our lives. I had always shied away from physical confrontations, even as a child, and I don't believe, at that point, anyone had ever called us "nigger" except at the CORE workshop. Even though I knew the organizers were only play-acting, it was strange to hear that hated, dehumanizing word leveled at us by white men and women. I felt myself bristling. But we believed it was all for a good cause. As it turned out, we would rely on those preparations a great deal in only a few short months.

The CORE workshop was not only theoretical—it was designed to put thought into action—so we took part in lunch-counter testing at Miami department stores and restaurants to see if Negroes would be served. I was one of the Negroes sent to test a Royal Castle, and Zev Aelony and a white woman went as observers to report anything they witnessed. When I sat at the counter and asked for food with a group of several Negroes, the manager looked at us closely. There were angry stares against our backs from other customers. I noticed that the manager looked nervous, with his jaw tight, but to my surprise, he actually took my order and served me a hamburger. None of the other Negroes were served.

"After they left," Zev recalls, "a white guy got up and went to the counter. He was just red with fury, and he said, 'Why did you serve her?' And the manager kind of gently pushed the cashier aside and said, 'If they pay taxes, I can't serve them—but if they come in and speak Spanish, I have to serve them by law.' "

Now, I had spoken with nothing but my usual Southern accent—and I certainly hadn't said a single word in Spanish—but I was wearing large hoop earrings and had long hair and olive-colored skin, so the manager had apparently decided to pretend he thought I was Hispanic rather than an American Negro. He then had an excuse to treat me like a human being.

The CORE workshop gave me and Priscilla a very strong conviction that we two could easily motivate other students in Tallahassee to take action against discrimination. Why should we have to attend segregated movie theaters with special balcony sections set aside for Negroes, or separate theaters altogether? Why couldn't we be served at lunch counters like Woolworth and McCrory's, especially since those same stores were more than happy to take our money when we purchased other items? Naively, we also believed that the university itself would support us. In any case, we were excited and ready for action.

Jim Dewar, a young, redheaded white man at the workshop, offered to give us a ride up to Belle Glade, which was roughly an hour and a half from Miami. Once we arrived, he asked if he and Harland Randolph, the other CORE workshop participant who was riding with us, could spend the night at our parents' house. Two-lane Highway 27 was known as "Bloody 27" because of all the terrible accidents, and he didn't want to drive all the way back to Miami in the dark. I said yes without hesitation. Priscilla says now that she had some misgivings about it, but she went along with me because I seemed so confident.

It was late when we arrived, and my family had already gone to bed. Jim and Harland slept in the living room while Priscilla and I retired to our respective bedrooms. As my mother recalled in an interview five years before she died, my grandmother, Alma Peterson, was the first to awaken the next morning, and she panicked when she saw the boys sleeping there.

"She woke up that morning and came into our bedroom, which was very unusual for her," Mother recalled. "She asked me did I know what was going on, saying, 'Those children are going to get us killed!' I said, 'What do you mean?' She said, 'They have two white boys sleeping in the living room!' "

Life for our family had changed already, and we hadn't even gotten started.

Three or four weeks after the CORE workshop, Priscilla and I went back to school for the fall term as two young women with a mission. As soon as our classmates began to trickle back to campus, we knocked on door after door in our dormitory at Wheatley Hall to encourage them to come to the first CORE meeting in Tallahassee. We must have talked to a hundred people, maybe more. CORE was an unknown organization at FAMU and in Tallahassee, but the students we talked to seemed eager to use the techniques used by CORE to eradicate a system that robbed them of their dignity and first-class citizenship. We had our first meeting right in the dorm. We were lucky to be on such a conservative campus, as all Negro colleges were, because young ladies had a curfew—I believe it was 9:00 P.M.—so we really had a captive audience. About thirty people came to the first meeting, and although Priscilla and I were disappointed at the time, we later came to learn that thirty people was actually a very large group for a meeting. (More often than not, you usually had a base group of only five or six people to plan civil rights protests, and larger numbers—hopefully—would attend the actual protests. But we hadn't learned that yet.)

In time, I also spoke to FAMU's assistant admissions director, Miss Daisy Young, who I knew was the advisor for the NAACP college chapter on our campus.[5] Miss Young not only helped us recruit white students from Florida State University, but she volunteered her own home as a meeting place. She also took me to a meeting of the Inter-Civic Council (ICC), a Tallahassee organization that had formed during a recent bus boycott. There, I explained the goals of CORE, and we were invited to hold our meetings at 803 Floral Street, where the ICC met in the office beside Rev. Dan Speed's grocery store. National CORE helped us get started by sending James T. McCain and Gordon Carey, the field secretaries who had helped run the summer institute, to meet with us. Many of us were students from FAMU and FSU, and our first president was a FAMU student named George Brown. Negro adults in Tallahassee's community responded to the call, too. For example, Rev. T. S. Johnson, another minister, was voted our vice president (and later became president), and an Episcopal minister, Father David Brooks, also allowed us to meet at his church, St. Michael's Episcopal Church on Melvin Street.

One of our most vigorous adult supporters was Richard Haley, an FAMU music professor with a distinct speaking voice, whom I had met while enrolled in his class on music theory. I had not excelled in Mr. Haley's class: He gave me the first "F" of my college career, and it was in his class that I realized I did not have a good "ear" for tone. But I did talk to him about CORE, and although he carried himself in a very sedate manner, he was excited about CORE from the start. Mr. Haley was originally from Chicago, and he wasn't nervous about getting involved, as were some other FAMU professors. "I'm not concerned about myself, because I can get another job," Mr. Haley once told Miss Young, advising her to be careful because she had family ties in Tallahassee.[6] (His words, unfortunately, turned out to be prophetic; Mr. Haley's activism would cost him his job.) Dr. James Hudson, FAMU's chaplain and a civil rights veteran, also became a charter member of Tallahassee CORE.

In all, there were twenty-one charter members, and our little fledgling group decided that our first project would be to test the desegregation of the buses in Tallahassee. The city buses had been a hotbed of controversy in recent years.

In 1956, shortly before Priscilla and I enrolled at FAMU, students Wilhelmina Jakes and Carrie Patterson refused to give up their seats on the bus to whites, and sat instead on a seat with a white woman right behind the driver. The driver told them to move to the back of the bus, and they were arrested when they refused to move after being told they could not have a refund.[7] That incident resulted in a bus boycott in Tallahassee very similar to the one Rosa Parks had sparked in Montgomery, Alabama, in 1955. One of our new CORE chapter's charter members, Rev. Charles Kenzie (C. K.) Steele, had been instrumental in planning and carrying out Tallahassee's boycott. Rev. Steele, who often wore bow ties, was the first vice president of the Southern Christian Leadership Conference and a friend of the young minister Dr. Martin Luther King Jr., who had garnered national attention during the Montgomery boycott. Dr. Hudson had also been very involved. The Tallahassee boycott had lasted eighteen months, and while it never received the same notice as the Montgomery boycott, 90 percent of Tallahassee's Negroes had refused to ride the buses—using carpools or simply walking—to prove that they would no longer be treated like second-class citizens.[8]

Yet more than a year after the boycott's end, Negroes were still riding in the back of the city buses in Tallahassee. Our CORE group decided to see what would happen to Negroes who tried to ride up front. We were somewhat surprised by what we found: None of the bus drivers or passengers bothered the Negro students when we sat at the front of the bus—except for funny looks, and we got plenty of those. While the desegregation order had held, our people were still segregating themselves. Most Negroes still rode at the back of the bus from fear or habit, or both. I guess no one wanted to be the only Negro sitting at the front of the bus because a shyness, a subservience, was so branded into us. Thinking back on it, that was a sad state of affairs, but at least Tallahassee CORE had conducted its first official activity.

To be truthful, we had hoped to have more of an impact.

Be careful what you wish for.

I'm still amazed all these years later how the actions of a very few people can have such wide-ranging repercussions. Rosa Parks, Wilhelmina Jakes, and Carrie Patterson were ordinary people who refused to give up their seats on the bus. Martin Luther King Jr. gave his voice to a newborn Movement. And in 1960, the entire South was ignited by the actions of four college freshmen in Greensboro, North Carolina: North Carolina A&T College students Ezell Blair Jr., Franklin McCain, Joseph McNeil, and David Richmond.

At 4:30 P.M. on February 1, 1960, those four neatly dressed boys sat at a lunch counter at a Greensboro Woolworth. They were told they could not be served unless they moved over to the stand-up counter reserved for Negroes, but they wouldn't. A Negro woman who worked at the restaurant became exasperated and reportedly told them, "You're acting stupid, ignorant. That's why we can't get anywhere today. You know you're supposed to eat at the other end."[9] Eventually, the store closed without further incident. About fifteen minutes after closing time, the boys left, saying they would return the next day with other students from their school. And they did. The Greensboro sit-in—the action of four boys—stoked a fever that raced through other Southern cities in the days, weeks, and months to come. The student sit-in movement had begun.

I heard about the Greensboro sit-in through the CORE grapevine, and I was very excited! Marvin Rich, who was the public relations person for

CORE, sent out press releases describing the situation in Greensboro, encouraging all CORE groups around the country to focus on picketing Woolworth to pressure them to change their policies in the South. We had a Woolworth right in Tallahassee, which also did not serve Negroes at the lunch counter, and we felt we could give these students support by sitting-in, too. After our CORE group had spent several months simply documenting discrimination policies throughout Tallahassee, this sounded like exactly the sort of nonviolent direction action we had trained for—and we were ready.

A regional "sympathy sit-in" day was scheduled for Saturday, February 13, and Tallahassee CORE took part.[10] About ten of us—students from FAMU and two Negro high school students—dressed in neat school attire—carried our schoolbooks and calmly walked inside the Woolworth store on Monroe Street. In 1960, signs above the lunch counter at Woolworth advertised sundaes for a quarter and an entire roast turkey dinner for sixty-five cents. We sat at the cushioned, straight-back counter stools and asked for slices of cake. The surprised waitress refused, but we remained at the counter. The whites around us, realizing what was happening, soon began to disappear. One white man remained to eat his food—and the waitress thanked him for tolerating that day's "indecency." The entire time, we sat quietly and stoically on our stools, our heads in our books. One white onlooker congratulated FAMU student William Carpenter, telling him, "I think you're doing a fine job. Just sit there." Afterward, a young white hoodlum tried to bait Carpenter into an argument, but Carpenter wouldn't respond. "I bet if I disjoint him, he'll talk," the hoodlum said. When Carpenter didn't respond, the hoodlum moved on. For a time, it was quiet.

"What are you niggers doing in here?"

One voice ignited the next, and suddenly shoppers at the store who had gathered around us began to taunt us, making threats. "Ya'll niggers want a whuppin'? You're stinking this whole place up. You better get the hell out of here." The waitress tried to ask the troublemakers to leave, saying, "You can see they aren't here to start anything."[11]

It's a strange experience to incite such negative emotion through such a simple, peaceful act. The longer we sat there reading in silence, the more incensed the crowd around us became, calling us hateful names, chiefly "niggers." The situation felt surreal. None of us could pay real attention to the words on our books' pages. I even saw someone holding a small handgun—which was shocking—and no one said a word to him about putting the gun away, even inside a public store. Was he going to shoot at us? We had entered new, dangerous territory.

As the threats intensified, the store manager panicked and closed the counter. We stayed for a total of two hours. Curious reporters came to see what the excitement was about, and then we all left. Someone eventually called the police, but we were gone by then. That was our first sit-in. Although we didn't realize it, the second would catapult us into national headlines.

Most of us were students, so we were careful to schedule protests around our classes. We decided we would go back on the following Saturday. We'd been lucky to avoid serious incident in our first sit-in, but we knew we couldn't take that luck for granted.

Using our experience from the first sit-in, as well as the tactics I'd learned at the CORE workshop in Miami, Mr. Haley and I spoke to potential sit-in volunteers about how to react in the face of taunts or violence that might ensue in the next sit-in. We designated two white students from Florida State University to act as observers. They would be seated before our arrival, and they would have an important function: By remaining seated alongside the Negro students after we arrived, we hoped they would demonstrate through example that there was nothing earth-shattering about Negroes and whites sitting next to each other. They would also report what was said about us after we left. This is just one of the many ways interracial cooperation was so important to the Movement.

Finally, the day arrived: Saturday, February 20, 1960.

Seventeen of us—mostly FAMU students, with two high-school students and a local forty-three-year-old resident, Mary Ola Gaines—arrived at Woolworth at approximately 2:00 P.M. None of us knew Mrs. Gaines, who was the only legal-age adult in our group that day. She'd heard about the planned sit-in through the Inter-Civic Council and had decided to join us after work. I was very glad, and surprised, to see her arrive. Although two of the participants were local high school students, Mrs. Gaines's arrival gave us even more legitimacy, since she was an established member of the Tallahassee community. A Georgia native, she had lived in Tallahassee since 1939 and worked for a white family as a housekeeper. She did not know anything about CORE, but she knew what she believed was right. "I was not afraid," she told me thirty years later, when I finally had the chance to ask her why she had come that day. "I was doing something I thought would help."[12]

Now, no one would be able to dismiss us as so-called "outside agitators." I heard the waitress say, "Oh, Lord, here they come again." We sat at the counter and ordered food, and the waitress seemed astonished. "Niggers eat in the back," someone told us, referring to a counter in the rear. The other white patrons got out of the way, leaving only the sit-in participants and our two white observers.

In no time, it seemed, a large crowd grew behind us. Maybe they had been waiting for us this time. Again, we sat and tried to read our books while people shouted threats at us. I was trying to make my way through *The Blue Book of Crime,* a criminology book I'd borrowed from another student, and Barbara Broxton was reading *How to Tell the Different Kind of Fingerprints,* which would become quite ironic later. "I thought I smelled niggers," someone called out. "You niggers sit in back!" someone else shouted angrily. We could feel the rage swelling behind us. Out of the corner of my eye, I noticed a man holding a baseball bat. The hoodlums who gathered around us were mostly younger men with upturned shirt collars, many of them wearing their hair slicked back in the style of the day. The crowd had become very big, very fast. I felt someone tug sharply on my clothing, but I sat stoically, not moving. The hoodlums were trying to pull us from our stools, trying to provoke us, but every single one of us held ourselves in check. We sat and read, all the while knowing that no one was likely to step forward to stop it if we were attacked.

Tananarive might ask, "Do you remember your heart pounding, your hands shaking?" Honestly, the answer is no. I can't speak for everyone there—and I know we all processed our fears in different ways—but I wasn't aware of the normal symptoms of fright. I was simply resigned, as if my feeling was "What else can you do to hurt me? I have to be free." That feeling was my bedrock.

About forty-five tense minutes went by, and after our two white observers decided to leave, the mayor of Tallahassee came into the store with other members of the city commission to ask us to leave. Some people might think, "Well, weren't you young people impressed that the mayor himself made the request?" To me, the answer was no. As long as he led a city with segregated policies, he had not won my respect. Most of us remained, except six students who changed their minds and decided to go back to campus. That left eleven, including me and Priscilla, Mrs. Gaines, six other FAMU students, and high-school students Charles and Henry Steele, who were sons of local minister Rev. C. K. Steele, pastor of Bethel Missionary Baptist Church and a charter member of Tallahassee CORE.

Four or five police officers arrived at 3:30 P.M. The mayor also came back and tried to direct questions to me, but Priscilla was our designated spokesperson, so she was the only one who could address authorities. She calmly told them that we would not leave until we were served. So that was that: All eleven us were arrested for disturbing the peace by "engaging in riotous conduct." Can you imagine? Simply for sitting at a lunch counter! We were walked a couple of blocks to the jail as a crowd of white Tallahassee residents watched us on the sidelines, applauding the police and making catcalls, but all of us held our heads up high. We may have been nervous, but though we had been raised as law-abiding citizens and had never been arrested, we certainly were not ashamed.

At the police station, we were fingerprinted and processed. The jail on Park Avenue in Tallahassee was in a building that had been a savings and loan, so the jail cell was nothing more than an old bank vault. In addition to the others I mentioned, there were several FAMU students: a brother and sister named John and Barbara Broxton, who were from South Florida; William Larkins, who was also from South Florida and was the incoming president of FAMU's student government association; Angelina Nance, from Greenwood, South Carolina; Merritt Spaulding from Alabama; and Clement Carney from New Jersey. Once we were inside the police station, officers continued to taunt and try to intimidate us. After some time, we were permitted to notify persons in the community of what had happened, so we called Rev. C. K. Steele and Rev. Dan Speed. To avoid publicity, police tried to sneak us out the back door when we were bailed out, but reporters circled the building to meet us.[13]

Our bail was set at $500 per person, which was very expensive in the 1960s. I do not remember how we paid our bail. We couldn't find any local attorneys willing to represent us, so CORE asked the American Civil Liberties Union (ACLU) in Miami to provide attorneys. Tobias Simon and Howard Dixon, who were both white, defended us, and the NAACP also assigned a Negro attorney in Miami, Grattan "G. E." Graves Jr. We were arraigned February 22, and we pleaded not guilty. Meanwhile, despite the fact that there was very little press coverage of the sit-ins in the *Tallahassee Democrat* (I think the editors intended to have a news blackout to keep word of our activities from spreading), both Negroes and whites in Tallahassee were growing more aware of what had happened. FAMU students voted not to go to classes so the entire student body could attend our March 3 trial. When word of that spread, our trial was postponed for two weeks.

Mother and Daddy Marion heard about what had happened even before we could call them, and we did our best to reassure Mother on the telephone that we would try to keep safe. But Daddy Marion wrote us a letter on February 21 that conveyed not only his fears as a parent, but his cynicism about the potential success of the blossoming civil rights movement:

> *I wonder if either of you has counted the cost. I know that you feel that you are doing a grand and noble thing, and looking at it from one point of view, you are making some headway. Remember this, if either of you get into trouble, the very people you are trying to help would never lend you a hand.*
>
> *The facts are really this: About 10% or 15% of our race are just about ready for what you are trying to accomplish; the other 85% or 90% don't care, are not at all interested, and would do nothing to aid the cause. They had just as soon walk all over you and even curse you for trying to help him. The great majority of them don't want help and wouldn't know how to appreciate anything you will have to suffer to accomplish.*
>
> *Yes, I know it looks big and you feel like you are doing something, but stop and take stock and put the matter in balance. Right now you stand chances of being expelled from school, as FAMU is a State School, run with State Funds, and dictated to from the State's governing powers. This might lead to your not being able to get employment anywhere in the State, unless you have money enough to open your own business, but right now all of us are living day to day with no preparation for tomorrow—financially nor for business. This thing could even come to the point of me losing my job—I do work for the County and State, you know—and I am too old to look for any type job now, nor would anyone employ me at my age. You may come out all right, but on the other hand you stand a great deal to lose and nothing to gain but short-lived satisfaction.*
>
> *The thing both of you should consider is to get through College, or get an education, make a place in life for yourself where you can be self-sustaining. You have this great*

> *opportunity now, so take advantage of it. Stop leaving too much to chance.*
>
> *I know both of you are going to do what you want to do. I think I know you that well. All I can say is to weigh the matter, consider all that might be affected, and then do what you are going to do. I know neither of you think Daddy Marion has any sense, but he has lived in this world a long time and what you are now doing is nothing new to him.*
>
> *Love,*
> *Daddy Marion*

Daddy Marion's conservatism was a bit of a surprise to us, considering how much he had influenced our thinking in terms of the rights and responsibilities of citizens, but he was a parent first. No one wants his children to be on the front lines. No one wants his own family to suffer. As much as it hurt us to realize that even the parents who had shaped our views were pessimistic at the time, we knew we had to press on. There was too much work left to do.

Robert Armstrong, a white Florida State University student, was arrested at a sit-in at McCrory's on March 5 that received prominent coverage in the *Democrat*,[14] and there were reportedly more than 200 people at the next Tallahassee CORE meeting, including many more whites who, I suppose, were beginning to realize that they could not be free, either, if all of us were not free. I was not in Tallahassee that day because several of us, including Priscilla and FAMU students, Merritt Spaulding and Charles Wilkerson, had driven to New York, where we participated in a press conference at the headquarters of the Brotherhood of Sleeping Car Porters on West 125th Street. Seven other Southern Negro students were with us, and we were all there to bring attention to the student sit-in movement. By then, about 200 Negro students in thirty-eight cities had been arrested in demonstrations in the South. Later that day, hundreds of demonstrators in Harlem picketed the Woolworth on 125th Street.[15]

My attention was still focused on Tallahassee, and soon I was back. With momentum building, the seeds for CORE's largest Tallahassee sit-ins were sown. After failed negotiations with the management of both Woolworth and McCrory's, we decided to stage sit-ins at both counters on March 12, a day that would be scalded into my memory for the rest of my life.

By March 12, the growing fervor on the FAMU campus was a far cry from the quiet, early days when we struggled to encourage thirty people to attend a meeting. Students were angry that other students had actually been arrested for simply trying to order food, and since negotiations with the store managers had failed, dozens had volunteered to take part in the sit-ins scheduled that day. (Those of us who were already facing charges decided not to subject ourselves to further arrest, at least for a while.) I did not fault those students who felt, for whatever reason, that they could not take part; I had a good friend, for example, who told me he couldn't be a demonstrator because he might not be able to adhere to our philosophy of nonviolence, and he didn't want to damage our efforts. Others shied away because of fears for their personal safety, which I also understood. But the rest of us *had* to participate. That need was simply in our souls.

I witnessed twelve other FAMU and FSU students arrested that day at the Woolworth lunch counter and taken to jail. They were marched down the street in interracial pairs, escorted by police on all sides, with police and onlookers branding the whites as "nigger lovers." "Hold hands with your nigger buddies you love so much," police taunted white FSU student Oscar "Bob" Brock.[16] A photographer captured the image of Brock walking alongside George Carter, a Negro student from FAMU. The solidarity between whites and Negroes was a very striking sight, but it was painful to see so many other young people's lives being disrupted for so simple an act. We had to try to show the powers that be that we would not be intimidated by arrest, or our cause would be lost. On FAMU's campus, our CORE group dispatched fifty more students to take over for those arrested at Woolworth, and fifty to sit-in at the lunch counter with white students at McCrory's. In accordance with CORE protocol, we also tried desperately to reach city authorities to negotiate a way to end the arrests and protests. No one would talk to us.

The students sent to McCrory's were arrested as soon as they arrived. At Woolworth, the president of the White Citizens Council (which, as far as I'm concerned, was a racist group no different from the Ku Klux Klan), Homer Barrs, was leading a mob of armed whites who had assembled to prevent more students from entering the store. The students had been stopped in their tracks, so they stood and shouted, "No violence! No violence! No violence!" Their voices rang against the other downtown storefronts, but all the while the specter of violence was gazing into their faces. The police officers on the scene refused to do anything about the knives, baseball bats, and axe handles being brandished by the angry whites. It looked like a recipe for a free-for-all.

We went back to campus to inform the students about what was going on. We got the word out to everyone who would listen and made placards in support of our arrested students: NO VIOLENCE. WE WILL NOT FIGHT MOBS. WE ARE AMERICANS, TOO. GIVE US BACK OUR STUDENTS. Standing on the steps between the stately columns of Jackson Davis Hall on FAMU's campus, I bared my heart and soul to my fellow students as I described the arrest of our classmates, and the students responded. Before long, our number had swelled to one thousand strong. With our placards painted and our spirits buoyed, we began a peaceful march, walking in pairs that stretched in a seemingly endless line.

I was proud of my fellow students. The feeling of impending change was so obvious on that day. With so many unified Negro students full of energy and determination, we could almost feel victory in the air. *We* were going to help bring about change. Finally, we were no longer going to sit and be intimidated. We began the two-mile walk from FAMU's campus, intending to reach downtown.

We never made it.

In Tallahassee, as in many cities, the railroad tracks serve as the line dividing the white town from the colored town. Near the Tallahassee railroad tracks dozens of police officers were waiting for us, forming a barrier all along Adams and Monroe Streets. The very people we had tried to reach to negotiate with had, apparently, prepared instead for a different sort of confrontation.

The teargas bombs began to fly. Officials later maintained that we had a three-minute warning,[17] but I remember no such warning. All I remember is that what had begun as a peaceful march turned to havoc.

I will never forget how one police officer, who apparently recognized me as one of the student leaders, stood directly in front of me and said, "I want *you*," before lobbing a tear gas canister into my face, point-blank. The thick, bitter chemicals filled my eyes, nose, and mouth. I coughed and choked, flailing and blinded, as other students around me screamed and fled. For a terrifying instant, I could not breathe at all. My eyes were afire.

They say all of us meet a guardian angel sometime. Most times, we never know who it is. I certainly met my guardian angel that day. A man grabbed my arm and pressed a handkerchief against my burning eyes. He began to lead me. "Don't touch your eyes. Don't rub them, or you'll just rub it in more. I was in the Army," the man told me.

The world was all darkness, but I could hear screams, shouts, and the pounding of running feet around me. "I can't see!" I told the stranger.

"I know. Your sight will come back. Just don't rub. Give it time to wear off."

With those reassuring words, he led me to a nearby church—I don't even know which one—and sat me in one of the pews. To this day, I do not know who he was, but I truly hope he will read this book and make himself known to me. His kindness still means a great deal to me.

The inhumane event, captured on film by local Negro freelance photographer Steve Beasley, appeared in *Ebony* magazine. It was also recorded by Virginia Delavan, editor of FSU's *Florida Flambeau*, who was later jailed herself for simply *talking* to Negroes involved in the protest.[18] Most of the students involved had not been civil rights activists before that day. They had never been to a CORE workshop to learn to deal with harassment, or attacks, or violence. They had never made the inner vow that they would risk their lives in this battle. Even with all my training and resolve, I had not expected what happened that day. How could they?

All around me, as I sat blinded in that church, I heard my schoolmates straggling in, sobbing. Their clothes reeked of tear gas. Many were treated for burns and other injuries at the FAMU hospital, rescued from the scene by faculty members. Later, I heard reports that the police had actually blocked the path of students trying to run back toward the campus during the tear gas attack. Thirty-five demonstrators were arrested, although the police did nothing to punish the armed whites who began using violence against the students. Clearly, the Tallahassee authorities considered it their job only to protect the interests of segregationist whites, not the interest of peace. Our own nation, it seemed, was at war against us.

All I could do was keep that handkerchief pressed to my face and grit my teeth against the stinging of my watering eyes. Though more than forty years have passed since that tear gas incident, I have felt so much sensitivity to light ever since that I have to wear darkened glasses even in a movie theater. The condition has only worsened with age. It is rare that I will drive at night, because even streetlights bother me, but dark glasses make it nearly impossible to see at all. All these years later, just as I did in March 1960, I have been forced to keep my eyes covered.

But I didn't know my future then. As I tried to recover in the church that day, I sat in silence with a pounding heart, feeling stunned, waiting until I could once again see the light.

Six

# Tananarive Due

**"Mama exhorted her children at every opportunity to 'jump at de sun.' We might not land on the sun, but at least we would get off the ground."**
***—Zora Neale Hurston***

"Hey, hey, U.S.A.—*Stop supporting Duvalier!* Hey, hey, U.S.A. . . . "

It was the 1970s, and my sisters and I walked in a purposeful circle with a handful of other protesters with hand-written placards in front of the Dade County federal building in Miami, chanting loudly in opposition to U.S.–backed Haitian dictator Jean-Claude Duvalier. I was about eleven, my sister Johnita was nine, and Lydia might have been seven. All of us wore our hair in neatly combed pigtails, and we pumped our placards in rhythm as we walked. "Hey, hey, U.S.A.—Stop supporting Duvalier!"

It was just another day in the Due family. Our parents gave us ballet lessons, drama lessons, piano lessons, etiquette lessons—and life lessons. From a very young age, we were taught that there were injustices in the world and that we could have a role in rectifying them. During the forty-five-minute drive to that protest from our home in Southwest Dade, our parents explained to us that Haiti was a very poor country, that most of its inhabitants were black, and that the United States government discriminated against Haitian refugees who tried to come here for a better life while refugees from Cuba were welcomed. Worse, we were told, the United States was supporting a terrible Haitian dictator named Jean-Claude Duvalier, who was corrupt and violent.

That was all we needed to hear. We joined the adults in the small picket line in front of the federal building, proudly brandishing our signs, chanting with youthful abandon. Passersby stared at us, but we did not feel shy or self-conscious. We had a message to spread, and we wanted people to hear it. "Hey, hey, U.S.A.—Stop supporting Duvalier!"

Roughly two years separate Johnita and me, and two years separate

Johnita and Lydia, so often we recall different childhood occurrences because of our age gap. While I remember a fairly regular barrage of racial epithets from white children after we first moved into Point Royal, Lydia, who is four years younger than I am, was bracing for that but got none. For Johnita and Lydia, most of their torment was from the mouths of other black children who called them "Oreo" and tried to pick fights, believing my sisters' careful diction and dedication to school must be proof that they considered themselves superior.

My sisters and I share slightly different memories of our family experiences. But the day we marched for Haitians' rights has been seared into all of our memories.

I felt strong, and free, and *right*. I felt like my parents' child.

For me and my sisters, childhood was about learning where we belonged in the world. We never questioned our parents' activism. We took for granted that this was something they did because it needed doing. We knew other kids' parents didn't have their names in the newspaper, or have people calling from all over the state because they needed help. Other kids' parents didn't march for Haitian rights, and hadn't been to jail. Perhaps, I thought, other kids' parents weren't quite so busy all the time, either, but that was all right, too. It needed doing, that was all. From time to time, when we weren't in school, my sisters and I would do it with them.

At meetings, my sisters and I usually sat in the back of the room. Our main job was to keep quiet. Once, my mother took us to a meeting in Opa-locka, a North Dade city (this was far, far away from our house, farther than downtown), with Mrs. Eufaula Frazier, an activist we knew very well, and we got a little too giggly during the opening prayer. That was one of the rare times my mother had to raise her voice at us in public. Another time, my father was hosting a meeting at the house. The only time people ever came over to our house was for meetings, and they came often and stayed late. My sisters and I amused ourselves by hiding just out of sight behind a big easy chair, giggling as we surveyed the visitors. That was one of the rare times we actually made our father angry, and he took us to the back of the house with swats on our behinds and a stern and firm good-night.

In 1976, when I was ten, my mother asked me and my sisters if we'd like to take the morning off from school. This usually only happened on Dr. Martin Luther King's birthday, when we set out early in the morning for a quiet observance downtown that culminated with the singing of

"We Shall Overcome," followed by breakfast at Howard Johnson. The singing and the eating were my favorite parts.

But this wasn't Dr. King's birthday. "You know who Jimmy Carter is, don't you?" my father said.

"He's running for president," I said, because I'd seen him on TV. "The peanut farmer."

"We're going to meet Jimmy Carter. He wants to see prominent blacks in Miami, so we're going to visit him at a hotel downtown."

Of course! Why wouldn't a man running for president of the United States want to meet my parents? I considered this a perfectly natural turn of events. If anything, I probably wondered why *we* had to go to *him* instead of *him* coming to *us*. John Due and Patricia Stephens Due were very busy people, after all. My only regret was that I wasn't already sitting in my classroom at R. R. Moton Elementary, where I could remark loudly to my classmates, "Oh, excuse me, I have to go. My family is going to go meet the man who might be the next *president.*"

"Do we have to?" Lydia whined. At six and a half, apparently, a trip to a hotel to meet a peanut farmer did not sound exciting enough to miss school. Johnita and I shushed her loudly.

Mom dressed the three of us in matching denim suits, and we set out for our appointment at the Konover Hotel on Miami Beach. I expected to find a zealous crowd of supporters waving red-white-and-blue streamers, but the setting was actually a very sedate hotel suite with only about a dozen people in sight. Lydia was the first in our family to spot him. "There he is!" she said, and we followed her pointing finger. People parted as Carter walked into the room. He was so soft-spoken as he talked to the people flanking him that I could barely hear the singsong of his Georgia accent until we were standing beside him. Since my sisters and I were too awestruck to speak, Mom asked him to sign autographs for us.

To me, it was all a bit anticlimactic. Jimmy Carter was not a large man, towering over everyone in the room the way I had imagined a presidential candidate might. He had a slight build, and he wasn't nearly as tall as Dad. We got a good look at his trademark smile, though. Carter posed for a picture with our family and Florida Representative Gwendolyn S. Cherry, my godmother and a close family friend. His hand rested gently on Lydia's shoulder as we all grinned for the camera.

"Hey, know what?" I said, making a sudden realization during the drive home. "If Jimmy Carter wins the election, we'll have a picture with the president!"

The three of us shrieked in delight, and a few months later, my prophecy came true. Johnita would meet President Carter again at a Democratic rally in Miami four years later, when his hair had gone white and the strain of his four years in office was obvious in the deep lines on his face. She showed him the picture he'd taken with us and asked him to sign it. "I'm sorry, sweetheart. The Secret Service won't let me sign it now," he said sadly, sincerely. "Mail it to me at the White House." By then, they both knew that he might not be in the White House much longer. True to his word, shortly before the end of his term, President Carter signed our photo: *With Best Wishes to the Due Family—Jimmy Carter.*

My parents' lives were not separate from ours, and by taking us with them to so many places they went, my parents gave us a consciousness many children our age did not have. I remember, when I was about eleven, my mother gave us T-shirts printed with a giant "X" across the image of an electric chair when we were about to drive to a state NAACP meeting. END DEATH PENALTY NOW, the shirt said.

"I can't wear that," I said.

My mother paused, surprised. She wasn't used to hearing objections. "Why not?"

"Because I'm not against the death penalty. If someone kills you, they should die, too."

My parents patiently explained to me and my sisters that the NAACP was against the death penalty because it unfairly targeted blacks and other minorities. A disproportionately higher percentage of blacks who committed murder were sentenced to the death penalty than were whites, they told me. And blacks were more likely to be poor, so they couldn't afford proper attorneys. They also told us the story of Freddie Pitts and Wilbert Lee, who had spent twelve years in a Florida prison, nine of them on death row, only to be proven innocent of the crime. The NAACP was also trying to help Pitts and Lee win reparations from the state, they said. In addition to being carried out in a discriminatory way, the death penalty sometimes sentenced innocent people to die, especially if they were black or poor.

"So you see?" my mother said. "I understand how you feel, but this is just another area where the system discriminates. And as long as that's true, we're against the death penalty."

As usual, my parents knew how to move me in a way that made their position crystal clear. There was *justice,* which is what my parents believed in, and there was *injustice,* which they were fighting against. It was as easy to understand as Superman and Wonder Woman outsmarting villains with the League of Justice on Saturday morning cartoons.

My opinion on the death penalty was formed at that moment, and hasn't wavered since.

---

In May of 1978, when I was twelve, I saw government at work. I was selected to serve as a page in the Florida House of Representatives under Rep. Gwendolyn Sawyer Cherry, one of the state's few black legislators. Rep. Cherry had received her law degree at the age of forty-four and was a forceful proponent of equal rights and reform on issues like the death penalty.

Most of my days as a page were spent scurrying back and forth between the snack bar and the House floor for the representatives' coffee, sugar, and nicotine fixes. During the brief moments between filling food orders, I heard snippets of the laws the legislators were debating. Most interesting of all was the question of whether or not to give former death row prisoners Pitts and Lee $75,000 apiece for their twelve-year ordeal. Mom and I attended an impassioned rally in their favor before the day of the vote, and I was later on the House floor to hear the cascade of loud nays that dashed their hopes in the Florida House, at least for that session.

*I think that's downright disgusting, but they're trying again next year, and they're going to keep trying until they get it,* I wrote in my diary. *Twelve years is as long as I've been alive. Pitts and Lee are asking for $75,000 mere dollars for all of those years of agony. I just can't imagine a government that would be so unfeeling to deny these two men not only their freedom . . . but justice.*

I didn't know it then, but I would be a grown woman—with a newspaper career behind me, and two novels published—and it would be on the eve of my wedding day before Freddie Pitts and Wilbert Lee would finally receive $500,000 apiece from the Florida legislature in 1998, after the tireless urging of Florida's black legislators. Pitts and Lee had been pardoned by Gov. Reuben Askew in 1975 after spending twelve years in prison, but they battled for decades to win compensation for those stolen years. After the police beat a confession out of them in 1963, Pitts and Lee originally were convicted by an all-white jury. Another man confessed to the murder they were charged with only a year after their sentencing, yet they sat on death row.[1] How can anyone calculate a price for such an invasion of one's life? And why did the state take so excruciatingly long to provide even that meager compensation?

Johnita was selected to serve as a page a couple of years after I did. She served a state representative from Jacksonville, Dr. Arnett E. Girardeau, a dentist who was a former NAACP vice president in Jacksonville. He later became one of the first black state senators in Florida since Reconstruction. (Lydia also later served as a page under State Rep. Humberto J. Cortina.)

Johnita's page experience had an ironic twist: Because Mom was working, she could not stay in Tallahassee with Johnita the way she had with me. So Johnita was hosted by Rep. Bill Flynn, a white Democrat from Miami, and his wife, Elizabeth. Between the Flynns, Dr. Girardeau, and especially Rep. Carrie Meek, Johnita was very well taken care of. But the decision to let Johnita live with the Flynns turned out to be controversial for my parents. Bill Flynn had been a strict segregationist in the 1960s, and my parents had two activist friends, William Miles and Odell Johns, who remembered Flynn threatening them with a shotgun in his South Dade barbecue restaurant because they wanted to be served. But Rep. Flynn begged my parents to entrust their daughter to him, saying he'd had a change of heart, and once Mom was certain it was all right with his wife, she agreed. "I just felt that this was what we were working for—change—so we could say, 'All right, you've changed,' " Mom said, explaining the decision. But when the news spread in the black community that the Flynns had offered Johnita a room and a bed in Tallahassee, my parents got a couple of nasty phone calls, and some of their civil rights friends didn't speak to them for some time. One of the activists, Clarence Edwards, brought it up again years later at a civil rights reunion my parents hosted in their home in 1997, "The Gathering." He said, "I forgive, but I don't forget." Johnita had no clue she was in the thick of a controversy. She only remembers that the Flynns treated her with kindness.

Despite my disappointment with the treatment of Pitts and Lee in Tallahassee—or perhaps because of it—my experiences at the state's capital helped inspire me to run for office myself.

My first elective endeavor was to run for president of the student body at Cutler Ridge Junior High School. I decided to run at the last minute, mostly because I saw an opportunity to make a speech, and I *loved* making speeches. I'd been winning oratorical contests for years, even though I found out later that my junior high school had refused to display my first-place countywide Kwanzaa Oratorical Contest trophy in the school trophy case, when the mostly black junior high schools across town did so proudly. My mother had kept this from me, so I had no reason to believe

I could not be voted student-body president at my school. As I wrote my speech, I gave myself instructions to "gaze out at the audience awhile before speaking." The way I remember it, my speech was a huge hit; it left the auditorium roaring as my topics veered between humor and fire while I impressed upon my classmates how much I cared. What a great feeling! My slate and I swept the vote after my speech. It never occurred to me back then to wonder about it, but I was the first black student-body president at Cutler Ridge.

I learned that I enjoyed winning elections. Soon after that, I ran for president of the Greater Miami NAACP Youth Council. Now that we were older, my sisters and I had meetings of our own to attend, and not just the Girl Scouts. I was probably in the sixth or seventh grade when my mother first began taking me to monthly meetings of the Greater Miami NAACP Youth Council, which met in the NAACP office in Liberty City. The group was never very large, but the same steady number of people attended each time. Some were very young, like me—brought, too, by their parents—and others were teenagers in high school, or perhaps just beginning college. They were young, but they were focused. They acted a lot like grown-ups, planning voter registration drives and other community activities. (As a sixth-grader, Johnita was crowned Miss NAACP for the Greater Miami Branch because she raised $3,000 for the organization.)

Honestly, I don't know why I ran for president. I pushed myself to try it, just to see how it felt. Maybe I believed my parents expected it of me, or maybe I really felt inspired to help make a change through public service. I won that election, too. It probably didn't hurt that my sisters could vote for me, and I might have been running unchallenged. In any case, I had become an NAACP officer. With guidance from the adult membership, and strictly adhering to Robert's Rules of Order at our meetings ("Yes, the floor recognizes Johnita Due."), the Youth Council set its sights on voter registration in the black community. The 1980 election was approaching, and Jimmy Carter was facing a formidable challenger in Ronald Reagan.

One sunny afternoon, I set out to make a speech with zeal, summoning my best suburbanized preaching voice as I held a megaphone to my lips: "You know, friends, there are some people out there in this day and age who don't understand the importance of—"

"Tananarive, what are you doing?"

I was riding in a car with Dr. William Perry, the president of the Greater Miami NAACP branch, and he'd given me the megaphone to shout out messages about voting while we drove slowly down Seventh Avenue in

Liberty City, one of the centers of Miami's black life. I liked Dr. Perry's wit and commitment, but I didn't like being cut off in mid-sentence.

"Telling people to go vote," I said, annoyed.

"When were you going to tell them?"

"I was *about* to tell them, Dr. Perry."

Dr. Perry laughed at me. "Girl, if you go on like that, we'll be at the next block before you finish what you're trying to say. Give me that thing. Let me show you." With that, the more seasoned activist began making choppy proclamations, with emphasis on all the key words. "The election is *Tuesday. Please* don't forget to *vote.*" Then, he handed the megaphone back to me. "Do you understand now?"

I sighed. Where was the creativity in *that?* When could I mention the marches of the 1960s? Or the suffering of generations of slaves who had never been permitted to vote? Still, despite my dissatisfaction, I imitated Dr. Perry's choppy, to-the-point phrases, keeping all my far-flung thoughts to myself. "The *election* is *Tuesday*. . . . "

I remained an NAACP Youth Council president for a while when I began high school. Then we started a new branch in South Dade. My father was the president of the adult branch, and my mother was the South Dade Youth Council advisor. Janet Reno, who was then Dade County's state attorney, occasionally came to his branch banquets and other events. Johnita and Lydia served as South Dade Youth Council presidents after me, focusing on voter registration in the area. Lydia even enlisted the help of her high school social studies teacher, Barbara Brown, in organizing her phone-bank campaign. Students from Ms. Brown's social studies class worked the telephones for Lydia during the campaign.

But I had already begun to lose my enthusiasm for leadership.

One day, my mother spotted a mural that outraged her, and she suggested that we needed to make a complaint as a youth council—which, as far as I remember, consisted of mostly me and my sisters, and perhaps a few others. A car detailing company with a prominent building on South Dixie Highway had a mural on its wall depicting a black man and a Hispanic man in a playful exchange, with stereotypical dialogue attributed to them. Something like "Yo, man, ya'll got the good deals? Qué pasa, homey? You got that right!" The black man had a big, gleaming gold tooth. No question: The mural was cartoonish, maybe even offensive. Mom wanted us to set up a meeting with the management to complain, but I was feeling slightly squeamish, though I had the cause of justice on my side! This would be my first experience with an actual one-on-one confrontation.

The meeting was set up, and one day Mom and I marched over there to talk to the owner. I steeled myself and voiced our youth council's concern as articulately as I could. The unshaven owner listened quietly, impassively, occasionally fidgeting with irritation as I spoke. I knew that the NAACP's name carried weight. If the NAACP was angry about something, it made the nightly news. At annual NAACP conventions, all the presidential candidates came to speak because they wanted to curry that organization's favor. No one wanted the NAACP on his tail, so I figured this man was irritated because he knew he was going to have to repaint his wall. I could understand that. That would take time and money.

When I was finished, the man shrugged and stubbed out his cigar in his ashtray. "Yeah . . . well . . . listen . . . we've been in this neighborhood for years, and nobody's complained. It's just supposed to represent the people who live around here, that's all. It's no big deal."

"But it's offensive." Suddenly, my voice sounded very tiny in my ears.

"To you, maybe. Sorry. Lighten up." He shrugged, having nothing more to say.

So much for my first confrontation. My mother was muttering about writing letters to the newspaper, but my insides had shriveled. First, I'd felt bad about bothering the guy, but then I was angry that he was planning to so thoroughly ignore me. No, not *me*—he was going to ignore the nation's oldest civil rights organization! There wasn't a single part of that conversation that had felt good to me, even airing my concern, because what if, after all, the mural wasn't offensive? What if it was just offensive to Mom, and she'd passed her indignation on to me?

I never pursued any further action on the mural, although the adult branch did. Eventually, some time later, it came down, but that experience remained with me.

I haven't run for office since.

---

"Come on, girls, put on your scarves," my mother said on February 23, 1980, after a flurry of telephone calls. "We're going to the Dade County jail."

My sisters and I were watching *Family Feud* when the news came that Dr. Johnny L. Jones, the first black schools superintendent in the county's history, had been indicted for grand theft and was ordered to surrender himself at the jailhouse. To my parents, Dr. Jones's indictment was just another attempt to discredit a black man in power, something that happens with curious frequency in Miami. Dr. Jones had been charged with misusing school funds to buy gold-plated plumbing for his home. When Mom had first seen the newspapers implicating Dr. Jones in what became known in the media as "The Gold-Plated Plumbing Caper," she'd been very upset. Something *else?* It could not have come at a worse time.

Based on a series of bad events, Miami's black community was already in a slow, churning boil. A black insurance executive named Arthur McDuffie was in the news. He'd died after a police chase in December, and police had claimed he'd died from injuries sustained when his motorcycle crashed. The *Miami Herald* had recently disclosed that the whole thing had been a cover-up. He'd actually been beaten to death. In another debacle, police had charged into a black schoolteacher's home and beaten everyone present, only to discover later that they had raided the wrong house. The *Miami Herald* also reported that a white Florida Highway Patrol officer had molested an eleven-year-old black girl and received virtually no punishment for his crime, not even a notation in his personnel record.[2] Was it open season on black people in Miami?

In 1979, in the midst of all this turmoil, Mom had been named coordinator for the 1980 NAACP national convention to be held in Miami Beach that summer, at the behest of Charles Cherry, the president of the Florida State Conference of NAACP branches. It was an immense event for which the city was ill-prepared. Mom had been working very long hours away from home, her stress level was high, and her mood was snappish. The tension in our home then was already thick, and now the most powerful black man in the county, in my mother's mind, was being lynched by the media. It was time for action.

Mom worked the telephone, calling Dr. Jones at home to ask when he was going to the jailhouse, then rallying volunteers to provide a human shield for him so he would not be mobbed by the waiting media. Johnita, Lydia, and I were going to be part of that shield. Dad was at a meeting, so he could not go with us.

I had a headache that night, but I didn't complain. We were part of a regiment, like the National Guard. When duty called, the Due family responded.

Dr. Jones and my parents were not friends. In fact, my mother had butted heads with Dr. Jones over parental involvement in the schools in her role as chair of the Dade County Title I Parent Advisory Council, when he asked her to buck proper procedure by signing off on a document without reviewing it first with her board. When she refused, he'd found a way to remove her from office. Personal feelings aside, my parents applauded Dr. Jones's efforts to improve education for children in general, being especially sensitive to the needs of poor and black children. My parents also considered the treatment he was receiving an outrage, and they were convinced the situation would have been handled very differently if Dr. Jones had been white. The Dade County School Board had made an unprecedented move, meeting on a Sunday to remove him from his position as soon as the allegation surfaced. Dr. Jones had not yet been tried, but his peers had found him guilty.

The one question that nagged at me as my mother drove me and my sisters toward the jail was *What if Dr. Jones* was *guilty?* I'd asked my parents that question when the news first broke, and they said absolutely not, but I still wrestled with that question. (Dr. Jones was convicted later that year, but in 1986 the Florida Supreme Court threw out the conviction because there had been no blacks on the jury. There was not enough evidence for a second trial. Dr. Jones died in 1993, never having fully recovered from the ordeal.)[3]

Once we arrived at the jailhouse, I hesitated briefly again as we passed the cluster of reporters waiting outside with their news cameras and notepads readied, waiting for Dr. Jones to appear. I was in the ninth grade at the time and was beginning to think I might want to be a reporter myself someday. Could that have been me standing out there, waiting to cover a story? Whose side was I on? Johnita, surveying about fifty supporters waiting for Dr. Jones to appear, had a different reaction, as she described in a school English essay: *I could* feel *the support in the air, and it made me feel self-satisfied.*

I chose my side. I decided there was a conspiracy against prominent blacks in Dade County, and the media was part of it, even if the individual reporters were not to blame. Dr. Jones deserved the privacy and dignity of being able to walk to his car without harassment after meeting with police.

We went inside the jail building and marshaled protectively around Dr. Jones with the other supporters, all adults except for me and my sisters. I gazed at this man I did not know except from watching televised school board meetings, noticing how red and glassy his eyes looked, how he strained to smile at his supporters. His smile looked tight; he was too tired and dazed to try to look like a composed politician that night. Introductions were made, and I shook his hand, holding tight to let him know I felt badly about everything that was happening to him. His attorney made a couple of dry jokes to ease the tension, and then it was time to go back outside to the waiting reporters.

"Okay, let's do it," someone said, and we were on our way en masse toward the exit.

At first, the reporters were caught off guard because they didn't see Dr. Jones in our midst. I was standing directly behind him, telling myself I would keep my eyes on his brown coat so he would always be in sight. We went outside to whatever was waiting for us.

I wouldn't remember any details about that night if I hadn't written an essay about Dr. Jones later that same year. Even then, I could recall so few details—to the point where I wondered if I'd gone at all, or if only Johnita and Lydia were there—and today I can't help wondering if I was slightly traumatized by that evening. Perhaps my experience was buried by the horror of the events in Miami that soon followed, making a February trip to a jailhouse seem trivial. Whatever the reason, my essay preserves details from my memory, at fourteen, that would otherwise be lost by now:

> *There was one urgent shout, and suddenly the reporters were upon us. That's when I first saw the ugliness. It seemed like everyone was talking at once amidst the bright lights and confusion. The pushing . . . the shoving . . . I was confused by all of it as I struggled to stay in back of Dr. Jones and keep my balance. It sounded like there was a fight going on, and I had a vision of us all being thrown in jail, but there was no fight. The reporters were standing in front of us, blocking our way as they tried to get good film, but we still walked forward, the ones in front shouting repeatedly for them to get out of the way. One of the cameramen, a large black man, kept saying over and over, "Come on, man . . . gimme a break . . . gimme a break. . . ."*
>
> *I felt so disgusted with him, I wanted to tell him how ashamed he should be and that he had no business here bothering us, but I didn't say anything. They tried to get pictures of Dr. Jones as he got into his car, but all of us held up our arms to block their view. The car drove off, his attorney driving.*
>
> *For once, we had won. Perhaps it was a small victory . . . but we had won.*

It's not a coincidence that Johnita and I both wrote essays about that night. She concluded by writing *My family went to our car and my sisters and I had relieved smiles on our faces.* Johnita's was for a class, and mine was longer, a researched essay detailing Dr. Jones's life, the conspiracy against black officials, Dr. Jones's trial, and how that night my family went out to shield him from the cameras and lights. Our emotions were raw, and writing the essays helped us order and settle them.

Because I could always find refuge in writing, nothing ever happened to me in vain. There was no such thing as utter uselessness or hopelessness. No matter what it was, or how bad it felt, I could write about it. And if I could put what I was feeling into words, I could at least give it all some kind of meaning.

By then, I really understood better what my place in life would be. I was not the bold firebrand who could confront anyone with ease, like my mother. I also did not live in the realm of philosophy, sociology, and law, like my father. I was a writer. I could escape through writing. I could teach through writing. I could air shared emotions through writing. I could tell people what had happened—*exactly* how it had happened—through writing.

As long as I could write it, people would know.

Seven

# Patricia Stephens Due

**"Until justice rolls down like waters and righteousness like a mighty stream."**
***—Dr. Martin Luther King Jr.***

Try to imagine a trial in which you and your attorney are openly called "niggers" during testimony. Or a trial in which the judge insists that the charges against you have nothing to do with race—when, in fact, the charges are *only* about race.

Priscilla and I, and nine others, had been charged with "disturbing the peace," among other charges, because we tried to order food at Woolworth. If not for segregation, and the fact that we were all Negroes, we would have been served without incident. At our trial on March 17, 1960, Judge John Rudd ruled that our lawyers should "get off that race question."[1] He also accused us of being affiliated with Communists because we had acted under the auspices of CORE, even though it was *not* a Communist organization. By the end of our one-day farce of a trial in a segregated courtroom in the segregated South, all eleven of us had been found guilty. Our punishment: a $300 fine, or sixty days in jail. I had not expected a fair trial in the South, but I couldn't help but be outraged by the blatant disregard for the facts in our case and the injustice of the entire system.

Mrs. Gaines chose to have her fine paid, although $300 was a steep fee in 1960 and her employer had already dismissed her from her job because of her arrest. "I was working and one day she said, 'Mary, I think I'm gonna try to do my own work.' She didn't want me involved," Mrs. Gaines told me later. Still, Mrs. Gaines decided she would not consider serving a jail term for what she had done. "That's the thing that went through my mind: 'We hadn't done anything. What are you arresting *us* for?' The people who were bothering us were the ones that needed to be arrested," she recalled.[2]

Priscilla and I, as well as six others, had made our decision before we entered the courtroom: We would not pay a fine to support a system that did not treat us as equal human beings. We would not pay for segregation. If we had to go to jail to further our cause, we would go to jail. If we went to jail, I thought, all of America might learn the truth about the South. Suddenly, our sit-in had turned into a "jail-in."

I was twenty years old, a college junior, and not yet a legal adult when we were sentenced to sixty days in the Leon County jail. Not only was this the first time we had been jailed, but it was the first time any activists in the student sit-in movement had chosen jail rather than pay their fine. We pioneered a tactic, becoming the first "jail-in" of the student protest movement of the 1960s. Locally, our jail sentence opened a lot of eyes, since the whole community was surprised. They expected us to be tried, pay our fines, and end it there. When we said we would go to jail, the reality of the plight of Negroes was much more clear.

The eight of us who had chosen jail over bail were me and Priscilla; Henry Marion Steele, a tall, gangly high-school student who was only sixteen; and Barbara and John Broxton, Angelina Nance, Clement Carney, and William Larkins, all students at FAMU. We did not have to report to the county jail until the next morning, so we had one last night of freedom. I knew that Henry was the son of Rev. C. K. Steele, and I had been friendly with some of the activists previously, but most of us really did not know each other on a personal level. Our association had been through demonstrations, when there wasn't much time to learn about each other's lives and personalities. Now we were about to undergo a very trying ordeal together. We met and held a prayer session at a local church, then we tried to prepare ourselves emotionally for whatever lay ahead of us, based on our CORE training. We shouted epithets at each other, pushed each other, pulled at each other's clothes—whatever we could think of to prepare us for what we thought jail might be like.[3]

Looking back now, clearly the preparations were not enough. You can never truly appreciate the value of freedom—even limited freedom in the segregated South—until that freedom is taken from you. The most intimidating aspect of jail is the degree to which your lives and safety are in the hands of others, whether it's other prisoners or guards. It became clear very quickly that some of our jailers felt a great deal of ill will toward us.

The verbal abuse began as soon as we entered the jail, with the jailer, a man named Mr. Chairs, and another woman, Miss Love, who processed us. I honestly think Mr. Chairs had some sort of sickness, and Miss Love's name became terribly ironic to me. She and Mr. Chairs were full of anything *but* love: *You niggers are causing all that trouble in town, but you won't last long in here, no sir. These folks in here don't like troublemakers. Ya'll make it bad for everyone else, and they're gonna make it bad for you.*

We were separated by gender. The jail was also segregated by race, but all of us were Negro. Each cell had four bunks, an open commode, and a sink, although our particular cell had no running water, and all were dank, dreary, and lonely. The thin, ratty blankets we were given smelled foul, as if they had never been washed. Food consisted of fatback, grits, and sweet breads, and it was awful. Most of us could not eat it. The males were forced to work on county roads, cemeteries, and ditches by day, and the college sit-in students were definitely worked harder than the other prisoners. Henry Steele recalls, "I felt so sorry for the other guys. [The guard] wanted them to look like they had been put through the mill so he could look good when he got back."

We females had to scrub what jailers called the "bull rank," the common area with tables outside the individual cells. At night, the concrete cells seemed very cold, and I had only a single sheet for a cover. Because of overcrowding, Henry Steele didn't even have a bed of his own. He had to sleep on a thin pallet on the floor, where he caught a terrible cold from the draft. In fact, according to Barbara Broxton's notes during the time, Angelina and Priscilla had colds within our first days of incarceration. I was ill, too, and a Negro doctor, Dr. Charles Stevens, was summoned to see me.[4] Not that it was easy to sleep at all. Jailers sometimes purposely rattled the bars to wake us up, calling us "bad niggers."

Our visitors were screened by race. After the first couple of weeks, none of the sympathetic whites were permitted to visit us, a further indication that they, too, were affected by discrimination. When whites were barred from visiting, says longtime Tallahassee activist Clifton Lewis—who is white—they gathered outside and sang inspirational songs for us. "We would be outside singing, and there would be policemen all around us. We were hoping you all could hear us in that jail," she told me later.[5]

Our jailers tried to use other inmates against us, which was a common tactic in Southern jails. One day, a mentally ill woman named Ruth was placed in our cell. *She is completely out of her mind,* Priscilla wrote of her in her diary. *She is a very dangerous person. She needs to be in an insane asylum.* The night Ruth arrived, we stayed up half the night trying to keep an eye on her, Barbara Broxton wrote.[6] After Ruth was removed from our cell because she refused to keep her clothes on, the jailers brought her back. This time she had a wire hanger. "I'm going to put your eyes out," Ruth promised, stalking us with that sharp hanger while we huddled to move out of her way. Ruth was our first real source of fear in jail because she threatened to kill us several times. We weren't just afraid of her because she meant us harm, but because we knew the only reason she could have gotten a wire hanger was through our jailers. Luckily, Ruth never followed through on her promise, although in the following days she did kick both Priscilla and Barbara Broxton. A prisoner and trustee I only knew as "Geech" was a real godsend to all of us, since he spoke to us kindly and tried his best to look out for us.

Once Mother learned we were in jail, she came to see us right away. Tallahassee is a twenty-one-mile drive east on Highway 90 from where my mother was raised in Gadsden County. Like most Negroes in the South, she grew up hearing tales of racist horror, so she was very frightened for us to be incarcerated in nearby Leon County. Some of those fearsome stories were from her own doorstep; she'd heard whisperings about her great-uncle John, who'd been dragged out of the house and lynched. No one ever told her the details, and it probably happened before she was born, but the story loomed large in her imagination.

As bordering states, Florida, Alabama, and Georgia had more in common than location; they were also well-known for their mistreatment of Negroes who tried to change the status quo. Between 1900 and 1930, Florida had more lynchings per capita than any other state in the nation.[7] I remember hearing about how Dr. William S. Stevens, a physician in Quincy, was tied to a tree in the 1940s after he tried to register Negroes to vote. Afterward, when Dr. Stevens built his own hospital to provide better medical care for Negroes, city fathers refused to allow him to open the facility's doors. Longtime residents also never forgot the spectacle of seeing a Negro man tied to the rear bumper of a Model-T Ford and dragged around the courthouse in downtown Quincy.

The terror had begun in earnest for Mother with our protests and arrests. She never shared it with us until later, but she had been wrestling with her own anxieties from the first time she heard we were leading the Tallahassee demonstrations. "Every time the phone rang, it was like someone shooting a gun. I jumped every time," she told us many years after the fact. Our names were in the news, and her neighbors had begun giving her their sympathies, treating our arrest and jailing like something shameful, which made her angry. Our grandmother was pleading with her to do something about our activism, telling her we had gone crazy. Daddy Marion, naturally, was being chastised by his superiors in the Palm Beach County school system, where he was then a principal, for not controlling his children. Mother was also very worried because Priscilla had just been prescribed a special diet because of her tendency for ulcers, and she was sure Priscilla would not be fed properly in jail. (She was right on this account, but we didn't want to alarm her. The food served to us in jail was not fit to eat. Despite the plentiful food later brought to us by visitors, Priscilla was sickly for a time and had to consult a doctor.)

In many ways, Mother never recovered from the days and years to follow. But despite her feelings, which she was struggling to keep under control, Mother didn't come to the jail to try to talk us out of what we were doing. Instead, she just wanted to stare us in the eye and make sure we were not being coerced by CORE or anyone else. After making the eight-hour drive from Belle Glade to Tallahassee, she gave us very tight hugs and searched our faces. "Girls," she said, "are you sure you want to do this?"

Priscilla and I reminded her that she and Daddy Marion were the ones who had taught us that all citizens must stand up for their rights. Further, we pointed out what we considered a painful truth: "Mother, if *your* generation had done this, we wouldn't have to do it now. It's time for all of us to be free."

Mother listened to us with sad brown eyes, knowing that she could not argue. "Well, then, girls, you have to do what you have to do," she said curtly, with only traces of fright in her voice. "Don't you worry about school. Don't you worry about the money we've spent on tuition. Whatever happens now, you're doing what you think is right."

Still, I felt a need to try to express myself better in writing. In a letter dated March 20, I wrote to Mother and Daddy Marion from the Leon County jail:

> *We cannot be contented with the condition here in the South any longer. Our very souls are being taken from us by discrimination. How can we be content, saying we'll put it off until we're independent? How many independent people are willing to make the necessary sacrifices for freedom? You know, and I know, that there are only a few, a very few. I hope my parents are included in that few. . . . We cannot sit back any longer. I'd rather not have an education if it is going to make me afraid to fight for my rights. We all would like to tell two great leaders that they were right when they said "Give me liberty or give me death" and "We've got to fill the jails to win our equal rights," respectively Patrick Henry and Martin Luther King.*

Daddy Marion visited us initially, but he could not come as often as Mother because his brother had just died and he had to make the funeral arrangements. What a stressful time for our family! But soon his letter arrived:

*March 23, 1960*

*Dearest Priscilla and Patricia:*
*One thing we want you to know and that is: We both love you very dearly and want nothing but the best for you. This, in itself, may make us seem pretty hard and objectionable to your ideas, since we know where such may lead in the final analysis. We, by no means, are letting you down. The fact is that we are stronger for you now than ever and will always hopefully be behind you and pulling for you.*

*We cannot come right out and say we are pleased with the whole situation, as we realize its worth and what such can do for the whole in general, but we are concerned as to how much you might hurt or suffer for such. Loving you as we do we can do nothing but be most concerned, anxious, and, yes, worried. I am a bit more outspoken than your mother. There are things she wishes to say but puts up fronts with her heart being torn to bits. She has lived her life for Walter and you, and has felt no sacrifice too great for either of you. There could come a time when she may break down under the tension or under the mental strain and anxiety. . . .*

*I came to the place on Sunday to see you, to tell you that I too love you both just as much as is humanly possible, but we were not allowed to see you. She buys every paper, listens to every broadcast, gets the ideas and thoughts of other people, all in an effort to assure herself that all is well with you as she and I, both, want the best for you. This is one of the reasons for the words that we feel sure you must still hear—Please count the cost. Cost does not always mean dollars and cents. Cost can mean anxiety as well. . . .*

*Write to us often and keep us posted on your situation and more about your welfare.*

*With love,*
*Mother and Daddy Marion*

As I reread that letter today, my eyes fill with tears because I realize how our actions, beginning in 1960, took such a toll on Mother. All of that worry may have shortened her life. At the time, as horrible as it felt that we might potentially be contributing to our mother's nervous breakdown or our stepfather's future lack of employment—as he'd mentioned in his previous letter, and such concerns were by no means unfounded—a bigger imperative was at work while we were in jail. All of us there knew it. But I must say, it is very difficult today for me to reread Daddy Marion's letter, which always brings tears when I realize how much stress Mother suffered during that time. My brother Walter tells me today that she and Daddy Marion never once mentioned our arrest or jailing in his presence in the beginning, so they somehow kept up a brave face in front of him. Although I had no time for tears in the 1960s, now I wish with all my heart it could have been easier for my parents.

CORE leadership tried to reassure our parents with a letter. James Robinson, the executive secretary, wrote to them: *"The faith shown in Tallahassee is a* major *factor in the growing pressure nationally to change Woolworth's policy. The chances are good that we shall win. If so, much of the credit must go to the Stephens sisters."* Richard Haley, my music professor and a CORE member, also wrote a letter to our parents on March 28, trying to reassure them that CORE was not a Communist organization and that our incarceration was not in vain: *"It is pointless for me to try to express my feelings for these young people. Long ago I exhausted my vocabulary of words with the strength and breadth and depth equal to my admiration for them. I would be proud—and humble—to be able to say of any of them, 'This is my child.' It is my hope that this is your stand, and that you will not be moved."*

If those of us in jail needed a reminder, we had received a very meaningful one only the day after we went to jail. A telegram had arrived to further demonstrate that we were not alone, that we were part of a far-reaching social movement, however young it might be. The telegram came from a thirty-one-year-old minister who had learned from his own experiences that the pressing needs of Negroes in the South must supersede personal concerns. He, too, had been arrested. His home had been bombed in Birmingham, while his wife and infant daughter were at home and might have been harmed. Like Daddy Marion, his own father had warned him to consider the cost. He wrote us:

> *I have just learned of your courageous willingness to go to jail instead of paying fines for your righteous protest against segregated eating facilities. Through this decision you have again proven that there is nothing more majestic and sublime than the determined courage of individuals willing to suffer and*

*sacrifice for the cause of freedom. You have discovered anew the meaning of the cross, and as Christ died to make men holy, you are suffering to make men free.*

*As you suffer the inconvenience of remaining in jail, please remember that unearned suffering is redemptive. Going to jail for a righteous cause is a badge of honor and a symbol of dignity.*

*I assure you that your valiant witness is one of the glowing epics of our time and you are bringing all of America nearer [to] the threshold of the world's bright tomorrows.*

*Dr. Martin Luther King Jr.*
*March 19, 1960*

*Today,* Priscilla wrote in her diary, *we received a wire from Martin Luther King Jr. congratulating us on our courage and willingness to go to jail.* In that day's diary entry, Priscilla also documented a strategy that may well have ensured our safety while we were in jail: Each day, we were told, two local ministers would visit us in jail at 6:00 P.M. This was unusual, of course, because jails have special visiting days set aside, but that demonstrates the unique nature of our imprisonment. The rules were different for us, in some cases. The local clergy—including Rev. C. K. Steele, Rev. Dan Speed, Father Brooks, and many others—wanted to make certain we would be looked after and prayed with.

Our third day in jail, a Sunday, hundreds of Tallahassee residents came to the jail to encourage us; they were white and Negro, young and old, students and community members alike. *The day of rest has finally arrived,* Priscilla wrote in her diary. *The special day set aside for God's Children to give all their praises and prayers. It is this and more to us. It is the day of visitors here in the jail. The day people get to express how they feel about us and this worthy cause. . . . They all made us feel very proud of them.*

Our welfare, as it turned out, would matter to more people than we had thought possible.

In March that year, baseball star Jackie Robinson concluded his weekly column in the *New York Post* by telling his readers that a letter had come to his attention, and he wanted to share it. Robinson had parlayed his fame as an athlete into a national forum for serious discussions on racial matters. The letter, he said, was from a Negro college girl. It had been addressed to James Robinson, the executive secretary of CORE. That letter was from me.

Dated March 20, it began with such a breezy air, anyone might have thought it was a casual note between old friends: *Dear Jim, How are things in New York? I hope the weather is a little warmer now.* But this was far from a casual correspondence, which soon became clear:

> *We do not plan to discontinue our fight. There are eight of us in jail: seven A&M students and one high school student. We are in what you call a "bull rank" with four cells in it. There is running water in only two of the cells. Breakfast, if you can call it that, is served every morning at 6:30. Another meal is served at 12:30, and I am still trying to get up enough courage to eat it. In the evening, we are served sweet breads and watery coffee.*
>
> *We are very happy we are able to do this to help our city, state, and nation. We strongly believe that Martin Luther King was right when he said, "We've got to fill the jails to win our equal rights." Well, I've got to dress for our visitors. We have two ministers visit us every day. Write when you can. Tell everyone hello for us.*
>
> *Yours truly, Pat.*
>
> *P.S.—My parents were here last night to get us out, but we persuaded them to let us stay. Priscilla, my sister, is supposed to be on a special diet and Mother is worried about her.*

My letter to CORE's executive secretary, which had been smuggled out of our cell by ministers who visited us each day, was one of dozens of letters I would write during my long jail stay. Serving out our sentence was only the first step. People had to know that in the United States of America, in the year 1960, peaceful Negroes could be jailed just for asking for a piece of cake at a lunch counter. As absurd as it seemed, it was the reality of the South. The more letters I received from shocked sympathizers, the more I realized how ignorant people were about life in the South. *I try and explain it to them,* I wrote to CORE leadership, *but my best in a letter is not enough. . . . There are so many things happening that people are completely unaware of.*

Jackie Robinson helped us tell our story, even sending us all diaries so we could document everything that happened to us during our incarceration. Many people remember Robinson only as a legendary baseball player, but he was also very active in the freedom struggle, and he sent money to Tallahassee CORE to help them carry out their activities. News of our jail-in appeared in outlets like *Jet* magazine, the *Pittsburgh Courier,* and dozens of other publications around the country, even around the world. Barbara Broxton also wrote impassioned letters called "Jailhouse Notes" that appeared in the *Southern Patriot,* a publication of the Southern Conference Education Fund. She wrote, *We do not consider going to jail a sacrifice but a privilege. Every night we thank God we are able to help those who are denied equal rights.*[8] We received a letter of support from as far away as Yokohama, Japan. We knew the nation was watching us, and parts of the world, too.

Also on March 20, Florida's governor, LeRoy Collins, had delivered a live radio and television address that resounded through the city and state: "So far as I am personally concerned," Governor Collins had said, "if a man has a department store and trade, I think it is unfair and morally wrong for him to single out one department and say he does not want or will not allow Negroes to patronize that one department. . . . People have told me that our racial strife could be eliminated if the colored people would just stay in their place, but friends, we can never stop Americans from struggling to be free."[9]

While many Negroes were hailing Gov. Collins as courageous and heroic for his remarks (which, admittedly, were unusual for a Southern governor during that time), they still rang hollow to me. For one thing, we were still in jail. Words have never meant anything to me without action to back them up, and Collins had also said that "public disorder" was harmful to the community. At least Collins was weighing in on the question in some form, and while he received many thousands of supportive letters from throughout the country, the reaction in his own backyard was lukewarm at best. The idea of a biracial commission, which the governor had recommended for municipalities statewide, was dismissed by Tallahassee Mayor George Taff, and the state senate leader, Dewey Johnson, called the governor a "strict integrationist" who would "sell his soul" for the prospect of higher political ambitions.[10]

Daddy Marion, though, was pleased with the governor's words. In his

March 23 letter, he wrote to us that the governor had made "a wonderful plea for the people of Florida to consider the moral values implemented in this tense situation." With the mounting publicity, we noticed a distinct change in Daddy Marion's tone. Despite his worries for our welfare and his job security, he soon seemed to feel more heartened:

*April 1, 1960*

*Dear Priscilla & Patricia:*

*It was lovely indeed to have letters from you and to know that you are in the best of spirits even if the surroundings are not the most pleasant in the world. May God bless you both.*

*Your mother has kept up with all newscasts, newspaper clippings, and the like, and has done all to keep up with your activities even if she has not taken the time to write. I would write more often if I could find the time when I am not so beat to my socks. Somehow I have not fully gotten myself together after my brother's death. I have had many restless nights, which is nothing unusual, but I awake disturbed and not always knowing the reasons why. . . .*

*Patricia, you are becoming nationally known. All I can say is: More Power to You and may God Bless all of you in your efforts. Such a nationwide endeavor is bound to have some great effect on the thinking of the people of this great nation. . . . Mother just read your published letter over the phone to me. Well written, old girl.*

*Give my sincerest regards to your enclosed friends. Our sincerest love to you both. Keep up your good spirits and pray. Prayers can move mountains if Faith goes along with them. Thanks for your letters and keep writing.*

*Love,*
*Daddy Marion*

Times were very tense, and I saw for myself how much tempers were flaring back on FAMU's campus. During a short-lived period during my sentence when Barbara Broxton and I were designated as "trustees"—which meant we had been assigned cleaning duties at the police station—a police car drove us back to the campus so we could get some fresh clothes. Somehow, word had gotten out that we would be brought to the campus, and a crowd gathered as the police car arrived. Students were furious when they realized we were there under guard. Once we were out of the car, they surrounded it, began battering it with their hands and pelting it with rocks, and rocked it back and forth to overturn it. I raised my voice to appeal to them, explaining why we were there: "We have not chosen to be released from jail!" I told the angry students. "We will *not* pay for segregation by paying our fines, and we want to stay in jail so people will know we're no longer going to put up with it!" The crowd cheered and the police whisked us away.

As it turned out, we lasted as trustees only one day since we refused to use the "Colored" bathroom and because the police chief accidentally tripped over my vacuum cleaner cord. Yes, it was an accident, but apparently they'd had enough of us by then. Since I was no longer allowed even the meager distraction of domestic work at the jailhouse, the days behind bars grew very long.

CORE sponsored a downtown boycott to protest our jailing. Although it wasn't nearly as effective as the bus boycott had been, the boycott and the memory of the sit-ins and protests incited the ire of local segregationists. In April, the *Pittsburgh Courier* published photographs showing the vandalism carried out against two of our supporters in the community, Rev. Dan Speed and Rev. T. S. Johnson. Someone threw a brick through the window of the Speed & Co. grocery store on Floral Street, which adjoined CORE's meeting place. "A lot of people don't know how that man suffered," Daisy Young said later about Rev. Speed. According to Miss Young, Rev. Speed was not only targeted by vandals, but his grocery suppliers stopped delivering goods to him, trying to put him out of business. The minister had to drive to Jacksonville—nearly 160 miles each way—just to stock his store.[11]

Vandals also visited Rev. T. S. Johnson, pastor of Fountain Chapel AME Church, and broke the windshield of his car with a large concrete block. After assessing the damage, Rev. Speed offered a prayer: "Father God, forgive those of your image that have committed the wrong in smashing glass in food store windows, homes, and automobiles, and many other sins upon their hands in this our Southland, for we are in love with them like our Christ, for they know not what they do."[12]

This vandalism was not happy news to us in jail, of course. But one important way we were able to raise our spirits in jail was through singing. In time, other inmates—both Negro and white—joined us in song. These women were troubled, and many of them were hardened, described in Priscilla's diary as "forgers, assassins, drunkards, and whiskey-sellers," but they sang with us. The lyrics of my favorite Freedom Song, "Oh Freedom," summarized the sentiment that helped give us our resolve: *Before I'll be a slave, I'll be buried in my grave.* In fact, we four women arrested at Woolworth wrote our own freedom song, which we set to the tune of the Dixie standard "Old Black Joe." The melody was befitting. Just as we intended to use the U.S. Constitution to tear down the walls of Jim Crow, we wanted to use the melody of a derogatory song to give us sustenance:

*Gone are the days*
*When tradition had its say.*
*Now is the time*
*For the South to integrate.*

*We will fight on,*
*For a better land we know.*
*For the Constitution tells us so,*
*Fight on, fight on!*

*We're fighting,*
*We're fighting,*
*For a better land we know.*
*For the Constitution tells us so,*
*Fight on, fight on!*

We felt so determined to stay in jail, and believed so strongly in our cause, that we were deeply disappointed when our number began to dwindle. We started with eight. Angelina Nance's mother finally prevailed in paying her fine to get her out of jail after she had already served more than two weeks. Angelina didn't want to leave, but her mother insisted, and we missed her terribly. Clement Carney left grudgingly to start the appeals process. Henry Steele, our youngest, also left for home to take part in an appeal, and I'm sure his mother in particular was relieved.

In the end, Priscilla and I, John and Barbara Broxton, and William Larkins remained. With ten days off for good behavior—and one additional day so authorities could stave off any publicity tied to our projected release date—we ultimately spent forty-nine days of our sixty-day sentence in the Leon County jail. I believe any of us would have been willing to spend a year, or longer.

Shortly before our release date, we had a surprising moment in jail. I've mentioned that some of our jailers were verbally abusive toward us, but one had been simply professional, neither more nor less. He came and did his job, and he never said much of anything for us or against us. Only days before we were to leave, that jailer, a tall, mature-looking young man whose name I do not know, unexpectedly showed up carrying a very young boy, perhaps as young as three or four. Since whites had been restricted from seeing us, it was a shock to see the jailer bringing a white child that young. Once they were closer, we could tell from the resemblance that the boy must be his son.

The jailer stood in front of our cell with his son on his arm, and the boy leaned his tiny face through the bars to gaze at us. The jailer asked the three of us who were jail-in participants to come forward. I braced for the worst, imagining that he was about to display us as an example of what happens to "uppity niggers," sowing the seeds of racism in the next generation.

The jailer began to speak in a gentle tone, pointing us out one by one. "Now, these ladies are sisters, Priscilla Stephens and Patricia Stephens, and this other lady here is Barbara Broxton," he said to his son. "Say hello to them."

"Hi," the boy said obediently, smiling.

"I know Daddy has told you only bad people go to jail. Well, you may be too young to understand, but these three ladies aren't in jail because they're crooks, or because they're bad people. They're in jail because they're trying to change the laws that say Negroes and whites can't eat together. They want to be treated just like anybody else. And they believe in what they're doing so much, they were willing to go to jail to make it right. So you try to remember that, okay? One day, you'll look back and realize how important it was for them to do this."

The boy nodded soberly. Perhaps he understood, and perhaps he didn't. But that jailer could have given no greater gift to those of us behind bars, nor to his son.

Now, with the help of CORE, we were going to tell everyone who would listen what had happened to us in Tallahassee to be sure that it would never happen again.

# Eight

# Tananarive Due

**"Or does it explode?"**
***—Langston Hughes***
**"A Raisin in the Sun"**

I was fourteen years old, watching Saturday afternoon TV, at the precise moment my childhood ended. It was May 17, 1980, and the local television station began scrolling a silent announcement across the bottom of the screen: AFTER DELIBERATING FOR LESS THAN THREE HOURS, A TAMPA JURY. . . .

My heart began to race, and I felt the taste of something sour rise in my throat. After a trial lasting six weeks, the verdict in the Arthur McDuffie case was in.

It wasn't his life, but his death, that had made Arthur McDuffie a household name in Miami that year. The thirty-three-year-old insurance executive had been beaten to death by Dade County police after he had led them on an eight-minute high-speed chase on his motorcycle. His beating was so severe, his skull had been cracked in half, from front to back.[1]

Arthur McDuffie was black. The four police officers on trial were not.

Realizing they'd killed McDuffie, police had tried to cover up the crime by bashing the motorcycle with "Kel-Lites," heavy police-issue iron flashlights, to make it appear that it had crashed. Officially, his death had been called an accident: He'd cracked his head open after flying off his motorcycle, police lied, just as they had for generations from Mississippi swamps to Florida back roads. Such lies have a long history.

This particular lie might have lived forever if not for a courageous and persistent *Miami Herald* police reporter, Edna Buchanan, who got a tip, so she met with McDuffie's family, examined the motorcycle herself, and saw the truth, which she printed in the newspaper for all to see: McDuffie had not died in a motorcycle accident. He had died at the hands of men.

The charge, inexplicably, was manslaughter. That in itself had caused a furor. When the subject of the manslaughter charge was raised at a candlelight vigil at our Unitarian church, I'd choked into sobs when I tried to talk about it. The judge determined that the case could not be tried fairly in Dade County, so it was moved upstate to the predominantly white community of Tampa in west-central Florida, where an all-white jury was selected to hear the evidence. If I'd had any fears at all about this trial—and, despite my parents' concern, I had utter faith in the strength of the evidence of a dead man's splintered skull and a tampered motorcycle—maybe it was that there might be a mistrial and the whole case would have to start again, or that the penalties for manslaughter would not be as severe as these officers deserved. (Eventually, one of the officers was charged with second-degree murder.)

I could not believe the words I saw at the bottom of the television screen on May 17, 1980: A TAMPA JURY HAS FOUND FOUR OFFICERS NOT GUILTY.

Did it say, could it say, *not* guilty? I blinked, stared at the screen, and blinked again.

"Mom!" I yelled, my limbs shaking, "It's not guilty!"

I'd only experienced a shock like that once before: When I was thirteen, I'd been barely awake as I listened to my favorite morning radio program on pop station Y100 and the newscaster announced that State Rep. Gwen Cherry had been killed in a car accident the night before after driving into a Tallahassee ditch. I'd heard this same newscaster morning after morning, but suddenly he was talking about someone I knew, and I'd felt as if I'd slipped into a strange, jarring dream. Gwen Cherry was my godmother. She'd sponsored me when I spent a week serving as her page in the state House of Representatives less than a year earlier. She'd posed with us in the photograph my family took with Jimmy Carter when I was ten. She was one of the Miami black community's favorite daughters, and my mother loved her like an older sister. Gwen Cherry's death was a personal tragedy to my family.

As terrible and unexpected as personal tragedies always are, they can heal. But May 17 was different, and I knew it. The Arthur McDuffie verdict was something beyond personal, deeper than personal. It was *staggering.* It wasn't just about McDuffie, a man we had never met. It was about all of the black people in Dade County. It was about all of us everywhere.

Arthur Lee McDuffie was a top performer at his insurance firm. He was a community volunteer. He was a former Marine who'd served as a military police officer. He had three children, and he'd been planning to remarry his former wife, a nurse. Aside from traffic violations, he'd never had any run-ins with the law. The night he died, he'd been doing silly stunts on his motorcycle, popping a wheelie like daredevil Evel Knievel, and he'd sped off when police spotted him. He led them on a chase.[2] For some reason, he was being a cowboy that night. Who can say what he was thinking? Did he think he'd just shake them and write the night off as an adventure to share with his buddies? He had to know it was foolish to run. He had to know he'd be in a pile of trouble, but I wonder what was going through his mind when he scooted his motorcycle to a halt near the expressway on-ramp and waited for the police to climb out of their cars, as if to say *All right, ya'll, I'm just playing.* Did he think he'd get only harsh words and a night in jail? Had he forgotten he was a black man?

Arthur McDuffie was unarmed. The police cuffed his hands behind his back. A dozen police officers stood around him and beat him to a pulp with heavy Kel-Lites and nightsticks, spraying blood and cracking his skull open so badly that the medical examiner would later say his skull looked like a "cracked egg." As one officer later described it, during the beating "they looked like a bunch of animals fighting for meat."[3]

They were going to teach this nigger a lesson, goddammit, but they got scared. McDuffie's injuries looked severe. The hospital said he was in a coma and would probably die (which he did, days later). According to an eyewitness who testified against the officers on trial, former Metro police officer Charles Veverka, the defendants tried to make it look accidental by smashing up the motorcycle. They killed a man and then conspired to lie about it.[4] Three former police officers who were eyewitnesses—the most prized kind of witness in any courtroom—testified against their fellow officers. One officer in particular, they said, had straddled McDuffie while he hit him with the Kel-Lite.[5]

Yet an all-white jury, with the speed and conclusion of its verdict, had in effect shrugged its collective shoulders and said, *Okay, we got no problem with that. Why did you waste almost three whole hours of our valuable time?*

McDuffie doesn't *matter,* I remember thinking. White people don't think he *matters.* My mind could barely comprehend it.

Dorothy McDuffie, Arthur McDuffie's sister, described her feelings to reporters in a way that captured what I believe most of black Miami felt: "It's like something unbelievable. . . . I feel like I'm nobody. I feel like my family's nobody. I feel like my people are nobody."[6]

Yes, my parents were civil rights activists, and I'd been brought up on a steady diet of black history lessons. I'd known all too well that there was a time, *long ago,* when such trials were commonplace. Lynchings didn't matter. Beatings didn't matter. Rapes didn't matter. I knew blacks had been considered nobodies in the old days of song singing and fire hoses. I knew my mother had been jailed for sitting at a lunch counter, and that her eyes had been injured when she was teargassed for marching down a public street. I knew my aunt had been kicked in the stomach by a police officer and that nobody had been willing to hear her grievance. That had been in the 1960s. Black people didn't matter in the 1960s.

But in 1980? In the world *I* lived in?

That moment of realization, that awakening, was when my childhood ended.

Immediately after the verdict was announced, the phone at our house began to ring. Shock. Disbelief. Rage. My parents learned there was going to be a protest at the Metro Justice Building in downtown Miami at 6:00 that night. The troops were gathering, yet again.

I couldn't muster any excitement over the prospect of carrying another sign, or yelling another chant. Not that day. My parents had been protesting and working for change all of their adult lives, and their work had still come to nothing more than this. A protest at the Justice Building? There *was* no justice. There never had been, and there wasn't now. No placards or megaphones or marches or complaints were going to change it. Maybe it would never change.

I had a terrible headache, at the edge of a migraine. When my feelings tried to surface, I locked them down tight. What good were feelings? What would tears do for me? What could anger bring me? I'd made plans with a friend of mine, a tall white girl who lived nearby, Michelle Ricciardi, to see a movie that had just opened, *The Nude Bomb.* It was a comedy about a bomb that made people lose their clothes when it exploded, and it looked very stupid in the commercials, so it was the perfect refuge from my feelings. Michelle was one of my most constant playmates while I skirted that line between childhood and young adulthood; like me, she loved the TV show *Emergency!* and indulged me in fantasies about meeting my favorite actor from the show, Randolph Mantooth. Without complaining, she read piles of *Emergency!* stories I wrote about dramatic rescues and fire-station drama. Michelle was a safe haven.

I had asked Mom if I could go to a movie with Michelle instead of to the protest, and although she was surprised I wanted to remain behind, she had said yes. Dad was already out in the field in his capacity as a county employee, so my sisters went with my mother, and I walked to my friend's house in the calm quiet of untroubled streets, where the McDuffie verdict was no more than an interesting topic of conversation in the living rooms I passed. I don't remember even bringing up the Arthur McDuffie verdict while I was with Michelle. I didn't care that she was white, or if she could understand how I felt. I didn't need her to understand. I wasn't looking for commiseration. I wanted an escape, if only for a few treasured hours.

Escape isn't that simple. I couldn't laugh at the movie the way I wanted. When Michelle and I got back to her house and began to eat dinner with her family, the local news was showing footage from a battle front. Burning cars. People running. A smoke-filled street. Like a scene from Beirut. The protest, which had begun peacefully, had turned into a riot.

"My family is there," I said to Michelle's family, disbelief wrapping around me. My friend and I were sitting in the white suburbs of Cutler Ridge, and my family was in the middle of a riot downtown. For a moment, my senses blurred.

Where were my parents? My sisters? Were they safe? My eyes searched the chaotic video footage of flames and running people, looking for familiar faces. A newscaster, speaking in that rushed, confused outburst that TV reporters use when they've stumbled onto an unexpected story, said that people had reportedly died. People had *died?*

"Oh, my God," Michelle's mother said.

That night, I was the most frightened I had ever been for my family's safety. For the hour or so between the time when I first saw the footage of the riot and I finally got a call from my mother, my separation from my family felt unbridgeable.

Lydia was ten years old, and Johnita had just turned twelve. They had been leaning against a police car in front of the Justice Building with Mom, watching the crowd and listening to speeches at the rally, when more and more people from the surrounding inner-city neighborhood began arriving, yelling their outrage. "The emotions were on the surface. You felt the mood shift," Lydia recalls. "You knew something was about to happen."

Johnita and Lydia remember that the car they were leaning against suddenly began to shake, then rock violently. People on the other side of the car were trying to overturn it, so they quickly moved away from it. The car was successfully turned over, and the crowd cheered. Another car was set afire. As soon as the violence erupted, my sisters were ushered to a nearby hotel by NAACP Regional Director Earl Shinhoster, who had come to Miami because of the tension in the black community. "That was our first exposure to anarchy, really," Johnita says. "I could understand the rage, but the part of me that had been raised to follow the rules and be a good citizen couldn't understand. There was a fear because I couldn't relate to what they were doing, and I knew that people could get hurt. They were burning and destroying their own community, even, and I felt so sad."

Even though she was the youngest, Lydia insists she was not frightened by the upheaval around her. Instead, she felt awed by it. "I don't recall being afraid. Instead, I was sort of shocked and excited—not excited in the sense of being happy, but because I knew something significant was happening I didn't have the words and emotional maturity to completely understand," Lydia says.

Paralyzed by conflicting emotions—despair and elation—I watched the three days of rioting unfold on television. I felt despair because my city was burning, and the seething ugliness Miami usually kept tucked beneath its paradisial image was thick and acrid in the air. Innocent blacks and whites were dying unnecessarily, just as Arthur McDuffie had. That first night, passing white motorists had been pulled from their cars and killed. In the following days, most of the two dozen people who died were black; my family had heard stories of pickup trucks full of shotgun-wielding whites out *looking* for blacks to shoot. Isolated as we were in a mostly white neighborhood sprinkled with Confederate-flag bumper stickers, I was almost afraid to go outside. Because Dad was working for the Community Relations Board, he was out in the inner-city streets with a walkie-talkie trying to urge calm during a time when calm was scorned. My sisters and I never knew from night to night if my father would make it home. Miami was living a nightmare, a chaos of hate and fear.

I also felt elation—yes, *elation*—because of one thought soothing my young psyche: *Well, someone's going to listen. Someone's going to listen now.*

In some ways, I was right. For a time, anyway.

President Jimmy Carter came. The U.S. Civil Rights Commission came. Janet Reno, upon hearing the verdict, had said she was "bitterly disappointed."[7] My parents testified, submitted documents, went to meetings. Meanwhile, more and more Cubans were welcomed when they came to make Miami their home—thousands upon thousands in the Mariel boatlift—while Haitians were still sent away. Arthur McDuffie was still dead. His killers were still free.

While administrators piped in saccharine-sounding Muzak to help ease tensions at my racially mixed school, I wished myself somewhere else by writing an essay about the society I wanted to live in, one that would be gentler to my heart.

> *I want to live in a society where "Jew" is no longer a dirty word. . . . And no one remembers what "nigger" used to mean. . . . A*

> *society where the executives never say, "You can't have this job because you're underqualified" and they really mean, "You can't have this job because you're Black . . . or a woman . . . or a Jew . . . or a Latin . . . or a homosexual. . . . In my society, when they say, "Some of my best friends are . . . ," they really are. But nobody cares because they're really all the same. Prejudice is something that the children read about in their history books and they shake their heads saying, "How foolish they were back then!"*

I wrote and wrote. I wrote about an end to pain, an end to hate, an end to discrimination. Blacks, whites, Hispanics, gays, Jews; all of us could live in peace, side by side.

> *That's where I want to live . . . maybe that sounds like Heaven, but if I lived there right now, I'd call this society Hell. You know why?* MAYBE IT IS.

My mother told me how lucky I was to be able to express my feelings in writing, that so many people had to resort to other means, or were strangled by the emotions gathered inside of them. Yes, I realized, writing would be my saving grace. Writing would keep me sane. I later wrote a ten-minute speech based on that essay and won county honors at school speech competitions telling the story of how I'd felt. Again, I had an outlet.

Later, as an adult and a reporter for the *Miami Herald,* I would have the added buffer of a journalist's objectivity to keep my heart safe from pain. Journalists are trained to be life's observers, never participants. Even involvement in community protests and advocacy organizations flew against my job regulations, so I contented myself to write about people I believed might never otherwise be heard—blacks, as often as possible—and I wore that as my shield.

But at the time, my discomfort with individual confrontation quickly steered me away from the kind of journalism that would put me in constant conflict with my sources. I would not be like *Miami Herald* Pulitzer prize–winning writers Edna Buchanan, who had uncovered the Arthur McDuffie story, or Gene Miller, who had first brought the plight of former death row prisoners Freddie Pitts and Wilbert Lee to public consciousness. Likewise, I would not be a fiery columnist, pointing fingers and ruffling feathers as a mouthpiece for my people. (By the time I would leave the *Herald,* I was probably best known for the column I wrote about dating and relationships.)

During the ten years I worked at the *Miami Herald*, I covered two civil disturbances, the recovery of bodies, car accident fatalities, and government scandals, and every minute I spent gathering news wore on me. I knew I had reached the point when I could no longer be a news reporter when I was sent out in a downpour to get a comment from the family of a well-respected school principal who had been shot to death by her husband. As I stood in the rain on this family's lawn, a young Hispanic man escorted his father out beneath an umbrella to talk to me. The old man had dry lips and hollow eyes, and he said something beseeching to me in Spanish.

"What did he say?" I asked the son.

"He said, 'Please don't bring our family any more pain.' "

I walked away with tears streaming down my face, filled with self-loathing. What business did I have intruding on the worst moment of this man's life, after the violent loss of his daughter? I didn't want my writing to bring anyone pain.

Instead I was drawn to the features section and human interest stories. I still take pleasure in the memory of the stories I wrote that I believe helped readers learn about people who might have otherwise been voiceless: Like Sharmanita Grays, the teenaged victim of a serial killer, who had been making a rag doll in class before she died, and the teacher who saw to it that her unfinished doll lived on as a cautionary tale to other troubled young students. Or the late Liberty City muralist Oscar Thomas, who labored in the community he loved to bring colors, beauty, and images of heroes—Dr. Martin Luther King, chained Haitian refugees, Alex Haley—to an otherwise dismal cityscape. Or how an elementary school in South Dade County braved its way through the disaster of the aftermath of Hurricane Andrew. I wanted to write about quiet triumphs, not adversity.

And I tried to forget about Arthur McDuffie.

In 1991, soon after Los Angeles riots incited by a videotaped police beating of a black man named Rodney King, Miami was the only city in the United States to snub Nelson Mandela when he made his tour after being released from a South African prison. While Mr. Mandela was being honored with parades in the streets of Atlanta, and addressing Yankee Stadium in New York, Cuban-American leadership in Miami signed a document denouncing Mr. Mandela because he had refused to distance himself from Fidel Castro, who had been supportive of the anti-apartheid movement. That leadership included Xavier Suarez, the mayor of the city of Miami.

Nelson Mandela was an international symbol of hope in the face of overwhelming racism, and suddenly the city I lived in felt like an island. My sister Lydia and I accompanied my mother and Aunt Priscilla to Miami Beach, where blacks were gathering to support Mr. Mandela to counter scheduled protests outside of the building where he was making an address. That day, I heard the hateful words *Go back to Africa!* lobbed at us. That same night, Johnita returned from Europe after spending a year at the University of Sussex while studying race relations in England for her master's degree in psychology. At Sussex, she had joined with her international student friends from England, Italy, South Africa, Zambia, and Costa Rica in celebrating Mr. Mandela's release and embracing humankind's progress—delayed though it was. When she saw our exhausted faces after our pro-Mandela demonstration, she told us sadly, "Yes, I'm definitely back in Miami again."

Still, I was more upset by the actions of Miami's leaders than by the careless words of a few emotional Cuban protestors who could not see beyond their own pain. Leaders are supposed to represent everyone. Weren't *we* anyone?

That nagging thought came to me again: Blacks don't matter.

I had a very strange dream on May 20, 1991, the date blacks in Florida celebrate as Emancipation Day because it was in May that the news of slavery's end trickled southward to our peninsula. Ironically, almost to the day of Miami's riots eleven years before, I described my dream in a wire-bound notebook I kept as a journal.

In the dream, I was shooting a film documentary. My father, or someone very much like my father, was pointing out the exact spot of the McDuffie beating.

> *The final phase of the dream was to be there, to see it. . . . I saw the slow-moving procession of police cars, sirens flashing—I knew it was time. I felt a surge of adrenaline, excitement. . . . I felt like a removed, detached journalist about to witness the one story blacks in Miami have never recovered from.*
>
> *I couldn't see what was happening for the crowd of officers. . . . Then, I had a view. A single officer stood over a dazed, bleeding McDuffie, who was on his hands and knees. The officer grabbed a handful of his hair to lift his face up, then he smashed his flashlight down on McDuffie's skull. A scream, a howl, rose from my throat. Simultaneously, I knew my anguished cry had become a part of the history of the event. . . . I had not seen the beating, I thought; but in reality I had been there all along, helplessly mortified and outraged*

*like the woman on her knees at Kent State, captured by a photographer. My cry in my dream woke me up.*

I had not forgotten. Eleven years after the fact, as a twenty-five-year-old woman, I woke up sobbing like a child. It hurt. It *still* hurt. I had never cried about Arthur McDuffie's unpunished death as I did that day, even on the day of the verdict, when my childish illusions about the world I lived in had been shattered and Miami began to burn.

In a dream, there is no place to hide.

---

For all the pain I felt as an adolescent thrust into the social and political fabric of Miami, my parents' activism also brought me unparalleled joy—because we were an NAACP family, through and through. With one of my book advances, I bought NAACP life memberships for both of my parents and my grandmother. And the NAACP gave me a wonderful gift.

The summer after the Miami riots, when I was fourteen and a high school sophomore, I entered the essay I'd written about former school superintendent Dr. Johnny L. Jones into a high school contest sponsored by the national NAACP called ACT-SO (Afro-Academic, Cultural, Technological, and Scientific Olympics). My essay was defiantly entitled "Dr. Johnny L. Jones: Come What May, We're Here to Stay," and I opened it with my favorite Frederick Douglass quote: *This struggle may be a moral one or it may be a physical one, but it must be a struggle.*

At the time, the NAACP's competition for high school students was new, but it gathered quick momentum because of the vigorous energy of its founder, pioneering Chicago newspaper columnist Vernon Jarrett, who has a deep love for young people. Jarrett, with his salt-and-pepper hair and high expectations, believed that young scholars should be celebrated for their achievements in the arts and sciences just as athletes were celebrated on the football field and basketball court.

The awards ceremony took my breath away. I had never seen anything like the energetic procession of young people behind their cities' banners as they marched into the auditorium to the cheers of their parents, chaperones, and friends. Reading winners' names with a dramatic timbre as the trumpets in "Fanfare for the Common Man" pealed majestically from speakers, Jarrett made all of us feel as if we were Olympians. I had won contests before, but never on a national level, and I won my first national prize at ACT-SO that summer of 1980: a gold medal in essay writing. I was greeted by pioneering scholar Dr. Benjamin E. Mays, the son of former slaves who grew up to become the dean of Howard University's school of religion and the president of Morehouse College.[8] Dr. Mays handed me my prize. I was also greeted by historian Lerone Bennett Jr., author of *Before the Mayflower: A History of the Negro in America, 1619–1962*, so I stood between two great figures in black history. My heart, which had been so battered by crises, soared.

To this day, when I hear Aaron Copland's "Fanfare for the Common Man," with its booming timpani drums and unforgettable trumpet salute, my memory takes me back to those grand ACT-SO award ceremonies at NAACP conventions. Nowadays, those ACT-SO ceremonies are televised nationally, although they were not when I was a teenager. But I didn't need the eyes of a national television audience on me. Those processionals were the proudest moments of my young life.

Even more important, my participation in the ACT-SO competition over the next three years gave me the opportunity to meet other young blacks in Miami and from all over the country. They knew about the NAACP, and just as I was dedicating more and more of my time to my writing, they were pursuing their own dreams of becoming scientists, singers, orators, photographers, chemists, inventors, leaders. I met a brilliant student from Miami Central High School, Ivan Yaeger, who invented a bionic arm for his ACT-SO project! (I always knew Ivan was special, and in 2001, he was featured in *People* magazine because he had modified the invention he first built in high school to give a young girl who was missing an arm the chance to live an easier life.)

During the time that I might have felt the most despairing because racial politics in Miami were so explosive, ACT-SO constantly reinforced in me that the next generation was ready to take on the challenges of the post–civil rights era. The world would be ours to conquer. Although I did not develop close personal relationships with many of my fellow ACT-SO competitors, I felt the glow of their ambitions and talents. I felt the glory of their company. At ACT-SO, I never felt alone or afraid.

To me, the words of James Weldon Johnson's great anthem "Lift Ev'ry Voice and Sing" were a rallying cry. Especially after the Arthur McDuffie riots—the event that demonstrated to me how far there was yet to go—I sang those words with renewed, near-fevered emotion at the NAACP gatherings: *Let us march on 'til victory is won.*

## Nine

# Patricia Stephens Due

**"Tomorrow is now."**
***—Eleanor Roosevelt***

There was no time for rest once we got out of jail in 1960.

We were released on May 5 to a hero's welcome among Tallahassee's Negroes, who staged a rally in our support. "Jail was an opportunity for us," I said to reporters as we were leaving the jail. "We had the time to think, to renew our faith in America and the power of nonviolence, to rededicate ourselves to the task of ending discrimination."[1]

As William Larkins explained to a *Jet* magazine reporter less than two hours after he was free, "All of us felt we were doing the right thing. We had a feeling of righteousness which didn't make us feel bad about going to jail. Some people—our parents—were very concerned, but staying in jail was the easiest thing for us to do. We didn't mind being cut off from society for a principle. We just wanted to get out and participate in more sit-ins," he said.[2] Even John Broxton's first haircut was considered newsworthy after our release, because the *Pittsburgh Courier* ran a photograph showing him sitting thoughtfully in a barber's chair, sporting a moustache and goatee in addition to his ample head of hair. The bespectacled barber, a Tallahassee man named Parker Hollis, had formerly been convicted on charges stemming from the Tallahassee bus boycott in the late-1950s, so they were two brothers in our struggle.[3]

Much to our disappointment, however, our jailing had not brought about real changes in Tallahassee. The city's lunch counters were still segregated, and Negroes were still second-class citizens. To further set back the clock, Gov. Collins's term had ended, and C. Farris Bryant, a firm segregationist, was the new governor of Florida. None of the jailed students were technically students at FAMU any longer because we had missed forty-nine days of classes, so we had all been asked to withdraw from school and re-enroll for the fall term. We were also on university probation. CORE leaders and FAMU students had retreated from further direct action, deciding to concentrate on the boycott instead.

Around the nation, the civil rights movement was taking root, especially the student movement. In April, while we were in jail, several delegations of student leaders had met in Raleigh, North Carolina, and formed the Student Non-Violent Coordinating Committee, or SNCC. The group was an outgrowth of the Southern Christian Leadership Conference, influenced by Nashville sit-in veterans such as Jim Lawson, a Vanderbilt Divinity School student and pacifist well-schooled in the philosophies of Gandhi, and Fisk University undergraduates Diane Nash and Marion Barry (who was elected SNCC's first president).[4] During this time, many students, myself included, believed that the court-oriented tactics of the older NAACP were not the entire answer; we needed more direct action. We were tired of waiting for change. And the Tallahassee students were ready to take our story to the nation.

Despite Mother's earlier nervousness about the time we had spent in jail, she allowed me and Priscilla to take part in a national publicity tour scheduled by CORE to bring attention to what had happened in Tallahassee—but only if she could chaperone us. We went home to Belle Glade for only a few days of rest, then began a tour that lasted most of the summer.

"It's like being in the oven and then going into the ice," Priscilla later said, describing how it felt to travel throughout the North relating our story to sympathetic audiences. Instead of being "niggers," we were now treated like young dignitaries from a backward, foreign place. And I suppose that was true, in some ways, since people outside the South seemed so uninformed. We were welcomed and celebrated.

Reading comments from other Tallahassee CORE activists in history books today, I now understand that there was some jealousy about the attention Priscilla and I got that summer, since we spent more time touring than the others. I think some observers may have misunderstood our enthusiasm during that tour, believing we'd been diverted by the so-called "glamorous" life in the public eye. I never saw it that way. I saw myself as a witness to injustice and a storyteller, trying hard to get the word out. I truly believed—as I believe today—that information is powerful and that events should be documented. That's why I was able to tolerate such a hectic pace: Some days we had a breakfast speech in one state, a luncheon speech in another, and then an evening church meeting in a third. "What city is this?" I remember asking before a speech in Chicago. We never saw much of any of the cities except the airport and perhaps a hotel. Mother stayed with us a month, but then she couldn't take the pace anymore, and we were on our own.

Originally, all of the jail-in participants were divided up, sent to different regions. Barbara Broxton went to Watertown, New York, where she made an emotional address to the annual meeting of Woolworth stockholders, including the company president, after leading a picket line outside of the building. "We will fight because we are right," Barbara, in her prim dress, told the meeting. She was a striking presence. "I've been to jail, and I'm willing to go back if necessary."[5] Based on Barbara's presence, several stockholders introduced a resolution supporting the desegregation of all Woolworth counters, both in the North and South. (Apparently, Woolworth's sales had already dropped 9 percent since the February sit-ins throughout the South).[6] William Larkins went to the Midwest, appearing on Chicago television and addressing various civic groups.

Priscilla and I went to Chicago, Washington, D.C., St. Louis, Philadelphia, New York, Ann Arbor, and probably a dozen or more other cities during our tour, garnering much needed press coverage almost wherever we went. We weren't only telling our story to the people who actually came to see us speak—which, in most cases, was preaching to the choir—but countless others who read about our appearances in newspapers. "We might be expelled from school and we might not be able to find jobs in Florida, but they can't stop us," I told the *Washington Post* during one stop.[7] Naturally, our appearances also served as a fund-raising mechanism for CORE, which was a cash-strapped organization struggling to find its own place among better-known civil rights organizations such as the NAACP and Dr. Martin Luther King's SCLC. Despite their similar goals, we came to learn that these organizations had rivalries. At one point, a high SCLC official took me and Priscilla aside and told us that CORE was only using us and that we should join his organization instead. But Priscilla and I never got caught up in that kind of thinking. We wanted to be effective, *period*, and CORE had been the first organization to present a plan of action we believed would enable us to carry out our goals. In the years to follow, I would work with several other groups, including the SCLC, SNCC, and NAACP. Affiliation wasn't nearly as important to me as commitment.

I will never forget several moments during that publicity tour, especially the warmth and interest of the people we came in contact with. We spoke in Harlem at the great Rev. Adam Clayton Powell's Abyssinian Baptist Church, the oldest Negro Baptist church in New York City, and Rev. Powell gave us scholarships to help us defray school costs. We had the pleasure of taking part in programs with Ezell Blair Jr., the very polite young man who had been one of the original Greensboro sit-in participants. I met John H. Johnson, the president of the Newspaper Publishers Association (and the publisher of *Ebony* magazine) when I addressed the publishers' banquet in Chicago. I met a New York attorney, Jeff Greenup, who helped present a $1,000 check on behalf of the social action committee of Grace Congregational Church; I could not know it then, but Attorney Greenup would come to Florida to volunteer his legal expertise and represent arrested activists in years to come. We were invited to a reception hosted by Harry Belafonte at his New York City apartment; I was told Belafonte had once been denied the opportunity to rent an apartment in the building because of his interracial marriage, so he had bought the building instead. At that party, I met the writer James Baldwin, who was very quiet and unimposing. A. Philip Randolph, the great labor organizer, was also there. I have never been one to feel starstruck after meeting celebrities, but I was very proud to see how involved they were. We had a unifying cause.

On June 20, we attended a fund-raising luncheon hosted by Eleanor Roosevelt at the Plaza Hotel in New York; Mrs. Roosevelt had sent out a letter encouraging patrons to attend by describing our jail-in: *Such courage deserves our admiration and respect*, she wrote. *More than that, it gives every one of us confidence in the future of our country. Her example tells us that nothing will stop the winning of full equality for all our citizens so long as girls like Patricia are prepared to make such a sacrifice.*[8] The former First Lady was elegant and very friendly toward us. Priscilla and I appeared at the luncheon with a white Florida State University student, Robert Armstrong, and the three of us reenacted the sit-in and the ridiculous trial, playing different characters such as hecklers, judge, and prosecutor. As always, our audience was very surprised to hear how freely the word "nigger" had been used during a legal proceeding. Daisy Bates, who had coordinated the integration of Central High School in Little Rock, Arkansas, and Jackie Robinson also attended that luncheon. I'm certain a lot of money was raised that day. I remember people asking me at that luncheon, "My goodness, aren't you nervous?" I kept saying, "Oh, no, I'm not nervous," but sure enough, I suffered an upset stomach and ended up in the bathroom.

That was a whirlwind summer, and it was very trying. I'm grateful to this day for a young man named Phaon Goldman, who was on the executive committee of the District of Columbia branch of the NAACP and was charged with our care for the evening we were in Washington. He was one of the few people, at the time, who seemed to view us simply as people and not larger-than-life figures. He had a much needed party for the visiting activists and told us, "Let's just pause for a while," because he knew how tired we were. At the time, it meant a lot to us.

It also meant a lot to us that CORE awarded the five jail-in students, including me and Priscilla, its Gandhi Award. Presented by activist Rev. Wyatt Tee Walker at CORE's annual convention in St. Louis on June 29, 1960, the award read, *"The five leaders have borne abuse and contumely with restraint and dignity. They have maintained a spirit of goodwill and understanding. They have not swerved from the objective of equal rights for all."*[9]

But our work was far from over. Only a few months after my release from a jail cell in Leon County, I was on my way to jail again—this time in Miami.

---

In April, Miami's biracial committee had brokered an agreement among major department stores and five-and-dimes—Woolworth, Kress, McCrory's, Grant, Burdines, Richard's, Jordan Marsh, and Sears Roebuck—to allow integrated seating at food counters. That group included Rev. Theodore Gibson, president of the Miami branch of the NAACP, Miami CORE Project Director Dr. John O. Brown, and Rev. Edward Graham, president of the Ministerial Alliance.[10]

But by the end of that summer, Miami was still far from integrated. When Priscilla and I returned to Miami for CORE's Interracial Action Institute, we were no longer curious young newcomers but tested veterans. The three-week workshop met in August, again at the Sir John Hotel, and although most of us there were college students, participants were as young as seventeen and as old as seventy-five. Even my younger brother, Walter, attended the workshop, encouraged by his big sisters' example. That workshop really opened his eyes, he told me later.

The first phase of the institute was the testing of lunch counters. We tested forty eating places and were served in only twenty-three.[11] One place that steadfastly refused to serve Negroes in its dining room despite a high number of Negro patrons was Shell's City Supermarket, billed as the "World's Largest Supermarket." It was right on Seventh Avenue in Liberty City, in the heart of one of Miami's ironically named Negro neighborhoods, so it became a focal point for picketing and sit-in demonstrations.

Priscilla and I, of course, were eager to take part in more demonstrations, but I remember that I did not want Walter to participate with us because I thought he would be too protective of us, which might lead to a confrontation.

Priscilla and I were among eighteen demonstrators who sat-in at Shell's City on a Wednesday afternoon, August 17, and waited for service. When our interracial group first sat down, the manager said, "Can't you see the waitresses are busy?" A half hour passed with no service, and then the police came. We were all escorted out of the restaurant, our names and addresses were recorded, and we were informed that we had been placed under arrest.

I honestly don't remember how much time we spent in jail in Miami. The CORE newsletter listed our trial date as August 26, so if we stayed in jail until then, we spent nearly ten days there. However, in 1963 I told a *St. Petersburg Times* reporter that I had spent five days in jail before the trial. Either way, Priscilla and I were once again in a jail cell for trying to be served food just like any other paying customer. I'm sure Mother was worried again about us, but our second jailing was not nearly as surprising as the first for her. She understood our dedication much better by then. In fact, I remember her telling me how irritated she was that she had a friend who continued to buy her liquor from Shell's City despite our arrest there.

At our trial, the judge told me and Priscilla that we were on probation for one year, and as long as we didn't get into any more trouble, the arrest would not remain on our records. I'm sure I was thinking, *Well, as long as discrimination exists in Florida, I'm sure this won't be the last time I get in trouble.* But I didn't say so then.

Days after the trial, at the Interracial Action Institute, I had the opportunity to meet Rev. Martin Luther King Jr., who came to give talks during the August 31 and September 1 sessions.[12] Dr. King was a slender, unassuming man dressed in a casual white short-sleeved shirt and dark slacks. While he spoke with great assuredness, we were told he had a cold, and consequently he was not able to attend all of the workshop sessions. The most lasting impression he made on me after my first encounter with him was that he seemed very tired, as I am sure he was.

Priscilla recalls another incident involving Dr. King some time later, when she was attending a gathering of activists in Pennsylvania. "I went to Mahalia Jackson's room and Dr. King was lying on the sofa sleeping. She said, 'Don't wake him.' She called him 'Black Jesus,' or 'Black Moses' or something. I remember how they would put him on a pedestal," she told me. To her, it seemed strange, because she was accustomed to relating to Dr. King as a *person,* a fellow soldier—yes, I had Dr. King's personal telephone number in those days, and I called him from time to time when I was in Atlanta—and the way others treated him bothered us. Priscilla was very aware of the idea that if she was not careful, the adulation of others might change her idea of who she believed *she* was. She did not want to lose sight of her goals, and we certainly never did anything because we hoped to see ourselves in the newspapers or so that people would treat us differently.

Priscilla also had lunch once in Atlanta with Dr. King and drew on her experience during our speaking tour to ask him how he coped with so much attention. "When we were first released from jail, they put us on a pedestal," she told him. "How do you handle it, because you have it a thousand times more than I do—about how you're so great and so wonderful, blah blah blah?" He thought and told her, "I do not know the answer to that. That is a very difficult thing."[13]

Walter, too, remembers an encounter with Dr. King not long after the 1960 workshop. At the time, Walter was enrolled at Morehouse College. "I was in the library one day and I met him. I reminded him I had met him previously, and my sisters were Pat and Priscilla Stephens. And he said, 'Oh, yeah, I know them!' I'll never forget how he stopped to say he remembered. The fact that he would do that for me as a freshman at Morehouse was awesome," Walter says.[14]

Walter took the lessons he'd learned in Miami to heart. He got involved with SNCC, participating in sit-ins and demonstrations in Atlanta. Although he was never arrested, he had embarked on a lifetime of community service in his own way. Forty years later, Walter would take thirty young black men from Boy Scout Troop #141, a troop he calls the "Buffalo Soldiers," on an unforgettable trip to Ghana.

In our family, activism was contagious.

---

FAMU President George W. Gore Jr. was "constantly" under external pressure to "expel all students and terminate any faculty members who were actively involved in the sit-in demonstration," according to Dr. Leedell W. Neyland, who wrote a book about FAMU at its centennial.[15] Dr. Gore and the rest of FAMU's faculty were Negroes, but they were expected to follow rules set by the state's white power structure. Still, despite resistance from Florida's Board of Control—the body that governed the state's colleges—Priscilla and I were permitted to register in the fall of 1960. We were officially college students again.

We received a wonderful boost of confidence from our fellow students. On November 20, 1960, Priscilla and I, John and Barbara Broxton, William Larkins, and FSU students Jefferson Poland, Richard Parker, and Robert Armstrong were awarded "Social Action Awards" from FAMU's Phi Beta Sigma fraternity chapter during its Annual National Social Action Program at an on-campus Vespers service. The campus administration had resisted, but the students had insisted on giving us the award. That made us all very proud.

I was ready to throw myself into my studies, which had suffered so much at the end of the spring term. But based on my newfound activism, I made a very difficult decision: I changed my major from music to sociology, where I thought I could do more good. I had been a serious musician, and I missed it, though, as I do today. I never have gone back to music, and I still consider it a great personal loss.

During the summer, while the students were away, the FAMU community suffered another great loss: Richard Haley, a faculty member and one of Tallahassee CORE's most ardent supporters, had lost his job. Haley's dismissal came as a surprise to the student body, since the student congress had voted him FAMU's Teacher of the Year only in May for "outstanding leadership of civil rights . . . and for general interest in the student as a citizen of the university community and his surrounding society"[16]—only a week before he was let go. Even the student activists had no true idea what had been going on behind the scenes with FAMU's staff, but Daisy Young and Richard Haley, who had become fast friends as well as CORE activists, were in the thick of it. They knew they were targets.

Daisy Young worked in the FAMU registrar's office, so she had seen Richard Haley turning in his grades over the years, but they had never gotten to know each other well until they were both drawn to CORE the previous fall. From the establishment viewpoint, the sit-ins, student teargassing, and jail-in had been an avalanche of bad publicity for FAMU and Florida. Although neither Miss Young nor Mr. Haley had participated directly in any of those events—except in assisting and observing—Dr. Gore was under pressure from the Board of Control to regain "control" of his campus. Gladys Harrington, a FAMU librarian, who was the secretary for the Inter-Civic Council and had been part of the Tallahassee bus boycott, eventually left Tallahassee because she felt the pressure from the FAMU administration, Miss Young recalled. (Harrington rose to prominence in CORE after she left Tallahassee, becoming chairman of New York CORE and the Northeast Regional Representative.)[17]

A spy from the university would drive past Miss Young's home to take note of who was leaving and arriving. License plate numbers of the cars parked outside mass meetings were routinely recorded. Miss Young once left an Inter-Civic Council mass meeting only to find a representative of the Board of Control actually standing outside to see for himself who was leaving, and she remembers one big-talking FAMU faculty member in particular who never attended another meeting after that night.

Miss Young says Dr. Gore called a meeting of everyone on the university's payroll at eight o'clock one Sunday night—the exact time the Inter-Civic Council held its mass meetings. Everyone convened in the Lee Hall auditorium, she says, filling it to capacity. After making a series of minor university announcements, Dr. Gore said the words Miss Young believed had been his reason for convening the meeting all along: "You know, we are like a ship. And I would advise everybody that's on the ship, if you want to stay on this ship, you stay *on* this ship. If you get off the ship, you may not be able to get back on. Because the times we are living in, the times are just not right to be doing some of the things some of you are doing. So, since you're on the ship, I advise you to stay on the ship."[18]

Miss Young interpreted his words as a direct threat, and she says it worked on a lot of faculty members who might have been considering more involvement. But not her. "That night, a whole group of us went right on to the mass meeting. As soon as the doors opened and he let us out, we went right on the way."

Miss Young remembers when the storm clouds arrived. It was her day off, shortly before the end of the 1959–60 school term, and she received a phone call from her boss. That day, she was busy at a task at the Inter-Civic Council office beside Rev. Dan Speed's grocery store. "I don't know what we were working on, but we were always working on something. And I got this telephone call, and it was [the registrar] Mr. Thorpe. And I said, 'Inter-Civic Council office.' And he said, 'Oh, Miss Young, don't say that.' He recognized my voice. 'Don't say that. Just answer the telephone. Don't give your name out.' And I said, 'What is it, Mr. Thorpe?'

"And I don't know, but I felt something. You know how you feel different? He said, 'I need to talk with you. Get here as soon as you can. I need to talk to you,' " she recalls. Dressed casually in jeans with a cap pulled over her head, she walked to the campus. When she got there, her boss had a warning for her: "You know, you're number one on the list. Mr. Haley is number two. Someone from the Board of Control has called Dr. Gore and wanted to know how in the world could we people be out protesting when we had full-time jobs."

Miss Young says that they weren't protesting—and even if they had been, what they did in their free time was their own business—but she wasn't surprised at the summons. After the large-scale arrests in Tallahassee on March 12, she and Mr. Haley had discussed the possible repercussions to them. Mr. Haley had told her and Gordon Carey, of national CORE, that he wasn't concerned about himself, but he was concerned about her because she had family and deeper ties in the community. Miss Young told him, "The Lord will take care of me. Don't you worry about me, now." They even laughed about it, she recalled.

Soon after the school term ended, Mr. Haley told her again how concerned he was about her. She again assured him she would be fine. That same day, he got the notice of his dismissal in the mail. "What Dr. Gore did, he waited until school was out," Miss Young said.

Of course, the dismissal mentioned nothing about Mr. Haley's civil rights activities, and some observers attributed it to personality conflicts and other problems. When even the American Association of University Professors weighed in to question why Mr. Haley's contract had not been renewed, Dr. Gore explained that it simply was "in keeping with the university policy dealing with non-tenured members of the instructional staff."[19]

After he was dismissed, Mr. Haley released an angry statement through Tallahassee CORE: "I have been employed at Florida A&M University for five years, and have maintained the most amicable relations with my department head. It's obvious that my work with CORE is the bone of contention. This is an arbitrary, unwarranted invasion of my personal freedom, and a clear threat to any other teacher—whether employed by public or private agency."[20]

Miss Young continued to hear warnings, too, both from her immediate boss and from other staff members who felt free enough to talk to her; all of whom said that if she didn't stop her activities, Dr. Gore would fire her. When I interviewed Miss Young in 1993 at her home on Pinellas Street in Tallahassee, her lively manner changed and her voice grew reflective as she recalled how harassed she felt. "Pat, it got so bad, nobody knew how the pressure did hurt me. It really did hurt me," she said.

And she wasn't afraid to speak her mind even back in the 1960s. As she once told her boss in the registrar's office, "Everything I do is after five o'clock. Now, if I'm not free to use my own time, then I know I need to stop fighting crackers and start fighting niggers." She told him she was never late to work, that she was up at 6:00 each morning even if she'd just gone to bed at 5:00 A.M. Much to her boss's horror, Miss Young made an appointment to talk to Dr. Gore. During the meeting with the university's president, she said, Dr. Gore was nervous, pacing his office, and he denied that he had been sending her any messages. After that, the warnings stopped, but Miss Young didn't receive any of her expected pay raises for two years, and she believes it was because of her civil rights involvement. To my mind, people like Mr. Haley and Miss Young, who were willing to sacrifice their livelihoods for their belief in the Movement, are every bit as heroic as anyone who faced physical harm. Without them, those of us on the front lines would surely have languished.

Although Mr. Haley remained active with national CORE and lived in Tallahassee, on and off, after his dismissal, our CORE chapter's morale was a little low at the start of the new school year. Clearly, we were fighting an uphill battle in Tallahassee. The city's lunch counters were still firmly segregated in the fall of 1960. By contrast, lunch counters had been integrated by July in Greensboro, the city that had sparked the national sit-in movement. Ninety cities in eleven Southern states were reporting changes as a result of the sit-ins, including North Carolina, Texas, Virginia, Tennessee, Kentucky, and Florida.[21] Change was visible in Miami, but in Tallahassee it was slow, slow, slow. It was such a great effort to push against the status quo, and we had to spend half our time fighting the white establishment and the other half, it seemed, fighting our own.

Despite our frustration, CORE did keep pushing for changes. On Tuesday, December 6, CORE organized a small, specially selected group of Negro students to picket Woolworth on Monroe Street, myself and Priscilla included. To prevent problems on the scale of what we'd experienced earlier in the year, William Larkins, president of the FAMU student body and one of our fellow jail-in students, passed out leaflets at FAMU discouraging other students from going downtown and to avoid violence or arrest. Those of us picketing were peaceful, of course, but during our three days on the line, white hoodlums shouted at and pushed us while police stood by and did nothing. In fact, according to the newsletter published in her home by Lorraine Calhoun—a white woman in Port Orange, Florida—to keep civil rights activists informed of developments around the state, an observer reported "flagrant fraternization and camaraderie between the police and the hoodlum element."[22] By the third day, the hoodlums felt bold enough to simply grab our signs and tear them up, but we continued picketing anyway.

At school, pressure was growing. On the morning our picketing began, I was summoned out of class to Dr. Gore's office. I expected him to lecture me about my involvement, but when I got there, much to my surprise, two no-nonsense white men in suits were waiting there for me. The men identified themselves as FBI agents and said they had questions for me. One of them tried to convince me that he was trustworthy by telling me that he wasn't from the South, that he was from Detroit. Then they proceeded to grill me about what activities our CORE group was planning. (This was only the first of many times I would find that I was once again being summoned to Dr. Gore's office to be questioned by the FBI.) I still have a souvenir from that day: the December 6 letter on FAMU stationery from Dr. Gore asking a professor to excuse me for being late that morning. *She was detained by me,* he wrote. But he didn't say why.

During that school term, I could feel that I wasn't at my best. Something was wrong. I often found myself rushing to the bathroom because my stomach was upset, and I had a bald patch on my head the size of a half dollar. A dermatologist told me it was caused by stress. Two weeks before the school term ended, I woke up and felt as if I couldn't think or move or speak. I'd had enough. "What do you mean you're going home?" Priscilla said, shocked. "Pat, you only have two weeks left! You can last two weeks."

I knew myself then as well as I know myself now. I could not go on. After nearly two months in jail and more months traveling to repeat the tale, I was emotionally spent.

I withdrew from school, feeling I had no choice but to waste all the effort I had put into my classes if I wanted to save my sanity. I packed my bags and went home. I needed to be with my mother.

# Ten

# TANANARIVE DUE

**"Children have never been very good
at listening to their elders,
but they have never failed to imitate them."**
***—James Baldwin***

I went to Northwestern University as a freshman in the fall of 1983 with dreams of becoming a student activist. I didn't intend to sacrifice as much of my schoolwork or social life as my parents had, but I was eager to add my voice to the thronging masses on a college campus, with its bevy of student causes and the tide of youthful idealism.

That wasn't exactly the way it turned out.

Northwestern is built at the edge of Lake Michigan in the peaceful suburban reaches of Evanston, Illinois. I saw no thronging masses of activists. When I arrived on campus, the only fever was from Rush Week, when students vied for invitations from soroities and fraternities. Unbeknownst to me, this was not very different from the way life had been on campus when my mother first arrived at Florida A&M University, but after a lifetime of admiring photos of the 1960s student civil rights and peace movements, I had expected more single-minded seriousness from the students.

Even before I set foot on the campus, I was out of the loop. Many of the other black freshmen had come to the campus early for various orientation programs like MEOP, the Minority Engineering Opportunity Program, but I had received no such invitation. By the time I arrived, those students had already formed fast friendships with other blacks they had met.

Soon after the start of the school year, a racial incident occurred on campus. Apparently, a black woman had been harassed by white members of a fraternity, but I heard only bits and pieces of the story. I also had no idea that black leadership had decided to hold a secret meeting to plan a protest march. Years later, I contacted my freshman-year roommate, a cheerful and graceful black girl named Charlie Jordan, and heard for the first time about her night of political intrigue surrounding that incident. While we were students, Charlie had heard about a meeting announced through a very secretive grapevine, but by a strange fluke, I hadn't—not even from her.

The black students met in a gym in near darkness, Charlie told me eighteen years later, with the older black students waiting for them like tribal elders. "Welcome to the family," someone told Charlie, squeezing her hand. At that gathering, Charlie learned about For Members Only, Northwestern's black organization, the history of black activism on the campus, and details of the fraternity harassment incident that had taken place about twenty-four hours previously: A group of white frat guys had jumped out and encircled a black woman passing their house, taunting and trying to frighten her. After hearing what had happened, the black students present mobilized for a silent march to the homecoming parade. When the float from the fraternity passed, a hundred black students raised their fists in solidarity while a frat member on the float shouted racial epithets at them. "What amazed me was the power of the network and how quickly all those people were galvanized together," says Charlie, who is today an independent film director living in Los Angeles.[1]

Where was I during all this racial unity? I have no idea.

I would have loved an initiation like that, but I received none. Meanwhile, I was searching blindly for familiar touchstones at Northwestern. There was no college chapter of the NAACP on the campus. I was thrilled when I saw a meeting announcement for the International Committee Against Racism, and I attended the meeting with Charlie—but that group turned out to be a Marxist revolutionary organization. We were neither Marxists nor revolutionaries, and the only other students in attendance, as far as I can recall, were white. Charlie and I took one look at each other and knew we wouldn't be going back there—although Charlie's name ended up published in the *Daily Northwestern* as a new member, much to her embarrassment.

I was frustrated by the campus's de facto segregation.

I lived in the Communications Residential College (CRC), a dorm where students had to apply for renewable membership. I was a journalism major with an interest in film, so I was attracted to the dorm because of its videotape and film editing rooms, darkroom, and audio production booth. CRC's residents were ambitious, talented students with very similar interests. I was program director for the dorm radio station I helped cofound, a pirate station we called WXLO, which is still on the air with an official sanction, today known as WXRU. While I lived there, I also wrote a screenplay and coproduced a video movie my friend Rob Vamosi directed, based on one of my short stories, and I spent many hours helping students finish their film and TV projects. To me, it was paradise.

Almost everyone in the dorm was white. A black film major named D. J. Wells lived in CRC, and I grew close to him and his best friend, Albert Mensah, a black premed student from the adjoining dormitory who shared D. J.'s wicked sense of humor. With peer pressure from D. J. and Albert, I had a brief stint patrolling Evanston's streets as a trained Guardian Angel, a manifestation of my civic duty that, in retrospect, was one of my stranger college diversions. But most of the blacks I met were like me: Their social circles were nearly all white, too. And none of my best friends, neither black nor white, were interested in political meetings or rallies. For that aspect of my life, I was entirely on my own. Even immersed in the company of friends who were as precious to me as blood relatives—a newfound family—I always felt something was missing. Charlie was often away, and she didn't live in CRC long. She didn't like the isolation from other blacks, so she moved out after one year. She wanted to live closer to her friends; if I had moved out, I would have been leaving mine.

Black students at Northwestern tended to flock to the Foster-Walker complex, the heart of black social life on campus. Charlie had also pledged Alpha Kappa Alpha, the traditionally black sorority, which my mother had encouraged me to pledge. After watching Charlie and her friends stay up until 3:00 A.M. making projects out of construction paper and running to Burger King on errands to please their AKA superiors, though, I didn't have the stomach for it. Instead, I pledged Chi Omega Rho, a co-ed fraternity that at the time had five or six other black members, making it the most racially mixed Greek organization on campus. I didn't have to perform any humiliating or stressful tasks to get in, but I was feeling more like an Oreo all the time.

I felt my Oreo-itis even more strongly when I checked out a couple of meetings of For Members Only, the black student organization to which Charlie had received such a dramatic introduction. FMO held regular meetings at "The Black House," which had a reputation for being very militant. Someone told me once that white people were not permitted to set foot into The Black House, even if they were reporters covering a story. I felt like a white woman in blackface when I set foot in FMO's meetings, given that I knew and liked so many whites. I did not go back to FMO after my freshman year, perhaps for no other reason than my belief that it had a meeting place where whites were supposedly banned.

I might have made a difference if I had approached FMO with the notion that I could help *shape* the organization, rather than simply accepting that it had already been shaped by others. Had I become active with FMO, I would have met exactly the sort of conscious, activism-minded black students I craved to meet. But I was intimidated, not to mention that I felt like the members would not approve of my circle of friends. I think I really believed I would be expected to entirely abandon my white friends to avoid alienation from blacks.

It seemed social forces on campus had conspired to make me choose between having white friends or black friends when I simply wanted to have both. I despaired in the cafeteria, noticing that black students ate at the tables with their friends and white students ate with their own, too. A few of us ate among interracial groups with others in our dorm, but we were in the minority. Blacks who sat with whites were also subjected to the occasional cutting glances of passing blacks, many of them strangers, who thought we had gone out of our way to make a statement by distancing ourselves. My frustration with constantly straddling a racial line caused me great discomfort during my college years. Since my mother's college experience was all I could draw from, I had envisioned opportunities to work for social change with both blacks and whites united.

Johnita became a freshman at Harvard University two years after I entered Northwestern, and she had the college experience I'd hoped to have: She was copresident of the Association of Black Radcliffe Women, regularly attended meetings of Harvard's Black Students Association, and traveled in black and white circles with equal ease, though for the first time in her life most of her friends were black. At Harvard, she didn't feel the same pressure to choose sides. "It was wonderful. It was a great feeling to be around others I had something in common with," Johnita says today. "I was exposed to black students with a social consciousness, and our views of the world seemed similar."

But Lydia, who went to Wesleyan College, a small liberal arts college in Middletown, Connecticut, found herself feeling cut off from black social life. She did not live in Malcolm X House, where most of the handful of black students opted to live. She was paired with her white freshman-year roommates by university housing, they became fast friends, and they lived together the entire four years they were in school. Like me, she longed for more black associations, but at the same time, she says, "I felt like an outsider."

I knew the feeling.

In a sociology class one day, the professor asked the students to raise their hands if their parents made more than $200,000 per year. To my utter shock, more than half the students' hands shot up. My father was making a good living as a county administrator, to the point where I was shy about mentioning his salary to anyone I knew, but he wasn't making that kind of money, and it was a real eye-opener to me that so many of my classmates came from such affluent homes. *Damn,* I thought, *these people here are* RICH.

That wasn't the case for most of the black students, whose families probably made less than mine. In fact, Northwestern seemed to have a very good record of bringing in promising black students from Chicago's economically disadvantaged areas. So, there we were: a campus with white students from affluent families who probably knew very few blacks at home, and blacks often from poorer backgrounds who probably knew very few whites. In retrospect, it's no wonder there seemed to be so little communication between them.

I felt one last gasp of optimism when I saw signs advertising a meeting for a new group: START—Students Together Against Racial Tension. It turned out to be an all-white meeting, and suddenly I was forced to be an ambassador, since all eyes were on me: "Why do black kids sit with only other black kids in the cafeteria? Why won't they sit with us?" someone asked me. That bothered me, too, but I knew it wasn't black students' responsibility to pepper themselves throughout the room so all the white kids would get a chance to "experience" them. I sighed inwardly and answered as patiently as I could that all students tend to sit with their friends. "You sit at tables with only white students, don't you? Why is that?" I said, and there were enlightened nods around the room.

That was the last time I went to a START meeting. I wasn't in the mood to give Sociology 101 lessons to a bunch of clueless white kids, no matter how well-meaning they were. I was still trying to figure it all out myself, and I wanted to be part of some kind of *action.* I longed to start a CORE group like my mother had belonged to in college, and I even wrote her about it, but CORE had changed so much by then, Mom said, she doubted it would serve my purposes. Instead, I could have tried to start an NAACP college chapter, but it seemed like too much work.

Instead, I gave up. I concentrated on socializing and working on arts projects in my dormitory, which became my cocoon. This was the first time in my life I was making real friends—the kind I had longed for in high school—who would remain my friends for life.

In 1985, my sophomore year, the anti-apartheid movement hit Northwestern. The conservative campus began to rustle restlessly, and before I knew it I was attending rallies that were drawing 200 students, spurred by a new group called the Anti-Apartheid Alliance and others. Northwestern, like many institutions, had money invested in companies that did business in South Africa, and students were raising their voices to demand that the campus divest its investments in apartheid. Finally! I was utterly electrified.

Exiled South African poet Dennis Brutus was on Northwestern's faculty at the time, and I remember hearing him read his poetry at a rally in his pained, melodic voice. As I scanned the crowd, though, I saw a schism: Most of the students at the protest were white, as were most of the students who wore red ribbons to symbolize their opposition to investments in South Africa. Somehow, even a movement designed to help end segregation and discrimination in South Africa could not overcome the de facto segregation at Northwestern. I couldn't believe the irony of it.

Not that I didn't understand what was repelling the other blacks. Many of the white students involved in Northwestern's anti-apartheid movement were sincere and hard-working, but there were also large numbers who simply looked flaky—draped in tie-dye, wearing flowers in their hair, strumming guitars, obviously trying to recreate their parents' hippie days. I'm sure most black students took one look at them and rolled their eyes, assuming their activism was nothing more than a fashion statement.

That didn't matter to me. All I cared about was the good that might come of it. And how much more good could we do if we all worked together? I read a skeptical quote from the president of FMO in the *Daily Northwestern*, about Northwestern's anti-apartheid movement, and I immediately fired off a response to him. *Yes, they're white, but they're sincere, and we all have a common goal*, I told him. The president at the time, a theater major named Harry J. Lennix, called me right away, and offered to get together to discuss my concerns. He had a deep, rolling voice, and I should have jumped at the chance! But instead, fearing a confrontation with a brother who was clearly more "down" than I was—writing a note is easier than a conversation, after all—I cowered away. We never met to talk, and yet another opportunity to build a bridge evaporated. I was pathetic.

Today, after tracking Harry down through Northwestern's black alumni network, I have come to learn that FMO was involved with behind-the-scenes negotiations to encourage the university to divest. Lennix attended those high-level meetings, though he says he grew annoyed with Brutus's criticism that FMO wasn't doing enough. "Back then, I tried—I did all that—but the bottom line is, charity begins at home," Harry says with his hallmark candor. (He is also an amazing actor who has since had roles in *The Five Heartbeats, Titus, The Matrix 2,* and a Showtime movie about Adam Clayton Powell, *Keep the Faith.)* "We've got enough problems right here."[2]

Unlike Harry, I was not ready to be a leader during that time. I always balked when the ball came back to me. I was not, it began to seem to me, cut from the same cloth as my mother.

Even with the anti-apartheid movement, I had no patience for meetings. At one Anti-Apartheid Alliance meeting, I watched students arguing over which tactic to employ when it seemed obvious that they should use both. When I meekly raised my hand to make the suggestion, they applauded as if I were a prophet. The constant tugging and negotiations between individuals trying to formulate plans of action has always frustrated me.

But rallies! I loved rallies. I loved the emotionalism that comes with hearing words you believe in your heart to be God's simple truth, and to raise your voice skyward to demand change. I loved the fellowship of like-minded believers. When I went to rallies, I felt transported, and I was certain that so much earnest belief could change the world again, just as it had changed the world in the 1960s. If I had been a college student during my mother's time, I thought, I wouldn't have been one of the organizers, but I would have shown up at the appointed time to hold my placard and march, or sing, or chant. And, yes, to go to jail.

At Northwestern, I finally got my chance to see what I was made of.

One rally drew the largest crowd ever, and we stood shoulder to shoulder in the courtyard of Rebecca Crown Center, the campus administration building visible from a distance because of its soaring, monolithic clock tower. I do not remember everyone who spoke that day, but Dennis Brutus was there, making the plight of black and "colored" South Africans all the more poignant through the gentle music of his poetry. In his speech, Brutus told the crowd, "It is a shame Northwestern University is profiting from the blood, the suffering, and the broken bodies in South Africa. It is time for Northwestern to clean up its act and get out of that bloody mess!"[3]

Other speech makers, including other professors, all overflowed with earnestness. A fever sweeps a crowd under the right circumstances, that same fever I'd yearned for since the first day I'd walked onto that campus, and the fever was there that day. I had tears in my eyes. When the drumbeat of the chanting began, with fists raised in the air—*Divest* NOW! *Divest* NOW!—I imagined I might have been in Tallahassee or Selma or Montgomery, and I felt myself pulled into a human current of students surging forward, driven by their passion.

I hadn't planned on it, but I was suddenly part of a student takeover. Inside the administration building, as secretaries scurried out of the way, I felt stunned, basking in the exhilaration and joy on the students' faces as we cheered our tiny victory. We had brought work at Northwestern's administration building to a halt. Now the university would have no choice but to pay attention to us, just as an earlier generation of Northwestern students in the 1970s had taken over the administration building to demand a black studies program. For most of us, I'm sure, this was the most drastic action we had ever taken, and we were all probably surprised at ourselves. We were putting ourselves at some risk for something we believed in.

When the telephone rang, a student answered, "Nelson Mandela Center!" and we all cheered again. Nelson Mandela might have been languishing in a prison thousands of miles from us, but he was in our hearts that day. Politically speaking, that was my happiest day at Northwestern. I felt an even bigger charge when a campus police officer made his way past the throng of students to tell us that the building would be closing at five, in less than an hour, and anyone who hadn't evacuated by then would be arrested and taken to jail for trespassing. Fine by me, I thought. Finally, I was about to become the person I'd always believed I could be. I was going to relive my mother's experience in Tallahassee.

More than a hundred students were inside the administration building, I believe, but I did not know any of them, with two exceptions. One was a member of my co-ed fraternity, Roger, and the other was Larry, a journalism major I had met when we participated in Northwestern's Summer High School Institute as high-school juniors. Both were white, and both were determined to be arrested. While my arrest would be a lonely experience, at least I would not be entirely alone.

As it got closer to five o'clock, the organizers made it clear that no one was being pressured to stay, that everyone would have to make an individual decision to be arrested. Slowly, some students began to drift out of the building, but my resolve was still firm. I would remain.

At about quarter to five, I heard someone struggling to have my name heard over the din of chatter. "Is there a . . . Ta . . . na . . . na . . . REEVE here?"

"That's me!" I said, completely startled, raising my hand.

"You have a telephone call."

Who in the world? Who would know to reach me here? I was mystified. To get to the desk, I climbed over the students sitting cross-legged on the carpeted floor.

When I picked up the phone, I could barely hear the tiny voice. "T? It's Kate." Kathryn Larrabee was my new roommate at CRC, a blonde-haired white girl, and it was completely out of character for her to try to reach me under such bizarre circumstances. She is now a gifted novelist, the author of *An Everyday Savior*,[4] and back then we were two starry-eyed kids who mostly talked about our dreams of being writers one day, not politics. I was convinced there must be an emergency at home.

"What's wrong?" I said, panicked.

"Geez, what's going on over there? I thought I'd never find you. I have a message for you from J. D. He says you guys are supposed to have dinner at 5:30. He can't do it any other time, and he's leaving early tomorrow. What should I tell him?"

J. D. Roberts was one of my best friends, a boy I'd had a crush on for a portion of my freshman year. He had been the driving force behind the dorm radio station where I had invested so many hours. I'd been looking forward to dinner with him. J. D. wouldn't be coming back in the fall, so this dinner was meant to be our good-bye. I hadn't expected him to plan it so early.

"What should I tell him?" Kate said again.

In that instant, it was as if the person I hoped to be was once again smothered by the person I really was. I was trying to make myself say, *Tell J. D. I have to cancel dinner because I'm about to get arrested.* I opened my mouth to say the words, but I couldn't.

"Tell him I'll meet him at 5:30," I said, my heart sinking.

My walk out of Nelson Mandela Center that day was long, indeed. Even though we'd been told we were under no obligation to stay, I imagined accusation in the eyes of the other protesters as they watched me winding my way toward the door. I knew I was leaving behind any dreams I'd had of following in my mother's footsteps as a college student. We simply were not the same people, and we did not live in the same times.

When I spoke to my mother on the telephone that night, I hesitated, but then I told her what had happened. I braced to hear her withering disappointment that her warrior stock had given birth to someone so weak of character.

"Oh, Tananarive-a," my mother said, adding the extra syllable to my name the way she and Mother often did. "I'm glad you didn't get arrested. Don't get arrested, do you hear me?"

"But *you*—" I began, and she cut me off.

"Darling, *I* went to jail so *you* wouldn't have to."

Ninety-five students were arrested that day at Northwestern. My two friends Roger and Larry were among them. Despite the way the university hassled the arrested students for months with legal appearances, the charges against them were later dropped. The college president mentioned their activism with pride at our commencement address, saying that their degree of commitment reflected well on the university. Eventually, Nelson Mandela was not only a free man, but the president of his nation.

I made lifelong friends at Northwestern. I fell in love and learned heartbreak for the first time. I helped adapt my own fiction to video. I had two creative writing professors—Janet Desaulniers and Sheila Schwartz—who made me believe I was already a writer, not a writer-in-waiting. But within those good memories, I see gaps, so many wasted opportunities, so many people I never knew. I took classes from extraordinary black professors—historian Sterling Stuckey, late novelist Leon Forrest, Guyanese novelist and playwright Jan Carew—but I was invisible, too shy to strike up relationships with them, and too young to appreciate how important that would be.

Still, I graduated with only one true regret: I wished I could go back in time and change the outcome of the day of the anti-apartheid takeover, to paint myself as someone who was fearless and committed and would gladly sacrifice a good-bye meeting with a friend for the larger cause. But in the years since, I've come to feel cleansed of the guilt that followed me. I might not make the same choice today, but what had I done wrong? During that precious college time, I was enjoying myself, making friends I cared for deeply, and preparing myself for my coming career in the arts, where there were a few trails of my own I hoped I could blaze.

I went to jail so *you* wouldn't *have* to, my mother told me.

My parents had given me a gift: I had the freedom to be a kid. I marveled at the magnitude of the gift I had been given, as I still do now, every day.

Eleven

# Patricia Stephens Due

**"Love is like a virus. It can happen to anybody at any time."**
***—Maya Angelou***

My life was so transformed by the fall of 1960, it's a wonder I still recognized myself. One major change was on the home front. After eleven years of marriage, Mother and Daddy Marion were separated. Having two daughters in and out of jail had not helped their relationship, I'm sure. Despite the fact that the problems between them couldn't be blamed on our civil rights activism, I have no doubt that Daddy Marion's fear of reprisals and Mother's heightened level of stress only contributed to their divorce. Mother and Daddy Marion had never been the kind of couple to argue openly in front of us when they had disagreements, but I had been aware that they had problems.

Mother never told us this at the time, but the main reason she had married Daddy Marion was to secure a father for her children. He had always known this, but he had hoped his love for her would win her heart and keep them together over time—and we could not have asked for a better father. But with Priscilla and me in college and Walter on his way to Morehouse in Atlanta, Mother decided she wanted a change. She had always been a very attractive woman, and there was no shortage of men who wanted to court her. Very soon after her divorce, she married a mortician named Leo Sears, who lived in Fort Myers, Florida, about 400 miles from Tallahassee. Daddy Marion remarried a former wife.

Unfortunately, my relationship with Daddy Marion was never the same after the divorce. Mother encouraged us to keep in touch, of course, as she had done with Daddy, but he began to withdraw from us. We might have withdrawn from him, too, but I firmly believe that his new wife felt threatened by his relationship with his stepchildren, so over time we became casualties of the breakup. We were not free to visit as much as we might have liked, and when we did, Daddy Marion asked us to come see him at his school rather than at home. I resented this, but

I loved him, so we complied with his wishes. Once again, in some ways, I had lost a father. (Daddy Marion retired from the school system in 1971, then I lost him for good when he died in 1973.)

My childhood was behind me, in every sense, and I had made the transition to adulthood. My life had taken on its own hectic pace, and now I had the prospect of my own family on the horizon. By December 1960, I was also engaged.

His first name was John, but I will only refer to his last name with the initial "B." John B. was a CORE volunteer I had met in New York, where Priscilla and I were loosely based during that summer of touring. John B. was a physics Ph.D. working in New York and, like most activists we met, he was extremely dedicated to the cause of equality. We met because he had been assigned to "entertain" me and Priscilla so we would not burn out during the tour. He told us we could go anywhere in New York we wanted. After some thought, I realized I wanted more than anything to go to Coney Island, and I had never been there. Now *that* would be a diversion! I was very excited.

Priscilla bowed out, having no interest in anything so childish. John B. did not seem so enthused himself, but he agreed to take me. When we got there, my eyes lit up when I saw the Cyclone, the monster rollercoaster that was the most famous in the world. I told John we had to ride it, and he agreed. What a ride! I must tell you, the Cyclone was worth the price of the ride. On a scale of one to ten, in terms of thrills, I rate it a ten-plus. I was so excited when the ride was over, I said I wanted to ride it again. My host, however, looked a little worse for the wear. "I'll stand here and wait for you," he said, "but I'm not going to ride that again." In fact, I think he had to run to the men's room.

That is my first memory of spending time with John B. I also remember him taking me to the zoo, where he listed scientific information about every animal we passed as if he were a tour guide. It's not hard for me to imagine that, to others, John B. might have suited every stereotype of a scientist: very smart, quiet, a bit standoffish—but he wasn't that way with me. When we were together, we laughed about simple things, and I got to know him. Our relationship continued after that summer, when he wrote to me at school. Our letters mostly discussed events related to the Movement, but he always began with his pet names for me, "Tallahassee Lassie" and "Black Princess."

By Christmas break, John told me he wanted to come to Florida to ask my parents for my hand in marriage. That impressed me a great deal. Being an old-fashioned girl, I was pleased that he wanted to get engaged the "proper" way. Even in the midst of a courtship, though, I realized that a marriage between me and John B. would not be that simple. Those outings we had shared in New York would never have happened so openly in Tallahassee, nor in any other place in the South.

I was Negro, and John B. was white.

Coincidentally, he had gone to school in Tallahassee, too, but he left before I arrived. In late 1956, John B. had been suspended from Florida State University because he had invited three Negro foreign exchange students to a college-sponsored Christmas party for international students. Because of that and other activities, he was considered a radical. "The boy is sick and needs help," FSU's college president said of him at a 1957 meeting of the Florida governor's Advisory Commission on Bi-Racial Problems,[1] all because he had become involved in the Inter-Civic Council with some other FSU students, calling for an end to Jim Crow!

After two decades of segregation, I had never had any sort of romantic inclination toward a white man before I met John B. When I tried to envision men I considered attractive, I never thought of white men. If anything, I probably considered white men stiff and somewhat cold.

Yet I liked John B., and we shared the common vision for this country's future that had become the driving force of my life, so I told him he could come to Florida to ask for my hand. Despite the fact that Mother and Daddy Marion were divorced by then—and that Daddy Marion was not even my biological father—John B. considered him my true father figure, as I did, so he set out for Belle Glade to talk to Daddy Marion first. I don't have a clear recollection of what Daddy Marion said, but I imagine his attitude was probably "Wait and see." He may not have thought we were serious. We also spent several days at Mother's house in Fort Myers. John B. wanted not only to ask for my hand officially, but he also wanted to spend a few days getting to know Mother. This, too, pleased me a great deal, since family is so important to me.

As I think back, Mother was unusually composed when I showed up on her doorstep with this dark-haired, mustached, baby-faced white scientist and he told her that he wanted to marry me. I was nervous. Unlike the last time, when I'd come with Billy H., praying she would release me from my obligation, I was older now and I wanted to get married. If she was horrified or amused, she didn't show it. She sat at first with an inscrutable expression and let us have our say.

When we were finished, Mother thought for a moment and said, very matter-of-factly, "You know, I've been married twice before, and I can tell you that marriage is difficult even when you have everything in common, such as your religion and racial group." Here she paused. "And the important thing is that you know an interracial marriage will be much more difficult. If you've discussed that, and you both think you're mature enough to handle that more difficult marriage, then you have my blessing." Mother had a great flair for handling things in the best way possible. If either of us had not given serious thought to the racial question, we would be forced to think about it now.

John B. and I looked at each other. We thought we knew what we were up against. In Florida in late 1960, a marriage between us would not even have been legal. We had talked about shielding ourselves by living in an academic setting, where people tended to be more open-minded, and John also had the opportunity to teach in London, where laws and customs were very different. Jackie Robinson (reluctantly, I believe) had told us he would host our wedding, if necessary. But with her own brand of finesse, Mother quietly planted seeds of doubt in my mind.

During that visit to Fort Myers, we got a taste of what our future lives together as a white husband and Negro wife might be like. We decided to go somewhere together to have a good time, but Fort Myers, of course, was completely segregated. As we tried to walk into a Negro nightclub, the man at the door, who was also Negro, stopped us in our tracks. "Hey, hey," the man said gruffly, "ya'll can't come in here bringing this white man. What are you thinking? This is my club, and I'm not getting arrested." Mother's new husband, Mr. Sears, saved the day. Pretending to be surprised, Mr. Sears said, "Oh, man—you think he's *white?* That's my wife's cousin! You know how that is." And, true enough, there has always been so much mingling among the races, legal or not (and consensual or not), that Negroes come in all shades. The man at the door took a close look at Mother's fair skin, glanced back at John B., then nodded. "Oh, yeah, I'm sorry, man. I'm sorry. Go on in."

The four of us laughed long and loud once we were inside. We discovered that John B. was not much of a dancer, which, according to stereotype anyway, would have betrayed his true lineage. We certainly got stares, but at least we had a few laughs getting in.

Joking aside, however, we had received a small preview of what was to come. John B. and I remained engaged, but we were not in a hurry to marry. He went back to New York, and I returned to FAMU's campus. I was excited to be engaged, but there was also serious business to attend to. I was eager to concentrate on my classes again, and of course I wanted to remain involved in civil rights.

Somehow, word of my engagement to a white man had spread far beyond the campus of FAMU. Only a couple of months after we got engaged, the Negro newspaper publishers met in Tallahassee, and I found myself summoned to speak to them. I had no idea why they were calling me, but I assumed it had to do with the Movement.

It did, but not the way I had thought.

Once I arrived at the meeting, I went to a conference room where about a dozen publishers and journalists were assembled. With very stern faces, they put their cards on the table right away: "If you marry a white man," they said, "your effectiveness in the Movement and your effectiveness as a voice for your people will be greatly compromised—if not totally deteriorated." In days of old, this was probably very close to what it felt like to be called before the tribal council. "Why are you marrying a white man?" someone asked me point-blank.

Ordinarily, I don't have the kind of personality where I allow strangers to ask me such pointed questions about my life. But because Negro newspapers had such an important function in the Movement, serving as an information source when white newspapers often would not print news about the unrest throughout the South, I respected this organization. And as an activist, I thought it was my duty to answer their questions.

"I'm in love with him," I said.

"Is being in love enough to sacrifice all the good you can do for your people?"

"I can still work for my people," I insisted, but they were not convinced. As I left that room, the mood was very somber, as if they were watching a fallen soldier.

Believe me, in those days it would have been newsworthy that a Negro activist was engaged to a white man. Negro newspapers printed their share of gossip, and they also saw themselves as community vanguards. (In his book *Bearing the Cross,* David J. Garrow points out that the *Pittsburgh Courier* issued a warning to Dr. Martin Luther King about traps to catch him during his suspected philandering as early as 1957, although it never named him directly: "A prominent minister in the Deep South, a man who has been making the headlines recently in his fight for civil rights, better watch his step.")[2] Just as the white newspapers very carefully chose what to print and what not to print, the Negro newspaper publishers had no intention of telling the world about my "fall from grace." Although everyone knew, no one ever printed a word about it.

The doubts planted by Mother intensified after that meeting, although I never let on. I knew I had to be very honest with myself about my feelings for John B. and what I wanted for my future. Frankly, I wasn't being very honest. Whether or not I wanted to admit it, I'd met another man—a Negro man who was also named John—I was also interested in.

The first time I saw John Dorsey Due Jr. was in the fall of 1960 at the Leon Theater in Tallahassee, where I worked at the concession stand. The Leon Theater was the theater that served Negroes, and the owner, a white man named Mr. Stone, was sympathetic to the civil rights cause, so he had offered me a job. One of the advantages of working at a movie theater was that I could get my friends in free as long as I asked permission. So Priscilla came one night with two male law students from FAMU. She'd invited along her date, Isiah "Ike" Williams III, and a new student named John Due, who only got an invitation, in truth, because he had a car. I had never seen John Due before that night, but he caught my eye.

John Due had recently enrolled in FAMU's law school after attending Indiana University. Little did I know that while growing up, the Terre Haute native had always considered himself a "studious nerd," and he had shed his eyeglasses for contact lenses to change his image from "Johnny," as his friends and family had always called him. In fact, John tells me now, during an unsuccessful stint at Indiana University's law school, he'd spent too much time socializing because he was trying to be "the Billy Eckstine of the period." He had beautiful, smooth brown skin with a hint of a reddish tint from a Cherokee forebear, very pleasant features, and he stood six feet, two inches tall. From his build, he could have been an athlete.

I'd caught his attention, too. Because my eyes were sensitive to light following the teargassing incident, I was wearing dark glasses indoors, which probably made me look like I was trying to be fashionable. Nothing could be further from the truth. I was also wearing a snug-fitting black sweater and black boots, which also gave the appearance that I was much more sophisticated and worldly than I really was. I noticed John Due's interested gaze. Although I couldn't tell initially which of the two men was escorting Priscilla, she was doing her best to play matchmaker. "Come see *Carmen Jones* with us, Pat," she said. "We'll save you a seat. Find us when you've finished working."

Well, I did want to see *Carmen Jones.* The all-black 1954 production starred Dorothy Dandridge and Harry Belafonte. I knew Belafonte was very supportive of civil rights, since he'd been involved with a major sit-in fund-raiser during the time Priscilla and I were in jail, joined by other celebrities such as Sidney Poitier, Mahalia Jackson, Shelley Winters, Ossie

Davis, Ruby Dee, and Diahann Carroll. Admittedly, while I had feelings for John B., I was interested in seeing more of John Due. To be honest, my immediate attraction for this man startled me. I already had a fiancé, after all. Why should I be interested in another man?

After the movie, Priscilla suggested that we all go somewhere else. John had planned to go home to study, but suddenly, he says now, he forgot all about studying. "Patricia was kind of short compared to the other ladies I got to know, but she was well-built," he recalls. "She was a very attractive young lady." Priscilla sat in the back seat with Ike Williams (the first time I realized he was supposed to be with her), and I sat up front with John while he drove. We ended up going somewhere to dance, and John danced with me.

John got a little fresh that first night. He tried to kiss me, which was considered very forward in the early 1960s, and I told him off. "What do you think you're doing?" I said. "You don't know me. I don't expect some man I don't know to be pawing all over me."

Believe me, that was the last time John Due got fresh for a long time. But I wasn't angry long, and I didn't forget him. There were now two Johns in my life. I thought of them as Black John and White John. Black John and I became very good friends, especially since we both had an interest in civil rights. After our first few meetings, he realized that Priscilla and I were the two girls he had read about in *Jet* magazine at his kitchen table with his grandmother. As a member of the NAACP in Indianapolis, John had followed the news of the sit-ins and our jail-in, so he knew exactly who we were, even though he had initially forgotten our names. He had already lost a job once with Indiana's Board of Corrections—where he had been the second Negro counselor at a state corrections facility—because he'd participated in a protest. (He'd won his job back under threat of lawsuit.) In fact, he'd come to FAMU precisely because he wanted to be in the thick of the civil rights movement in the South, leaving behind everything and everyone he knew. Rev. Steele had already invited him to speak before the Inter-Civic Council. But John had been warned by the dean of the law school, Dean Thomas Miller Jenkins, that he should not get arrested or do anything to jeopardize passing the bar exam, and his strategy was to get his law degree and become a lawyer so he could be more involved on the legal front of civil rights. John was five years older than I was, but he was one of the few people close to my age whom I could really talk to.

I have to admit, when those Negro publishers and journalists called me in to explain my love for a white man, I did walk away feeling more confused. How could I really love White John when I was getting so attached to Black John?

To complicate matters further, John B.'s parents were distraught when they heard about our engagement. He was from Fort Dodge, Iowa, and his father was a respected entrepreneur in the dairy business. He told his son that if he married a Negro woman, it would destroy him. Further, he made it clear that if John B. married me, he would no longer be his son, and he decreed that if anyone else in the family attended our wedding, they too would be cast out.

John B.'s mother tried a more gentle approach, but she was also very opposed to our union. She wrote letters to me directly, hoping to appeal to me woman to woman. She said she wasn't prejudiced, that she had Negro friends. She told me she knew I must be a person of high caliber if John was interested in me, but she pointed out that although John B. was a few years older than I was, he was very inexperienced socially. Under any other circumstances, she said, she would be delighted he had found someone he wanted to marry, because he had never paid much attention to women. But in the end, because she knew her husband's attitude, she said, "Please don't marry our son. This will ruin our family." And, she reminded us, what would become of our children?

I did not feel any anger toward John B.'s parents, especially his mother, whose letters were so passionate and sincere. Naturally, though, I would not have been swayed by a mother's plea if I really believed John B. was the person I was destined to marry. Ironically, it was John B.'s own reaction that gave me pause. "Pat, I've been financially independent for years," he said. "I'm going to marry you, and if my parents don't like it, that's just unfortunate for them. Even if they disown me, it wouldn't matter to me."

On the surface, those words might have sounded romantic, but not to me. I wondered why John B. wouldn't at least consider reasoning or negotiating with his parents in some way. I could not fathom having such a cold attitude if my parents had been in such emotional turmoil. A voice in the back of my mind said, "If he could be that cold to them, could he be that cold to me someday?"

John B.'s mother eventually decided to defy her husband and attend the wedding if we were determined to marry, and one of his brothers was also planning to attend. His family was literally being split over the question, and I found myself forced to do some deep soul-searching. How could I marry John B. and potentially destroy his family if I wasn't sure how I felt about him? And how could I marry one man when I knew full well that I was still attracted to another?

Unfortunately, Tallahassee's lunch counters were still segregated in 1961, a year after our jail-in. Henry Steele had been briefly served at a lunch counter at the Neisner's department store the previous June, when he dined with a group of FSU students, but that turned out to be a fluke. A group of white ministers had also become involved, forming a biracial committee to encourage downtown merchants to bring about integration without further direct-action protests. That effort had failed, in part because merchants had received no assurances of police protection in the face of the public outcry they expected from whites.[3] National CORE was concerned with the lack of momentum in Tallahassee, and although I wasn't on the campus during that time, Priscilla and the other students were hoping to breathe new life into the organization.

I had already served my jail time because of the sit-in arrest at Woolworth, but our attorneys appealed our convictions all the way to the United States Supreme Court. Tobias Simon and Alfred I. Hopkins, two of our lawyers, held that no arm of the state government—in this case, Tallahassee's mayor—could use its power to impose racial discrimination against a private citizen. In 1948, the Supreme Court had ruled that real estate covenants designed to prevent Negroes from moving into certain areas could not be enforced in court, so why should our arrests at a lunch counter on the sole basis of race be any different?

In March 1961, a year after our initial arrest, the Supreme Court made a decision: It would *not* overturn our convictions.[4] Apparently, in the eyes of U.S. law, it was perfectly legal for a town mayor to enforce Jim Crow policies. I was not surprised by the Supreme Court's decision, but I was disappointed. Whatever progress had been made during our speaking tour and fund-raising drives, it seemed, could be negated with the stroke of a pen. If the law wasn't on our side, then what was our hope?

Since we weren't going to tolerate discrimination any longer, the laws would have to change. Period.

We might have been considered only kids in those days, but clearly it was going to be up to us to help change the laws.

Twelve

# Tananarive Due

**"Sometimes a person has to go back,**
**really back—to have sense, an understanding**
**of all that's gone to make them—**
**before they can go forward."**
***—Paule Marshall***

One of the most extraordinary experiences I've ever had while researching a book was in 1999, when I was writing *The Black Rose,* a historical novel fictionalizing the life of self-made black beauty tycoon Madam C. J. Walker. I was at the Indiana Historical Society, searching through old microfilm of *Indianapolis Recorder* newspapers from the early 1900s, and my eyes were peeled for any references to Madam Walker, her husband C. J. Walker, or her attorney, F. B. Ransom (whose son, Willard Ransom, was one of my father's mentors). I was in a particular hurry because I hadn't realized the historical society was closing early that day, so I had two hours less than I'd planned. It was my last day in town, I still had a lot of film to go through, and I had to leave in twenty minutes.

Suddenly, a name jumped out at me from the screen: *John Due.*

The newspaper was from April 25, 1912. The name topped the "Society Gossip" column, which chronicled weddings, births, deaths, illnesses, parties, and any other events in the black community that the social editor deemed newsworthy.

The reference was tiny, but it stilled my heart: *Mrs. John Due is seriously ill at her home at 112 Emmett Street,* it said. Alongside the notice, a real estate salesman's ad proclaimed BOOKER T. WASHINGTON ADVISES HOME BUYING. Beneath that was an ad for a laundry company that delivered its clothes with a horse and buggy.

Here was a snapshot of my family's history, right before my eyes.

After being immersed in the world of Booker T. Washington and horses and buggies for so many months while I wrote *The Black Rose,* the sight of my forebear's name made me feel as if I'd been sucked into a time portal. Suddenly I could imagine my feet touching those historical streets, as if some part of me had been walking there all along. It was a feeling of deep connection on the level of spirit and ancestors, which is rare during an era when we all routinely scatter so far from the places of our roots, and when we often don't learn who came before us.

I asked my father about it, and he told me that the Mrs. John Due in the newspaper was his great-grandmother. I had stumbled blindly onto a reference to my own great-great-grandparents while doing research on a book that had nothing to do with me.

After floating on a surreal cloud of elation after the chance discovery, I remembered that I've always known my father's roots in Indiana go deep. Even my reasons for agreeing to write *The Black Rose*—a book based on the research and notes of *Roots* author Alex Haley and therefore not a project entirely of my own creation, unlike my other novels—were entangled with the story of my father's family in Indiana. Mom was the first family historian in my life, but my father and my great-grandmother Lydia Graham (my sister's namesake and the woman who raised my father) told me stories, too.

I did not know Grandmother Lydia well or see her often. My only real memory of spending time with her is that she had emphysema and asthma, so when I once spent the night with her in her room, I lay awake terrified that I would hear her labored breathing come to a sudden stop. I do remember her as a cheerful woman, I enjoyed our telephone conversations, and when I was eleven she was a voice of history when I needed her help on a school project I called "My Own Roots."

It was 1977, in the wake of Alex Haley's book and the miniseries that had kept the entire nation captive, and I was electrified by the idea of learning my family's history—not only the 1960s sit-ins and arrests I'd heard about, but from Before. From slave times. After seeing *Roots,* I was obsessed with images of Kunta Kinte, Kizzy, and Chicken George, and I started writing a piece of fiction I called *Lawdy, Lawdy, Make Us Free,* about a young African girl's experience with the Middle Passage and slavery. I was thirsty for a feeling of connection with black people from that time, imagining how they'd suffered—thereby giving the circumstances of my own life deeper resonance. I was developing a long-term perspective.

I asked my father if he knew any stories about his ancestors.

"There sure is a story," my father said, his face lighting up. "Did I ever tell you about Lyles Station?"

I shook my head.

"Well, I'll tell you about it, but we should call Grandmother Lydia, too."

I couldn't believe my luck. My father was eager to share an unknown part of his life with me! And I was lucky enough to have a great-grandmother who could tell me where I'd come from. I didn't realize it at the time, but Alex Haley's *Roots* and my school assignment had inspired me to honor my ancestors in a way that would never cross most children's minds. To my ears, my father's story revealed itself like a glorious, unwritten chapter of *Roots.* I was not disappointed.

"Way back in the 1800s, not long before the Civil War," my father began, "a slave master in North Carolina decided to set his slaves free. He'd decided he didn't believe slavery was right. But he also knew there was a lot of prejudice against black folks to prevent them from making a good life for themselves, so he bought them a parcel of land in Indiana under his own name. He did that because there was a law in North Carolina that required him to take responsibility for his slaves after they were free. Now these freed slaves had somewhere to go, land where they could build their own houses and start their own farms. So they packed up everything they owned and drove in a wagon train all the way from North Carolina to Indiana."

My eyes widened. A wagon train! The scene unfolded in my imagination, the dust kicking up under their wheels, the jouncing of the wagon, the sounds of *"Yee-haw"* as the driver coaxed his horses to go faster. I could see grandfathers and fathers and mothers and children, free for the first time in their lives, savoring every sight that came before their eyes.

"When they arrived," my father went on, "they began to farm the land. Now, these slaves knew the land, they knew farming, and the ground was fertile, so they had bumper crops, better than they expected. In town they sold what they grew, so they were not only feeding themselves, but they were earning money. And they were so prosperous, they started attracting attention to themselves. The white farmers who lived around them started getting jealous. And this came at a time when a lot of folk in Indiana were putting pressure on the governor to make it a slave state. Indiana was a free state, you see. And people who already wanted Indiana to be a slave state were very unhappy to have to compete with these freed slaves. They started thinking, 'Now who are these niggers making all this money?' Poor white folks didn't like to be shown up by black folks. That's when trouble always started."

*Uh-oh,* I thought, beginning to realize I might not like this story. I had heard stories like this before, about the Ku Klux Klan and lynchings and burning crosses. I'd heard stories about trouble. Stories like those didn't have happy endings for black people.

"Well, sure enough," my father said, his voice dropping to give the story drama, "one night after it was dark, the neighbors of those freed slaves came in a surprise attack. The freed slaves were sleeping in their beds when the shooting started."

*Yep,* I thought, *here it comes. This is where all the black people die.*

"But these freed slaves did something that was very smart: They had thought about what to do in the event of something just like this, so they all ran to what's called a 'round house.' That was a big, sturdy building where they stored their farming equipment. They had their rifles in there, too. Once they were all gathered inside, the men passed out the rifles and shot at their attackers through the narrow windows of the round house, while the women climbed up into the loft and reloaded the guns. Back in those days, guns could only fire once and had to be reloaded. That's why they had worked out a system. But even with all of them shooting, they couldn't keep all of the whites from getting to the round house. The whites started to break down the door, and the blacks knew that once they got inside, they would try to kill everyone."

I might as well have been inside that round house, too. I could see myself crouching behind bales of hay in the loft while I covered my ears to block out the sounds of shooting and shouting below. I could imagine their faces hardened with determination, and the terrified beating of their hearts as they fought for their lives.

"What happened?" I asked, nearly breathless.

"Suddenly, the door came crashing down. The armed white farmers began swarming inside. But again, the freed slaves were ready for them. They had lined up on either side of the door with battle-axes raised high over their heads. When the farmers broke in, they swung those axes down. And they kept swinging until all those jealous farmers were dead."

"They won the fight?" I said, hardly daring to believe it.

"They won the fight."

"But what happened to them? Did they get in trouble?"

"Well, it caused a big problem, of course. Even the governor had to get involved. He didn't blame the freed slaves for what happened—they'd been attacked on their own land—and he knew he would have to take some precautions to keep the peace. He helped them move to a settlement called Lyles Station. Freed slaves from all over came to Lyles Station to settle in a place where their neighbors wouldn't bother them. They built a thriving community. And my grandmother was born in Princeton, Indiana, which is near Lyles Station. They still have family reunions at Lyles Station."

Did the story really happen? I may never know. I should point out that I haven't been able to verify my father's story with the Lyles Station Historic Preservation Association, which is actively working to preserve both the oral traditions and buildings of the Lyles Station settlement in Indiana. But as Jeanne Killebrew, the association's founder, pointed out to me twenty-five years after my father first told me the tale, Lyles Station is full of stories, and not all of them are known. Settled in the 1840s, she says, Lyles Station is the only incorporated black town in the state of Indiana. The definitive book about Lyles Station, written by Dr. Carl Lyles (a descendant of one of the original founders), is entitled *A History of Lyles Station, Indiana*. There is also a children's book based on Lyles Station by Scott Russell Sanders, *A Place Called Freedom*. My father still stands by his account of the attack and relocation. It's a story his grandmother told him, and her mother told her.

While I was researching my school project, my great-grandmother wrote me two letters to add her knowledge to our family's history. We still have the letters, which she wrote painstakingly in her shaky script: *I have been looking for papers giving names and dates of the family. When I find them, I will send you some history of your roots. I will have to write it because I have no tape, and my eyesight is poor so you will have to be patient with me.* Grandmother Lydia related that the families who had come from North Carolina and other slave states to take up territories in the wooded lands included the Hardimons, who were "Irish and Negro." They settled in Gibson County, among others. One man, John, had eight sons, and one of his sons, Alexander, married Lydia Walden, a girl from a large family of mixed white and Indian blood. *In 1857 a daughter was born, Alice; in 1860 a son, Horace. In 1861, when the Civil War was declared, young Alex, then nineteen, was drafted, leaving a wife and two babies. They lived in a thick woods, in a one-room cabin. They stayed in this wooded place, which was three miles from the next log cabin, all summer—but as fall came, they were afraid, for most of the white people were very mean and there were only pig paths to travel. Lydia Hardimon, then seventeen, took her two children and went to live with her parents, who lived ten miles farther into civilization.*

Grandmother Lydia listed names and little-remembered facts that she had culled together from papers I would have no idea how to find today. *William Henry Stuart, who was called "Colonel," also came from a large family of mixed races. His father escaped from an old wicked slaveholder who sold his wife and some of the children and sent them away. He and three of his boys were helped by some good white people who gave them some shoes and clothes, also a sack of food. They helped them to a free state.*

To me, my great-grandmother's words were distant echoes from a nearly forgotten past. She died at the age of eighty-nine in November 1980, when I was a teenager, that tumultuous year of the Arthur McDuffie riots, but I don't remember asking her about family history again. Her daughter, my grandmother Lucille, died in 1992. My father's great-great Aunt Melva Richardson died in 2001 at the age of 112, but I hadn't seen her in years.

As close as I was to Mother, my maternal grandmother who died at the end of 2000, I can think of a million questions I never thought to ask her. What did she think of the changes she'd seen in her eighty years of life? What was her happiest memory as a child? Whom did she most admire in her lifetime? My grandmother's death has taught me that no matter how many hours I have spent with my mother in interviews and conversations, there will be only a roaring abyss left behind once she is gone, too. And my father. That's the only time we realize how much we never knew. How much we never asked.

The story my father told me about Lyles Station when I was eleven was exactly what I'd hoped to hear. I wrote my report and my parents helped me build a large plywood display, which I adorned with family photographs and ink-pen sketches my father had drawn for me: a black man driving a wagon with a horsewhip, the desperate battle inside the round house. I worked harder on that project than I'd worked on anything up until then. Somehow, it mattered more than anything I'd ever done for school.

I concluded the "My Own Roots" report with earnest zeal. *Some of your relatives may know of their history. Do they sometimes sit around and tell stories the way Alex Haley's grandmother did? If they do,* listen!

I couldn't express that thought any better today.

# Thirteen

## Patricia Stephens Due

**Where is the Jim Crow section**
**On this merry-go-round,**
**Mister, 'cause I want to ride?**
**Down South where I come from**
**White and colored**
**Can't sit side by side.**
**Down South on the train**
**There's a Jim Crow car.**
**On the bus we're put in back—**
**But there ain't no back**
**To a merry-go-round!**
**Where's the horse**
**For a kid that's black?**
***—Langston Hughes***
**"Merry Go Round"**

I left FAMU's campus and went back to Fort Myers to be with Mother in early 1961, and there was more stress waiting for me because she and Mr. Sears, her new husband, were already having problems. Mr. Sears was a very respected businessman in the local community and shared Mother's belief in the importance of civic involvement, but they also had serious conflicts, and I was not happy with her new situation. I felt that Mr. Sears was an intruder in Mother's life, and in turn in mine, especially since she had left Daddy Marion for him. After staying with them for a short time and seeing how often they argued, I resented their marriage even more. Mother had sacrificed a great deal to raise her children, and I wanted her to be happy in her own life now that we were adults. But one thing I appreciated was the way Mother talked to me like a confidante instead of a daughter while I was there, and our relationship began to shift into the cherished friendship it would remain for the next forty years, until she died. Despite Mother's anxious state regarding Mr. Sears, I enjoyed being with her, away from school and the civil rights movement.

My respite from Tallahassee didn't last long. One day in March, I got a call from Priscilla, who had taken the lead of Tallahassee CORE. During that time, for whatever reason, Tallahassee CORE's membership had become more limited to students, with less input from the adults in the community. "Pat," my sister said in her breathless, enthusiastic way, "you just have to come back here. We need you for demonstrations."

I flatly told her no. "I need a break from all that," I said.

"But we *need* you!" she said. Because she was my sister, Priscilla probably was the only person who could have persuaded me to come, and that did take some persuading. Finally, I agreed to go back to the battlefront.

I arrived in Tallahassee expecting to find Priscilla ready to direct me, but she was nowhere to be found. She had a class she didn't want to miss, which annoyed me, but I learned there were to be lunch counter demonstrations at Sears & Roebuck, McCrory's, and Neisner's. Only five of us had volunteered to take part. This was a far cry from the days when we'd had dozens of protesters, but we decided to press on. On March 4, our small group visited the stores one by one. We arrived at McCrory's at 11:45 A.M., and after we sat down we were asked to leave, which we did in an orderly way. At Sears, the management had a much more hostile attitude to our presence; instead of asking us to leave the snack bar, management emptied it by sending both employees and diners away, then they locked us inside—but not before turning up the heat as high as they could. It was March, which is technically winter, but Tallahassee's weather is mild, so it wasn't long before all of us felt like we were suffocating in that stifling heat. We were trapped inside for nearly three hours, until police finally brought us out at about 3:00 P.M. We were held for a time, but we were not arrested and were soon released.

That left one more store: Neisner's. By then it was late in the day, and the only other student remaining with me was a FAMU political science major named Benjamin Cowins, a thin, energetic young man in black-rimmed eyeglasses who had grown up in a Negro neighborhood in Miami known as Bunche Park. Ben had first come to the campus in the wake of the FAMU student's rape in the late 1950s, so he had become politicized right away. At his home neighborhood in Miami, he recalls, he had everything he needed at his fingertips: a movie theater, a shopping center, everything. There was no need to venture into white neighborhoods to be subjected to the insult of a WHITE ONLY sign, so he'd been very sheltered, except he'd noticed how his grandmother corrected anyone, Negro or white, who tried to call her "girl."

Tallahassee was different, he says. Negroes had to patronize the white downtown area because Frenchtown, the hub of Negro life in Tallahassee, did not offer nearly the same range of goods and services. Also, he says, because he studied political science, he was that much more aware of the unconstitutional oppressiveness of Jim Crow. "Those of us who had the strength, who had the guts, simply volunteered to become a part of all of that," he says, although he admits he'd "probably think twice today, because I remember being in churches at CORE meetings and at CORE functions when white folks were riding around the church. I recall being downtown participating in sit-ins when there were whites standing around with sticks and with guns and rifles, you know, on their trucks, in their cars, and we were just nonviolent. We had been taught to be nonviolent."[1]

At the time, he recalls, he was particularly annoyed with the Negro student athletes who had so much power to raise excitement on the football field and other sports venues, but who refused to get involved with civil rights activities. Their coach discouraged it, he says. And it really irritated him that women were so enamored of those athletes. "I didn't think very much of the kind of relationships they had with some of those guys who would not even come down and stand around to provide somewhat of a protective atmosphere," says Cowins, who is today an educator with a doctorate who still lives in Miami. "The young ladies who were participating in the demonstrations at that time sometimes would be spat upon, sometimes would be pushed, sometimes would be hit by the hecklers who were always there. And I felt that the least those guys could do was come and observe."

That Saturday in Tallahassee, Ben and I were alone, without the protection of athletes or anyone else, as we walked into Neisner's for the last attempt of the day. The lunch counter was empty, and we sat down to be served. I'm sure we were wondering what was in store for us next, and we didn't have to wait long to find out. Just like in the earliest sit-ins at Woolworth, a crowd began to gather. "What are you niggers doing in here?" whites shouted at us, mostly young men. "Niggers can't eat here!"

Two police officers arrived quickly and stood behind us for a while, but they left. Ben and I decided to leave, too. Suddenly the hecklers, who had been tugging on our clothing, got more violent, probably because the police had already come and gone. Hands grabbed at us and pulled us from the stools. One man challenged Ben to a fight, and he was thrown roughly to the ground by two men, who began punching him, knocking off his glasses. Ben, of course, had been through CORE's workshop on nonviolence, but apparently he'd succumbed to his anger and self-protective instincts, because he began punching back in the face of the uneven attack. The police returned and stopped the fight right away.

Ben was arrested for fighting. I was arrested because there was a broken glass at the scene of the skirmish and I was "in a position to have thrown a glass," a charge that was pure fabrication. A very large crowd, perhaps 200 people, had gathered outside of Neisner's by then, and they all jeered at me and Ben as we were led away by the police. Apparently, one of the white assailants and his two sisters also attacked one of the police officers.[2] I know of no whites who were arrested, however.

Once again, I would spend the night in jail. Since I hadn't eaten in several hours, I called John Due right away and asked him to bring me a sandwich. "Patricia, what are you doing here? I didn't even know you were in town," he said, and I told him what had happened. He was concerned I was in jail, but he sounded happy to hear from me.

On the men's side of the jail, Ben says he was determined not to be locked up even overnight. "I remember stating to a jailer or policeman that I thought I had glass in my eye, and I was elated because I thought I would be taken to the doctor and I would get out of jail that night," he says. "The policeman took me out back to a water fountain and said, 'Nigger, wash your eye.' Then I went back to jail."[3]

Ben was arrested on a Saturday and apparently spent three days in jail. The entire time, he was still wearing the neat suit he had worn during the demonstration. On Monday morning, he says, he was rounded up with the other Negro prisoners and led to a truck to be taken to the rock quarry to work. "I was not going to participate in any foolishness like that, carrying rocks or busting rocks, and this made the driver very, very angry," Cowins says. "He had a lot of things to say to me about what he was going to do to me if I did not participate. He [said] was going to beat me upside the head with a stick. Anyway, he ended up having to drive me back to jail, and he didn't like that. But he took me back to jail, and I'm almost sure I was placed in a very, very small cell, in isolation. But I was not about to get my suit dirty on that particular day." He spent only about a day in that isolation cell before his court date.

In court, Ben and I were found guilty of disorderly conduct and fighting. Because of my previous record, I suppose, I was sentenced to 120 days in jail, while Ben was sentenced to thirty. We both stayed out of jail on appeal, but in October the court upheld Ben's conviction. (Mine was thrown out for lack of evidence). Ben was ordered to begin serving his jail sentence, and he was immediately suspended from school.

Ben's misfortune helped galvanize Tallahassee's Negro community again. Although he had been dismissed from FAMU's faculty, Richard Haley continued to be active on behalf of Tallahassee CORE. Mr. Haley wrote letters complaining about Ben's treatment to both FAMU President George W. Gore and the national CORE leadership. Eventually, Mr. Haley's efforts resulted in an article about Ben in the *St. Petersburg Times.* On November 12, Rev. R. N. Gooden and St. Mary's Primitive Baptist Church hosted a community-wide "Ben Cowins Day" to raise money for Ben's expenses and court fines. Several organizations also joined their voices: CORE, the NAACP, the Inter-Civic Council, and a new organization called the Non-Partisan Voter's Crusade sent an open letter rallying teachers to stop being called "gutless invertebrates" and join the Movement.[4] Because so many middle-class Negroes were educators, their absence on the civil rights front was marked and critical.

Daisy Young and former professor Richard Haley were stalwart supporters, as was Dr. James Hudson, the college chaplain and a professor of philosophy. Make no mistake, we were visited and supported by FAMU faculty during our forty-nine days in jail, too.

For example, a FAMU physical education instructor and long-time family friend, Carrie "Tot" Meek, was one of our most faithful visitors with her mother, Mrs. Carrie Pittman. They often came to see how we were, bringing books and gifts. I also received a very kind letter from Anita P. Stewart, an instructor who assured us that we were in her prayers each night. Dr. William Howard, who taught a course on contemporary Africa, was very understanding when I had to miss classes because of my civil rights activities; Priscilla tells me that he also assured her she shouldn't worry about the school time she missed during the 1960 jail-in. Dr. Howard recalls sending William Larkins schoolwork to help him keep up with his studies in 1960. Priscilla reminds me that art professor Herman Bailey was also very supportive. And sociology professor Victoria Warner was active in another interracial organization to which I belonged, the Tallahassee Committee, which was also dedicated to change.

Some FAMU faculty members seemed to resent our push for civil rights. Those professors went so far as to ridicule us in class, which was very painful. It was one thing to hear insults from outsiders, but from your own?

Ben Cowins remembers Professor Bonds, the political science department head, who told students involved in the demonstrations, "Whatever those white hecklers are doing to you out there, you deserve that and more." Imagine! These students were risking their lives and safety in the demonstrations, and they had to hear that. Ben dreaded going to Professor Bonds's class because of the verbal abuse he would suffer, but those classes were impossible to avoid because they were germane to Ben's major.

Yes, Professor Bonds had a very sharp tongue. I know male students always rushed from the demonstrations to get to his classes because he seemed to delight in embarrassing the young men if they came in late. But when it came to me, Professor Bonds always said, "Good afternoon, Miss Stephens," and that was the end of it. Meanwhile, if a male activist came in with me, Professor Bonds would roar at him, "And where have *you* been?" To this day, I'm puzzled by the disparity.

Sociological studies show that oppressed people will often take on the characteristics of their oppressors, a phenomenon evident in this country during the days of slavery, with Negro overseers behaving as badly as, or worse than, the white ones. I definitely believe some of that was at work during my days at Florida A&M, but as I've gotten older, I've also learned to appreciate that the Negroes in "authority" were in a very delicate position in the 1960s, because there was truly no such thing as Negroes in authority. They were beholden to the white power structure—the white power structure giveth, and the white power structure taketh away. In the course of researching this book and interviewing former students, I have heard surprising stories of generosity and support involving faculty members who did not seem supportive on the surface.

Ben Cowins told me one such story about FAMU's director of student activities, a minister named Rev. Moses G. Miles, who had a reputation for being very conservative and trying to dissuade students from getting involved in the Movement. After Ben served his jail sentence, the university apparently began receiving telephone calls from the all-white Board of Control, inquiring whether or not Ben was still enrolled at FAMU, which he was. Then the word came down: Cowins *must* be suspended, the Board of Control said. Rev. Miles was the one who called Ben into his office, and he looked grieved. "The white folks have called to see if you're in school, and you're being suspended for the rest of the semester," Rev. Miles told him. "I regret being the bearer of bad news, but I promise I will assist you in returning."

When Ben was ready to return to classes for the new semester, Rev. Miles's church congregation took up a collection. "They paid the tuition," Cowins says.

Yes, it was frustrating to have to fight so many of your own. But it was also that much more gratifying when help came from unexpected places.

I remember sitting with John Due on the porch of Daisy Young's house at 1314 Pinellas Street in Tallahassee, not long after my arrest with Ben Cowins at Neisner's. Miss Young's home had become a gathering place for student activists, a place to plan strategies, socialize, or simply rest. Miss Young was folksy and warmhearted, and she was also fiercely intelligent, with a sharp memory. I had met her when we first began organizing the Tallahassee CORE chapter, and we had become very close.

It was nearly summer, and I had decided I was not going to Mother's house in Fort Myers because of the ongoing stress between her and her husband. I decided to attend summer classes at Howard University, so I accepted an invitation from good friends, Wendolyn Johnson and her husband, former FAMU professor Dr. Randy Johnson, to stay with them and their three children in the Washington, D.C., area. I was going to leave Tallahassee soon, and I was telling Black John all about my plans for the future with White John. Black John had already written me little notes about how he wasn't the marrying type and how he wanted to dedicate his life to the freedom struggle, but I think I wanted him to try to stop me from leaving. I wanted a sign that he cared about me the way John B. did.

John Due was sitting on a chair on the porch, and I was sitting on his lap. "We're moving to England for at least three years," I told him. "John is going to be teaching there."

"That's great," he said in a very dull tone. "It's good to travel."

"And John is such a planner, he's already planning our entire family. He says he'd like to have two-and-a-half children. That's how he puts it, you know. We're both trying to imagine what they'll be like."

"Don't go."

The words came so suddenly, so unexpectedly, that I thought I had heard wrong at first. I gave him a very confused look. "Don't go," he said again, gazing into my eyes in a way he never had. He definitely did not look like we were just friends anymore. "We can make it here at school. We both have scholarship money. We could live in Polkinghorne Village together. Marry me, Patricia."

*Marry me, Patricia.* Those were the words I'd secretly prayed to hear, so I'll never know why I did what I did next. I guess I was just so shocked, and probably I was also feeling shy and embarrassed at such an unusual outpouring from John Due. I couldn't make a sound for a moment. Then I laughed hysterically. I was mortified, but I couldn't help myself.

To poor John, it was like a slap in the face. He stood up and dumped me out of his lap and went back into the house. For all I knew, I had just missed my chance to marry the man I thought I might really be in love with.

I stayed with the Johnsons and went to Howard University's sociology department that summer, where I was awarded a scholarship to pay for my tuition and travel expenses. I was only a couple hours' train ride away from John B., but somehow, with my shifting priorities and a new man in my life, John B. and I just drifted apart.

---

Summer at Howard was busy. I became involved with NAG, the Nonviolent Action Group, an affiliate of SNCC chaired by Marion Berry, who later became the mayor of Washington, D.C. NAG conducted sit-ins and demonstrations in the Washington area. It seemed like I was on a different picket line every day.

By fall, I needed a change. I had been offered a job in New York as a girls' group worker for the Lower East Side Mission of Trinity Parish, so I decided to take that opportunity. The job called for a college degree, and although I had not yet graduated, I was hired based on my civil rights experience. As a group worker, I was part of a contingent that lobbied in Washington, D.C., for better benefits for the residents of the Lower East Side and New York City, but for the most part, my life was suddenly removed from the civil rights arena completely. Instead, I concentrated on the young people who were serviced by this large organization. The Lower East Side Mission of Trinity Parish was reportedly one of the richest church organizations in the country and had a huge staff serving the New York area. I also had a very busy social life, meeting young African dignitaries from emerging independent nations at the U.N. I swear, sometimes it seemed I had one date for breakfast, one for lunch, and one for dinner. During this time, I even considered going to Africa to serve in the Peace Corps.

Back in Tallahassee, the civil rights movement was still marching forward while I was away. White activist Jeff Poland, who'd been arrested during the 1960 sit-ins, returned to Tallahassee voluntarily to serve out his sentence in May 1961, after the U.S. Supreme Court appeal failed.

(He had transferred to another college after his suspension from Florida State University.) In jail, Jeff staged a hunger strike lasting nearly a month to protest segregated lunch counters. Sixty-eight ministers, including Rev. Steele and Rev. Alexander Sherman, fasted on Fridays in sympathy and encouraged others in Tallahassee to do the same.[5]

Priscilla was still in Tallahassee, too, although she had graduated from FAMU. She became involved in CORE's next phase of the civil rights struggle: the Freedom Rides. In the South, Negroes had to ride in the "colored" section at the back of the bus or in segregated train cars. In response to a December Supreme Court ruling, *Boynton v. Virginia* (which banned segregation during interstate travel in buses, trains, and terminal accommodations), CORE and other organizations launched an ambitious Freedom Ride throughout the South. White and Negro riders volunteered to ride buses and, if arrested, remain in jail rather than pay their bail. The Freedom Ride gained a great deal of publicity, but it also brought reprisals: The buses were often met by angry mobs, and a Greyhound bus riding toward Birmingham, Alabama, was set afire. On a Birmingham-bound Trailways bus, eight white men boarded the bus and beat two of the Freedom Riders with metal pipes. (James Peck, who later wrote the book *Freedom Ride* about his horrible experience, was knocked unconscious and needed fifty stitches as a result of his beating.) Other Freedom Riders were arrested and jailed, more than 360 by the end of the summer. Even the new CORE national director, James Farmer, was jailed in Mississippi.[6]

Tallahassee was one of the designated stops during the Freedom Rides, and a bus carrying ten participating ministers and rabbis rolled into town in June. The morning after their arrival, the Freedom Riders sat at the municipal airport restaurant to order food, but they were all arrested for "unlawful assembly." Priscilla, Jeff Poland, and another Negro activist were waiting to greet them, and all three were arrested, too. Additionally, Priscilla was charged with interfering with a police officer and resisting arrest. Judge John Rudd, who had tried Priscilla before, gave her a mandatory five-day jail sentence and an additional thirty-day sentence stemming from a probation violation.[7] (The clergymen were sentenced with fines of $500 apiece or sixty days in jail. Although they chose jail, when they came back to serve their terms in 1964 after losing their appeal, the clergymen were freed after only a few days in a surprise court action.) In November, when the Interstate Commerce Commission prohibited all segregation in travel terminals, Richard Haley came back to

Tallahassee and worked with Priscilla, Ben Cowins, John Due, and Robert Armstrong from FSU to test how communities were complying.[8]

I was away while this was going on in Tallahassee, and I'm sure some of my fellow civil rights activists believed I had dropped out of the scene completely. But it wasn't that simple. Sometimes when you're a soldier—and I saw myself as such—you're on the front lines all the time. You burn yourself out. Sometimes you're so weary that you aren't as effective as you could be, and you can be more effective if you just step aside for a little while. So that's exactly what I did. During my year in New York, I never went to a CORE or NAACP meeting. I concentrated on my job, and in a way that was an extension of what I was trying to do, what I was fighting for. I wanted young people to have the opportunity to do things they had not done before. Those young people who lived on the Lower East Side had never even been to Carnegie Hall! It was only a couple of subway stops from where we were. So I made it my business to try to expose the young people—and I say "young people" even though some of them were almost as old as I was—to things they needed to be exposed to.

Sometimes civil rights includes those quieter battles, too.

---

By 1962, John Due was in Washington working as an intern for the U.S. Department of Labor, and I was ready to visit him to see if his feelings about me had changed since our disastrous night at Daisy Young's house. Even though several young men had expressed interest in me at that time, I still felt unresolved. Once I got to Washington, John told me he was in love with someone else, and I said, "Okay, that's fine. I just needed to know how you felt." Although it wasn't what I wanted to hear, I was relieved when I went back on the train. I had been dating a Nigerian physician on and off, and now I felt more free to open my heart to him.

I had met my Nigerian beau, a physician from Lagos, when I attended a party with Priscilla. Like many of the Africans we met, he was surprised to see American Negroes attending an African party—many Africans thought American Negroes were ignorant about them, that we had learned everything we knew about Africans from Tarzan movies. He was not very political, but he was proud of our involvement. During this time, many African nations were fighting for and gaining their independence from colonial rule, so they were happy to see American Negroes fighting for freedom, too. My Nigerian friend was a graduate of Harvard Medical School, and I enjoyed his company though I had not been dating him long.

A couple of weeks later, my telephone rang, and it was John Due telling me he was in New York and wanted to see me. We went out for spaghetti and meatballs at a little restaurant right near my apartment. John was in New York on his way to a friend's wedding in Boston, but we talked so long that he missed his connection and got to Boston late. After that visit, I started wondering "Why is he coming to see me?" It was weird. But I let it go. I didn't pursue it.

I had other things on my mind. I had gotten an offer from the Henry Street Settlement to work with pre-delinquent children, who today we would call "at-risk" children. While I was pondering that, I received word that I would be permitted to go back to school at FAMU. I was excited about that for two reasons: First, I thought it was important for me to demonstrate that activists could be involved *and* finish their studies at state-supported institutions. Secondly, I was excited because I assumed John Due also would be back at FAMU.

In more ways than one, our school year at FAMU at the beginning of the fall of 1962 was going to get off to an explosive start. Much had changed in parts of Florida, but not in Tallahassee. In a state where larger cities had desegregated public facilities and lunch counters, Tallahassee was refusing even to appoint a biracial commission, as other cities had, to tackle the race problem, choosing instead to live with its head in the sand.[9] Two years after the jail-in, Tallahassee's facilities were still segregated. This was the situation facing us in the fall when we went back to school, and some of the most significant demonstrations of Tallahassee's civil rights movement were going to take place during the upcoming school year. Many students' lives were about to change forever, including mine.

I went back to campus to register in Lee Auditorium, where the registrar's office was. While going upstairs, I ran into John Due. He casually said, "Hi, how are you?" No big deal on his part. He seemed to be going his separate way, and I felt my stomach sink. For the next month or two, it really seemed he wasn't interested in me. He was in the graduate department because he was in law school, and he was dating other women in the graduate school. We didn't even seem to have a close friendship anymore. Priscilla decided to go to New York to do graduate study at Banks Street College, so for the first time I didn't have my sister's company at school, either.

As disappointed as I was, I didn't have much time to mourn the apparent end of my bond with John Due. The school year was barely underway when I was arrested again on September 25. This time, in an effort to make sure public travel facilities were truly desegregated, we'd targeted the Trailways station in Tallahassee and the Carousel restaurant inside.

Aside from the Freedom Rides, Tallahassee CORE had been very quiet in the previous months. I think many other activists were truly afraid of CORE because our tactics always led to confrontations, and usually to arrest, but we believed this was the most effective method for change. So again, just as it had been at Neisner's, there were only a handful of us at the protest. We had a core group of activists working to revitalize the Tallahassee chapter, and all of us were Florida A&M students. Besides myself, the group included a political science major from Lake City with a boyish sense of humor, Rubin Kenon; a smooth-faced student named Julius Hamilton ("Ol' Prettyboy," Rubin called Julius); a student from New Jersey named James Hamilton; and a FAMU political science club member named Ira Simmons. We became a very close group over time, although our relationship had almost nothing to do with socializing. We gave each other strength and emotional support, and we shared a purpose.

Our CORE group decided to test the new travel desegregation rules at Carousel, a privately owned restaurant inside Tallahassee's Trailways bus station. Neatly dressed, as always, the four of us went to Carousel at about 9:00 P.M., sat down at a table, and tried to order food. I was the spokesperson, so I put in the food order, but the manager told us to move to the other side because we were in the "white" section. When we didn't move, the manager called the police. We were charged with "disobeying a police officer" and had to spend the night in jail. Once again, we were brought before Judge Rudd, who set our trial for October. Our bond was set at $100 apiece, and payment was arranged by Rev. Dan Speed.[10]

This time, we thought, how could we possibly lose? The law was on our side, and even the president of the restaurant chain had sent a letter to the Interstate Commerce Commission, insisting that he had warned its Tallahassee operators to stop discriminating on the basis of race.[11] When Judge Rudd convicted us anyway, we filed a $1 million lawsuit in U.S. District Court. We charged that Tallahassee operated under "apartheid principles, policies, and practices." Our brief also quoted the Langston Hughes poem "Merry-Go-Round." We asked for $100,000 for actual damages and $900,000 in punitive damages. Even though we didn't win our lawsuit, we never had to serve our sentences.

Each and every victory was so hard fought. And the real battles were only beginning.

When I returned to FAMU in the fall of 1962, I lived in Tallahassee with Rev. C. K. Steele and his family, which gave me a rare chance to be part of a civil rights family and draw conclusions about what hardships and challenges related to the Movement I might expect when I had my own family. I feel so very fortunate to have gotten to know the Steeles. As crowded as their house was—with Rev. and Mrs. Steele, four of their five sons, and one daughter—the Steeles took me in when I needed a place to live. The Steele children at home were Henry, Clifford, Darryl, Derek, and Rochelle, whom we called "Pat," and they lived downstairs while I lived upstairs, paying $45 a month for my room and board.

I cannot say enough good things about Rev. Charles Kenzie Steele, who died in 1980. He was very courageous, a man of principles and tireless dedication who would not back down under pressure. To me, he was also a perfect example of a man who was not nurtured and appreciated enough by his own community while he was still alive. In truth, I think Rev. Steele received much more respect outside of Tallahassee than he did in his own city. He was the pastor of Bethel Missionary Baptist Church, and as the president of the Inter-Civic Council, he had been one of the main organizers of the Tallahassee bus boycott of the late 1950s. He was a friend of Dr. King's, had hosted Dr. King and his wife, Coretta, at his home, and was also the founding first vice president of the Southern Christian Leadership Conference. His home was a beehive of activity during the height of the bus boycott, his son Henry recalls. Henry remembers seeing an "ugly little man"—who later turned out to be James Baldwin—hanging around his family's front yard. Scores of reporters and other out-of-town activists also camped out at the Steeles' home as part of an open-door policy. As a boy, Henry loved the excitement and was too young to be daunted by the potential dangers that came hand in hand with his father's activism.

Henry, who was about thirteen during the boycott, considered all of the commotion at home part of what was necessary to fight injustice. "I was too excited about it to be really scared about anything," says Rev. Henry Steele, who is today a minister himself. He recalls how, as a youngster, during his annual summer visit with his grandparents in Montgomery, he'd witnessed the height of the Montgomery bus boycott and attended the mass meetings of thousands led by Dr. Martin Luther King and Rev. Ralph Abernathy. He felt change in the air, and he wasn't too concerned about the consequences. In that way, perhaps, Henry was his father's son. (Henry's first job, in fact, was as an assistant to Rev. Abernathy at West Hunter Street Baptist Church in Atlanta, in the wake of Dr. King's assassination in 1968.)[12]

But life was very hard for the Steeles as a result of Rev. Steele's activism.

If a brick came crashing through the family's window in the middle of the night, it was no big deal to Henry. In the event of such attacks, the family had a plan. They ran into the hallway, where there were no windows, and crouched there together until the crisis had passed. And there were many crises. About six months into the Tallahassee bus boycott, he says, his family was forced to move out of the church parsonage because of so many rock-throwing attacks, threatening phone calls, and shooting incidents. Appearances by the Klan were regular. Klan members drove past their house on Tennessee Street, or Highway 90, on their way to Klan rallies, and long lines of hooded Klansmen gathered outside the house to harass them. Once, the Klan burned a cross on their lawn, right in front of the church. As a precaution, some deacons stood guard at the Steeles' house at night. Henry recalls that bullet-riddled venetian blinds hung in their window for years after the boycott, lingering evidence of the price his family had paid. Henry also remembers his father sitting by the window with a Smith & Wesson in his lap to do what he would have to do to protect his family, preacher or no preacher.

That aside, though, Rev. Steele was also known for his lack of malice toward his tormentors. In *The Pain and the Promise: The Struggle for Civil Rights in Tallahassee, Florida,* Glenda Rabby writes that when there were threatening phone calls, "instead of hanging up, Steele would often preach to the callers over the phone, telling them about nonviolence, redemptive love, and the life of Christ, even inviting them to call back after he finished his meal."[13]

It's not surprising that Henry's mother had a nervous breakdown during this time. It's so unfortunate that Mrs. Lois Steele died in 1983, before she could share her trials and tribulations in her own words. She was only fifty-nine when she died, and she was one of the Movement's quiet heroines. I do believe the stressful circumstances of her life probably cut her years short; she became a wife and mother very young, got swept into the civil rights movement, and then had to nurse her husband through a long illness before he finally died. And she outlived her eldest son, Charles, making her burden all the greater.

The youngest Steele son, Derek, fell into a life of drug abuse for several years as an adult, spending time in jail before he went clean and became a chaplain, counseling addicts in Tallahassee. He told the *Tallahassee Democrat* in 1998 that he certainly didn't blame his father's notoriety for his troubles, but he felt the weight of his father's achievements on his shoulders.[14]

Besides the emotional toll, which was especially high on Lois Steele, there was also a financial toll. Mrs. Steele was trained as a teacher, and she'd worked hard to complete her schooling, despite several pregnancies after her marriage at the age of sixteen. When she appeared for job interview after job interview, principals refused to hire her. Negro principals at Negro schools had to follow the orders of their superiors and the white power structure. One day a principal took her aside and confided, "Mrs. Steele, actually, we have been *told* not to hire you." His family went without a lot of things, Henry says. He feels that the church, rather than rallying behind their pastor to see that his family was cared for, instead put pressure on Rev. Steele to curtail his activities. Members were afraid they might lose their jobs for belonging to his church. One church member, ironically, was FAMU's president, Dr. George W. Gore.

Because the church deacons wanted to curtail Rev. Steele's civil rights involvement both inside and outside of Tallahassee, they attempted to restrict so-called "outside groups" from holding meetings at the church. They also tried to limit the number of times Rev. Steele could ask a guest minister to take his place on Sundays. When Rev. Steele had disagreements with the deacons, he took up the matter with the congregation, and the parishioners supported him, but the deacons controlled the church finances and punished Rev. Steele's disobedience by refusing to give him raises and by not providing monies to make repairs to the parsonage.[15] The penalties were not put in place by whites, but by other Negroes. This is the other side of the civil rights movement many young people are unaware of today. Even on the threshold of so many important changes, often some of our most difficult battles were with our own.

When I moved in with the Steeles in the fall of 1962, I believe the money I paid them, however little, helped ease some of their financial burden. I got up and hitchhiked to my 8:00 A.M. class on FAMU's campus, which was several miles away. Mother and Daddy Marion had divorced, and Mother's relationship with Mr. Sears had already ended (she had bought a house in Miami), so it was comforting to spend time in a family situation during that time, eating at the dinner table together and such. Although Henry was four years younger than I was, we had both spent time in jail after the Woolworth sit-in. We both had a playful streak, and we'd sit outside overlooking accident-prone Highway 90, guessing which cars would crash.

Most memorable of all, I think, were the long conversations I had with Mrs. Lois Steele, often while she cooked in the kitchen. She enjoyed having another woman to talk to, and she confided many of her frustrations to me—frustrations that, in time, I would learn on a more personal basis. One thing I loved about Mrs. Steele was that she wasn't a traditional minister's wife, nor was she traditional in any way. She was a free thinker, which meant that she didn't even always go to Sunday services to hear her husband preach! And she said what was on her mind.

Mrs. Steele told me how frustrating it was to have a husband who was often traveling, and how when he *was* at home, he was swept into the needs of his church and community. Mrs. Steele thought the community was largely ungrateful for the sacrifices Rev. Steele and his family had to make. "You know, Patricia," she told me many times, "family has to come first." She impressed the point upon me further, but I already knew that I wanted life to be different for my family. When my time came, I would have to find a way to balance both activism *and* being a wife and mother.

That became my vow, and it was a vow I never forgot.

---

By December 1962, I'd had enough of John Due's aloofness. I wanted to pay attention to my studies and the Movement, but I was too distracted, in emotional limbo. I decided I would leave FAMU. *As much as I hate to go,* I thought, *if I want to get my education and do other things, I need to get away from here.*

I told John I was going to New York. I had already arranged a ride with a male student I did not know. "Oh, no, you can't do that, Patricia," John said.

"Well, I'm going," I said adamantly.

"Okay, I'll drive you," he said. "But first, we'll have to stop in Indiana."

Naively, I agreed. I should have looked at a map, because Indiana is nowhere near New York. Indiana was where his mother lived, and that was where he wanted to take me. While we drove, he suddenly looked at me and said, "Patricia, let's get married." This time, I did not laugh. I had been waiting more than a year to hear those words again! But I was still surprised. I asked him why he'd been treating me so nonchalantly.

He sighed, staring at the roadway. "Well, I hadn't wanted to get involved with you because I want to finish law school and carry out my civil rights work. I didn't want a wife, a family. I'm not the marrying kind. But when you said you were leaving, I knew that meant I'd never see you again. Well, I didn't want that to happen."

John took me to Indianapolis, Indiana, to meet his mother, Lucille Graham, a very tall and fair-skinned woman who had been certified by the Madam C. J. Walker School of Beauty Culture in 1941. She had studied at Indiana State Teachers' College for eighteen months, but she left college because she needed to make a living to support her baby boy. She had later worked for a company that made supplies for the United States Navy. Mother was fair, but John's mother was even lighter.

"Well, Mother, we're getting hitched," John announced, hooking his arm around me.

*Getting hitched?* That term sounded so funny and country to me. I noticed his mother's gaze upon me, and I could nearly read her mind: She thought I was too dark. John B.'s parents had not wanted to accept me because of my race, and now another Negro woman did not approve of my complexion. She did not want to say anything to offend her son, but her reception was cool. (As the years passed, my relationship with John's mother was just fine, and she apologized to me for her earlier coolness. She even lived with us for a short time toward the end of her life. She died in 1992.)

I was thrilled about our engagement. John Due and I would be married! I would have a partner in the civil rights struggle, someone who would understand my dedication. I would never have to worry that my husband might disapprove of what I was doing and try to convince me to stop. To me, we seemed like the perfect match.

I called Mother and told her we would get married in April. She had met John once, so she knew a bit about him even if she didn't yet know him well. She trusted me, telling me that I should get married if that was what I wanted, but she wanted our wedding ceremony to be a Baha'i wedding, within the Baha'i faith she had adopted.

Mother never completely abandoned her Christian roots, but she adopted the Baha'i faith after some friends introduced it to her and she studied it. Founded in the Middle East in the 1800s, the basic tenet of Baha'i is that humanity is a single race, and that God has ordained that it is time to eliminate prejudice and build a peaceful global society.[16] Mother took the best of the religions' offerings and molded them to fit her life. I did not understand the Baha'i religion, but Mother introduced me to a white couple who hosted many meetings at their home on Star Island, and I thought they were very good people. Their religion seemed to embrace many of the same ideas I believed in. I never thought about becoming Baha'i myself, but I didn't have any objections to being married according to their customs.

John stayed in Indianapolis for a while to visit his relatives. I went to New York, where I stayed with William Larkins (a former Tallahassee activist who was an aspiring actor) for a time because Priscilla was out of town and had forgotten to leave me the key to her apartment, but I took ill with tonsillitis and Larkins called John to come retrieve me. In late December of 1962, during our entire drive back to Florida, we talked about our wedding plans. Once we got back to campus, we told the FAMU housing authority that we would need married housing for April, but things weren't done that way. "When you show me that piece of paper, that's when you can reserve an apartment," said Mr. Matthews, who was in charge. He was actually a family friend, but that made no difference. Rules were rules.

"Well, gosh," we thought, "if that's the case, if we're not certain we're even going to have a place to stay, we might as well go and get married now."

That was on a Friday. We called Thomasville, Georgia, which was about thirty minutes away from Tallahassee, to find out if we could get married. We'd heard you could get married there without a waiting period. The woman on the phone asked, "Well, is it an emergency?" In my mind it was, although I guess she was asking if I were pregnant. So I said, "Yes, it's an emergency. We need to get married. Is it possible to get married there?" She said, "Yeah, well you can come tomorrow."

Needless to say, we did not have a very traditional or a Baha'i wedding. I called my mother that Friday night and said, "Mother, John and I are getting married tomorrow. Can you get here?" Of course, Mother couldn't get there. I said, "Well, we're going to do it anyway, and then maybe we can have another ceremony later." John's mother couldn't come, either. Since we didn't have family members there, we brought our friends in their stead. Three men from the law school stood up for John. One was Edward Rodgers, who is Judge Rodgers now, another was Ike Williams, and one was John Moss, a law professor. With Priscilla in New York, I didn't have anybody there for me. It was January 5, 1963.

I tell you, the woman conducting the ceremony spoke so rapidly, I don't remember anything she said except "I now pronounce you man and wife." And I told John, "It doesn't feel like we're married yet." Right after we left Thomasville, we went back to Tallahassee and asked Rev. Steele to marry us in his church. Again, none of our own family members were there because of the sudden timing, but at least he spoke slowly enough that we could feel that something was different. I just wanted to feel as if it were official. (Derek Steele, about eighteen months old, was the Steeles's youngest child and kept chanting "Spook, spook!" at our wedding ceremony. I guess he had heard the word so often, leveled against his father and the other activists, that he'd adopted it into his vocabulary.)

That was how John and I began our lives together. We had joined not only as man and wife, but as a combined force for change. The fact that we had such a scaled-down wedding ceremony, that we had no honeymoon—even that we'd had very little of a traditional "courtship"—demonstrated our mind-set at the time: The civil rights movement came first. In time, that way of thinking would become very trying for me.

But in the beginning, John Due and I both had only freedom on our minds.

## Fourteen

# Tananarive Due

**"A man must be at home somewhere**
**before he can be at home anywhere."**
***—Rev. Howard Thurman***

In my novel *My Soul to Keep,* my protagonist, Jessica, lost her father at a very young age, when she was eight. In one scene, where Jessica is remembering her admiration for her father when she was young, I wrote, "Jessica had known he was a genius before she really knew what a genius was. She'd always looked forward to the day—maybe in fourth grade or fifth grade, she'd thought—when she could sit down and impress her father with how smart she was too."

When I wrote that, of course, I was thinking about my own father. I remember vividly how I used to watch my father scribbling in his legal pads, or marking pages in the sociology, philosophy, and history books that always littered his bathroom, waiting for the day when I would be smart enough to truly engage him in a conversation. "What I did in school today" was not good enough for my father, I believed. His attention would drift, and his eyes would glaze as a thought flew into his head and took him somewhere else, to the words of Frantz Fanon, Friedrich Nietzsche, Thurgood Marshall, or W.E.B. Du Bois. There's a line in the Des'ree song "You Gotta Be" where the singer advises, "Read the books your father read." That was exactly what I wanted to do, when I was old enough. So we could really get to know each other.

In the meantime, though, Dad was somewhere else. Oh, he lived with us, to be sure, and we saw him every day, but his true existence was always elsewhere, enmeshed in the Struggle.

We both happened to go to the NAACP convention in New Orleans the summer of 2001. I was there with my fifteen-year-old stepdaughter, Nicki, whom I'd brought with me while I served as a playwriting judge and presenter for the national ACT-SO competition, and Dad was there for a legal workshop. Dad and I both had hectic schedules, but we were able to carve out a couple of hours to share a traditional New Orleans meal not far from my hotel.

At dinner, after I talked to Mom on my cell phone so I could feel like we were all sitting at the table together, I remarked to Dad that he had a very good memory for details of the events in the 1960s. I'd been listening to the tapes of his interviews Mom and I had conducted over the years and, I said, I was impressed.

"Well, yes, because it was my life," he said. "Unlike with Patricia, it was my whole life."

"I'm sure Mom might take some issue with that one," I teased him. I thought he was feeling a surge of competitiveness.

He shook his head. "No, it was my *life.* Patricia's always talking about that, how it's my *whole life,"* he said. Yes, I'd heard Mom say that many, many times, usually when she was frustrated. Charity begins at home, Mom was always reminding him. "That's all I wanted to do."

Suddenly, I realized what he was saying, and I sat with his words for a moment.

Civil rights was all he'd wanted to do.

There was a time, I'm sure, my chest would have swelled with rage to hear him put it so baldly: *Yes, nothing was more important to me than my civil rights work*. But I didn't feel rage. All of us knew that about him. Dad's life was in the garage, in his stacks of papers that sat in towering columns all around his desk. When he wasn't at meetings, he was always hidden in his papers in the garage, and from what little I could gather, he'd been that way most of his life. When I spent my Thanksgiving or spring breaks from Northwestern University with Grandmother Lucille in Indiana, she used to say, "Oh, you like to close the door, too—just like John."

And I gained insight from her words. I was closing my door because I was visiting a set of grandparents I didn't know nearly as well as Mother because of our distance. When my conversations and meals with Grandmother Lucille and Grandpa George were over for the night, I closed the door to my room to relax back into myself and grow accustomed to my new surroundings. I have never slept well in new places, and privacy gives me my bearings.

But why did Dad close *his* door? I remembered how Mom used to be so adamant about not allowing us to close our doors when we were children, to the point where we once petitioned her for the right. As an adult, I realized she'd spent years facing Dad's closed garage door, and she sure as hell wasn't going to allow herself to get the closed-door treatment from her three children. For whatever reason, Dad's door has been closed.

Yet, when I hear him make jokes, I remember how I used to think he was just like Bill Cosby. And he's a music lover, just like Mom. In fact, that summer in New Orleans, I put on a Miles Davis CD in my hotel room because he doesn't make time to listen to music and I knew he would enjoy it. He *loves* music, and he helped teach me to love it, too. (When I told him as a girl that I didn't like country music because it was redneck music, he chided me, "Music is music. Music doesn't have a color. All music is for everyone.") I can understand his missing movies and watching little television except the History Channel and CNN, but how can my father keep himself away from something as magical as music?

His work is more important to him than music. More important than laughing and making jokes. When we were younger, it probably seemed to us that it was more important than his three daughters. His work is everything. It's his whole life, as he said.

"Wasn't that funny?" I said to Nicki after Dad made a joke in New Orleans, then excused himself to find the men's room. "My Dad has always had this great sense of humor, but he doesn't share it much. He's always so serious. He's trying to save the world."

"One piece at a time," Nicki said, intuitively.

"Yes. One piece at a time."

What makes someone that way? Mom tempered her life to make room for us, and thank God she did, because we needed her so badly, and she gave us so much of herself. But Dad could not. He stayed with us, and he got a job to pay for his activism, but he would have done it for free. He was going to be working to help people his entire life, and that was that. He was going to attend meetings and draw up proposals and write briefs, and do it for no money if that was the way it was, because that was what he must do.

It was no surprise to me, then, when Dad mentioned during our New Orleans visit that he was considering trying to get into a seminary after he retires. Really, in some ways, my father has been a monk his entire life.

---

John Dorsey Due Jr. was a lonely child. He was the only child of a stately, attractive woman named Lucille Graham and a charismatic entrepreneur,

John Dorsey Due, who had his own shoe-repair shops in two cities and a shiny Buick while his mother was a student at Indiana State Teachers' College during the Depression of the 1930s, no small feat. His parents divorced when he was only five, so he and his mother moved in with her parents in Terre Haute, Indiana, while she worked in the Madam C. J. Walker School of Beauty Culture for her certification, which she received in 1941. When Dad was seven, his mother moved seventy-five miles away to Indianapolis to work in a defense factory and run a beauty shop from her home, so Dad only saw his mother on weekends, or less frequently. He referred to his grandmother as "Mom," his biological mother as "Mother," and his grandfather as "Gramp." He didn't see his father for years after John Dorsey Due Sr. was drafted to serve in World War II, and he saw him only on weekends after that. Next to his grandfather, the most constant male figure in my father's life was Glenn Graham, his mother's brother. My parents share similarities in their early upbringing, having been born into broken homes and having grandparents step in to assist while their mothers worked at a distance and lived apart from them. That arrangement hadn't lasted very long with Mom, but the living arrangement lasted for Dad until he graduated from high school. His mother remarried when he was about eighteen, but he and his stepfather didn't get along.

Dad was related to Shirley Graham, who married W.E.B. Du Bois. Dad's grandmother, Lydia Graham, was a refined and nurturing woman. His grandfather, James Graham, was very emotionally withdrawn, and he seemed defeated by forces my father did not understand as a boy. Dad and his grandfather did not talk very much. Dad remembers feeling lonely as a child, and climbing a tree in his grandfather's yard to escape to the world of intellect and imagination. Sometimes I think Dad never fully emerged from that remote place from which he learned to view the world.

My father's grandparents lived in an integrated working-class neighborhood in Terre Haute. His grandmother was a housewife, and his grandfather worked in a foundry, pouring molten iron, which was grueling work. It's no wonder he had little to say when he got home after spending the day in that excessive heat. Still, Dad's grandparents were perceived as a higher class than the poor whites who lived around them. The family attended Spruce Street AME Church—located in a Terre Haute neighborhood of middle-class and professional Negroes. The church was in a popular neighborhood, but his grandparents preferred to live in the integrated area. So my father, unlike a lot of other Negroes of his day, grew up knowing white children.

My father's racial awakening came in a series of blunt little blows, the sort of incidents that were commonplace but still painfully unique to any child forced to endure the experience. When he was about six, before he had started school, a white girl he often played with asked why there was a difference in their skin color. The palms of their hands looked very much alike, she noticed, but the other sides were strikingly different. He had no explanation, so she said she'd find out at home.

"The next day," my father told me, "I heard That Word from her."

The word, of course, was "nigger." She'd apparently heard the word in response to her inquiry to her family. My father had never heard that word before, he says, "But the way she said it, I could tell it must be a bad word. And we weren't friends anymore."

When it was time for him to start going to school, he noticed that the white children who lived near him were sent to a school much closer to where they lived, but he had to walk nearly two miles to attend Lincoln Elementary, an all-black school. That was curious to him, but it didn't really bother him on a significant level until the day his teacher, Miss Harris, rounded up all his classmates and told them they were going to see *Snow White and the Seven Dwarfs* at a movie theater across the street from a park where she often took them to play. His class cheered. It was supposed to be a good day for them.

It was 1942, my father says. Even in the days before television, he and his classmates had heard about Disney's *Snow White* on the radio. World War II was underway, and my father's grandparents, like many families, kept their radio on constantly to hear updates on the war effort. Between news bulletins and programs like *The Shadow,* my father had heard the cheerful, alluring advertisements for *Snow White.* There were probably few children in the country who weren't eager to see that film. Miss Harris lined up a combined class of kindergarteners, first-graders, and second-graders and walked them in single file to the nearby movie theater, where she went to the ticket window to purchase tickets.

The man behind the ticket window said something to Miss Harris, and my father saw her face change. Something was very wrong. Visibly surprised and upset, the teacher turned to the children, looking like she hardly knew what to say. "I'm so sorry, but we can't go see the movie, children," she told them. "Colored people aren't allowed in this theater."

Shock waves traveled through the assembled youngsters, and many of them, including my father, began to cry. It was one thing for a friend to call him a bad name, but how could anyone keep them from a movie that had been made especially for them? "I felt very upset and resentful, because at the time we thought that movie was supposed to be so important for children, for *us.* And we were denied the opportunity to see that movie," my father says.

Not satisfied by his teacher's explanation, when he got home, he asked his grandparents to explain this terrible occurrence. Their response, in retrospect, was very understated, trying to minimize the incident. Like many Negro families, they wanted to shelter their grandson from the realities of racism. And his mother did not have the kind of relationship with him where she would talk about such things.

So Dad filed it away, gradually forming opinions both about himself and how he could expect to be treated by the world around him. He could sense this big Thing all around him, and no one seemed to want to discuss it openly or name it for the ugly injustice it was. Dad was too young to realize it, but Negroes in Indianapolis and other parts of Indiana had made accommodations and developed their own survival mechanisms. A fairly high number of them were prospering, and few people wanted to rock the boat. The region enjoyed a high number of doctors, nurses, and lawyers, and Indianapolis had been home to the Madam C. J. Walker Manufacturing Company, one of the nation's top Negro businesses. Even Negroes who worked as domestics for whites often considered themselves superior to people like my father's grandfather, who toiled at the foundry. Negroes in Indianapolis supported arts programs and attended socials and speeches by visiting dignitaries like W.E.B. Du Bois, but they had made their painful peace with the status quo. Not only was the Negro middle class very conservative, but Dad felt his share of snubbing from other Negroes because his skin was dark brown and not light like his mother's and grandmother's.

Still, from time to time, Dad heard subtle messages that steered his consciousness. At the "colored only" Lincoln Elementary School, the colored principal, Mr. Lewis, was Dad's algebra teacher in sixth grade. Mr. Lewis, who was also the music teacher, took a special interest in Dad, encouraging him to play the trombone. He arranged for Dad to represent the school in a radio discussion where he had to make the case as to why it is important to hire the handicapped, giving Dad his first opportunity to do research at the library. Mr. Lewis also had a unique way of teaching math, designed to give his students problem-solving tools that went far beyond algebra.

"The way he taught algebra, he also taught black history," Dad says. "For example, he was saying, 'If the city of Indianapolis is twenty-five percent black, one-fourth black, what would that mean if people would unify their votes?' He was a very black-conscious principal."

He was also controversial, Dad recalls. "Mr. Lewis was retired, and they brought in another black lady to be principal of that school. And I always remember being conscious of the fact that it was like a sense of getting even, of retaliation, because this lady was not like Mr. Lewis. She did not talk about current events during that short time I was still at Lincoln School."

Mr. Lewis's seeds had found fertile ground in my father. He won a spot as the only Negro student in Terre Haute's citywide band. When he went to a mostly white junior high school, Woodrow Wilson, he noticed that the white counselor was trying to steer him toward general courses, designed for students bound for a technical high school, and he spoke up.

"I had enough sense at the age of thirteen to realize that this was not what my grandparents would want," Dad says. "So I enrolled in the college preparation academic program in junior high school. I remember that all my colleagues from Lincoln sat in the back of the room. I realized then I couldn't sit in the back with my Lincoln School friends, so I sat in the front of the class and was very assertive about classroom questions and being involved, to the point where one day Miss Shortridge, a white teacher, asked me to come out into the hallway. She wanted to talk to me. And she said, 'I'm very proud of you. One day you're going to be a leader of your people.' I didn't know what she meant by that, but I remember how excited that made me feel."

Having grown up near whites, like my sisters and I did, Dad was not intimidated by white children the way his other classmates from Lincoln were, but he wasn't protected from other universal experiences encountered by Negroes. He was assigned *Huckleberry Finn* for an English class, and he thought the book was well-written, but there was something about the book's tone that bothered him and made him feel like an outsider, the way *Amos and Andy* did on the radio. And once, he did a favor for a white girl he had a crush on by writing a paper for her in class. The paper she passed off as hers, which Dad had written hurriedly, got an "A"—but his own paper, which he thought he'd written much better, was marked "C." The unfairness of that smarted.

In high school, he had another turning point: He was again at a mostly white high school, Wiley. On the first day of school, he and a white friend, Glenn, left the school grounds in downtown Terre Haute to have lunch, heading to a popular local café near the railroad tracks. Glenn, a stickball pal Dad got along with very well, was probably his best friend—one black, one white, but race was of concern to neither of them.

"We both ordered navy beans and something else, and they put his plate on the counter, but they had put my beans in a sack they wanted me to take out," Dad says. He looked at the sack, shocked, and then looked back at his friend to see his reaction. "I remember him sitting there eating those beans like nothing was going on, like he forgot who I was. So I began to realize that your so-called white friends, whenever it comes to a point of choice, might just let you down. . . . And I can still see his gray eyes today. It's like I want to cry even today. I'm sixty years old, and I almost want to cry today because he just kept eating those beans. But what was even more humiliating was that I accepted the sack and took it back to school to eat secretly. I was so embarrassed about complying, conforming. I think from that day on, I took peanut butter and jelly."

Despite his small awakenings, Dad was still shocked to hear the attitude of a Negro friend of his when the two boys were at a Terre Haute movie theater. It was 1952, and the Korean War had just begun, so while they climbed the stairs to the theater's balcony, the only place where Negroes were allowed to sit, the two high school boys were mulling over whether or not they would be drafted. Dad's friend, whose name was Manford Carter (and is today a Washington, D.C., minister), suddenly muttered angrily, "I'm not going to get drafted and get killed for America. When I graduate from high school, I'm going to join the Air Force because I'm not going to get killed fighting for so-called democracy."

Dad was shocked by his friend's words. He knew that joining the Air Force was a less risky proposition than being drafted into the infantry because only officers could fly planes into combat. A Negro enlisted man in the Air Force would probably be a mechanic, safe at a base. But at the time, Dad didn't understand his friend's bitterness. Why didn't his friend believe America was a true democracy worth fighting for?

He and Manford both attended meetings of the NAACP Youth Council in Terre Haute, but they did not participate in any kind of civil rights activities. Mostly, the NAACP was a place to socialize and to learn about racism in an abstract sense.

The summer after Dad graduated from Wiley in 1952, he enrolled in Indiana State Teachers' College because his grandparents wanted him to be a teacher. But Dad knew he wanted to be a minister or a lawyer—even if he had only a vague notion of what a lawyer did—so he transferred to Indiana University in Indianapolis after a year. Dad still hadn't found his political footing. He followed the music fads, went to jazz clubs, and began meditating and experimenting with Zen Buddhism, which was the rage on the campus. Colorful pastel shirts were his trademark fashion statement.

Then he had the nerve to try to join the Young Republicans Club, since his grandfather and uncle were Republicans. However, the Republicans in the club did not feel hospitable, and again Dad felt like an outsider. "I remember attending that first meeting, but based upon the body language—they were very diplomatic—I could tell I did not want to be with them," Dad says. Their eyes gave them away. Silently, they snickered at his clothes: his "Mr. B" wide-collar purple shirts (named after jazz singer Billy Eckstine) and knit ties.

Dad began to give more thought to what he *did* want.

"I think Booker T. Washington had a lot of impact upon people of my grandparents' generation—which was if you work hard and earn credentials, you'll be respected. Although when I was at Indiana University I called myself a liberal, I wanted to be a lawyer who would be involved in labor relations. I was concerned about the poor more than I was concerned about the interests of black people, because I thought that black people's interests could be resolved, and the problems we had were just isolated situations. I didn't wake up until after 1955 when I was in the Army."

Dad had volunteered for the draft to get GI benefits to finish his college education. At the beginning of what would have been his senior year, he reported for duty and was sent to Fort Bragg in North Carolina. "That's when I began to feel the dual system. Although we worked together, black and white, during the day, at night, and on our own free time, whites went into their separate world. Also in 1955, that's when the gruesome murder of Emmett Till came up in Mississippi. I remember how the *Charlotte Observer,* which was supposed to be a liberal or moderate newspaper, condemned the NAACP, saying it was just as bad as the Ku Klux Klan in raising 'racial' issues about this murder. So I began to get sensitive. Then, while I was in North Carolina, that's when Montgomery, Alabama, came up."

Montgomery, Alabama. Rosa Parks. Dr. Martin Luther King Jr. The bus boycott. The beginning of the era that became known as the modern civil rights movement. Dad hadn't been impressed by the 1954 *Brown v. Board of Education* Supreme Court decision because he had already been attending integrated schools, and he knew school integration wasn't the whole answer. But Rosa Parks's determination not to give up her seat on the bus moved him.

"I began to become rebellious to authority unconsciously. I was not comfortable being a traditional soldier and I couldn't conform, so in order to do something with me, they assigned me to the library or K.P., Kitchen Patrol. That's where I had plenty of time to do a lot of reading and understand what was occurring. That's when I began to read books like *The Black Metropolis,* about Chicago, and Carl Rowan's book about the race riots in Tennessee, so I began to educate myself about racism while I was in the Army. When I was released from the Army as a private to go back to college in 1956, the first thing I did was to join the college chapter of the NAACP at Indiana University."

*The main goal of mine is to be a leader, or a community leader, though I haven't shown much talent for it yet,* Dad wrote to his grandmother in June of 1956, shortly before his release from the Army. *The future will show itself soon.*[1]

Through the NAACP, Dad began taking part in sit-ins at segregated restaurants, even though in 1956 the NAACP as a whole did not embrace the direct action approach. The strategy of Dad's NAACP college chapter was to enter the restaurant to document whether or not they were served. If they were asked to leave, they got up and left. They planned to ask the university to sponsor a boycott of those restaurants in its literature for incoming students. It was all very measured and polite.

Through the Indiana University college chapter of the NAACP, Dad met his civil rights mentor, John Preston Ward, a Negro Indianapolis attorney, one of the first Negro professors at Indiana University. At that time, a girl Dad had yet to meet, named Patricia Gloria Stephens, was still a high school student in Belle Glade, unaware of her future in civil rights, but just as Mom would be electrified by CORE's summer workshop in 1959, Dad was electrified by John Ward.

John Preston Ward was a political science professor at Indiana University, and he also served as the director of Indiana's ACLU chapter and as adviser to the NAACP chapter. To Dad, Ward seemed tireless and very focused on what he wanted to accomplish. He was a young man when Dad met him, probably only about five years Dad's senior. Their friendship continued after Dad graduated from Indiana University in 1958, when Dad remained in Indianapolis to continue his work with the NAACP. Further influenced by John Ward's legal profession after volunteering with him at the Indiana Civil Liberties Union, in 1959 Dad enrolled at Indiana University's law school.

In early 1960, the student sit-in movement in the South swept national headlines, and Dad read about two sisters named Priscilla and Patricia Stephens, students at Florida A&M University, who had been arrested in Tallahassee, Florida, and sentenced to sixty days in the county jail. "Will you look at this?" he said to his grandmother, showing her the *Jet* magazine while they sat at her kitchen table. For Dad, seeing those pictures in *Jet* gave the Movement a human face, the same way the picture of Rosa Parks had—one of sacrifice and putting one's future at risk in order to be considered human. His grandmother seemed to feel what he was thinking.

"I don't know about all that, Johnny," his grandmother said.

He knew the rest without her having to say it: the Booker T. Washington philosophy of building capital with education, avoiding trouble. But Dad wanted to stir up trouble, and he was growing frustrated. He was involved with the Indianapolis branch of the NAACP, but the old alliance of Negro and white radicals he'd known in the beginning had been swept out, replaced by more conservative Negro ministers. Those ministers had little use for Dad and others like him. When Roy Wilkins, the NAACP executive secretary, sent telegrams to the NAACP's northern branches asking them to support the student sit-in movement in the South, the Indianapolis branch balked. To be certain they wouldn't be associated with the sit-ins, the ministers met and arranged for somebody to pay for a full-page ad in the *Indianapolis Star*—a major white-owned newspaper, where advertising wasn't cheap—and they signed their names denouncing the sit-ins. Dad later heard that ad was worth $5,000. He was deeply disillusioned.

A young man named William Raspberry, now a famed *Washington Post* columnist, was head of the Indianapolis NAACP Youth Council. Dad worked with him and other young men and women who had launched sympathetic pickets against Woolworth stores—the same stores that refused to serve Negroes at their lunch counters in the segregated South—at Indianapolis's business hub, Monument Circle. Many of the Youth Council members were no more than adolescents, but as was often the case, young people were willing to venture where the elders would not tread. The Youth Council did its best to push for change even with the vacuum of more progressive adult leadership.

Dad's schedule in recent months had been too trying. He had worked at the post office during the day, attended law classes at night, and spent his free time volunteering in civil rights activities and socializing. By the end of his first year of law school, his grades were plummeting. "I don't say I failed—I didn't succeed. There's a big difference," Dad says with his characteristic good humor. By the time he was twenty-five, Dad had flunked out of law school.

Afterward, he worked as one of the first Negro counselors at the Indiana State Farm, a correctional institution in Greencastle, Indiana. But the Monday after he took part in the Monument Circle demonstrations, his boss asked him to resign. "Why?" Dad asked. "You were seen making a spectacle of yourself picketing, and that reflects poorly on us," his boss said, and he began writing up termination papers, where he stated the reason for Dad's dismissal.

That was his boss's mistake, Dad says. Since all new employees were probationary for the first six months anyway, his boss needn't have bothered offering an explanation, and it was an explanation that seemed clearly discriminatory. When Dad went to John Ward to ask advice, Ward said he would help him sue.

"I pictured myself going all over the state of Indiana speaking in relation to this issue, when I was called by the supervisor to come to work," Dad says. "I knew that although I was called back to work and everything allegedly was forgiven, they would find some other reason to get rid of me."

Besides, Dad was ready for a change. He had been displeased with his law school's highly conservative leanings, and since the civil rights struggle didn't really seem to be catching fire in Indianapolis, Dad began thinking about going South. He felt that Indianapolis's Negro leaders had sold out. He wanted to go where the action was, like the demonstrations he had read about in Florida. He wanted to become part of the direct action of CORE.

Coincidentally, a lot of Negro students from Florida were enrolled at Indiana University during that time. As Dad tells it, the state of Florida was trying to dodge the United States Supreme Court's order to desegregate its graduate schools by paying the tuition of its Negro college graduates to attend graduate schools *outside* of Florida. One of those students was George King, who taught history at Florida A&M University in Tallahassee and happened to be working on his doctorate at Indiana when Dad was there. Through him, Dad learned about FAMU's law school, which the state had created to avoid desegregating the University of Florida's law school. There were not many students at FAMU, Dad was told, and the school would be happy to admit him. Dad wrote to the dean, Thomas Miller Jenkins.

"He advised me, 'Get prepared, and don't make the mistake you made at Indiana University College of Law. Learn as much as you can, and just don't get involved with civil rights activities until you get your law degree and become admitted to a bar. If you get involved before you pass and take the bar, you won't be able to be successful,' " Dad recalls. "So, I told him, 'Yes, you're right, Dean Jenkins. I'll just study and I won't get involved.' "

He believed that. He also believed he would get his law degree in Florida, then return to Indiana to make changes in the state of his birth.

In life, things rarely go as planned.

My mother was never allowed to have any illusions about my father, because he told her on many occasions exactly how he felt: He wasn't the marrying kind. He didn't want a family. All he wanted was to fight for his people's rights.

My parents didn't "date" in any real sense. He didn't court her or buy her roses, and she never put on special dresses or had her hair done when she was going to see him. In many ways, they were just friends. But they spent countless hours in conversation and strategy sessions, envisioning the world they wanted to help build, and they glimpsed each other's souls. It became more and more clear to my father that this attractive firebrand had feelings for him, and he couldn't ignore his feelings for her. Those feelings were problematic. He had blurted out a proposal the night they'd been sitting on Daisy Young's porch as summer approached in 1961, and her laughter had hurt his pride. He'd decided maybe he'd dodged a bullet. Maybe it was all for the best. Maybe she deserved someone else, someone with broader interests than his.

But when Patricia Stephens announced that she was going to leave FAMU and go to New York at the end of 1962, Dad knew his life was at a crossroads. As it turned out, it wasn't his soul or his heart that made the decision to marry Patricia Stephens. Once again, to boil it down, he relied on his intellect and his powers of observation.

Dad had seen a few things that stuck with him during his days in Indiana with John Ward. Ward had been a mentor beyond his dedication to the struggle; Ward was also a mentor in his handling of his personal life, as a cautionary tale if nothing else. Ward had been married briefly while Dad knew him in Indianapolis, and it had not been a pretty union to witness.

"John Ward sacrificed his life, his family, his marriage," Dad says, explaining that Ward had not paid enough attention to his wife, spending too much time away from her with other women, and the marriage had lasted only a few years. On the one hand, Dad thought, he could look at Ward's example and avoid marriage entirely. After all, the kind of energy and focus it would take to make a real impact on American society would not leave much time for a home life.

On the other hand. . . .

Ever the voracious reader, Dad had read *The Rebel* by Albert Camus, in which the French existentialist writer discussed how all revolutions eventually become corrupt. Since Dad saw himself at the forefront of a social revolution, he knew those lessons would apply to him. "You know, the Russian Revolution turned out Stalin, who just killed millions of people. He purged so many of his officers in the Russian Army that he almost lost Russia to Hitler's invasion in World War II. Fortunately, he didn't kill the officers that were fighting the Japanese, so he just had to bring them back to Moscow to save Moscow. And of course we know about Castro—complete idiocy. There's so much arrogance in feeling the righteousness of your cause," he says.

What did that have to do with marrying Patricia Stephens?

"I said to myself, 'If I let Patricia go, I'm going to be my worst enemy. People will be looking for me. I'll be in prison somewhere.' "

In marrying Mom, Dad believed he could safeguard both his future and his soul. She would help keep him anchored to the world of practicality so he would not lose course and fly off completely into the world of ideals and beliefs. And because their shared belief in the cause ran so deeply, he thought they could avoid some of the pitfalls he had seen plague John Ward.

He almost calculated wrong.

In 1972, when my parents had been married for nine years, had three children to care for, and had more bills than money, my father simply vanished one day. He had been suspended from the Florida bar as a result of a trap laid for him in response to his civil rights activities, and the rebel in him was burning strong, as it had throughout the 1960s. In the earlier days of their marriage, my parents had considered prolonged separation a fact of life. My father was used to traveling on a shoestring, sleeping in his car, on people's sofas, on the floor if he had to, and my mother had often done the same. Dad was used to losing himself in the Struggle.

Life was different by 1972. My parents had children now, mouths to feed. My mother had no idea where he was, and after two weeks she was frantic and beyond furious.

While my mother was wringing her hands in Miami, Dad was organizing a statewide welfare rights organization, traveling throughout northern Florida. He'd gone to St. Petersburg first, and Joe Waller, a client and activist with J.O.M.O. (the Junta of Militant Organizations), a Florida black militant organization, had given him enough money to travel from St. Petersburg to Jacksonville to talk to welfare mothers about what their rights and expectations should be. My father's family was in Miami, but his mind was on making changes for other families and other children.

Then, my father says, he had an epiphany. He was about to sit in on a meeting for his people called by a professional organizer who had been brought in from New Orleans, but he was stopped at the door. "No, Mr. Due, this is just for the welfare mothers," a woman told him.

Dad went back to his hotel room and let it sink in. *He didn't belong there.*

"That's when I came on back to Miami, and I said, 'Look, I need to rearrange my priorities somehow,' " Dad recalls. "I remembered how John Ward's life was all messed up, so I said, 'No, I need to try and stay home. I need to stay home and see what I can do.' "

In 1973, he was offered a job with the Metropolitan Dade County Community Relations Board. The director, Robert Simms, asked him, "Do you believe you can carry out your mission in life by working *within* the system?" Dad knew the CRB was comprised of movers and shakers who wanted to know what should be done to keep the peace without the police violence of St. Augustine or Birmingham. Dad also knew that his grandmother's concern was coming to a head. Finally, he also remembered the conclusion he'd come to in the sixth grade when doing research on why it was a good idea to hire the handicapped: It was "good business" to hire the handicapped. Taking the job at CRB would give him access to movers and shakers, to show them that it was good business to do the right thing. He took the job.

As it had on my mother, J. Edgar Hoover's FBI had been keeping a dossier on my father since the early 1960s. His affiliation with more radical groups in the later 1960s earned him FBI categorization as a "subversive," citing "prior acts or conduct or statements indicating a propensity for violence and antipathy toward good order and government."[2] (My father had never committed a single act of political violence, but the Black Power groups of the late 1960s scared the government.) When he'd worked for Legal Services of Greater Miami, the FBI regularly called his director and clients to tell them Dad was attending meetings to "overthrow the government." We discovered after reading his files years later that people he worked with and considered his allies were informing on him to the FBI. The agency kept tabs on him, constantly noting his whereabouts. He was considered outside of the mainstream.

At the Community Relations Board, Dad would be inside mainstream life again, and it was an adjustment for him. He was afraid he was selling out. Father Theodore Gibson, a longtime Miami civil rights activist, was very upset with him for taking the position for precisely that reason. He wanted Dad to be independent of the county in reorganizing the Miami branch of the NAACP. But Dad's new job paid the bills. It provided for his family. By 1974, the FBI finally stopped monitoring my father's activities, no longer considering him a threat. Over the years, my father made peace with his choice while doing all he could as a volunteer.

But making peace is never easy.

As of this book's publication, my parents have been married forty years. In a society where divorce runs rampant, I see my parents as a shining example of partnership that truly *can* last a lifetime. At least, as their child, that is my hope. I heard on *60 Minutes* recently that not a single one of Dr. Martin Luther King Jr.'s four children has ever married. Hearing that, I couldn't help speculating that those four children of the Struggle probably didn't emerge from their traumatic childhoods with a notion of marriage they wanted to emulate. Those kids had not really had a father, even before his assassination. Their father lost his life, and Dr. King was so often absent that Coretta Scott King, in many ways, was a widow long before her husband died.

There are probably many times when my mother feels like a widow, too.

My sisters and I have all married, and we are building our own families. I have a teenage stepdaughter, Nicki, and my husband and I intend to have more children, both biologically and through adoption. Lydia has two young sons, Justin and Jordan. Johnita, too, plans to have children soon. To me, more than for anyone else, this book is for our children.

My sisters and I all know my parents' marriage has not been easy on my mother in particular. That was never a secret in our home. But we love both our parents, even if Dad is sometimes still a mystery to us, and if Mom is the one we're used to hanging out with and sharing our joys and anxieties with first. We talk to her almost every day about anything and everything. When we talk to Dad, the conversation is almost always rooted somehow to the Struggle.

But my sisters and I believe in the dream of soul mates and family as fervently as we believe in Dr. King's dream. The quest for racial equality that brought my parents together also nearly tore them apart, but somehow it never did.

The home my parents built for us wobbled and groaned from time to time, but when the storms blew over, it always stood tall.

Fifteen

# Patricia Stephens Due

**"In every human breast, God has implanted**
**a principle which we call love of freedom;**
**it is impatient of oppression and pants for deliverance."**
***—Phillis Wheatley***

John Due and I didn't have a honeymoon, even for a weekend. In fact, although I didn't know it, I would be going to jail again less than three weeks after our wedding. The Movement was picking up momentum in Tallahassee, and as two newlywed civil rights activists, there was nothing more important to us.

It had been a busy time. On January 15, after years of negotiations with CORE and other organizations—and without rallies or marches or celebrations—Tallahassee's lunch counters were finally integrated in 1963.[1] It had seemed like a very long wait to those of us who were first arrested at Woolworth in 1960, but in retrospect it was the year before the 1964 Civil Rights Act, so our work was paving the way for others.

Only three days after my wedding, I'd been selected as one of the local Negroes who would take part in a quiet test of city restaurants and lunch counters, sanctioned by the city. Throughout the day, we sat and asked for service, and city officials and police stood by, ready for reports of white mobs getting upset. Since we were all Americans, it always annoyed me that city officials were so concerned about the emotional reactions of racists rather than the rights of Negroes, but that was the way it was. We were treated like the last priority, as if the fear and hurt feelings of a white crowd were more important than democratic principles. That time, however, nothing happened. Much to our relief, we ate in peace, and Tallahassee's city fathers decided the city was finally ready to open its lunch counters and accept that, at least on that basic level, Negroes were people, too.

I suppose city officials might have hoped they were rid of CORE after that. But as soon as they were probably congratulating themselves on getting rid of that pesky "Negro" problem at the city's restaurants, CORE began picketing the city's segregated movie theaters. Believe it or not, every battle was separate. We had to try to gain our humanity one small step at a time.

We moved on methodically, following CORE guidelines: We couldn't assume we would not be given entrance at the theaters, so we had to conduct tests. In the testing, I tried to purchase a ticket at the Florida Theatre at 118 N. Monroe Street, and I was refused. The next step was to try to negotiate with the management, but as usual the management was not interested in talking to us. When negotiation didn't work, it was time to have direct action demonstrations. Although I was married to John and he was just as determined to win equal rights, he had only four months left of law school, and we were both very concerned that if he got more directly involved, the state would not allow him to become a lawyer. In fact, a police official threatened him directly during that time: *I'll see to it you won't ever pass the Florida bar.* So, John was ready to work behind the scenes, explaining legal ramifications to protesters and helping them if they got arrested, but he could not afford to get arrested himself.

On January 23, FAMU student Julius Hamilton and I, armed with movie tickets that had been purchased for us by a white activist, tried to enter the Florida Theatre. We were stopped, and management called police when we refused to leave. We were charged with criminal trespass, and we spent a night in jail before being arraigned. The case was dropped within days, however. Our lawyer, ACLU attorney Tobias Simon, was told by Tallahassee's city attorney that they were "tired of suits and litigations." Maybe they thought they could avoid more bad publicity, but sue is exactly what we did. We filed a $1 million discrimination suit against city officials. Rev. Steele counseled us to try to use our suit as a bargaining chip, which we did: We offered to drop the suit if the city would desegregate its courtroom. The judge agreed, but later reneged. When Julius, Rubin Kenon, and I came to the courtroom, we were removed from the side reserved for whites.[2]

It seemed that officials wanted to play games with us, but we were in no mood for that. We began scheduling regular pickets at the Florida Theatre and State Theatre. We picketed after classes and on Saturdays, careful to try to preserve our academic schedules. As usual, we had only two or three people in the beginning, but over the course of more than a week, our pickets grew from a few people to a dozen people, and then from a dozen to two dozen, and so on. The more of us there were, the more we were noticed.

During this time, civil rights activists had cause to celebrate. I wrote about the momentous turn in a May 21, 1963, letter to my former professor, Richard Haley, who was now based in Louisiana and still very involved with CORE: *Yesterday, the United States Supreme Court overruled laws against sit-ins. That is, they said it is unconstitutional to arrest demonstrators to enforce local segregation laws, which are, in themselves, unconstitutional.*

Could the tide be turning in our favor? Would the courts finally be our friend?

A May 29 theater demonstration drew about 400 students, with all of us singing, clapping, and chanting for freedom while hundreds of white onlookers stood by and watched. We definitely were an intimidating sight to anyone hoping to purchase a ticket for a movie. An editorial in the *Tallahassee Democrat* the next day characterized our peaceful protest as "very much like a football pep rally, or an old fashioned camp meeting, or a college sing. . . . The words this time didn't praise the old-time religion, nor the old Fam-U spirit, but something we across the street didn't quite make out about freedom to go where they want and do what they want to do."[3] The article noted that the white street toughs on the scene were kept away from protesters by police.

Still, after several days of protests, the panicked theater owners were successful in convincing Judge Ben C. Willis to issue a temporary restraining order against me specifically, as well as other members of CORE. The order also officially banned protesters from using derogatory signs, or signs that urged a boycott of the theaters.[4] But we were determined to keep protesting, especially since the film *The Ugly American* was now playing at the Florida Theatre on Monroe Street. What better backdrop for a civil rights demonstration?

As I learned later, by May 30 Tallahassee Mayor Sam Teague considered Tallahassee to be in a state of emergency. He took control of the police department, calling the sixty-eight-member force to a meeting at 5:00 A.M. Despite ridiculous warnings from the FBI that infiltrators at FAMU with plans "printed in Cuba" were going to try to disrupt his city, Teague said in a 1978 interview for an oral histories collection, "I realized as mayor that 99.9 percent of the students out here were well-meaning American citizens trying to improve their lot in life." His biggest worry was for public safety, he said, so he told his officers to leave their cattle prods at the station, and he forbid them to use their nightsticks. Many of the officers were reportedly enraged, but Teague told them, "I want you to uphold the law, I want you to be dignified, but I don't want anybody getting rapped on the head with a nightstick." He had also asked city ministers to try to prevent confrontations at the demonstration between whites and Negroes.[5]

The Florida Theatre demonstration drew hundreds of FAMU students, Negro high school students, and a white student from Florida State University. Again, we came with hand-painted placards, of which my favorite read, ARE YOU AN UGLY AMERICAN? We picketed and sang in front of the theater while crowds gawked at us, some of them with curiosity and some with anger. Again, as in previous demonstrations, there were so many students there that I did not know many of them personally. While I did know the students in the inner circle—students such as Rubin Kenon and FAMU student Arthenia Joyner, who were two of the real lieutenants in the Movement—we still did not share many parts of our lives with each other during that time. We had a single focus: freedom.

For example, it was almost forty years before Rubin Kenon admitted to me that his fear was so great he became sick to his stomach and often had to vomit before he set out for protests. Or how he would survey his dormitory room before each demonstration, always believing he might be seeing it for the very last time, careful to leave specific items out where friends or relatives could find them later. Then he joined us on the front lines, despite his nausea and despite his fear.

Rubin came to Florida A&M University in 1960 after growing up in Lake City, Florida, which he had always heard was the state's lynching capital. When Tananarive and I interviewed him in a Lake City restaurant in 1997, he surveyed the room with awe as we sat at a table undisturbed, surrounded by both whites and blacks. "If someone would have told me that one day I'd be sitting next to these white boys over here in this place, I would have never believed it," Rubin said. He told us a story about how the University of Florida moved its campus from Lake City to Gainesville in 1906 because there were simply too many dead black men swinging from Lake City's trees. "I don't think the administrators were so concerned about black people getting lynched," Rubin said. "It just offends their sensibilities as they walk to class that they look up in a tree and see a black man hanging."

When he was thirteen or fourteen, Rubin was beaten up by Ku Klux Klan members. As a result of that incident—and the countless stories he'd heard of how Negroes were treated by his town's whites, including how a white man had impregnated a Negro woman and then simply shot her to be rid of the problem—Rubin was afraid of white people. The fear he learned for police officers lingers to this day, he says. His mother, a schoolteacher he called "T. K.," tried to teach him to stand up for himself, both through words and by her example. If she felt she was treated differently than a white customer at a shop, she took her money elsewhere. Once, at the icehouse, the iceman gave the block of ice to six-year-old Rubin to carry to his mother's car instead of taking it himself, as would have been customary. Furious, his mother bought her own refrigerator two weeks later. "She never went back to that icehouse again," Rubin said.

When Rubin stumbled into FAMU's civil rights activities in the 1960s, the two sides of his personality were at war. On one hand, he *did* believe in standing up for his rights, but on the other hand, he was downright terrified, and there was good reason to be afraid. Rubin, like me, could tell that the May 30 *Ugly American* demonstration was going to attract attention. Experience had taught us that racist mobs might form and try to harm us, but that was the risk we were all willing to take.

Sure enough, across the street from the theater, a group of angry whites began to grow, and some of them were quite close to us. We picketed and sang, and they shouted and threatened. Some onlookers were waving Confederate flags, a reminder of the slaveholding mentality that was still flourishing in the South nearly a century after the end of the Civil War, a symbol that is still incorporated into some state flags, and people wonder why blacks find it so offensive! A good number of young white men flanking the protest were wearing their hair slicked back and their shirttails out: in those days, sure signs of hoodlums looking for trouble. "The air was so electrically charged at times that just the flick of an eyebrow was enough to set off an explosion," Rubin recalled about that protest and others like it. "It was a time when we just didn't know if we were going to survive." After a few hours, the city decided to try to shut the protest down. Circuit Court Judge Ben Willis issued an injunction order informing us that we could not block entrances, we could not attempt to enter the theaters, we could not display signs pertaining to the policy of the theater, and so on.

The students chose not to obey the order. We assembled to march from FAMU up the boulevard toward the capitol, where the State Theatre was located. I was in front of the march with Scout, the beautiful German shepherd I had bought to celebrate John's graduation from law school. We have always had dogs. I couldn't leave Scout in the apartment because John was studying at the library and then would go to work, and Scout's stomach was upset because he had just been wormed. It wasn't long before I began to realize that bringing Scout might have been a mistake. When the capitol press corps saw us approaching with Scout at the head of the march, they began pointing and yelling, "Reverse Birmingham!" (In Birmingham, Bull Connor's police had turned German shepherds on child demonstrators.) Seeing a situation that could be damaging politically, a FAMU student named Arthur Teele—who would later become a high-level Reagan appointee to the Department of Transportation, a state NAACP official, and executive chair of the Miami-Dade County Commission—did some quick thinking. He drove up in his car, took Scout's leash, and carried our dog away.

That day, 220 of us were arrested, including me, Rubin, Doris Rutledge, and a freshman from Miami named Betty Jean Tucker, who later became a Miami-Dade County Commissioner under her married name, Betty Ferguson. But even arrest didn't dampen our spirit of protest. While the police walked us down the street to the jailhouse, we shouted, "Free-dom! Free-dom! Free-dom!" Again, as in 1960, word got back to the FAMU campus that students had been arrested, so a sympathy march formed. This time, about 200 students were in the march, compared to 1,000 in 1960, but Mayor Teague decided nonetheless to disperse it with tear gas when students would not turn back. Thirty-seven more students were arrested and joined us at the jail.[6]

Once again, much to the city's dismay, I'm sure, Tallahassee was making national headlines because of civil rights arrests. The protest and arrests were described in the *New York Times*, and a photograph of me being lifted from a passive crouch by three police officers outside of the theater appeared in *Time* magazine and the *Miami Herald*. I was wearing dark glasses and a neat dress and pumps, hardly the picture of someone who posed a threat to the community. The *Herald's* photo of my arrest accompanied a story about how Negro agitation was making civil rights a more important part of the national agenda, how President John F. Kennedy planned to push for new civil rights legislation in Congress, and how Secretary of State Dean Rusk had stated that the civil rights problem was putting our nation's "leg in a cast" in the race against communism. "Our voice is muted, our friends are embarrassed, our enemies are gleeful because we have not put our hands fully . . . to this problem," Rusk said.[7]

Meanwhile, John had graduated from FAMU's law school and was studying for the bar and working part-time at a steakhouse, the Silver Slipper, a gathering hole for local politicians. John had not been arrested with us, but he did go to the courthouse to try to get an appointment with Judge Ben Willis to get a clarification of his arrest order. John thought that would be the end of his involvement, but he was wrong. When he arrived back at our apartment, a deputy sheriff was waiting to serve him with a summons. He had been named a codefendant! Someone was making trouble for him.

The next day, when John reported to work, his boss called him aside. "What you do on your own time is your business," his boss said, "but when your business affects my business, you have to go. My customers saw you leading a march downtown with a German shepherd dog!" John was barely making any money as it was, but now he had been fired on the basis of a lie.

At the contempt-of-court hearing before Judge Willis the next day, the charges were dropped against all 257 of us. Judge Willis told us he didn't believe most of us had purposely ignored his injunction, and he clarified that the signs we'd carried had not defamed the theater. "They said 'Segregation is unconstitutional,' which is an expression of opinion, not derogatory or defamatory. Another said, 'Are you an ugly American?' and that was not defamatory. I'm glad no one asked me that. I'd have had to say 'yes,' " the judge said, which sounded like his effort to make a joke. "Another sign said 'Freedom,' and there is nothing objectionable about that."[8]

But he also slowed our effectiveness by instituting rules to govern our protests, limiting the number of participants and outlining very specific guidelines for where we could stand and what we could say. For example, only eighteen students would be permitted to protest at one time at the Florida Theatre, and only ten at the State Theatre, which was only symbolic. At the time, one of our attorneys, Tobias Simon, proclaimed to gathered Negro onlookers in the courthouse that the ruling was a "tremendous victory. This is the first and only time in a Southern state has the right of a Negro to picket a white establishment been recognized and put into an order. I predict [the protests] will be effective and the day of segregated theaters in Tallahassee will come to end very shortly."[9] I always saw the ruling as an attempt to silence us to the point of ineffectiveness. Protests continued under the new guidelines, but they were definitely more lackluster.

Besides, the end of the spring school term meant that many students who might participate were leaving Tallahassee for the summer. John and I remained behind, and Rubin Kenon was there that summer, too. We were also once again joined by Priscilla, who came to Tallahassee to visit me after she had surgery. This was a rare opportunity for us to spend time together again, but it's a decision I believe my sister came to regret, and one that would make her vow to never again be involved in the Movement, at least for a time. She has described her visit to Tallahassee that summer as a turning point of her life, and not in the positive sense.

Priscilla is one of the most open and warmhearted people I have ever known. She is certainly not without faults, as none of us is, but to me her big strength is that she has always enjoyed people very much. As someone who was not nearly as sociable, I was likely to be labeled as cold by people who did not know me well. Someone in the Movement once told me I was "as cold as an icicle," but that has never been true of Priscilla. She has a radiant smile, and she is generous with it. Especially when we were younger, she always seemed to believe that people operated under the best of motives, and Mother worried that she was too naive. Despite everything she and I had witnessed in the past few years, Priscilla brought that same optimism back with her to Tallahassee in the summer of 1963.

After her arrival, Priscilla and I visited with each other and probably had some fun, although, to be honest, I don't remember much in the way of fun during those years. It wasn't long before she became involved in civil rights again. Since the movie theater demonstrations had petered out for the summer, she and Rubin took part in small demonstrations to protest Tallahassee's segregated so-called "public" swimming pools.

On May 30, the same day of all the arrests at the Florida Theatre, three white Florida State University students had quietly waged a protest of their own by trying to purchase tickets to swim at Tallahassee's "Negro-only" swimming pool. Saying they were not a part of CORE, students Anne Hamilton, James Walker, and John Parrott told police and reporters they only wanted to patronize the municipal pool closest to where they lived, which happened to be the pool designated for Negroes. "We thought the municipal pools were open to everybody and we wanted to go swimming," Hamilton said. They were fingerprinted and released.[10]

In June, Priscilla and Rubin decided to try the opposite tactic: They would try to swim at the "whites-only" Meyers Park swimming pool, something they called a "wade-in." They tried to gain admission for three days, but were unsuccessful. On the third day, already wearing her swimming suit, Priscilla managed to slip past the gate and made her way toward the water. Police stopped her before she made it.

In the beginning, at least, there was nothing noteworthy about Priscilla's arrest. She allowed herself to be handcuffed, and the officer pulled her toward his parked police cruiser. He opened the door, and she began to climb inside. For some reason, Priscilla recalls, the officer thought she wasn't moving fast enough. In front of a crowd of dozens of white onlookers, the officer kicked her in the stomach.

Priscilla was almost too shocked to feel the pain right away. She had never before been physically abused by a police officer, and she could hardly believe that a *man* would strike a *woman*, especially a woman in handcuffs. Sitting in the police car, Priscilla looked out at the witnesses. "I looked at the crowd, and I said, 'My god, you allow this? I'm doing nothing,' " she recalls. No one was cheering, but the faces that stared back at her in the bright sunshine that day seemed completely indifferent, except for one woman she noticed. That woman was staring at Priscilla with what looked like a sympathetic smile. "Oh, this lady is going to come forth," Priscilla says she remembers thinking. "She's going to tell what happened!"

At her trial, exactly as she'd believed, Priscilla was excited to see the very same woman in the courtroom. Priscilla was not allowed to speak on her own behalf, as was always the case in these arrests, so as much as she wanted to complain about the officer's behavior, the judge gave her no venue to do so. Instead, Priscilla kept looking at the white woman in the audience, expecting her to declare why she had come, what she had seen. The woman simply sat and watched, wearing the exact same smile. She never spoke.

"The whole thing was over, and I had been sentenced, and this woman had said nothing. So my conclusion was the smile was just a smile," Priscilla says. Had it always been a different kind of smile altogether, and Priscilla just hadn't seen it? Had the woman come to gloat instead of defending her? To Priscilla, the woman's lack of sympathy was even more troubling than the police officer's kick because it meant she no longer trusted her own judgment of people. It was a disillusioning moment that Priscilla says she has never forgotten.

Priscilla doesn't know exactly how much time she spent in jail as a result of her "wade-in" experience, but she remembers that she was thrown into the isolation cell because she wouldn't stop singing. Instead of having me and other students in jail with her this time, she was by herself, and the loneliness she felt was keen. To keep her spirits up, she sang "Oh, Freedom" and the song we'd made up during the 1960 jail-in to the tune of "Old Black Joe," but the guards didn't like her singing and put her in the tiny isolation cell. Her incarceration (and, no doubt, the kick) had aggravated her surgery, and she felt herself becoming inflamed. But she lay on the cold concrete floor, she says, singing and singing.[11]

I was outraged about what had happened, of course. Priscilla, Rubin, and I went to a city commission meeting to file a police brutality complaint, but we never had the chance to speak because two city commissioners left the meeting, shutting it down. Instead of rebuking the police department at the meeting, the mayor offered praise.[12]

The city closed the white pool rather than face more protests. After that, for five long years, no one could go swimming to escape the hot Tallahassee sun.[13]

In July 1963, the Tallahassee CORE office got word that a crisis had arisen: A friend and CORE colleague named Zev Aelony had been arrested in Ocala, 182 miles southeast of Tallahassee. We had to go to Ocala right away to check on Zev's welfare. As Priscilla's recent police experience had only reinforced, a lone activist in police custody was not in safe hands. Rubin came with me in our worn 1952 Plymouth to see about Zev. That car was in such bad shape that the floor was missing, and you could see the road passing beneath your feet, but we were students, and it was the only car we had.

During the three-hour drive, we worried about Zev. The Movement was heating up around the country, and it was looking more and more like a domestic war. In May, Birmingham police, led by notorious segregationist Bull Connor, had turned high-powered fire hoses and set dogs on children as young as six; 600 Negro children had been arrested and jailed in one day during those demonstrations, which Dr. King had spearheaded. President Kennedy, after seeing a photograph of a police dog attack, had said it made him "sick."[14] During that time, the home of Dr. Martin Luther King's brother, Birmingham minister Rev. A. D. King, had been bombed, although he and his family had not been injured. Later, in the same city and on the same night, Dr. Martin Luther King's hotel was bombed, but he too had been lucky enough to escape injury. It's ironic to me: With all of today's worry about terrorists, many people in this country forget that civil rights demonstrators were subjected to terrorist acts by American racists on a regular basis, and as far as I'm concerned, they were often encouraged by police and government officials. On June 11, 1963, President Kennedy had been forced to dispatch National Guardsmen to the University of Alabama because of Gov. George Wallace's attempt to block the enrollment of two Negro students, Vivian Malone and James Hood. Governor Wallace set the tone from above, and the terrorists only took his hate-filled rhetoric to the next level.

That night, President Kennedy made a historic televised speech celebrating the Alabama students' enrollment, urging Americans to understand that Negroes could no longer be treated as second-class citizens. But just after midnight on June 12, 1963, only hours after President Kennedy's speech, the Movement suffered a horrible blow that was only a precursor to the very tough and violent times ahead for all of us: An NAACP field secretary named Medgar Evers, who had been leading demonstrations in Jackson, Mississippi, died after being gunned down in the driveway of his home.[15] He died surrounded by his wife and three young children, who were hysterical.[16] Even if President Kennedy was finally beginning to set a tone from above, who was going to protect us in the meantime?

So much was happening so quickly, and all of these developments were on our minds as Rubin and I drove along Highway 27 toward Ocala from Tallahassee, wondering what had become of Zev Aelony. We thought he might be in particular trouble because of the special animosity racists reserved for other whites. Zev was a Jewish pacifist I'd first met at the CORE Miami Action Institute in 1959, and we had corresponded over the years; he had tried to convince me to visit the peace-oriented kibbutz in Israel where he had lived for a time. In truth, I really had hoped I could see it one day, but I never did. Rubin thought of Zev as the most "Godlike person" he had ever known because of his very gentle spirit and righteousness; to Rubin, a Christian, Zev was living according to the example of Christ. Zev's social awakening had come when he was very young because his parents had worked with refugees from Nazi concentration camps who moved to the United States in the mid-1940s, and during that time Zev also met Japanese-American kids who were emerging from America's internment camps. "The camps came as quite a shock," Zev told me. "I was kind of brought up listening to the radio and reading comic books and so on, with good guys and bad guys, and we were supposed to be the good guys." As a teenager, he'd become involved in an interracial folk-singing group, and he remained socially active throughout college. Later, he was a conscientious objector and very active in civil rights, especially in CORE.[17]

By 1963, when the call came about his arrest, Zev was twenty-five years old and based in Americus, Georgia. He had come to Florida at my request, to help where he was needed, and then he'd heard that a sister chapter of CORE in Dunnellon, a tiny, isolated Florida town, needed help trying to desegregate a restaurant. He'd readily agreed to go.

That Dunnellon call came from a young Negro activist named Bettie

Wright, who had heard me speak at FAMU during the school term and had participated in theater demonstrations, and then had gone home for the summer to Dunnellon, the town where she'd grown up, to try to make changes there. She started a fledgling CORE chapter in Dunnellon, only the third CORE chapter in the state. "When it started, it was me alone," Bettie said in an interview. Bettie, who was then a nutrition major between her junior and senior years in college, went to church after church to recruit young people for CORE. (Today, Bettie Wright Blakely is an assistant professor in the Department of Human Ecology at the University of Maryland Eastern Shore. Her specialty is still nutrition.)[18]

When she expanded, she'd invited Zev to Dunnellon because he was a more experienced CORE worker who could conduct training in nonviolence, but Zev ran into problems as soon as he stepped off the bus, he recalled in a later interview with me. The police were watching the bus station, and a cruiser immediately followed Zev and Bettie as they crossed a bridge over the famed Suwannee River. Still, not allowing himself to be intimidated, Zev went to a meeting and agreed to take part at a protest at the restaurant. Someone from the Movement was taking photographs to illustrate that the protest was peaceful, just in case someone tried to accuse them later of rowdiness or violence. A police squad car pulled up while the photographer was asking for Zev's assistance with his camera. The police immediately approached Zev, who stood out because he was white. The officer asked if Zev was a newspaper reporter, and Zev said no. Then the officer asked, "Do you know what the vagrancy statute is in this county?" The next thing Zev knew, despite his insistence that he wasn't a vagrant (and he had pay stubs to prove it), Zev was arrested for vagrancy. He was told to get into the police car, and the police drove him away. That was when Bettie called me.

Zev was eventually transferred to the car of another officer, this one from the Ocala Police. "I remember him because he had a very angry attitude and snarling kind of personality," Zev said. Much to Zev's relief, at the police station, the officer asked permission to turn on a tape recorder. A recorder meant some measure of protection, Zev thought, but after a brief interview, the officer turned off the tape recorder and said, "We operate according to the law, but if it was up to me, I'd slit your throat." Then, he took Zev back to the cell where about four or five other white men were locked up. Before he left, the officer announced to the other inmates, "He's a Freedom Rider. He's the one." Then, he left Zev at their mercy.

The next thing Zev remembers is being attacked by the other prisoners, who kicked him and began smashing his head against the porcelain toilet. Zev tried to protect himself by curling into fetal position, but he could not have fought the men off even if he hadn't been a pacifist. No one can say how long the beating would have continued, or how much worse it would have been, if a visiting white woman had not called for help. "They're killing somebody in there!" she screamed. Without treating his injuries, the jailer first put Zev in a large, empty cell, then moved him to a very small all-steel isolation cell with no windows or light switch on the inside, and only a small steel hatch on the door that his jailers could open or close. When Zev tried to curl on the floor to sleep, jailers turned on the bright light to wake him up. After he was awake, the light would be turned off again and the steel hatch door closed to leave him in darkness. The cell was very narrow, he recalls, only about seven feet high and three feet across.

Rubin recalls arriving on the grounds of the Marion County jail, and being allowed to see Zev the next morning. The police really must have had no shame, because Rubin was very upset by Zev's appearance. "When he walked out, both of his eyes were blackened. I mean, you could see the blood had settled under his eyes. They whupped him. They beat him badly. And when I saw that, I got scared, because, I mean, they might *kill* this white boy because he's in there by himself," Rubin said.

We needed to bring attention to Zev's incarceration quickly. We met with Rev. Frank Pinkston, the NAACP branch president, and with members of Ocala's NAACP Youth Council, including the president, twenty-year-old Charles Washington, and a twenty-year-old Clark College student, David Rackard.[19] They were very courageous and serious-minded young people. Most were teenagers, but some were as young as eleven or twelve, and they were eager to go to Zev's assistance. Rubin and I, leading nearly forty young people, set out for the Marion County jail, where we sang freedom songs as we walked on the vast grounds. "We shall overcoooommme. . . . We shall overcoooommmme. . . . We shall overcome soooomme dayyyyyyy. . . ."

Zev, in his cramped cell, heard our singing. "I wasn't sure if I was hallucinating, but I heard the singing of freedom songs, and I started listening and I realized that it wasn't a hallucination because if I put my ear up against one wall, it was louder," Zev recalled. The singing lifted his spirits, he said. "It was such a spectacular change from what it had been."

We had hardly set foot on the grounds—and we were nowhere near the jail building—when police arrested us for trespassing and unlawful assembly. We were later charged with interfering with county prisoners, and I was charged with resisting arrest without violence. Rubin and I, along with eight others in the group who were not minors, were held at the jail. The others were sent home to the custody of their parents, with police muttering about how the adults were leading them astray. (Which is exactly what police thought of the children's marches in Birmingham, when, in fact, young people are often more militant than their elders.)

Because Rubin and I were in no position to provide for our own defense, the NAACP assigned a team of Negro attorneys to defend us, including Tampa-based attorney Francisco Rodriguez and Daytona Beach attorneys Horace Hill and Joseph W. Hatchett. Authorities had investigated my previous civil rights arrests, so despite our very competent team, Rubin and I were both sentenced to two years in the county jail. We appealed that conviction, of course—and you could pay to stay out of jail pending the outcome of your appeal—and the case eventually made it all the way to the United States Supreme Court. The court eventually ruled that we did *not* have the right to picket the jail. We lost that case so, technically speaking, I suppose there's still a warrant out for me in Ocala, Florida. For years, John has teased me about that whenever we drive through the town.

Our demonstration in Ocala accomplished our goal, though, which was to ensure Zev's safety. Stories about our arrest appeared in several Florida newspapers, probably because so many children had been arrested. Two weeks after his initial arrest on July 26, Zev was finally released.

Zev's brushes with the law didn't end there. He returned to Americus, Georgia, and in August he and three other civil rights workers were arrested for an archaic charge of "attempted insurrection" against the state of Georgia, based on a local 1930s-era law that made sedition a capital crime. They were actually under threat of the death penalty! The outrageous charge made international headlines, causing the nation embarrassment. It was brought to the attention of Attorney General Robert Kennedy, but he did not intervene. Zev and the others had to spend three months in jail until their lawyers convinced a federal court that the charge against them was unconstitutional police abuse.[20] In 1964, Zev was badly beaten after another arrest in Americus. He certainly collected his share of physical bruises in the 1960s.[21]

But bruises were not going to stop us.

By August 1963, every activist we knew was talking about the March on Washington for Jobs and Freedom scheduled at the end of the month, when thousands of civil rights activists from all over the country would gather at the base of the Lincoln Memorial. It would be the first march of its kind in my experience, and we hoped it would put pressure on Washington, especially President Kennedy, to push through legislation to protect the rights of Negroes. Everyone wanted to go, of course, but if there was one similarity that characterized civil rights activists, it was that we were usually broke. John could not work as an attorney because he had not yet received his bar results and since he had been fired from the Silver Slipper for the false claim that he had led a demonstration, he was excluded from getting work elsewhere in town, too. His GI bill had expired, and my scholarship from CORE and the Southern Education Defense Fund barely covered our living expenses. While we fantasized about how wonderful it would feel to be part of that historic march, we didn't think it would be possible.

A week or so before the march, John and I went to Miami so he could scout for potential work, since he was considering moving there after he passed the bar. We were invited to a meeting at the residence of Thalia Stern, whom we had met earlier through CORE. Jack Gordon, another CORE veteran, was also there. After hearing our financial plight as John and I talked about the March on Washington, someone in the group suddenly exclaimed, "We can't go, but we can send you two!" They all helped us go to the march, as well as some supporters from northern Florida, and we were thrilled. The meager help was really only enough to cover the train trip, but what a trip it was! Some of the others who left with us from Miami were Miami CORE President A. D. Moore, Rev. Edward Graham, Rev. H. E. Green, *Miami Times* columnist Blanche Calloway (bandleader Cab Calloway's sister), and Weldon Rougeau, a CORE field secretary.

The trip was one of the greatest experiences of my life. Our train left Miami and made its way north, stopping in West Palm Beach, near the town where I grew up. We changed trains in Jacksonville to a train dubbed the "Freedom Train," then we went on to Waycross, Georgia; Savannah, Georgia; and Charleston, South Carolina, with marchers pouring in at each stop. Charleston alone sent 218 delegates. They were young and old, men and women, people from all walks of life. Some of them had fresh bruises from police brutality during protests or jail stays. Some young men even boarded dressed as women to try to elude police.[22] As people boarded, they marched up and down the aisles singing freedom songs: "Woke up this morning with my mind set on Free-dom!" The rest of us clapped and joined in, excited to feel the growing momentum as the train cars filled. In fact, I was so worn out by the excitement of the ride on the Freedom Train that by the time we got to Union Station in Washington, D.C., on August 28, I was exhausted. But we were still singing when we climbed off.

I was told that there had been some discussion that Priscilla and I, and some of the others who had spent forty-nine days in jail, should be permitted to speak at the march. In the end, though, we were not given a spotlighted role, as were John Lewis and Dr. King, not to mention Hollywood celebrities like Marlon Brando and Charlton Heston. Still, John and I received VIP seating passes, so we had very good seats where we would not miss a moment of the program.

Nowadays, of course, almost all anyone seems to remember about that day is Dr. King's "I Have a Dream" speech. It's a lovely speech, but it isn't what I remember most. Rather, I remember National Urban League director Whitney Young's speech on unity, education, voter registration, and economic development. But all the speeches were wonderful. Even though I dozed off a few times because I was so tired, it was a truly marvelous experience to see the hundreds of thousands of people who came that day. It was a refreshing change, really, to feel that there were no responsibilities on my shoulders. I was in a happy, half-waking state for much of the time, listening to speeches, feeling contented, and thinking, over and again, "Well done!" I was so proud of all of us.

When I look back on what I most enjoyed about the fellowship of that day, it wasn't really the march itself. The spirit of brotherhood and sisterhood continued after all of the songs had been sung and the speakers had all had their say. John and I made our way through the crowd, having decided we would find a way to New York instead of heading straight back to Florida. (John thought he might want to pass the bar in two states, New York and Florida, so he would be a more effective civil rights attorney.) In those days, the best form of transportation for people without money was hitchhiking, and no sooner had we positioned ourselves by the road than a white couple pulled over to pick us up. They had just attended the march, too. Not only did they give us a ride, but they gave us food to eat. We were all filled with love for each other. It was just a beautiful, beautiful time—the kind of event that really helps you feel there is hope for a better tomorrow.

Only two weeks later, a bomb blast rocked through the Sixteenth Street Baptist Church in Birmingham, Alabama, killing four Negro girls: Denise McNair, Addie Mae Collins, Cynthia Wesley, and Carole Robertson. Governor Wallace had embroiled the city in yet another battle with the federal government over school integration, and that church had become a target because it was the headquarters for the city's civil rights movement. In the aftermath of the bombing, two white Eagle Scouts—young men who had reached the highest, most coveted rank of Boy Scouting—were leaving a segregationist rally when they shot at two Negro boys on a bicycle, killing a thirteen-year-old. Police also shot and killed a young Negro man who was running away from them.[23]

Bobby Frank Cherry, a former Klansman, became the third man convicted of the church bombing thirty-nine years later. But if the March on Washington had given us a glimpse of the nation we were trying to build, the terrorist bombing of that church and the senseless killing of those four little girls was a horrifying reminder of the nation we still lived in. In 1963, Dr. King's dream was just a dream. I still don't believe we live in the nation we all dreamed about the day of the March on Washington, when we felt our combined love and strength, but we were definitely much farther from that dream on September 15, 1963.

And the killings were not over. The killings were just getting started.

---

I'll be the first to admit that over the years, many of the faces have blurred when I think about the 1960s. Tananarive is always pressing me for details about the people I knew, asking about their mannerisms, their dress, their personalities; and I can remember some of those things, but mostly I remember the work we did. I remember our trials together and our common goal.

One person I wish I'd had the opportunity to know better was only a high school student when I met him, about seventeen years old, much younger than I was, but old enough to stand up for what he believed in. His name was Calvin Bess.

I met Calvin in the most unlikely of places: I was teaching Sunday school at Rev. Steele's church, Bethel Missionary Baptist Church. During the time I had lived with the Steeles, Rev. Steele had always tried in vain to coax me to come to his services each week, despite my argument that I overheard him rehearsing his sermons each Sunday morning anyway. I had been raised African Methodist Episcopal, not Baptist, but that wasn't the reason I stayed away. Rather, Sunday was one of the few days I could sleep in, and I cherished my peace. Rev. Steele's coaxing hadn't stopped when I moved out of his house, but he figured out how to intrigue me when he offered me a chance to teach. He wanted to baptize me, but I adamantly refused. I simply could not see myself being submerged in water when I had already been sprinkled with water in the AME church.

So there I was, an AME girl teaching Sunday school in a Baptist church. I always felt tickled when I imagined what the other members of his church would think if they knew. Not only did I teach Sunday school, but I took particular pleasure in leading a youth group of older students who met at my apartment once a week to socialize and to discuss current events. We called it the Young People's Progressive Club, and our first meeting was held in January 1963. Naturally, with the prominence of the local and national civil rights struggle, our conversation often turned to Jim Crow and the Movement. I was only a few years older than these young people, and I was invigorated by their energy and idealism. These youngsters truly believed they could have a part in helping to change life in America forever.

Of course, some students were more interested in civil rights than others. As I look back at the minutes of those meetings, the young people voted to host a party just like any other young people would. But one thoughtful, bright, and serious-minded young man stood out to me. He was a bookish seventeen-year-old with a slightly reddish complexion and a shy smile, the son of a long-haul trucker and a schoolteacher. His full name was George Calvin Bess, but everyone called him Calvin. He had very careful diction and carried himself with dignity. Like many Negroes in Tallahassee, this young man came from a struggling family, but he was dedicated to his studies, and became just as dedicated to civil rights. After learning more about CORE through the Young People's Progressive Club, he took an interest in Tallahassee's theater demonstrations and decided, on his own, to take part. I never put pressure on anyone, no matter how old or young, to participate in demonstrations if they were uncomfortable about it. But even though I could not acknowledge his presence in the midst of the hectic protests, I was happy to see Calvin. At one point, he was arrested at a theater demonstration.

His involvement didn't end with the theater demonstrations, either.

Rubin says he remembers that Calvin was hesitant to leap headfirst into activism the way Rubin himself had, but despite what Rubin recalls as some reticence on Calvin's part, they spent a lot of time talking about civil rights. Calvin was willing to accompany Rubin to meetings. At one meeting in Lake City, Rubin says, Calvin came to an AME church where Rubin was waiting to make a civil rights announcement. Rubin had already appeared at the church and pleaded with the membership to be supportive, even if it was in terms of donations, but so far the church hadn't responded. He had come to give it another try, awaiting his turn to speak. When it was time for announcements, Rubin raised his hand and waited to be acknowledged. The preacher ignored him, he says. So, being assertive, Rubin stood up and began speaking anyway. The preacher went on, ignoring Rubin, trying to drown out his words. At this, even the congregation felt sympathetic to Rubin. "Let the man talk!" some members complained. But the preacher persisted, grabbing Rubin's hand to forcibly remove him from the sanctuary. If not for the presence of a bishop that day, Rubin says, that preacher looked mad enough to hit him.

Suddenly, Calvin stood up and began to speak in Rubin's place, his voice filling the room, and all eyes turned to him. "To me, that was an act of bravery on his part, because Calvin was not bodacious like me," Rubin says. "Calvin stood up. And he really gave me the impression that he didn't want to be part of the group. Yet, on the other hand, he was irresistibly drawn to it. I think after that night, Calvin became a radical."[24]

In addition to being socially active, Calvin was so brilliant that he eventually won a graduate scholarship to Harvard University, but he never had the chance to take advantage of it. I couldn't have known it in 1963, but four years later, Calvin and another young man would be found dead in a car in a Mississippi swamp. They had been trying to register people to vote with the SNCC, the Student Nonviolent Coordinating Committee. Calvin died at the age of twenty-two, leaving behind a son he had never known he conceived, and leaving his family, especially his mother, in emotional shambles. Ironically, Calvin's family lived on Liberty Street.

Even many years later, his mother couldn't find joy in her heart when Dr. King's birthday finally became a national holiday, recalls Calvin's sister, Cherrye. "I don't *want* to celebrate Martin Luther King's birthday," their mother told her. "Nobody celebrated my child's birthday. He worked just as hard as Martin." A few years after Calvin's death, when Cherrye was twelve, she walked into the kitchen and found her mother standing with a knife, poised to hurt herself. "She'd be talking to Jesus, I reckon," Cherrye says.[25] Mrs. Bess's grief over her only son's death remained with her until she died in 1997, the year after we found Cherrye and her father and interviewed them. Mrs. Bess was too ill for me to interview her that day, and I think it's best I didn't force her to dredge up bad memories. I've learned the hard way, in researching and writing this book, that old hurts can overwhelm when you dig them up. Mrs. Bess was so angry after Calvin's death, as John reminded me not long ago, she came to our house after it happened to tell me to my face that it was my fault. And I've asked myself since: Was it?

When I first met Calvin Bess in 1963, and those young people in the club were busy planning their party, Medgar Evers was still alive and those four little girls at Sixteenth Street Baptist Church in Birmingham thought they had their whole lives ahead of them. Most of the civil rights casualties had not yet begun to mount, so Calvin understood even less than I did how dangerous his activism might be. Perhaps, as so many young people do, he thought he was invincible. Or perhaps, like me, he did not feel truly alive because his people were not free.

I've often felt guilty about what happened to Calvin, as if those meetings with an impressionable young man eventually led to his death in the Mississippi swamp. But I have a feeling that even if I could have sat Calvin down and told him his future, he still would have wanted to fight. His father, like my parents, had taught him to stand up for his rights. He'd grown up on Liberty Street, after all. And as Rubin said, Calvin stood up in church that day.

He stood up.

# Sixteen

# Tananarive Due

**"No one can leave his character behind him when he goes on a journey."**
***—Yoruba proverb***

During my senior year in college, when I was bound for Lexington, Kentucky, to earn school credit by working as a reporter for the *Lexington Herald-Leader,* my family's code dictated that a young black woman did not drive alone through the South. So, although I was twenty years old and had worked at the *New York Times* and the *Miami Herald* in summer internships, my parents decreed that my father would drive with me to Lexington, and my mother would fly out to Lexington at the end of the term to drive back home with me. Period.

I was appalled at their plan, believing I was being babied. I tried to explain that times had changed, that the New South was the most integrated region in the country. They didn't want to hear it. Years of civil rights training had taught them that.

I tried to make the most of it. When my father took me to Lexington in the fall of 1986, we enjoyed a rare visit together during the two-day drive through the mountains and farmlands of the South, admiring the trees as their leaves made their spectacular visual sojourn from green to yellow, rust, orange, and red. It was a beautiful sight. I don't think I had ever spent that much time alone in my father's company, with no distractions for either of us, and it was a good time, filled with easy conversation. I was always happy to have Dad all to myself, far from his meetings and responsibilities, when he could release himself to his sense of humor. My father has a loud, abandon-filled laugh, and I've often wished he'd given himself more freedom to laugh every day the way he does when his thoughts are away from the world's troubles.

When Mom came to drive me back home, it was a different story. I swear, sometimes I think trouble goes out of its way to seek that woman out.

Although I could not have known it then, in many ways the drive home from Lexington with my mother was a prelude to numerous trips we would make in the years to come, researching this book together. At the time, although I'd heard many of the stories, thoughts of chronicling our family history were far from my mind. I was trying to finish my education, eager to launch my own career so I could move beyond the shadow of being John Due and Patricia Stephens Due's oldest daughter and find out who *I* was. I wanted to be a novelist.

By that time, I was glad Mom was with me for the drive. The unreliable Plymouth Horizon I'd been driving in Lexington had given me nothing but trouble, needing jump-starts from AAA on cold mornings at least once or twice a week. Mom, as usual, was behind the wheel. She couldn't relax when I was driving, she said.

The music stations faded in and out, and when they faded in, they were playing tinny-sounding country music instead of the Prince, Michael Jackson, or Tina Turner my mother and I would have preferred. Our only company on the road was a cheap plug-in CB radio my mother had given me as a safety precaution before I left Miami; it was powered by the cigarette lighter, and the antenna stuck on top of the car with a magnet. Its range reached the next few lanes and not much farther, but it was enough for us. With nothing else to do, we listened to that thing for hours, fascinated by the hidden world of the road and its mysterious language.

But it got old. After hearing endless trucker chatter peppered with sexual exploits and the N-word, there were times I thought about switching over to the Oak Ridge Boys or Alabama on the FM stations. "That's a shame," my mother said when she heard truckers comparing women's talents or warning each other about the whereabouts of Smokey Bear. But then, as if to prove my point about the change of heart in the South, we suddenly heard a white trucker rebuke a fellow trucker's litany of racial hatred.

"I don't have to listen to this crap," the man cut the racist off. "Why don't you bug out?"

*See?* I said, beaming at my mother. The New South.

Still, there was no mistaking the hot stares we received at a small-town Tennessee diner, where the white patrons went silent when we appeared in the doorway. In that instant, I could relate to what it must have felt like when my mother first walked up to a Tallahassee, Florida, lunch counter in 1960 to order food, precipitating her first arrest. We were served twenty-six years later—and we defiantly took our time while we ate—but we did not feel welcome.

Yes, it was time to get back home to the suburbs of Miami, I thought. We had entered some sort of alien territory where I did not understand the customs, and I'd had enough already.

The car had different plans. A tire blew out at 55 miles per hour on the expressway, forcing my mother to steer over four lanes to the shoulder with her usual aplomb under pressure, face set hard, eyes unblinking. I thanked God several times that I wasn't by myself. How would I have steered a car with a blown-out tire? Do you *pump* the brake or *floor* the brake?

After we'd come to a stop, we left the car running and climbed out to examine the blown-out tire. Instead of stopping, other cars flashed their headlights and honked as they passed. "Wonder what's wrong with them," I said, bracing for some insults. I felt very self-conscious and exposed as we stood beside our car.

My mother noticed the problem first: We were still in a traffic lane for merging, and cars were barreling toward us fast. "Let's move!" my mother cried, and we ran back to our seats, barely taking the time to close our car doors as my mother scooted the car over about six yards to the grassy shoulder, finally clear of the roadway.

Neither of us knew how to change a tire. My mother had learned during a driver's ed class in the 1950s, but she'd forgotten. We were nowhere near a phone, in the days when mobile phones were still a novelty. We were in the middle of Georgia, but neither of us knew where. Unless one of us was going to stand by the roadway with a hiked-up skirt used to flag down a passing car—and my mother and I both had watched too many horror movies to want to do that—all we had was the CB radio.

"This is, uh, Red Bird. We're a . . . four-wheeler, and we just blew a tire," I said uncertainly into the CB, exhausting the extent of the jargon I'd learned so far.

"What's your twenty, Red Bird?" a man's voice came back.

"Pardon me?"

"Where are you located?"

I read him the exit sign, and suddenly we were celebrities. The radio came alive with the talk of two ladies in a four-wheeler stuck with a flat. Really, it seemed like no time after our distress signal that a small panel truck pulled up behind us. A white man and his thirteen-year-old son hopped out and changed our tire, refusing any payment except our gratitude.

"We don't usually stop for motorists anymore," the man confided. "Nowadays, people just aren't grateful like they used to be." Well, we were grateful, and we sent them on their way with friendly waves. Just people helping people. We were amazed at the truckers' responsiveness to a plea for help. This was a side of road travel we had never been privy to.

When my mother stuck her key in the ignition, Red Bird didn't so much as chirp. Now it was the battery! That battery had beleaguered me throughout my internship, and now it was dead again. We were still stuck on the roadside, and the panel truck was long gone. We cursed and moaned, and Mom tried the ignition again. No luck. We went back to the CB.

"Negatory, Red Bird, we can't help," a trucker radioed in apology after our new plea. "I'm an eighteen-wheeler, and I'm too big to jump you. I'll give Smokey Bear a shout."

Good ol' Smokey Bear. Truckers spent all of their days and nights trying to dodge the state highway patrol, but they knew how to contact Smokey if there was a problem. And Mom and I were very glad to hear it.

"Thanks a lot, Good Buddy," I said, meaning it in the most literal sense.

About twenty minutes later, a state patrol car eased behind us. I saw a white trooper with large jowls and a western-style hat in the driver's seat, his eyes hidden by reflective sunglasses. He sat in his car, scribbling notes. We waited for him to get out of his car, but soon it became apparent that he wasn't moving anytime soon.

I gave Mom a questioning look. "Guess I'll go talk to him," I said.

I walked to the trooper's car and leaned into his open window. "Thanks for coming," I said. My voice sounded nervous to me, even though I had no idea why I should feel nervous. "This battery always acts up. We just need a jump and we'll be fine."

The patrolman scribbled on, not looking up or speaking. Yes, now I was definitely nervous. I paused, waiting to see if there might be a delayed response, but there was none. *Okay,* I told myself, *time to just back off and go sit in the car with Mom.*

"What'd he say?" Mom said as I climbed back inside our stalled car.

I shrugged. "Nothing."

So we sat and waited. Not talking. Not laughing. Just waiting.

As we sat and endless minutes passed, I imagined the pervasive intimidation my mother, and others like her, had met in the South. I had never had a personal issue with the police, not even one. In junior high school, at the same time I knew that Arthur McDuffie had been murdered at the hands of police, I was a member of my school's "Future Police Officers' Club" and anticipated visits from the club's sponsor, Officer Rosendale. I did not fear police. I never connected those cops who'd killed McDuffie with Officer Rosendale, who obviously cared about children. But in those long moments on the shoulder of the expressway somewhere in Georgia, I realized what a helpless, infuriating feeling it was to be wary of someone designated to protect me, and to feel the gnawing of his quiet hostility when I was most vulnerable.

How had my parents done it?

Many years later, when I had become a novelist, I taught on the faculty of the Imagination creative writing conference at Cleveland State University, and I met a Native American writer who told her own story of an encounter with a police officer on a lonely road. She was near the reservation, in a very deserted area, when a police officer turned on his lights to stop her car. She saw the lights and stopped. When the officer strode up to her window, instead of citing her for speeding or a broken taillight, he said, "Would you step out of the car?"

Get out of her car? Why? What was the problem? What had she done? There was just something in his tone. Something in his departure from procedure, which should have been to ask for a driver's license and registration. Something about losing the protection of her car when there wasn't another soul in sight, being asked to stand out in the open. She did not get out of her car. Instead, she slowly drove away. The police officer did not chase her. He let her go.

I know there are many Americans who would never understand what prompted her to behave as she did. But I understood, based on what had happened to me and my mother in Georgia as we drove my car home from Kentucky. For some of us, usual rules do not apply.

At last, there was movement from the trooper behind our car. He circled our car until he was facing us. Battery cables in hand, he popped his hood. We popped ours, then watched him link our batteries. One jolt did it. Our car's engine roared back to life.

I have no memory of that trooper speaking a single word to us. He never smiled. We might as well not have been there. It was as if as an officer of the law he was duty-bound to help us, but he was determined not to give us the tiniest measure of respect.

"Redneck," my mother and I muttered when he was gone.

Maybe he'd had a bad day. Maybe he'd jumped six cars since breakfast and could have told us to call AAA instead. But I felt an unease after that brush, one that sat in my stomach like a rock. My America was not the same one my parents had known, but the remnants of meaner times lingered on that expressway.

As the miles on the road passed, separating us from the spot where our car had been stalled, my mother and I felt our moods improving. The day belonged to us again. Our chatter resumed, and eventually our laughter. Because the CB radio had been so good to us, we turned it back on to hear our new friends. Nothing had changed since we'd listened last. The chatter we heard was bawdy and coarse, in merry Southern drawls, red-neck to the core.

I spotted a highway patrol car crouching in the bushes, so I grabbed the CB. "Watch out for Smokey around the bend," I said, just doing my part for our friends.

Seventeen

# PATRICIA STEPHENS DUE

**"Sticks in a bundle are unbreakable."**
***—Bondei proverb***

I had just been arrested again when I heard about the bombing of the Sixteenth Street Baptist Church in Birmingham in September 1963. For a moment, I felt paralyzed with disbelief. As much as we'd been going through, I still couldn't believe the people who opposed us could go to such lengths, bombing a church and killing innocent children.

Theater demonstrations had brought me to jail again. By now, mass demonstrations were becoming a more common sight across the United States. In addition to the demonstrations in Birmingham and the March on Washington, thousands of people were taking part in marches and pickets all over the South. Injuries against protesters were mounting, and jails were being filled to capacity.

In Tallahassee, students returning to campus after the summer break turned out in impressive numbers to be arrested in theater demonstrations, in wave after wave. First, on Saturday, September 14, about 200 of us went to the Florida Theatre to protest the theater's segregation policies. I'd had a wisdom tooth extracted that morning, but I went straight from the dentist's office to the Florida Theatre. Even though I never got my painkiller prescription filled, I didn't give my tooth another thought.

This time, the movie showing was *The Day Mars Invaded Earth*, and I'm certain it must have felt that way to many white onlookers who gazed at the thronging crowd of Negroes. A photograph of that day clearly shows me and John at that protest. I am wearing my dark glasses, as usual, and there is a very determined expression on my face, and a crowd of students is behind me, clapping and singing in front of the theater. Many of the students there, like FAMU business and education sophomore Doris Rutledge (who would later become a lifelong friend), brought money to purchase a movie ticket, then remained to protest when refused. When police tried to disperse us based on the injunction issued the spring before against large-scale protests, some of the students opted to leave, but 157 of us were arrested, including me, Doris Rutledge, Rubin Kenon, and Calvin Bess. Doris has told me how a police officer struck the inside of her left leg with his nightstick while she was being herded into a police van. Nothing was broken, she says, but it was so painful that she was afraid she might lose the leg, and the bruise lingered a long time. She suspects that her leg never healed properly from the blow; she had never had leg problems before, but her left leg remained weak and has thrown her off balance in the years since. "I'm thankful I have this leg," she told us at a civil rights reunion at my home in 1997, surrounded by activists who had stories of their own to tell. "It is a memory of trying to go someplace where everyone should have had a right to participate: going to a theater. I was beaten by a cop because that was all I wanted to do."[1]

Word of the arrests spread back to campus, and 450 students came to the jail to protest. Of those, ninety-one were arrested for disturbing the peace when they marched near the jail. The following morning, the day of the Sixteenth Street Baptist Church bombing, 250 students returned to the jail to protest. Most of them left after Rev. C. K. Steele, Rev. E. G. Evans, Rev. David Brooks, and some Florida A&M deans pleaded with them to avoid arrest, but a hundred students refused to leave, sitting calmly on the ground or praying, and they were arrested. The total number of students arrested in those two days was 348.[2]

Tallahassee's involved adults had their hands full with the mass protests, and it was considered a crisis in the city. Rev. Steele, remember, had been supportive of our direct action protests in the past, but clearly he believed our actions at that time were becoming too radical, resulting in expensive arrests. Some of our other adult friends in the community also believed we should have adhered to the judge's injunction, but we felt that our willingness to face arrest would accomplish more than programmed demonstrations of fewer than twenty students.

The decision was controversial, since the split between the more conservative NAACP and organizations like SNCC and CORE was growing at that time, and we had to rely many times on the NAACP and its lawyers to help us get our students out of jail. (One of the NAACP lawyers who was often there for us was Charles Wilson of Pensacola.) But Miss Young, FAMU's assistant registrar, understood. She made pleas on our behalf, telling NAACP officials, "These students, they want to do something. They're daring, and they want to do something, and this is what they did."

On October 3, Judge Ben Willis handed down his convictions. He was hardest on me and Rubin because we were considered the organizers. We were sentenced to $1,000 fines or six months in jail. The others who had been arrested at the theater were divided into groups. Those who had participated in the May theater demonstration, like Doris Rutledge, were fined $500 or three months in jail. A third group was sentenced to $250 or forty-five days in jail. The remaining 119 students received suspended sentences because Judge Willis believed they had been victims of "faulty leadership." He warned them, "You are not forgiven. . . . You are given the opportunity to prove you can conduct yourselves in a lawful and peaceful manner. You have many opportunities to serve your race, your community, your state, and your nation, all of them dignified and peaceful."[3]

Immediately, thirty-seven of the students decided they would go to jail rather than pay their fines, including Doris. It was a difficult decision, but Rubin and I decided we could do more good if we did not spend that time in jail. Not only did we hope to remain active as organizers, but we both were scheduled to begin student teaching in the field. I had an internship in Jacksonville, I was finally scheduled to graduate in January, and I really wanted to prove that activists could take part in demonstrations *and* complete their studies. But where would we find the money to help get so many students out of jail? CORE, as usual, had very little.

Miss Young and fired FAMU professor Richard Haley worked frantically to raise money, spending late nights at the CORE office on Floral Street waiting for telephone calls from the national NAACP office, the national CORE office, and any other organizations that would hear their pleas. Very late one night while they worked, Miss Young recalled, there was a knock at the door. They both looked at each other, nervous.

"Haley told me to go in the back, in the mimeograph room. He said, 'Go back there and unlock that back door, so if there's trouble, you get out of here. I'm going to answer the door.' It was just that dangerous during that time," Miss Young said. When Mr. Haley opened that door, he got one of the surprises of his life: Two white Tallahassee residents, a banker named George Lewis II and an entrepreneur named James Shaw, were standing outside the office in the dead of night. The men gave them $7,000 in cash.

"They didn't want it to be known," Miss Young said. In fact, I discovered later, it was such a secret that even Mr. Lewis's wife, a very liberal woman named Clifton Lewis, knew nothing about her husband's donation at the time. "He might have had to borrow it, or he might have had to sell stock. I don't know what he did. And I didn't know he did it, but I sure am glad he did," Mrs. Lewis told me years later, when we interviewed her not long after her husband died.

Despite being firmly established in Tallahassee's white power structure, at the time of the theater demonstrations George Lewis had recently suffered his own setbacks because of his political beliefs and activism. Mr. Lewis had chaired a committee that released a document entitled the *Report on the Florida Advisory Committee to the United States Commission on Civil Rights,* which severely criticized state officials and the lack of civil rights progress in Florida, comparing the state's practices to those in Mississippi and Alabama. As a result of his position on that committee, Mr. Lewis was removed as president of Lewis State Bank, the family bank. (He was named chairman of the board, but that was a nonvoting position, and therefore one with less power.) CORE had its account at Lewis State Bank, and it was one of the very few institutions that was willing to lend Negroes money in times of need. But on that night, George Lewis and James Shaw had come through with an outright gift, not a loan.

"I'll never forgot that night," Miss Young told me. "We sat there after they were gone. I said, 'Haley, there's a God somewhere. There's a God somewhere. There's a God somewhere.' "

One thing many people forget when they think in terms of the civil rights movement is that there were many whites, as well as Negroes, who put their lives and livelihoods at risk. All of us worked together, whether it was the white FSU students who bought movie tickets for Negroes to try to gain entrance, white students who went to jail, or the white community members who gave time and money to help the cause. But you see, I never simply saw it as a *black* cause, because any system in place to oppress blacks ultimately oppresses everyone. I have always believed that none of us can be free until all of us are free. Many Tallahassee whites had learned that lesson during the 1960 jail-in, when they were not permitted to visit us to show their support. The white ministers and rabbis who came to Tallahassee during the 1961 Freedom Ride learned it when they were trying to order food at the municipal airport, and they later served jail time for that "offense." James and Lillian Shaw (who later became two of Tananarive's godparents) had always understood the oppressive nature of discrimination, and so had George and Clifton Lewis.

George Lewis II was president of Lewis State Bank and chairman of the Florida Advisory Committee of the U.S. Civil Rights Commission, and the Lewises were both very involved. In May 1963, for example, Clifton Lewis participated in what CORE called the "Courtroom Project," where whites purposely sat in the all-Negro section of the courtroom to protest segregation. They had long-standing community connections: George Lewis had been the college roommate of C. Farris Bryant, who later became a segregationist governor of Florida. The Lewises' activism was a cause of concern among some whites in Tallahassee. They were once warned by a newspaper reporter that their telephones were wiretapped because of their involvement. Asked to describe one of the most frightening experiences of her involvement, Clifton Lewis, who at eighty-two, at this writing, is still politically active in Tallahassee, remembered being at home alone at dusk when she got a telephone call from an acquaintance. "He said, 'Mrs. Lewis, are you there by yourself?' And I said, 'Yes.' He said, 'You have a lot of glass in that house, don't you?' I said, 'Yes,' " Mrs. Lewis said—the caller was aware that her secluded Frank Lloyd Wright home had an entire wall made of glass. "And he said, 'Well, I've just gotten the grapevine from Gainesville. You better get down in that cellar. They're headed your way with a bomb from Gainesville. I've just called to tell you.' " Then the phone clicked off.

"I didn't have a car," Mrs. Lewis says. "I was here by myself. I don't know where George was, but thank heavens there were no children here. And we didn't get a bomb. But that was very scary."

Their young son Ben, too, paid a price because he attended Leon County High School after it finally integrated in the fall of 1963. In part, Ben was targeted because everyone knew his father was on the Civil Rights Advisory Committee, and in part because of his own beliefs. When three Negro students were scheduled to attend the school, school administrators warned the Negro students' families that they could not take physical education or have physical contact with white students, and that they should avoid the bathrooms because their safety could not be guaranteed. As for the white students, the principal told them they should ignore the Negro students. No one was to speak to a Negro. No one was to smile at a Negro.[4]

In the cafeteria, if a Negro student tried to sit at the table, the white students got up and moved, and young Ben Lewis didn't agree with that. He tried to do his small part to make the Negro students feel welcome, his mother says. "Ben would go sit at that table with them. But he wouldn't talk to them or smile," she says. Still, that small gesture was enough to arouse white students' ire. "He was afraid for his life to go to the restroom at Leon High, because that's where they would get him," Mrs. Lewis recalls. As Ben was leaving school to walk home one day, a car pulled up beside him and four young white men jumped out. Much to Ben's horror, they forced him into their car at gunpoint. After the car screeched away with Ben held in the backseat, the car passed a group of Negroes standing beside the street. The captors rolled the back window down. "Go on, say it, you nigger lover! Call them niggers. Call them coons. That's what they are. *Say it!"* they ordered. Reluctantly, but honestly afraid that the gun might fire even accidentally, Ben did as he was told. *"Niggers!"* he screamed out the window.

Only then did the young men let him go. Ben didn't tell his mother that story until he was in his forties, after his father had died. But his parents did know about another incident, when Ben's car got stuck in the sand at Alligator Point, a secluded spot where he'd gone to "spoon" with his girlfriend, his mother says, and some white men beat him up and destroyed his car. His date, luckily, was unharmed.

Despite the threats to their family, like the Steeles, the Lewises always stayed involved. George Lewis died in 1996 at the age of eighty-two, before I could interview him for this book, but he and his family were more unsung soldiers in the civil rights cause.

---

In the fall of 1963, only hours before the theater demonstration and the resulting arrests, some white students from the University of Florida in Gainesville, 150 miles southeast of Tallahassee, came to town. One was a tall woman with white-blond hair named Judith (Judy) Benninger, another was her boyfriend, a curly-haired man named Mike Geison, and the third was a lanky, pleasant-featured young man named Daniel (Dan) Harmeling. After spending the summer working with the Ocala NAACP branch and Bettie Wright with Dunnellon CORE, Judy and the others had come to Tallahassee to learn leadership skills and to take part in activities. "I was opening up my paper at least once a week, or once every two weeks, and seeing yet another demonstration or action Pat was involved in, so I actually went looking for her," Judy told me and

Tananarive in an interview in 1990, explaining how we had met. At the time we interviewed her, Judy was very ill with breast cancer, and her friends had assembled a video crew to document this brave woman's place in Florida history, both in civil rights and women's rights.

Judy had taken the lessons she learned in civil rights to the women's movement, coauthoring a paper with Beverly Jones in 1968 entitled "Towards a Female Liberation Movement," which has been widely anthologized and is credited with helping to launch the women's liberation movement. She cofounded Gainesville Women's Liberation in 1968, the first women's liberation group in the South. She also became another of Tananarive's godmothers. (Tananarive had several, since so many people I knew from the Movement wanted to feel like a part of our daughter's life.) "I was sort of pushing myself on Pat, and following her around trying to learn from her, and also trying to get to know her because I had never seen a woman lead like that. I had spent the whole summer watching men lead and do a very good job of it, but there was something for me about the fact that she was a woman. And she was also, as far as I was concerned, the best that I had seen, male or female, in terms of really teaching as well as mobilizing," Judy said.[5]

A demonstration was planned the very day Judy arrived in Tallahassee, so the group from the University of Florida got a very sudden, unexpected initiation from us. As Dan recalls, he and his twin brother, Jim, had recently started attending NAACP meetings in Ocala, and Dan had come to Tallahassee to get even more deeply involved. Tallahassee was an eye-opener to him, Dan told me later. "In Gainesville, when we would have ten or fifteen people, with each person who joined the picket line, we'd feel just this enormous sense of strength. Now we were in a group that had literally hundreds of people willing to demonstrate," he says.[6]

The next thing he knew, the demonstrators in front of the Florida Theatre were being warned that they were about to be arrested. Immediately after the warning, before Dan could make a conscious decision, he realized he was being herded toward a police van. Dan hadn't planned to get arrested in Tallahassee, but once he realized he was getting arrested, he wanted to show his solidarity with the other students. Because there were so few white demonstrators, there was room for Dan at the Leon County jail instead of the fairgrounds, which was where I'd been sent with many other Negroes. He was jailed along with two other white male participants, Florida State University students Steve Jones and a soft-spoken young man with a slight build named Frank O'Neil, who would soon take my place as chairman of Tallahassee CORE. Once he was inside his cell, Dan says, the sobering reality of what had happened finally hit him. "Realizing I was being locked up, I just felt this overwhelming sense of being a prisoner," he says. "All these gates were things I couldn't open, and I was in a place where I was being held—whether I willed to be there or not. I remember waking up all night long listening to that clanging of the doors as they brought more people in."[7]

Neither Dan nor Judy had ever been jailed before that day, and neither had many of the other participants from FAMU. Some had taken part in the May protests, but others had only become involved as a result of recent mass meetings and rallies. John and I had tried to get the word out that arrest was a possibility, explaining that CORE did not have the funds to bail people out of jail, but some of the students who participated had not been present at those informational sessions, unfortunately. As I mentioned earlier, this became a real bone of contention with groups like the NAACP, because frantic parents deluged the NAACP with telephone calls, expecting to get their children out of jail. As far as the NAACP was concerned, CORE whipped the students into an emotional frenzy, but then took no responsibility for them. Besides, the NAACP had long held that courtroom action, not direct action, was the means to equal rights, and we students were considered too unruly.

Judy's mother, Ernestine Benninger, had been raised in the Baha'i faith, and she believes she passed on that religion's principle of equality among the races to her daughter. Still, she was completely unprepared for the 2:00 A.M. telephone call that awakened her and her husband in Gainesville. The man on the phone was Dr. Marshall Jones, and he was a faculty member at the University of Florida who was very involved in that campus's student movement. He told them that Judy had been arrested in Tallahassee and that she was in jail, but he gave no other details. "Our first reaction was 'Oh my God!' " Mrs. Benninger recalled. She hadn't known her daughter was in Tallahassee, much less why. She and her husband called the Leon County jail immediately, only to be told it was closed until 9:00 A.M. "So we lay there like boards until about 6:00 or 6:30, and got up and went up there. And she was really scared, because that was a Saturday night, and the women in the jail knew why these girls were there, and they really harassed them about what they were doing and why they were doing it."[8]

Judy's arrest reached the newspaper in Gainesville, to her family's mortification, but they were relieved to discover that Judy's name was misspelled. Still, some people her family had considered friends simply had nothing to do with them after that. Later, Judy's father, Lawrence Benninger, told his wife and daughter that he'd been in line for a vice presidency at the University of Florida, where he was a professor, but he was withdrawn from consideration after Judy's arrest.

Judy was among the students from the theater demonstration who chose to stay in jail rather than paying her fine after the trial. After their convictions, Judy and the three other white women arrested at the demonstration—including FSU students Rosemary Dudley, Mary Ann Stevens, and Elaine Simon—were tormented in jail. The guards promised that any prisoners who beat them up would be granted favors, so at night two women in a nearby cell tied razor blades to broomsticks and jabbed through the bars, stabbing at the civil rights demonstrators from a distance. Judy and the others were forced to crowd together at the edge of their bunks to avoid the weapons.[9]

Judy stayed in jail for a week after her trial before her parents came and paid her fine to free her. She later told me she was furious when her parents paid the fine, calling their act "unforgivable." She and others had agreed they would stay in jail until everyone could get out. "A lot of people had gotten out by that time, but I felt that the white people should stay until the end. I was very embarrassed that my parents had done that," Judy said.

Dan Harmeling, Steve Jones, and Frank O'Neil also chose to go to jail rather than pay their fines, a decision that became frightening right away. As soon as they were escorted to the cell block, the other white inmates began screaming to the guards, "Let them in! We'll take care of them!" Their stay after their initial arrest had been without incident, but the mood had changed drastically. Dan recalls that Steve Jones insisted, "We're not going to go in there. If we go in there, all we'll get is beaten up." The guard agreed. Instead of locking them in the regular cells, he took them to what he called a "security area," which was solitary confinement. Dan and Steve Jones were placed in one cell, which Dan says was like "a closet," and Frank O'Neil was alone in the other. Inside those cells were no lights.

"Our food was brought to us and put through a slot in the door, and then if we wanted to see what we were eating, what was on our plates, we had to hold our food out of the slot and then look as the dim light shone on the food," Dan recalls. They got no exercise because they were not allowed to leave their cell. They had only beds, a commode, and a small sink for drinking water. After five days, they agreed to pay their fines.

20 The Philadelphia Tribune [illegible] May 24, 1960

Put On Weight In Jail:

# Sisters Jailed In Student Lunch Counter Protest Visit Here; Tell Of Experiences

By RUTH ROLEN

The stout-hearted Stephens sisters, Priscilla Gwendolyn, 21, and Patricia Gloria, 20, were refused lunch counter service at McCrorey's and Sears and Roebuck in Tallahassee, Fla., before they received 60-day jail sentences for participating in student protests there.

Priscilla and Patricia are juniors at Florida A&M College where they are majoring in Elementary Education and Instrumental Music, respectively. Accompanied by their mother, Mrs. Lottie M. Hamilton, they are on tour under auspices of the Congress of Racial Equality.

**WORKSHOP**

The sisters were introduced to CORE while vacationing in Miami last September. After attending a National CORE Workshop on the non-violent technique of protest against discrimination, they joined the cause.

On Nov. 1, Patricia organized the off-campus chapter of which she is now secretary in Tallahassee. While most of the ministers, physicians and other professionals enrolled are colored, the majority of students are white. These students are from the all-white Florida State University.

Faculty members from both of the state-supported schools belong to the chapter. While A & M's president, Dr. George W. Gore, does not express disapproval of CORE, he intimates that his job comes first.

**FIELD SECRETARIES**

At the chapter meetings, the first of which was held on October 22, CORE field secretaries were present. They incl[illegible] Carey

became t trusty, and Priscilla have a common complaint—townspeople brought them so much food that they got fat.

"To The Bitter End"

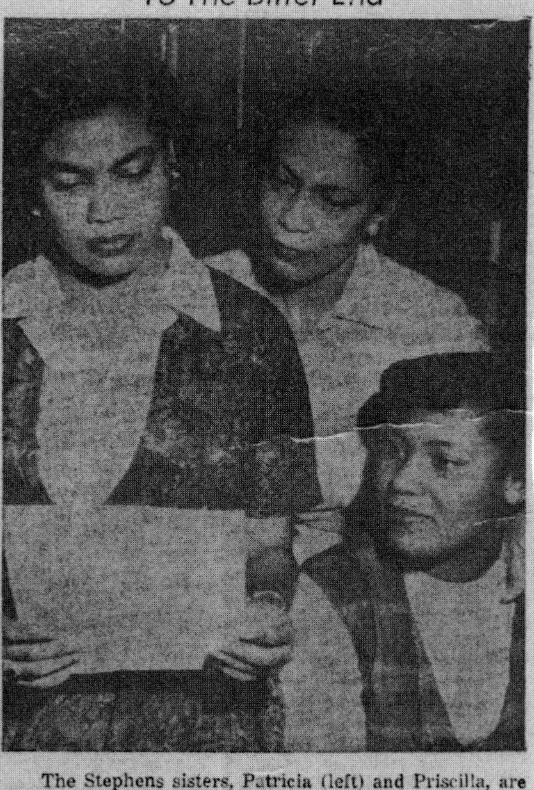

The Stephens sisters, Patricia (left) and Priscilla, are shown with their mother, Mrs. Lottie Hamilton, during a visit to this city while on tour from Tallahassee, Fla.

(Left to right) *Patricia Stephens, Mrs. Lottie Hamilton (mother of Patricia and Priscilla), and Priscilla Stephens. The Stephens sisters were on a national speaking tour after spending forty-nine days in jail for sitting-in at a Woolworth lunch counter in Tallahassee, Florida. Their mother accompanied them on the tour because they were minors.*

*(Photo from The Philadelphia Tribune, May 24, 1960)*

(Above, left to right) *Priscilla Stephens, Walter Stephens, Lottie Hamilton (their mother, standing behind them), Patricia Stephens, their stepfather, Marion Hamilton, and, seated, their grandmother, Mrs. Alma E. Peterson (Mrs. Hamilton's mother), posing in front of their home in Belle Glade, Florida, in Palm Beach County around 1955. (Due Family Collection)*

*Richard Allen Powell, the father of Lottie Hamilton, the parent who raised her. (Due Family Collection)*

*Patricia Stephens holding her favorite doll as she stands with her sister, Priscilla, and their mother, Mrs. Lottie Hamilton, in their yard in Belle Glade around 1950. Mrs. Hamilton went out of her way to get Negro dolls for her girls to make certain that they loved themselves. (Due Family Collection)*

(Below, left to right) *Priscilla Gwendolyn Stephens, Marion Hamilton (Daddy Marion), and Patricia Gloria Stephens in band uniforms in Belle Glade, where Daddy Marion was band director as well as the Social Studies teacher. He had once played with Lionel Hampton's band. Priscilla played the flute and Patricia played the trumpet and bassoon. Patricia and Priscilla both raised money to buy the band uniforms. (Due Family Collection)*

*A 1959 photo of the Congress of Racial Equality (CORE) workshop at the Sir John Hotel in Miami's Overtown, where Patricia and Priscilla Stephens first learned about CORE.* Seated, left to right: *Mrs. Shirley Zoloth, one of the people who persuaded Mrs. Hamilton to let Patricia and Priscilla participate; Patricia Stephens; person unknown; Vera Williams from St. Louis CORE; and Priscilla Stephens.* Standing, left to right: *Jim Dewar; Zev Aelony (interviewed for* Freedom in the Family*); person unknown; James T. McCain, a CORE field secretary from Sumter, S.C. who celebrated his ninety-seventh birthday in March 2002; and Gordon Carey, CORE field secretary. (Due Family Collection)*

*Patricia Stephens, a student at all-black Florida A&M University, talks to a student from all-white Florida State University while picketing for the right to eat at a lunch counter in December 1960 in Tallahassee, Florida. (Courtesy of the Florida State Archives)*

*Patricia Stephens looks on as Priscilla points at a police officer during the December 1960 demonstration. Officers had refused to respond to hecklers threatening students on the picket line. (Courtesy of the Florida State Archives)*

*FAMU students on March 12, 1960, as they marched downtown to protest the arrest of fellow FAMU students. On the far right, behind the sign that says "Give Us Back Our Students," is William Larkins, incoming Student Government Association President at FAMU, and one of the students who later spent forty-nine days in jail for the February 20, 1960, arrest at Woolworth. Patricia Stephens had teargas thrown in her eyes during this march. (Courtesy of the Florida State Archives)*

*St. Augustine dentist and activist Dr. Robert Hayling speaks as John D. Due Jr. and other activists look on. Dr. Hayling was badly beaten by the Ku Klux Klan in the 1960s. (Courtesy of the Florida State Archives)*

*Florida Theatre demonstration held after an injunction limited to eighteen the number of people allowed to picket. Patricia Stephens Due is shown in black dress and dark glasses; John D. Due's head appears above the cap of the police officer. This demonstration resulted in six-month jail sentences for Patricia Stephens Due and Rubin Kenon, both FAMU student leaders. Under pressure from the Board of Control, FAMU president Dr. George W. Gore suspended them from school after their arrests. (Courtesy of the Florida State Archives)*

*During a protest against segregated lunch counters in December 1960, FAMU student Nathaniel Williams is pushed from the sidewalk to the street by racist white hoodlums while holding a picket sign that says "Join Us in Our Fight for Freedom." To his left is Henry Marion Steele, a high school student who had been arrested earlier at a Woolworth lunch counter. White CORE member Barbara LaCombe climbs into her car to escape the melee. (Photographer: Stephen K. Beasley)*

*With money in his hand, FAMU student Benjamin Cowins tries to get service at a McCrory's lunch counter on February 21, 1961. He looks toward the waitress, who is ignoring him. Two weeks later he was arrested at a Neisners lunch counter, which led to his spending thirty days in jail. (Photo from the collection of Benjamin Cowins)*

*Calvin Bess, who died under suspicious circumstances in 1967 while registering black voters in Mississippi. (Photo from the collection of Cherrye Bess Branch)*

MRS. FRANKLIN D. ROOSEVELT

May 31, 1960

I would like you to join me for luncheon on Monday, June 20th to take action in the emergency situation confronting the Congress of Racial Equality (CORE). For the past year CORE has led the struggle in the South and throughout the country to bring full equality to all our people. In the course of their struggle, CORE staff persons and the young college students with whom they have worked have done what every one of us wish we had the courage to do. They have peacefully assembled in a series of now-historic sit-in demonstrations. They have used non-violent tactics to assert their human rights. Many have gone to jail in what I believe to be the truest American tradition -- to sacrifice oneself for the right even though alone in the struggle.

At our emergency conference we will have an opportunity to meet and hear Patricia Stephens, a 21-year-old Negro student at Florida A. & M. University. Patricia has just finished serving, together with her sister and three other students, a 60-day sentence for participation in a sit-in demonstration. This girl, believing fervently in the justice of her cause, refused to appeal to a higher court because she strongly believed in the Rev. Martin Luther King's words: "We must fill the jails in order to win equal rights."

Such courage deserves our admiration and respect. More than that, it gives everyone of us confidence in the future of our country. Her example tells us that nothing will stop the winning of full equality for all our citizens so long as girls like Patricia are prepared to make such sacrifices.

Understaffed and underfinanced, CORE has stretched its meager resources to the breaking point to meet the many demands for guidance from college students like Patricia. Today CORE faces a summer of financial crisis. It is to take action to help CORE that I am inviting you and other friends to meet Patricia Stephens and myself for luncheon at the Plaza Hotel, Fifth Avenue and 59th Street, in New York City on Monday June 20, at 12:30 P.M.

I hope that we will all show equal readiness to sacrifice in helping CORE even if our sacrifice is small compared to that made by Patricia Stephens and her fellow students. Will you please let me know at your convenience that you will be with me for lunch on Monday, June 20?

Sincerely,

Eleanor Roosevelt

(Above) *Letter inviting supporters to a luncheon to hear Patricia Stephens talk about her forty-nine days in jail. Mrs. Eleanor Roosevelt hosted the gathering for CORE to raise funds for activists in the South. Jackie Robinson and Daisy Bates, organizer of the Little Rock Nine who integrated Central High School for the 1957–58 school term, also attended. (Due Family Collection)*

(Left) *Patricia Stephens Due and John D. Due Jr. in April 1963, four months after they married. (Due Family Collection)*

(Above) *James and Lydia Stewart Graham, who raised John D. Due Jr. (Due Family Collection)*

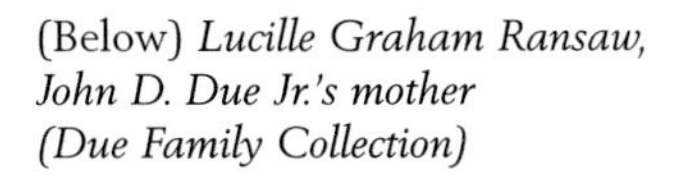

(Below) *Lucille Graham Ransaw, John D. Due Jr.'s mother (Due Family Collection)*

(Right) *Rev. C. K. Steele congratulates John D. Due Jr. as he graduates from FAMU's law school in April 1963. (Due Family Collection)*

*John D. Due Jr. speaks on FAMU's campus to remind students of the consequences of their actions in demonstrations.* Looking on, left to right: *Doris Rutledge, who was arrested several times and later became a CORE field worker; Patricia Stephens Due; Rubin Kenon, suspended from FAMU for his activism; and others. (From the collection of Doris Rutledge Hart)*

*Tananarive's dedication, 1966.* Back row, left to right: *Mrs. Susan Ausley, an activist at a time when it was dangerous for whites to be involved (she later became Johnita's godmother); James and Lillian Shaw, activists and Tananarive's godparents (James Shaw secretly gave bond money to Richard Haley and Daisy Young to get students out of jail); Rev. Grant A. Butler, the minister, and Mrs. Candaisy Blackshear; Horace Walter Stephens, Tananarive's uncle; and Dr. Irene Johnson, one of Patricia Stephens Due's FAMU professors.* Front row, left to right: *Wanda Crutcher, daughter of Rev. James and Addie Crutcher, Quincy, Florida, activists; Mrs. Dorothy C. Jones, one of Tananarive's godparents and former elementary teacher of Patricia Stephens Due (Mrs. Jones allowed Patricia to live with her in the early sixties when it was very dangerous); John D. Due (holding Tananarive); Patricia Stephens Due; and Mrs. Addie Crutcher holding Stephen Crutcher. (Photographer: Stephen K. Beasley)*

*The 1971 Poor People's March from Miami to Tallahassee, sponsored by the Southern Christian Leadership Conference to demand prison reform, an improved welfare system, and greater political representation. Lydia and Johnita Due, daughters of Patricia and John Due, headed the march, being pushed in a double stroller by Rev. Ralph Abernathy, head of SCLC, and Miami community activist Mrs. Gladys Taylor, with Rev. James Orange and other SCLC staffers participating. Lydia learned to walk on this march. (Johnson of Miami)*

(Below) *Johnita Due sits with lawmakers as she serves as a page in the Florida Legislature.* Left to right: *Rep. William "Bill" Flynn from Miami, a former restaurant owner who, in the 1960s, threatened blacks with bodily harm if they came in his restaurant, but repented later and asked the Dues to allow Johnita to stay with him and his wife in Tallahassee; Rep. Arnett Girardeau, Johnita's sponsor, from Jacksonville (a dentist and member of the NAACP Executive Board, one of the first black senators in Florida); Johnita; Rep. Carrie Meek, who later became Florida's first female senator and now sits in the U.S. House of Representatives; Rep. Joe Kershaw, from Miami, the first black in the Florida House since Reconstruction. (Due Family Collection)*

(Above) *Fourteen-year-old Tananarive Due speaks at the seventy-first NAACP convention in Miami Beach after winning a gold medal in the Afro-American Cultural, Technology, and Scientific Olympics, dubbed ACT-SO, in the area of Original Essay. ACT-SO, an Olympics of the mind, was the brainchild of Vernon Jarrett, a journalist from Chicago, who wanted black youth to compete in the academic arena as they do in the sports arena. (Lee's Photos / Columbus Lee)*

*Tananarive Due receives a gold medal in the ACT-SO essay competition at the 1980 NAACP Convention. Dr. Benjamin Mays, former president of Morehouse College, stands to her left; to her right is Lerone Bennett Jr., historian and author of* Before the Mayflower. *(Lee's Photos / Columbus Lee)*

(Right) *The Due family meets presidential candidate Jimmy Carter in October 1976.* Left to right: *Tananarive; John D. Due Jr.; Patricia Stephens Due; and Rep. Gwendolyn Cherry, one of Florida's first black representatives. Lydia Due sits in front of Carter and Johnita Due sits in front of Rep. Cherry. (President Carter later signed this photo.) (Johnson of Miami)*

*Judy Benninger* (left) *of Gainesville, Florida, former student activist and CORE worker, feminist activist, civil rights lawyer, and one of Tananarive's godparents, chats with Patricia Stephens Due. (Due Family Collection)*

*Tananarive Due presenting the John D. Due Jr. and Patricia Stephens Due Freedom Scholarship to FAMU. Dr. Frederick Humphries, on Tananarive's left, looks on with Patricia Stephens Due and John Due. (Photographer: Keith Pope)*

Right to left: *Patricia Stephens Due with Kwame Turé (Stokely Carmichael) and his mother, Mrs. Mabel Carmichael. (Due Family Collection)*

*Photo of Patricia Stephens Due that appeared in the Tallahassee Democrat surrounded by articles about her Civil Rights involvement. (Tallahassee Democrat, Mike Ewen)*

*Patricia Stephens Due raises her arms as she makes a point at the memorial service for Judy Benninger in Gainesville, Florida, in June 1991. (Due Family Collection)*

*The Gathering was a reunion of civil rights activists hosted in the home of Patricia Stephens Due and John D. Due Jr. in Miami, Florida, in 1997.* First row, left to right: *Miles McCray, Mrs. Athea Hayling, Doris Rutledge Hart, Patricia Stephens Due, Mrs. Lottie Hamilton Sears Houston, and Priscilla Stephens Kruize.* Second row, left to right: *Johnita Patricia Due, Jeff Greenup, Clarence Edwards, Ulysses Baety, John D. Due Jr., Dan Harmeling, Tananarive Priscilla Due, Mrs. Vivian Kelly, and Dr. Robert Hayling. (The Gathering is covered in detail in Chapter 24.) (Photographer: Lee A. Waters, Jr.)*

*October 15, 2000: The Due women at Johnita Due's wedding.* Left to right: *Lydia (pregnant with Jordan, her second child); Johnita, the bride; Mrs. Lottie Sears Houston, the proud grandmother of the bride; Patricia Stephens Due, mother of the bride; and Tananarive Due, sister of the bride. This was the last group photo with Mrs. Lottie Sears Houston and her family. Mrs. Houston died at the age of eighty on December 25, 2000. (Lee's Photos / Columbus Lee)*

*Due shares a moment with her grandchildren,* left to right: *Tananarive's stepdaughter, Nicki, and Lydia's sons, Justin and Jordan, during the Christmas and Kwaanza celebration in 2001. (Due Family Collection)*

*Tananarive Due and her mother's Great Dane, Samson, await the beginning of the next interview in the home office and library of Patricia Stephens Due. (Due Family Collection)*

*At the ninety-seventh birthday celebration for James T. McCain in March 2002, the student leaders who became CORE field secretaries in the 1960s are reunited.* Left to right: *Patricia Stephens Due, Dave Dennis, Thomas Gaither, and Rudy Lombard. (Photo from the Due family collection)*

*The Due family portrait in January 2000.* Front row, left to right: *Lydia Due, John D. Due Jr., Patricia Stephens Due with grandson Justin Greisz, Mrs. Lottie Sears Houston (Patricia's mother)*; back row, left to right: *Jonathan Greisz, Lydia's husband; Tananarive Due and her husband, Steven Barnes; and Johnita Patricia Due and Mark Willoughby (now her husband). (Photographer: Lee A. Waters, Jr.)*

Doris Rutledge, a Negro student at FAMU, was determined to stay in jail, but she too could remain only a little more than a week because her mother paid her fine, and she was forced to leave. So many people were in jail, Doris recalls, that a Negro woman locked up with them complained that police had gone out and arrested her just so she could cook for all the inmates. To protest her incarceration, Doris staged a hunger strike during most of her stay.

There was one point of relief: Word circulated among them that higher-ups had given orders that no harm should come to any of them, in no small part, I'm certain, because of the fear of bad publicity. Still, some of the civil rights prisoners did not just adjust well to being in jail, and Doris remembers hearing one woman crying. Impatient with the woman's tears, Doris brashly announced, "I don't feel sorry for anybody except Ruby McCollum!"

To Negroes in Florida, Ruby McCollum was a legendary example of how a Negro woman had been wronged by a racist system. The noted Harlem Renaissance writer Zora Neale Hurston had written about Ruby McCollum's trial for the *Pittsburgh Courier* in 1952, and my family had followed that trial closely.

On August 3, 1952, Mrs. McCollum, a Negro woman from Live Oak, Florida, whose husband had built a small fortune running numbers, shot a white doctor dead. The doctor, Clifford LeRoy Adams, was a popular man planning to run for governor. She never denied killing him, and prosecutors claimed she'd done it over a doctor bill she didn't want to pay, but the case had never felt right to those of us who heard about it. It came out later that Mrs. McCollum had been sentenced to die without having the opportunity to tell her version of what had happened: that she and Adams had a long-standing affair, he was extorting money from her, he beat her, she'd already had one child by him and was pregnant with another, and she had reason to believe he was planning to kill her. (Mrs. McCollum lost Adams's second baby in jail.) Live Oak's white establishment was desperate to keep their relationship a secret, so those details were not permitted in court, just as Mrs. McCollum's history of mental problems had never been brought out. After a long fight by journalists and her attorney, Mrs. McCollum's death sentence was overturned and she was committed to a mental hospital.[10]

When Doris said she didn't feel sorry for anyone but Ruby McCollum, the other protesters got the message and grew silent. At that instant, Doris noticed a quiet woman she'd known from the campus, Kay McCollum. Doris had a sudden realization: This was Ruby McCollum's daughter. She had never made the connection before, but she suddenly recognized Kay's name from the book she had read about Ruby McCollum. Doris and the soft-spoken young woman made eye contact. "I apologized to her, and she said there was no need to," Doris says. "That was a real different kind of experience for me, because there was just so much pain and history. In my mind, even though I thought I had experienced some kind of discrimination by not going to the theater, these people have destroyed her life."

Kay McCollum, in her willingness to go to jail to change the system that helped destroy her family, was taking her life back. Maybe, to her, that was a way she and her mother would both be free.

---

In the fall of 1963, I was assigned to a student internship in social studies at a high school in Jacksonville, where I was ironically assigned to civics teacher Rutledge Pearson, who happened to be the state NAACP president. Mr. Pearson believed in having his students see their government at work, and consequently my first official activity was to accompany him downtown with his civics classes to Mayor Haydon Burns's office. (Burns later became governor of Florida.) I had been in Jacksonville only about a week when I was called back to Tallahassee, where I was notified that Rubin Kenon and I had been indefinitely suspended from FAMU.

The Board of Control wanted us out, and Dr. Gore bowed to their pressure. Although I wish he had been stronger, I have tried to appreciate, over the years, what a difficult position he was in. It was bad enough that after our arrest Dr. Gore told the press, in a statement showcased on the front page of the *Tallahassee Democrat*, "What [the students] have been doing is a waste of their time and ours and is not in the best interest of our institution or of the students."[11] Giving lip service to the power structure was one thing, but now he was interfering with my ability to complete my studies. And I was so close to finally getting my degree! Rubin, too, was crushed. "It was a thing that broke out tears," he says.

Rutledge Pearson, the state NAACP president and my student teaching director, was also outraged. He wrote a letter to President Gore, stating,

"It is not our intention to idly stand by while these two young Americans are caused to suffer for rebellion against a system of living which is not of their making." He then threatened if we were not reinstated to launch a statewide boycott of FAMU's famed annual Orange Blossom Classic parade in Miami. He sent copies of his letter to both President Kennedy and Attorney General Robert Kennedy, but Dr. Gore was not swayed.[12]

Unfortunately, Rubin actually suffered a nervous breakdown. Soon after learning he had been suspended from school, all the stress of the previous months caught up with him. He committed himself to a mental hospital in northern Florida, but during his two-month stay, he never lost sight of his goal of equality. When he wanted to visit the institution's library, he was told there was one library for white patients and one for Negro patients, and he was enraged. He organized patients into pickets to protest the segregated libraries. "I'll never forget, the administrator was a Harvard graduate, and he said, 'I want to help you get out of here. What can we do to get you out of here?' " he recalls.

Rubin's hospitalization was very hard on his mother. "My mother cried all the time. She would come to see me and start crying," he says, pointing out that she had remained calm during the large-scale protests, when he felt the danger was much greater. "And I would wonder why she was crying, because I was okay. *Now* you start crying!" he says.

I can only imagine how Rubin's mother felt. At this point, with more bombings and attacks against civil rights activists in the news, my own mother probably would have been happy to see me leave behind my life as a civil rights activist the way Priscilla had after the police officer kicked her. But Mother never wavered in her support, and after I poured out my heart to her on the telephone, she sent me an inspirational postcard printed with the saying, "TOUGH TIMES NEVER LAST . . . BUT TOUGH PEOPLE DO!" On the back of the postcard, she wrote her typical encouragement, *Have Hope and remember the saying on this note—there are better days ahead.*

Rubin and I tried to fight through legal means. Right away, Tobias Simon filed a temporary restraining order in U.S. District Court to try to enjoin the Board of Control, Dr. Gore, and FAMU from carrying out the suspension. A month later, a federal judge in Tallahassee dismissed our lawsuit, refusing to allow me or Rubin to return to FAMU. Some FAMU students showed their support for us by staging a "sleep-in" outside Dr. Gore's home, but to little effect. FAMU's faculty senate met and issued a vote of confidence in Dr. Gore, supporting our suspension. For now, at least, Rubin and I were out of school.

I had at least one bit of good news: On November 15, 1963, John officially became a member of the Florida bar and a practicing attorney. Since we were no longer eligible for student housing, John and I rented our first real house at 3108 Galimore Drive in Tallahassee. We got a second German shepherd we named "Freedom."

One afternoon in November, I was at home having a rare moment of relaxation, watching *As the World Turns,* when a newscaster interrupted with shocking news from Dallas: President Kennedy had been shot. It was November 22, 1963. I sat for a moment in disbelief, then I called John in St. Augustine, Florida, where he was defending his first official client. We could hardly believe what had happened. I held my breath, praying that the president was still alive, that he would survive. Soon the word was official: President Kennedy was dead.

President Kennedy's actions on the civil rights front had often been too slow for our liking, but we had held out hope that he would carry out his promises to push through civil rights legislation. Like many Negro activists in Florida, I'd written President Kennedy a letter that June, asking him not to grant federal money to a 400th birthday commemoration scheduled in 1965 in St. Augustine because it would signify "federal support to this celebration of four hundred years of slavery and segregation."

I was stunned. I could not believe it. It was pure chaos. In my lifetime, this was the first time a president had been killed while he was serving in the nation's highest office. I knew politically who would succeed him, but John and I both had the same thought in our minds: What would happen to the nation and the struggle now? We realized how many others felt the same way as our phone continued to ring for weeks and weeks, with callers asking that same question. Although President Kennedy had moved much more slowly than I had wanted him to, a lot of us thought he was a good friend, and that this possibly would be the end of an era when we would have access to the president and to Attorney General Robert Kennedy, who dispatched federal help in times of need. The tone for justice had been set from the top.

The day after the assassination, November 23, I received a telegram from James Farmer, who was at that time the national director of CORE. (In 1961, Jim Robinson had been removed as CORE's leader, in no small part because the organization decided it should have a Negro director.)[13] Farmer's note really captured my feelings. It read, *The assassination of a president is a tragedy not only for his family but for all Americans. . . . We believe this assassination was the result of the president's efforts to bring about a more democratic America and we hope that this nation will rededicate itself to those ideals of his. Our prayers go out to Lyndon Johnson in the difficult days ahead.*

And the days ahead would be difficult, indeed.

---

John had been scheduled to appear in court the same day President Kennedy was assassinated, and he knew something was wrong when he arrived at the St. Augustine office of his client, a fiery Negro dentist named Robert Hayling. He found Dr. Hayling red-eyed and teary.

When we spoke on the telephone the day of the assassination, John told me that not a single one of the prosecutor's witnesses—some of whom he believed were Ku Klux Klan members—appeared in court after news of the president's death. "Maybe the reason the prosecutor's witnesses didn't show up is because Kennedy's assassination shocked them enough for them to realize that they, too, have been part of this nation's madness and they were ashamed to come to court," John told his client at the time.

Dr. Hayling scoffed at his young lawyer's naivete. "Due, the reason those suckers didn't show is they are out celebrating Kennedy's assassination," the dentist said.[14]

Dr. Hayling, the advisor for St. Augustine's NAACP Youth Council, had been badly beaten at a large Ku Klux Klan rally staged to celebrate the bombing of the Sixteenth Street Baptist Church in Birmingham, where the four little girls died. Can you imagine anyone wanting to celebrate such a horrible terrorist act at a rally? Dr. Hayling had tried to observe the rally with three colleagues, but instead was captured by Klan members and badly beaten. His activism had very nearly gotten him killed more than once. One night, someone drove past his house and shot through his doors and windows, killing the family dog, a boxer who had rushed, barking, to the front door inside the house. If his wife hadn't left their bedroom moments before to use the bathroom, he says, she would have surely died in the shotgun blasts, too, because their bedroom was riddled with bullet holes. His harrowing story, unfortunately, set the tone for the violent days to come.

Dr. Hayling, who'd been raised in Tallahassee, first moved to St. Augustine, the nation's oldest city, in 1960 with his wife and two children, opening a dental office as part of a program to repay his state-funded student loans to traditionally Negro Meharry Dental School. St. Augustine had grown progressively more dangerous and violent in the early to mid 1960s, when his NAACP Youth Council, and later, Martin Luther King's Southern Christian Leadership Conference, began challenging the segregated policies of public accommodations.

At the time Dr. Hayling first moved there, on the surface St. Augustine appeared to him to be one of the more tolerant cities in the South for Negroes. There were integrated neighborhoods, with Negro and white families living side by side; and more than half of Dr. Hayling's dental patients were white. A popular dentist who preceded him had also been Negro, and residents were accustomed to being treated by a Negro dentist, rare for the time.

But Dr. Hayling wasn't satisfied with moving to town and opening a thriving practice. A former Air Force lieutenant known for his short temper when it came to matters of segregation, he became the advisor to the NAACP Youth Council, made up of adolescents and young adults, and he guided them on their quest to integrate the city's restaurants and motels.

They had the perfect platform: In 1963, two years before the city's 400th birthday, the city was seeking federal funds to celebrate its quadricentennial in style. With banquets and major events in the planning, Dr. Hayling outraged the white establishment by contacting federal authorities to insist that St. Augustine should not receive federal assistance because it was so segregated. National NAACP leadership urged Dr. Hayling to keep a low profile. The message: "Don't rock the boat. Let these people have their celebration."

However, Dr. Hayling's profile was anything but low. In response to fears that violent whites might retaliate for the effort to block federal funding, Dr. Hayling was quoted in the local newspaper as saying, "I and others of the NAACP have armed ourselves and we will shoot first and ask questions later." Dr. Hayling denies that he ever said such a thing: "Anyone who knew me knew that didn't sound like Dr. Hayling," he says, dismissing the statement as a Wild West embellishment. (The accurate quote, he says, was that he'd said he would use "all the vim, vigor, and vitality at my command" to protect himself and his family.)[15]

Dr. Hayling and other activists pressed, picketing and protesting, and it wasn't long before sleepy, "tolerant" St. Augustine showed its true nature: "When we said we wanted to sit down at a restaurant or go to a hotel or motel, we uncovered a hotbed of Klansmen," Dr. Hayling recalls.

In September of 1963, soon after the Sixteenth Street Baptist Church tragedy, downtown St. Augustine was blanketed with leaflets advertising a large Ku Klux Klan rally in a cow patch about a mile and a half south of St. Augustine, where Dr. Hayling recalls that a large, towering cross had been erected and set afire. NAACP Youth Council members who had been picketing downtown came to Dr. Hayling with the flyers, and Dr. Hayling and three other Negro civil rights activists—Clyde Jenkins, Jimmy Jackson, and James Houser—decided to drive near the rally site to monitor it from a distance. "People have asked me, 'Why did you try to go to a Klan rally?' " Dr. Hayling says, but he insists they never intended to attend the rally, just to spy on it.

They would all get a much closer view than expected.

As they drove, they noticed several cars parked on the shoulder. White men with shotguns posted on the side of the road saw them coming. The man driving Dr. Hayling's retractable hardtop Ford sports car got nervous and said he thought he knew a side road, so he gunned the gas and veered off the highway, U.S. 1. None of them realized that ditches had been dug into the ground to keep intruders from sneaking close to the rally undetected, and their car got stuck. Before they knew it, they were surrounded by another group of men armed with shotguns.

*Niggers, get out that car.*

The four activists were searched, their wallets taken. Unfortunately, Dr. Hayling recalls, the foremost piece of identification in his wallet was his NAACP membership card. Not only had they stumbled into enemy territory, but they could not hope to claim ignorance. Suddenly, their lives were in real danger. "So much happened so fast, I don't think we had time to be frightened," Dr. Hayling says.

Like prisoners of war, they were marched to the rally site. Dr. Hayling, remembering his military training, tried to maintain a psychological advantage by marching in a proud and authoritative manner, hoping to intimidate the group, but only moments before their arrival, a Klan leader had been berating the approximately 250 townspeople attending the rally, telling them that if they had any guts, that "nigger dentist" who was stirring up all the trouble would end up with a bullet in his head. Now, as if by script, Dr. Hayling arrived in person, and standing near the front of the crowd was a girl on whom he'd recently done some crown work, alongside her mother, and they both recognized him immediately. Instead of trying to defend him, they pointed their fingers and began shouting, "That's the troublemaker! That's Dr. Hayling!"

With the women goading the men, the attack began. Dr. Hayling and the others were piled together "like a cord of wood," Dr. Hayling says, and a barrage of blows from fists, feet, baseball bats, and axe handles began to rain down on them. Pounded across their heads, faces, chests, and torsos, the men grew bloody and semiconscious. Dr. Hayling heard someone say, "He's a right-handed dentist!" and his attackers set out to cripple his hand with their blows. *Have you ever smelled a nigger burn? Go get some gasoline!*

The racial tension in St. Augustine, as in many southern cities at the time, was like a noxious gas wafting through the air, and the poison was feeding upon itself at that rally. It was a recipe for death.

Yet Dr. Robert Hayling was not to be martyred that day. By chance, he and the members of his party weren't the only ones who had decided to monitor the much publicized Ku Klux Klan rally. Also in attendance, shocked at the violent turn of events, was a white minister from Daytona named Rev. Irvin Chene Jr. A civil rights sympathizer who recognized that a calamity was about to happen before his eyes, Rev. Cheney slipped away from the rally and found a telephone to call for authorities.

He didn't call local police, Dr. Hayling says; he knew full well that members of the St. Johns County Sheriff's Department, including the sheriff himself, were Ku Klux Klan sympathizers, and a few were probably already in attendance. In fact, according to FBI files cited in *Bearing the Cross*, Sheriff L. O. Davis was friendly with Holsted "Hoss" Manucy, who was the Exalted Cyclops of the Klan in St. Augustine.[16]

Instead, Rev. Cheney called the Florida Highway Patrol in Tallahassee and asked that officers from surrounding police jurisdictions be dispatched right away. When news of the police officers' approach crackled across police-band radios in St. Augustine, Sheriff Davis finally stepped in to pull the crowd away from Dr. Hayling and the others. He arrested several Klansmen for assault, but Dr. Hayling and the others were also arrested for the same charge.

Police drove them to the nearest hospital in St. Augustine, where they were treated for their injuries, but authorities didn't think it was safe for them to stay there, so a local Negro mortician was enlisted to drive them to a Negro hospital in Jacksonville the next day, his hearses substituting for an ambulance. Dr. Hayling's injuries included such facial disfiguration that he could not work for weeks, and there was damage to the muscles and ligaments in his right hand.

"I still have indentations from sutures in my skull I'll take to my grave," Dr. Hayling says today of his violent encounter.

Dr. Hayling's car was destroyed by Klansmen, but a police search turned up a .25-caliber pistol in his glove compartment. Dr. Hayling had not reached for that weapon in self-defense when the armed Klansmen pulled them out of their car; he'd forgotten all about it, he says, and even so he would have known it was no match for shotguns. Putting their heads together to defuse a public relations nightmare, St. Augustine authorities told Dr. Hayling he would not be charged for illegal weapon possession if he and the other activists dropped assault charges against those who had beaten them at the rally. Still, in November, while the Klansmen went unpunished, a jury convicted Hayling for assault and the judge levied a $100 fine.

Despite the odds stacked against his client, John had gone to St. Augustine to argue the dentist's case. But at a time when life itself was so tenuous, justice was too much to ask.

Contrary to the inspirational note I'd received from Mother not long before that awful November, very, very difficult days were ahead. Two weeks after President Kennedy's death, his successor, Lyndon B. Johnson, stood before Congress and proclaimed, "No memorial oration or eulogy could more eloquently honor President Kennedy's memory than the earliest possible passage of the civil rights bill for which he fought so long."[17] The eventual passage of the Civil Rights Act of 1964—guaranteeing that Negroes could not legally be barred from employment or service in restaurants, hotels, and other public facilities on the basis of race—was President Johnson's first priority. Many of us hoped the new law would bring a hasty end to the discrimination we had been fighting. But the civil rights movement was about to get bloodier than ever.

# Eighteen

# TANANARIVE DUE

**"There would be no one to frighten you if you refused to be afraid."**
***—Mohandas K. Gandhi***

Two weeks after Hurricane Andrew devastated much of my parents' neighborhood and vast portions of southern Dade County in August 1992, my family faced a standoff that made it difficult to remember that much time had passed at all since the 1960s. The police picked the wrong house that night.

My parents still live in Point Royal, about a mile north of the shambled Cutler Ridge Mall, which President George Bush (the First) had visited just days before to declare South Dade a national disaster area. What was left of their community after the lashing dealt by that powerful, destructive storm bore none of the dignity of what had been a palm-lined residential neighborhood. All that remained was splintered plywood, crumbling concrete, littered streets, billows of smoke, uprooted trees, twisted street signs, and the silent anguish of collective loss. The backyard I'd known in childhood, I wrote in my journal, looked like the scene of a forest fire: *All throughout the neighborhoods, dead trees baking in the sun have filled the air with a sharp scent of dry leaves and brittle timber. . . . Dade has been bombed out. . . . We have all lost so much, it is barely comprehensible.*

The hurricane had also wrought fear. Any storm clouds brought a new fear of the sky; and the loss of electricity, which lasted for a month or more, brought a new fear of the night.

Because natural disasters attract looters, the National Guard had been called in to enforce a curfew. Nervous homeowners, camped out like squatters in the shells that used to be their homes, occasionally fired guns to ward off real or perceived intruders. Many homes posted hand-painted signs: LOOTERS WILL BE SHOT. Vietnam veterans unfortunate enough to live in the hurricane-destroyed areas would later report horrible flashbacks. How could they not? Soldiers were patrolling the streets, helicopters were constantly beating their propellers overhead, and the prolonged power outage left everything enveloped in a curtain of darkness for miles north, south, east, and west. At night, South Dade not only looked like a war zone, it was under martial law. Anyone caught breaking curfew was subject to arrest.

All of my closest relatives in Miami, including my parents, lived in the midst of this. My Aunt Priscilla had spent the duration of the hurricane screaming in an upstairs closet while her house fell apart around her. My grandmother, who lived ten minutes northwest of her, fared somewhat better in her solid, concrete 1950s-era home, but it had still taken a battering, her roof and dining room badly damaged. My parents had structural damage, too, but there were no gaping holes—and with four bedrooms, they had the most space, so their house had become the family base. I lived thirty miles north, having moved to North Miami the year before from a Cutler Ridge apartment destroyed in the storm. My new neighbors and I, suffering only a few days' loss of power and the uprooting of the frailest trees, were aghast at the video footage from South Dade.

Out-of-state family members came down to help my family rebuild what we could, and they all camped at my parents' house. My Uncle Walter, my mother's brother in Atlanta, drove down with his teenage son, John. My cousin Muncko, who was a Navy recruit based in Hawaii, flew in with his wife, Carol. During the day, life focused on roof repair, finding and preparing food, and salvaging what could be salvaged. At night, there was only the disabling, pervasive darkness and a wet summer heat barely diminished by the sun's absence.

My cousin Muncko, the only one in the family with weapons training, slept with a black Remington shotgun at his bedside. When there were unfamiliar sounds outside of the house, he investigated to make sure no intruders were on the property.

At the cusp of midnight that fateful night, my mother heard a noise through the shattered, open windows. While everyone inside slept, the Chihuahua, Frisky, was outside barking furiously. Frisky wasn't the sort of dog who barked out of boredom, or for attention. He barked at strangers, unlike the Great Dane, Samantha, who was untroubled by noises and sound asleep in my parents' bed.

*Someone must be out there,* my mother thought, climbing over the dog to get out of bed.

Every time my family members sit around and talk about this particular night, we always remark how lucky it was that it was my mother, not Muncko, who heard the barking first. By the time Muncko and his wife stirred, they heard my mother opening the front door to go outside. Muncko and Carol had glanced out of the window a few seconds earlier and seen only darkness, but suddenly, from somewhere, came a glare of white light.

A man's voice came, shouting an order: "Okay, freeze!"

The men outside looked like soldiers, but they were police officers, Florida Highway patrolmen. There were twelve of them, and their bulletproof flak jackets were on, their revolvers aimed. "We have you surrounded! Tell everybody to come out of the house!"

Imagine, we always say when we remember, if Muncko had opened the door first and walked outside with his shotgun. Imagine how different that night might have been. *If I had not heard a noise and investigated, they were going to storm the house, and someone would have died that night,* my mother would write later in the black-owned *Miami Times* newspaper.

My mother was outside wearing only the slip she'd been sleeping in. She had no idea why a small army was ready for combat in the front yard, rattling the fence, threatening her family, but she was about to find out.

First, she, too, barked instructions to the people in the house. "Stay inside," she said. She told Carol to get on the telephone to call me in North Dade, so they could establish contact with someone who was not in the house, a witness, which had been part of her civil-rights training. She told my uncle and father to stay inside. The instructions she rattled were second nature, self-assured, calm.

Then she turned her attention back to the men with the guns. "What do you think you're doing in my yard?" her litany began.

The group's leader, a white lieutenant, told her to be calm and asked to speak to the man of the house. My mother rejoined loudly, "*I* can handle this."

My father is a quiet intellectual, and I have never heard him raise his voice at anyone. But it was not merely because of personalities that my mother stood between him and the armed police officers that night; it was a common-sense tactic, as far as she was concerned. In an unfamiliar situation, when emotions are running high, you do not send a black man into the path of the police. Black men are the molded image of what America fears most; they are the robber, rapist, and drug dealer America sees on its television screens at night. And that night, despite my father's clearly marked Metro–Dade County car parked inside our gate, it was the hunt for black men that had brought those police officers to our doorstep.

Later, watching the John Singleton film *Rosewood,* I thought of my mother's face-off with the police when Esther Rolle's character, Aunt Sara, goes outside to reason with a mob gathered beyond her fence demanding that she send her son outside. The similarities were almost uncanny, and my mother, like Aunt Sara (who, incidentally, was shot—both in the movie and in real life), faced the police alone.

"Listen," the ranking police officer told my mother gruffly, "a black man in a white van with a Georgia tag was spotted stealing machine guns from the National Guard campsite. We need everyone out of that house right now."

Naturally, a white van with a Georgia tag—my uncle's—was parked at the end of my parents' driveway. "It's still warm, it's still warm," one of the officers was saying, feeling the hood of the van as if to confirm that, yes, indeed, this must be the getaway vehicle.

It wasn't only National Guardsmen that had been assigned to Dade County's streets. Hundreds of regular Army troops in South Dade were also enforcing the curfew, helping citizens remove debris, and coordinating public hot meal lines. Transport trucks loaded with soldiers rumbled up and down the streets day and night. Just days before, my mother had befriended a squad of soldiers who'd been wandering the neighborhood, and she'd offered them cold drinks in exchange for help clearing debris from the backyard. The photograph she posed for with them on our front porch—a woman in a purple housedress beaming a beautiful smile in the midst of the group of grinning, youthful men in camouflage uniforms, rifles slung across their shoulders—was a shocking contrast to the combative stance these police officers took that night.

But my mother wasn't concerned about being arrested, or about being shot. She was just full of rage. She was indignant. How *dare* these men disturb her household. My relatives, who watched the exchange from a huddle inside the dark house, say her tirade at the front gate lasted at least twenty minutes. She demanded to know their names, what agency they represented. She told them, in no uncertain terms, to whom she was about to report them first thing in the morning. She told them to get off her property.

One patrolman, the only black man in the group, obviously annoyed she was speaking that way to his superior, felt obligated to step forward to chastise her. As soon as he opened his mouth, my mother tore into him: "Listen," she snarled at him, "I *got* you this job."

I can only imagine how the irony must have made her feel. After all she and my father had sacrificed to see to it blacks could win police jobs, or any jobs, without being discriminated against, this man was going to stand here and try to scold her on her own property?

Oh, no.

That was the end of this brother's contribution to the conversation. The rest of the night was my mother's. All the armed men could do was listen to my mother's verbal thrashing in a sheepish, uncomfortable silence. Her deep voice, which flows with a texture as dark and rich as molasses, can be soothing when she's calm—on the basis of her voice alone, people often mistake my mother for Maya Angelou—but it's a mighty weapon whenever she raises it in anger, and she brandished it like a torch that night.

After all of the outrages suffered by blacks in riot-torn Dade County for so many years, this intrusion was the final outrage, the last indecency.

The hurricane itself had already brought its own injustices. My parents and NAACP observers believed white neighborhoods like affluent Country Walk were receiving more attention than equally battered poor black areas in Goulds, Naranja, West Perrine, and Richmond Heights. It was already painfully clear to my parents that while insurance claims could repair the damage to their waterfront home, there were so many uninsured and under-insured poorer families—often *black* families—who would never fully recover.

All that fueled the anger and indignation my mother battered those police officers with at her front gate that night. Here, in the midst of this chaos, in a city with a history like Miami's, a pack of police officers would descend upon her home simply because of a vague coincidence—and because she and all who lived there were black.

Black and white. Yet again. And again. And again.

As the lieutenant's radio squawked that night, my mother learned that the report of the stolen machine guns had been embellished by imagination, like so many other strange myths that had grown out of the hurricane. The theft had been thirty-six hours before, not that night, as the officers believed. The van's warm hood was irrelevant, proving nothing.

Eventually, with nothing to go on and an obstacle in their path, the police left. The following day, representatives from Metro–Dade Police visited my parents' house to make an embarrassed formal apology. They also tried to explain the circumstances.

The Florida Highway patrolmen who had surrounded my parents' house that night were not from Dade County at all. They'd been recent arrivals from Orlando, brought in because help was so sorely needed.

They did not know to respect the official county car parked near the van, or that John Due, the man they believed was harboring gun thieves in his home, was a respected civil rights attorney and the director of Dade County's Office of Black Affairs. They did not know that his eldest daughter was a reporter for the *Miami Herald*, the city's daily newspaper.

And they did not know that Patricia Stephens Due, the woman who stood in their overwhelming spotlight that night in a short, sheer slip as though she wore a bulletproof vest, had fortified her soul by standing unarmed against guns and worse threats long ago, during the era when anyone bold and black was begging for harm, very nearly *expecting* it.

My mother had never flinched before, and she sure wasn't about to start.

# Nineteen

# Patricia Stephens Due

**"I am not truly free if I am taking away someone else's freedom, just as surely as I am not free when my freedom is taken from me. The oppressed and the oppressor alike are robbed of freedom."**
***—Nelson Mandela***

If Tallahassee's white power structure expected me to be silenced because I was no longer enrolled as a student at FAMU, they were sorely wrong. If anything, now I had more time to dedicate to the civil rights struggle. I turned my attention to an area that was potentially much more powerful than a movie theater's segregation policies: voter registration.

By the end of 1963, all over the country, civil rights activists' agenda was shifting from public facilities to voter registration. The presidential election was coming up in the fall of 1964. Although we didn't know it at the time, President Johnson would be running against a reactionary Republican candidate, Barry Goldwater, who, like Alabama Governor George Wallace, would ride the backlash against civil rights. I had a much broader role throughout all of northern Florida, not just in Tallahassee, because I had been named a CORE field secretary. I was now on CORE's staff, not simply a volunteer. I have been told I was one of the first female field secretaries in the organization's history—another was Mary Hamilton, a fiery speaker who had been involved with the freedom rides and came to stay with John and me in Tallahassee when she was needed—but I never gave much consideration to the fact that I was a woman. Society wasn't discriminating against me because I was a woman. Society never saw past my skin color. I saw myself as a *Negro*, period.

CORE was launching a voter registration drive in North Florida, and I was named project director. I wanted to base my headquarters in Gadsden County, where the majority of the population was Negro. After years away from the county of my birth, I was finally back home in Gadsden County, but I did not receive a very warm welcome when I returned, even from blood relatives and some people who had known me since I was a child. By then, after reading my name in the newspapers since 1960, many people were afraid to be seen talking to me. When I asked them about providing me with housing or office space for the voting project, they said absolutely not. No one wanted to be associated with me.

In the beginning, the only person who reached out to me was a former elementary-school teacher, Mrs. Dorothy Chandler Jones. Mrs. Jones, who was still teaching in 1963, also ran a grocery store on the property beside her well-kept house in St. Hebron, outside of Quincy. Mrs. Jones had been a friend of Mother's for years. She was raising her fourteen-year-old daughter, Mary Lee, alone after her husband's death. She divided her time between being a mother, teaching, her church activities, and keeping alive the tradition of Community Grocery, the tiny grocery store her husband had opened in the 1950s. I knew Mrs. Jones's home very well because Mother had sent me to her house for piano lessons when I was young. She had a large property, an acre or more, and I can still see myself climbing the steps to her house, my hair in ribbons, wearing my neatest dress, with little ankle socks. She spanked my hands whenever I hit the wrong note, although I rarely gave her reason to. Those days felt very far away by 1963.

When I came back to Mrs. Jones's house to tell her what I needed, she invited me right inside. I sat at her kitchen table with a man she'd invited to meet me, Rev. D. H. Jamison, who first provided the contact names in several counties of the ministers and community leaders who would be crucial to help initiate a massive voter education drive in North Florida, people like Rev. James Crutcher in Quincy and Mr. E. K. Bass in Suwannee County. I can't express what a godsend Mrs. Jones was at that time. She let me sleep at her house, giving up her own master bedroom and bathroom to make me comfortable. She also allowed me to bring my dogs, Scout and Freedom, to stay in her backyard. I will never forget that kindness and bravery.

"Some of my neighbors talked to me and said, 'What you trying to do? Get hurt?' I said, 'I'm just trying to make things better for everybody,' " Mrs. Jones recalled when I interviewed her at that same house more than thirty years later. (During a later interview with her when Tananarive was present, in 1996, Mrs. Jones was recovering from a stroke, speaking in a painstaking way, often frustrated when she could not express herself as clearly as she wanted. She was as tenacious about regaining her powers of speech as she has always been about everything else. As a young woman, she had worked in tobacco fields and taught school to put herself through college, attending classes only in the summers. It took her many, many years, but she finally got her degree. Likewise, in only a few short months since her stroke at the age of eighty, Mrs. Jones had worked hard enough to make herself understood.)

"Some of the neighbors would say, 'Well, we're getting on all right. We don't need anybody coming here trying to start something.' That's what they'd say—start something," Mrs. Jones said, still looking amazed at the silliness of her neighbors' words. "I'd say, 'We *need* to start something.' "[1] True to that belief, Mrs. Jones later took part in a demonstration at Quincy's Leaf Theater, standing outside in plain sight of everyone in the small town.

She caught grief at her workplace. Her principal called her in to explain why she was being seen demonstrating against the theater, which only allowed Negroes to sit in the balcony, and why she was allowing civil rights workers, both Negro and white, to stay at her house. "My principal told me, 'We heard you're letting white folks stay in your house—*white* people.' I said I'd let stay there who I wanted to stay, and he didn't have anything to do with it," Mrs. Jones says. "And if he could do anything about it, he could do it. If he wanted to get taken to court, it's all right with me." She told her principal she dared the school superintendent to come to her classroom to talk to her himself if he had problems with her involvement. "And the next time [the superintendent] came, he passed by my room and looked the other way," Mrs. Jones says.

As the registration drive escalated, Mrs. Jones woke up one morning to realize that someone had burned a cross in front of her house, a common scare tactic in the South. Her neighbors were terrified, but not Mrs. Jones. "It didn't frighten me. In the Bible, fear is mentioned 365 times—*Do not fear*—and that has always gone with me. I don't fear. I'm not afraid of rattlesnakes. I'm not afraid," she says.

But Mrs. Jones's daughter, fourteen-year-old Mary Lee, had fears. Because they had a grocery store, Mary Lee didn't worry about her mother losing her teaching job, but she worried about other things, like having crosses burned in her yard. And whether or not a racist might run me or her mother off the road one dark night while we were on our way home from a civil rights meeting. But aside from her fears, Mary Lee didn't feel a personal connection to the Movement. When her mother took her to mass meetings, she often curled up and fell asleep on the church benches. The Movement was not about *her,* she believed. She was oblivious to its impact on her.

Not long afterward, Mary Lee would learn that her mother's involvement was *very* personal. In high school, she got a memorable taste of racism. When Mary Lee was in eleventh grade, her mother insisted on signing her up for a new option called "Freedom of Choice," where Mary Lee could choose any school to attend—Negro or white. "My mom was determined I was going to go to the 'white' high school, because she wanted to see what they were getting that we weren't getting," says Mary Lee, who is today Mary Lee Blount and has two adult children of her own. Mary Lee wasn't enthusiastic about integrating Quincy High School, but she agreed.

She hated the experience, she says. She and the handful of other Negro students felt completely isolated. Younger white children who tried to talk to her on the school bus were chastised by their older brothers and sisters, so no one would talk to her. At worst, the other whites at school were hostile. At best, they might smile at her, but that was all. The entire auditorium stirred with resentment and disbelief when teachers inducted her into the National Honor Society. The school staged a private prom at a country club instead of holding the prom at the school as usual, purposely excluding the Negro students. "It helped me learn myself and know myself," Mary Lee says of the experience. "It helped me be all I could be. I became a better student. I had to study my lessons, because I felt if I didn't they were looking for any reason to knock me down and say, 'Oh, she's mediocre.' So I really learned independence."[2]

Mrs. Jones, Mary Lee's mother, can no longer live on her own, so she lives in Tallahassee with Mary Lee, an accountant and university instructor of accounting and taxation. I will never forget the help she gave me, and I know the Movement took a toll on their family.

Even after I enlisted Mrs. Jones as an ally in the voter registration campaign, I knew I needed another foot soldier to help me. Luckily, I also knew the right person to ask.

Judy Benninger was about to leave the University of Florida after losing her scholarship and being placed on academic probation because of her involvement in the Tallahassee theater demonstrations. I'd worked with Judy long enough to realize that she had the drive and organizational skills to be a useful ally. She became the assistant secretary for what we called the "Big Bend Voter Education Campaign." In Tallahassee, our steering committee included Dr. James Hudson from FAMU, a Negro school principal named Sam Hunter, and white couples George and Clifton Lewis and James and Lillian Shaw. Mrs. Lewis allowed us to use her Tallahassee apartment as a temporary office. Then we got help from Susan Ausley, a white woman married to a prominent attorney, John Ausley. Mrs. Ausley intervened when we had trouble getting a city permit to rewire an old building we would use in Frenchtown.

Our goal was to register as many new Negro voters as possible in Gadsden and Leon Counties. At the time, fewer than half of Leon County's 14,000 eligible Negro voters were registered, and Negroes made up 33 percent of the population in 1960.[3] Gadsden County was even worse. Fewer than 500 Negroes were registered there, a county where their population of 24,000 outnumbered the 17,000 whites![4]

Why was Negro voter participation so limited? While it appeared that Negroes in Florida were free to vote, a history of intimidation had prevented many from registering. Florida had a poll tax until 1937, which had prevented many Negroes from voting, and after that, Negroes complained about threats when they tried to vote. Certainly, quite a few wondered if voting would make any difference, since Florida's one-party Democratic machinery was all white and could effectively eliminate Negro participation in primary elections.[5] Everything was stacked against us, which is why the charges of voter discrimination in Florida, even during the 2000 presidential election, were particularly painful to me—and rang so true.

The task before us in 1964 was obvious, but before we could go to the community with our cause, Judy and I had to work on a few social differences. I very much agreed with CORE's interracial strategy, which held that our efforts would be more effective if whites and Negroes worked together. But as a white woman with only limited contact with Negroes throughout her life between Oklahoma, Alabama, and Gainesville, Florida, Judy had a lot to learn about how to approach Negroes. Many of our meetings were held in churches, for example, and I knew that her casual way of dressing would turn off many potential voters and activists. The clothes I considered casual wear, like jeans and a blouse, were what Judy considered her "dress-up" clothes. She couldn't go to a Negro church dressed like that.

Negroes, especially in that era, were very conservative in appearance and public behavior, which was a big part of our problem as civil rights activists. When we asked Negroes to break the law, or to draw attention to themselves publicly, we were asking them to break deep social taboos. At the very least, the people we approached had to understand that we were not so different from them. In terms of religion, Judy considered herself a "nonbeliever," so she did not attend church. When she visited Negro churches with me, every single custom was foreign to her. She had to learn to wear a dressy dress, and she had to learn to address people she did not know by their courtesy titles, not their first names, which was more formal than she was used to. It was a cultural learning experience for both of us.

Obviously, Negroes and whites would have to learn to work together if we were going to set any kind of example for the community at large, and I think interracial involvement was a very important part of the civil rights movement. It was also much more dangerous because of the extra attention we drew to ourselves. Our project started getting in trouble right away, when we'd barely had a chance to start.

In January of 1964, John and I brought Judy, FAMU student Julius Hamilton, and white students Rosemary Dudley and Dennis Flood to a Negro-owned tavern, the 40 Club, in a town between Quincy and Tallahassee appropriately named Midway. The place was really bustling. There must have been at least a couple of hundred people there, which made it the perfect place to get the word out on voter registration. If you wanted to reach the people, you had to go where the people congregated, and it wasn't always at church. The tavern's owner was a distant relative of mine, so I asked if we could go inside to make an announcement encouraging people to vote. I'm sure he looked at us with distrust—we were two white women, one white man, one Negro woman, and two Negro men—but he told us we could come in. We all sat down, and at a lull in the music, we were told we could make our announcement. Julius began making his pitch for Gadsden County voters.

In no time, a sheriff's deputy showed up. Dennis managed to slip outside, but Judy, Rosemary, and Julius were arrested. (Dennis was arrested later, when he came to visit the others at jail.) John and I were the only two in the group who weren't arrested, and we speculated that it might have been because I was from Gadsden County and rumored to be remotely related to the sheriff through blood. More likely, it was because the police knew me by reputation, and no one wanted the extra publicity that would be brought by my arrest and an extended jail stay similar to the Tallahassee jail-in. The others were carted off to jail, which was very demoralizing for our group. When they asked why they were being arrested, the deputy replied, "Being in the wrong place."[6] They were held for three days without bond before they were charged with trespassing.

In a newspaper story about the incident, Sheriff Otto Edwards was quoted as saying there was "no need" for a voter registration drive in Gadsden County because "the county had no restrictions against Negroes registering to vote."[7] That was laughable, considering the stir we caused just by bringing up the issue, not to mention that 94 percent of Negroes were not registered. Newspapers also claimed that the proprietor asked us not to come inside, which simply wasn't true. I believe either the proprietor or someone else inside the tavern panicked and called the police so they wouldn't be associated with us. That's how fearful people were. But I never would have thrust our group upon an unwilling party. The way it was portrayed, anyone would have thought we had barged in uninvited and caused a disturbance, and I didn't operate that way, not unless it was a planned demonstration.

So, Judy got her education very quickly when it came to the nature of our work. When I interviewed her in 1990, she recalled a similar incident, when we decided we wanted a decent meal while we distributed flyers encouraging people to vote, so we went to a Negro restaurant in Quincy, the Fountainette, owned by someone I knew. The owner allowed us in, but the police showed up and arrested Judy for trespassing. It seemed that this happened everywhere we went.

This time, the deputy drove her to the station and parked his car outside. I followed in my car, and then called John, who came, too. John asked the deputy, "How could she be trespassing when the owner invited her to buy her lunch there?" The deputy didn't answer. Leaving Judy in his car, he walked inside the jailhouse and vanished. By Judy's recollection, it was nearly 100 degrees that day, and while she sat sweltering in the police car, John and I stood outside, puzzled, while we waited for the arresting deputy to come back. He didn't. As Judy recalled, "Pat finally came and opened the door, and backed her car toward the police car, and I got in her car, and went on. And that was the end of that."

Judy wasn't so lucky the next time she was arrested. She and Rosemary Dudley suffered a terrifying experience after giving a speech one night at a club in Gadsden County. They were charged with disturbing the peace and taken to jail, where they faced a nightmarish scenario. A mere trustee was in charge of a small jail with only a part-time jailer. At first Judy and Rosemary were placed in a cell for women, but then they were taken to the men's cell, where eight white men were locked up.

The situation was tense for all of them, Judy recalled, including the men. "They were terrified they would be charged with rape," Judy said. "They said, 'Don't worry, we know they want us to rape you, but we won't.' They beat on the window to attract the attention of the people on the outside, and eventually raised so much commotion that we were taken out and put back in our cell." Meanwhile, Julius Hamilton was arrested when he went there to protest their incarceration. Eventually, John and I got them all released, and the charges were dropped.[8]

My marriage to a lawyer was a big help during this time, just as John and I had hoped it would be. We were a wonderful team. My expertise was in frontal assaults, and John's expertise was in much-needed legal assistance. In the case of the tavern arrests, for example, John asked by way of a petition of removal to have the case moved to federal court. This was a tactic John helped pioneer because state courts were breaking the backs of civil rights organizations with legal costs. (Ultimately, the case was dismissed by the clerk for lack of prosecution by the state.) If we could not cut down on our court costs due to arrests, as you can see from the police harassment, I probably would not have had a staff very long! As it was, many people were intimidated by the police tactics.

Yet other people in the community were outraged and made even bolder under the face of intimidation. When our interracial groups first began appearing in Quincy, Negro onlookers couldn't believe their eyes, but then they grew excited and sometimes shouted, "We've been waiting for someone to come!" or "The freedom riders are here!" By February 1, four hundred new Negro voters had registered in Gadsden County.[9] And Negroes would continue to register, despite the police harassment that included not only following me and arresting the project workers, but deputies who sat outside of church meetings and voter registration offices and took down the license plate numbers of cars parked outside. Community members involved in the voting drive began complaining about losing their jobs.[10] As Judy pointed out in a letter to the editor at *The Nation* magazine, the voter registration office at the *Gadsden County Times* newspaper office was only "one block from the city police station and two blocks from the county jail."[11]

None of that could keep the momentum from building. On Sunday, February 2, 1964, CORE sponsored a series of very successful workshops at churches in Quincy, where more than 500 young Negroes learned how to conduct themselves during direct action protests.[12] I organized young people into the CORE Freedom Choir, which sang freedom songs at our gatherings, even though I have never had a good singing voice. I have always loved music, so I used records to teach the singers the civil rights songs. Oh, they were good! *Keep your eyes on the prize, hold on, hold on.* That era was one time you could really feel the power of those songs. Songs unified us and gave us strength. Our headquarters was at Mt. Moriah Baptist Church in Quincy, where Rev. James Crutcher, one of our main supporters, was pastor. CORE also held meetings at Arnett Chapel AME Church in Quincy. We also stepped up our efforts in Tallahassee, in Leon County, sending out letters urging 100 percent of FAMU's faculty and staff to be registered by April 4 (an effort that Dr. Gore, FAMU's president, was willing to support).

On March 23, 1964, Arnett Chapel AME Church hosted Quincy's first national civil rights speaker when James Farmer, the national director of CORE, made an appearance there to help bolster the voter registration drive. Years later, when I interviewed Mrs. Jones, she told me what "a thrill" it was for her to recall how Farmer ate a meal in her home and rested in her master bedroom before going to the meeting that night. The meeting was a great success, with hundreds in attendance. Farmer was a very dynamic speaker, and he left all of us energized for the long road ahead. By April, we had registered 975 Negroes in Gadsden County, which was more than twice the number that had ever been registered there before. But there were still 10,800 who had not registered, which was very significant, considering that Negroes outnumbered whites.[13]

Our foes continued to strike at us however they could, trying to both scare us and humiliate us. In April, CORE worker Doris Rutledge, who had also participated in the Tallahassee theater demonstrations, was arrested in nearby Live Oak for writing the wrong date on her driver's license application. It was a simple mistake, only off by one day, but she was taken to the jail where she believed Ruby McCollum had been held in the famed Florida murder case. It was so bad to be jailed in Suwannee County that civil rights workers were terrified of being stopped for any reason by the police—which many Negroes considered notorious. Since Doris believed she was at the jail where it was rumored McCollum had been mistreated and lost her baby, she defiantly told her jailers, "I know the story of Ruby McCollum!" That made them very angry, she says.

"I didn't sleep that night because I knew I could die. I wasn't pregnant, but I figured I could have been raped. Anything could have happened to me," Doris says. "So the only thing that I could do was stay awake, and if someone did try to do anything, I could fight them off. I had already said to myself, 'If something happens, they will have to kill me.' I would not submit to anybody just to save my life. Just kill me." She was released without incident after a night in jail.[14]

That same month, an official with the Leon County Health Department began contacting Judy Benninger at the Big Bend Voter Education Campaign office in Tallahassee, claiming there was "serious evidence" she had received a communicable disease through "intimate contact." Judy dismissed the first calls, but then a man with a medical bag from the Alachua County Health Department showed up on Judy's parents' doorstep in Gainesville, telling her mother that Judy probably had syphilis. Judy was mortified that such a lie was being spread not only to me, her employer, but also to her parents. A similar claim was made about Rosemary Dudley, another white woman who was working with us, and a male volunteer who was a member of Tallahassee CORE. When Judy and I went to the health department in Tallahassee to deny the claims, health department officials demanded that Judy take a blood test or face arrest. "The next time you hear from me, it will be through the sheriff's department, and that's all I have to say," an official said.

Judy didn't want to face more publicity or an arrest, but she also didn't trust the health department to provide a truthful blood test. Instead, she went to a Negro physician, Dr. Charles Stevens, and explained the situation to him. Dr. Stevens tested her under a false name, and the test results came back negative for syphilis. As Judy had said all along, the whole thing was a lie. Still, Judy's mother was very upset by the ordeal, in part because she believed her husband might be angry enough to take action against Judy's accusers if he found out. One night after speaking to both Judy and the health director in Alachua County, Mrs. Benninger suddenly felt weak and found blood on her pajamas. She later discovered she'd suffered a hemorrhage, which she believed was brought on by the emotional stress of the situation.[15]

For people involved in the civil rights movement, black or white, our families suffered right alongside us.

---

While Judy battled the health department, another group of us from Florida felt compelled to take part in an April demonstration at the 1964

World's Fair in New York. Our voter registration workers were suffering daily harassment and intimidation, but the governor of Florida, C. Farris Bryant, was planning to tout Florida as a "paradise" at the World's Fair, hoping to drum up tourism. *Paradise?* Florida might have been a paradise to whites on vacation, but it was hell to the Negroes who lived there.

The New York chapters of CORE, which were quite militant, had planned what they called a "stall-in" to block the bridges with stalled automobiles and keep people from attending the fair. (Again, this was considered very radical; the SCLC, for example, thought such tactics would have a negative impact on the Movement.) We only had three cars from our group to offer to the demonstration, but about ten of us, including Doris Rutledge and Rosemary Dudley, drove to New York to take part. Tentatively, I called Priscilla, who was still living in New York, to ask if she would join the demonstration. My sister hadn't had anything to do with civil rights since her kick in the stomach by a Tallahassee police officer the year before, and I didn't know how she would react to my call.

To my surprise, Priscilla agreed to help us. Once again, it was a decision she would regret—and it would change my family forever.

An hour and a half before the 9:00 A.M. opening of the fair, a protester pulled the emergency cord on a subway bound for the fair at Jackson Heights, a busy hub. Other protesters then lay across the tracks and tried to block the train, but police had the subways moving again within eight minutes. I do not remember what happened in the effort to block the highways, but I assume we simply did not have enough cars to make much impact. The "stall-in" didn't work out as the organizers had hoped.[16]

The fair opened on a cold and rainy day. Three-thousand police officers and Secret Service agents were on hand to keep order, especially since President Johnson was there to make an address that day, along with former president Harry S. Truman. At the Florida pavilion, a group of us assembled with picket signs to make our views known. Florida's exhibit at the fair featured porpoises playing in tanks and a huge orange on top of a pole that seemed to be 200 feet tall. We held up signs, sang freedom songs, and shouted "Governor Bryant must go!" when the governor appeared.

Still, we were peaceful and probably would have avoided arrest if not for one young man—who was not anyone I recognized—who actually scaled the huge pole. I counted everyone in our group, and we were accounted for, so the man had not come with us from Florida. I originally thought he might have just been a thrill seeker, but I learned later that he was a member of the South Jamaica chapter of CORE in New York.[17]

I have forgotten if the man was Negro or white, but as all of us peered upward to see what in the world he was doing, the police descended upon the demonstrators and loaded us into paddy wagons. Priscilla and I were under arrest yet again. In all, 294 CORE members and others were arrested that day.[18]

As many times as I had been arrested and spent time in Florida jails, nothing had prepared me for New York. This was the worst jail system Priscilla and I had ever seen. Doris Rutledge remembers being shuttled from facility to facility throughout New York's boroughs, and having matrons put their hands all over her body to search her. When Priscilla and I first arrived to be processed, the jailers told us we were expected to submit to a vaginal exam. I honestly thought I must have heard wrong. Why should we need a *vaginal* exam? I can only imagine they were planning to look for drugs or weapons, but we refused. "Then you're going to isolation," the jailer said.

That sounded like a punishment to us at first, until we were walked past the crowded cell block and got our first gritty taste of what a true life of incarceration would be like. Compared to Tallahassee and other small-town Florida jails, the New York jail was a different world. The jail was crowded, loud, smelly, and dirty. As we walked past the cells, women were reaching out through the bars like wild animals in cages, trying to touch us and grab us. *Hey, sweetie, why don't you come in here? You look good, sweet meat!*

Priscilla and I were shocked. Believe it or not, although we had been threatened during our 1960 jail-in, we had never experienced sexual advances from women in jail before. We knew immediately that this was not somewhere we would want to stay a single minute longer than necessary. We weren't going to refuse to pay our fine. The sooner we got out, the better. Needless to say, we were very grateful that we were going to be placed in isolation. Even while we were in an isolation cell, women continued to try to grab us through the bars. And the food was more terrible than ever. For breakfast, they served sauerkraut, which we had never even tasted.

There was another serious problem. As Priscilla recalls, we were not even permitted to use the telephone. Of all places, Priscilla laments, we had to spend three days in that New York jail before we could even call our lawyers or families to tell them where we were. John and Mother knew we were at the World's Fair, but they had no idea what had happened to us. We had simply disappeared in the outside world. By coincidence, photographs of both me and Priscilla had appeared separately in the *New York Times* story about the civil rights demonstrations, but that was the last anyone had seen of us. By the third day, when we notified our lawyers, we were set free. "It was terrifying," Priscilla says today. "I promised myself, and I have never broken that promise, 'I will never, ever go to jail again.' "

Our problems in New York didn't end with the jail stay. I was summoned to New York for arraignments several times to answer to the same charges. Each time I was called, I had to drop everything in Florida and return to New York. When I arrived, the court was always confused, calling for both "Patricia Stephens" and "Patricia Due." No matter how many times I tried to explain, the court never did understand that we were the same person. That system was the most disorganized I have ever known.

It was even worse for Priscilla, even though she still lived in New York. For one arraignment, she was ill and couldn't make it, so I submitted a note from her doctor explaining why she was not there. The court accepted the note, and there seemed to be no problem. But then, the next time we were arraigned, Priscilla was arrested because she had failed to show up for the previous arraignment! The whole experience proved to be too much for Priscilla. She'd pushed herself too hard. One day while I was back in Quincy, I got a phone call from her, and I could tell something was wrong by the sound of her voice. "Pat, I have to get out of here. I have to leave," she said. "I can't stay in this country another day."

Although she didn't have any money, Priscilla was determined to board a ship bound for Ghana in West Africa, the land from which she had heard one of our ancestors had been kidnapped in the 1840s. If she could not be treated like a full American citizen, she reasoned, she would live somewhere else. "If I had stayed, I knew I would die," Priscilla explains today. "I knew I would not have an opportunity to live a full, rich life with all my potential. I didn't understand how things could be affecting me so badly, and I knew I could not change my feelings toward these things. I knew they would have killed me. So, I wanted to live."

She asked me for money, and John and I had very little to give her. Mother was ill during that time, already in the hospital, when she got a call from Priscilla. Daddy Marion had recently made arrangements for Priscilla to begin teaching with him in Florida—something everyone was very happy about—so Mother was unprepared for Priscilla's call.

"She called to tell me she was going to Africa, and I'm lying there helpless and I say, 'Well, this is the most absurd thing I've ever heard of! This child is going to Africa. She doesn't have any money. She doesn't have anything. Why is she going to Africa when she already has a job at home?' " Mother said, recalling her feelings in her 1996 interview.

Priscilla had at least one voice of support, though. Daddy Marion had written Priscilla a letter in March, after she had apparently toyed with the question of possibly going to Africa someday: *Africa is a long ways off, but if that is what you really want, by all means go to Africa. . . . Know thyself, and be true to thyself, and you can be false to no one.*[19]

Although I did not want Priscilla to go to a strange place by herself, I tried to understand why she felt she had to leave everything behind, including us. With a very heavy heart, I sent her what little money I could. Then, the woman who was both my sister and my best friend was gone. On the rare occasions Priscilla traveled back to the States to visit after 1964, her skin broke out in hives as soon as her ship left international waters and she drew closer to U.S. soil. That's how emotionally shattered she felt by her civil rights experiences in her own country.

Priscilla finally came back to the United States to live in June of 1977, but the sister I grew up with never returned. Priscilla was never the same.

## Twenty

# TANANARIVE DUE

**" 'What became of the black people of Sumer,' the traveler asked the old man, 'for ancient records show that the people of Sumer were black? What happened to them?' 'Ah,' the old man sighed. 'They lost their history, so they died.' "**
***—Proverb from Sumer***

When my mother told me she wanted to spend the weekend at a dude ranch in central Florida with real-life cowboys and a rodeo, I thought she was crazy. Mom wanted to go somewhere she could ride a horse the way she had as a child growing up in Quincy, and the River Ranch Resort sounded perfect. It was a three-hour drive from where we both lived in Miami, near a town called Yeehaw Junction. I knew it was the last place most citified black women would want to go.

In a more important way, it was perfect for us. That trip was a symbol.

It was 1996, and this was my first road trip with my mother since I'd taken a long-awaited leave of absence from my job as a newspaper reporter at the *Miami Herald* to help her write a book about the civil rights movement. My whole life, my mother had told and retold the stories about herself and the other activists she knew, vowing to write a book about those experiences one day. For years, in fact, she'd already been traveling throughout the state to interview people she'd worked with in the 1960s, hoping to preserve their stories before it was too late.

I think I've known I would be the one to help her fulfill her vow ever since I began writing short stories as a child. Of my parents' three children, I was the only writer. (My sisters Johnita and Lydia, who'd both written about her in school research papers, never pursued writing, becoming lawyers like our father.) In May of 1996, when my mother and I set out for that ranch, I'd sold two novels and finally had enough money to support myself during my leave of absence, so we were ready to get started. I had just turned thirty, my mother would soon be fifty-six, and we were about to become coauthors and chroniclers. We would transport ourselves from the 1990s to the 1960s.

In some ways, I felt as if I'd been drafted. Six years earlier, in 1990, I'd been working for only two years as a full-time newspaper reporter at the *Miami Herald* and was miles away from the slightest inclination to start researching a book on my family history. I wanted to write novels and, based on the barrage of rejection slips I was receiving for my short stories, that would take some time. My priorities at that time were my fiction, my job, and my love life, and that pretty much covered it. I was in my early twenties, discovering life, trying to build a future.

My mother called me one day and told me that my godmother, Judy Benninger Brown, was very sick. Judy and I had never been particularly close because of the distance between Miami and Gainesville, where she lived, but we had exchanged letters over the years, and she'd sent me a college graduation gift. Still, I knew that the most significant relationship with Judy was not mine, but my mother's. My mother is a woman of few true friends, and Judy was one of them. In the 1960s, she and my mother had been soldiers together. Once, I'd been told time and again, Judy had saved my mother's life.

"How sick?" I asked her gently.

"She must be very sick. She has a video crew to document the Movement, and she'd like you to conduct the interview," Mom told me. It's hard to deny a dying woman's wish, and I was flattered to be asked. Besides, under the circumstances, I wanted to see Judy again.

It was a hard, hard experience for me.

Judy Benninger Brown was fighting cancer. The image of her constantly holding an ice pack to the raw nerves where her left breast had once been—a routine to cope with daily pain as natural to her as the way I wore my eyeglasses was to me—will never leave me. She was clearly tired and in great discomfort, and she sat with me and my mother under hot lights for hour after hour, day after day, reciting the stories. The theater demonstrations. The voter registration drives. Some of the stories I had heard from Mom, some of them I had not. Often, as I sat perfectly still beneath the hot lamps while the cameras rolled to preserve this brave woman's legacy, the situation felt unbearable. I was fidgeting. I wanted to be away, to be anywhere else. I felt horrible about Judy's suffering during the long taping, and I felt horrible about her suffering during the 1960s. I felt smothered by the weight of it all.

Afterward, I wrote this in my journal:

*Where this will lead, I don't know. Perhaps this journey will be the first of many. Or perhaps the moments of hardship and burden spent here will outweigh the advantages when I return to my cocoon and all its comforts. . . . I believe I am at a crossroads. I still don't feel the genuine passion for this documentation like the politicos and activists and idealists who spent so many hours planning this weekend; but I have an unavoidable personal interest, and I feel a responsibility to see that this story is told. I will keep and treasure the videotape footage that results from these long hours of interviews, although I am not eager to view them again soon.*

A year later, Judy was dead. I did not know it then, but I would have to grow accustomed to hearing about the deaths of people we had interviewed. It would happen often.

By 1996, as happy as I was that I had accomplished my goal of building a good career and then liberating myself from it so I could dedicate myself to working on a book with Mom, I was also scared to death. The memory of Judy's interview sufficed to make me understand that the process would be full of pain. Mom and I both knew we had a lot of work, stress, and soul-searching ahead of us.

The River Ranch Resort was our last chance for escapism before we dove into our real journey together, and we embraced our trip to the dude ranch with the enthusiasm of two college girls on spring break. My mother's carefree college years had been cut very short by civil rights, and her inability to blink away from injustices in life has afforded her few real chances to be playful. Now, finally, she could be.

We even dressed the part. At the ranch gift shop, I bought my mother a striking black cowboy hat ringed with steel studs, and she admired its stylish fit in the mirror. For myself, I'd brought along a fashionable Western-style shirt, my black riding jeans, and some faux cowboy boots. Neither of us had been anywhere near a horse in years, but we were determined to be convincing.

I'll never forget that weekend. There are probably few people—even my sisters and I—who have seen my mother as she was for those three days. My mother's no-nonsense demeanor has been characterized as everything from cold to unnerving, depending upon the source. When we were children, my cousin called her a "drill sergeant" because he thought she was such a strict disciplinarian. And during the civil rights movement, my mother found out later, her own staff people tiptoed around her and kept secrets from her, fearing her reaction if she knew they were breaking the organization's rules against dating and socializing with people in the communities they were there to help. But there has always been a reason for her demeanor: There was serious business at hand.

My mother's single-minded sense of purpose is what has enabled her to so effectively accomplish everything she has, whether it was standing up to Jim Crow or raising her daughters. There's a time for fun, as far as she's concerned, and a time for business. The line has always been very clearly drawn, even when she called weekly "family meetings" at home so we could all coordinate our busy schedules (my sisters, father, and I always rolled our eyes when she whipped out her notes from the previous meeting). It didn't matter to her that we were all just sitting around the family-room table; to her, family issues needed to be discussed with the same purposefulness as a meeting of the board of directors of the Ford Motor Company.

That demeanor vanished at the ranch. With her video camera, she bounced around our plush, two-bedroom "cabin" to tape our lodgings: We had a sunken living room, a screened patio, three television sets, a washer and dryer, central air-conditioning, and a full kitchen with a microwave and ice maker. "Yep, we're roughing it, pardner," was her recurring joke that weekend. My mother decorated the cabin with family photographs and copies of books she'd brought, including my novel *The Between;* she'd also brought a book on the history of CORE, just in case we ever found ourselves in a scholarly mood.

We never did. We did, however, find ourselves at the rodeo, where the announcer instructed the audience on the fine art of shouting "Yeeeee-hawwwww" with the proper inflections. We both cringed during the cruel-looking cattle-roping demonstrations. As for the bull riding, we were secretly rooting for the bulls. And we made it to the horse trail, where my mother finally got her chance to ride. I took pictures of her sitting happily astride a tired-looking brown mare as she clopped behind the cowboy who guided us on the trail and chatted to him about the horses of her youth. She was *girlish*. For a few days, at least, there was no visible weight on her shoulders. She was free to be herself.

From habit, yes, we noticed that there were no other black faces at the resort. I thought I'd spotted a black child darting beneath the bleachers on rodeo night, but he'd vanished before I could point him out to my mother. However, once we adjusted to our solitary status and received nothing but smiles and politeness from everyone we greeted, race was no longer on our minds.

Then, I went to the saloon. It was a true-life saloon with a wooden facade and a live country band inside. The fiddle player was burning up his bow with "The Devil Went Down to Georgia," and the dance floor was packed with cowboys and cowgirls fresh from the rodeo. The dance floor broke up into lines of synchronized movement, and I realized I was having my very first exposure to the intricate foot tapping of line dancing. I stood in a corner, feeling more self-conscious than I had since my mother and I had arrived. In fact, I felt like I'd stumbled onto the scene in *48 Hours* when Eddie Murphy walks into the cowboy bar and everyone swivels around to stare. I didn't actually notice anyone staring, but I felt like a foreigner. I didn't know the music, for the most part. I didn't know the dance steps. I've known whites my entire life, but this was a part of American life I had not seen. It made me wonder how much, as black and white Americans, we share a nationality but live in different worlds.

Needless to say, I did not expect any dance invitations. And I received none.

I left as soon as I finished my drink. It wasn't until I was walking back toward the cabin to join my mother that I realized I'd felt uneasy because a lifetime of negative racial experiences had trained me to expect a glare, an uttered epithet, some outward sign of resentment. *What are you doing here? You don't belong here.*

Yet I had received none.

"How was the saloon?" my mother asked, surprised I was back so soon.

"I thought I'd better leave before I got lynched," I said. I was only joking, but this was one of those moments that begged for reflection on how our life experiences, in some respects, had been so very different. In my mother's day, I knew, I never would have crossed the threshold of that saloon. I could have expected a beating, or worse, for having the audacity to simply walk up to that bar and order a drink.

That still seemed like a far-off bad dream to me, hard even to imagine. Yet my parents, and their parents, and their parents before them had been forced to live as this nation's unwanted stepchildren every single day. Born and raised in the South, I was a part of the first generation of African-Americans who had grown up with sweeping laws protecting my rights and opportunities, even if those laws had not also miraculously changed everyone's hearts or repaired the legacy of inequity. I was also part of the first generation who had begun to forget what life for most blacks had been like before, to lose sight of the magnitude of their struggle. I've heard my mother's stories my whole life, as if they were milk from her breast, and still they didn't seem quite real. At times, I could gaze at her as if she were a stranger.

For that reason, the River Ranch Resort was a good place to begin our book. We knew we had a lot of pain to explore in the next year or two. In another way, I knew that we'd already spent a weekend experiencing one of the precious few instances in which, in the end, a lot of my mother's real work has already been done. We'd been treated with respect in a place where many black people might have assumed they would not. We'd had a good time just being human.

"This is the best vacation I've ever had," my mother said into the video camera as we stood outside our cabin, ready to leave. Her grin beneath her cowboy hat stretched for miles.

Twenty-One

# PATRICIA STEPHENS DUE

**"Freedom is not something that anybody can be given. Freedom is something people take, and people are as free as they want to be."**
***—James Baldwin***

"It's going to be a long, hot summer."

Those prophetic words were my concluding quote in a *New York Times* article in May of 1964, when a reporter interviewed me for a story about our voter registration drive in Quincy. In the article, I complained about the intimidation of local residents through their jobs and the constant, paralyzing police presence.[1] That summer—which would become known by civil rights workers throughout the South as "Freedom Summer"—was going to be a deadly one. It was a summer many of us were lucky to survive, and I was no exception.

By the summer of 1964, John and I had a long-distance marriage. In March John had been given a one-year Eleanor Roosevelt Fellowship by the National Association of Human Relations Workers, a position based in Atlanta, and I was still living in Quincy. Assigned to the Voter Education Project of the Southern Regional Council (headed by famous civil rights attorney Wiley Branton), John traveled throughout the South to do field research and send back reports on voting rights for Negroes. Because of John's relationship with Branton and CORE General Counsel Carl Rachlin, he also ended up acting as backup counsel to local attorneys in Mississippi and North Florida. Sometimes John and I did not see each other for a month at a time, but we had always known that lengthy separations might be a cost of our activism. During that time, the needs of the Movement were much more critical to us than the needs of a young married couple.

"Don't you get lonely, what with your husband bein' gone all the time? I could keep you company," a grinning police officer said to me after pulling in front of my car to stop me on an out-of-the-way dirt road in

Gadsden County. This deputy was one of my regular tails—going wherever I went, staying as long as I stayed—so I recognized him right away.

"I know I'm always following you, but I'm not your enemy. I'm your friend," he said. "Don't you want some attention? I know women like attention."

I was very annoyed to be pulled over for such nonsense. This arrogance was common in the South, where some white men were brazen about sexual overtures toward Negro women in a way they would not dare with white women. By contrast, the slightest suspected overture by a Negro man toward a white woman could be deadly for the Negro man. "No, thank you. I can manage fine," I said curtly. "You do your job if you feel you have to, and I'll do mine. That's the only reason I'm here." And I backed up and drove away. He allowed me to pass, but he followed as usual.

In the voter registration campaign, I knew that whatever resistance we were already meeting was about to get much worse. Since we had received a grant from the Voter Education Project of the Southern Regional Council, we were going to expand our staff in the coming months, and we were going to have a much more visible presence in a wider area. In March, Judy and I had gone to a CORE meeting in New Orleans to train for a larger-scale voting campaign. We met at a motel for Negroes, the Mason Motel, which was willing to host an interracial group. When the day's programming was over, the organizers suggested several places we might visit in New Orleans.

As Judy told the story that day Tananarive and I interviewed her, she sat in the back seat with a Negro man from Southern University, and I sat in the front seat with the white male CORE field director who was driving. Like me, the white activist was married. The driver and I were speaking casually about issues related to the Movement. Frankly, I had never considered civil rights meetings a place to socialize or "date," unlike many other activists who got on my nerves because they seemed to always be on the prowl. This was Judy's first visit to New Orleans, and she was excited to see some of the famed spots she had heard about. We parked the car, she said, and went to nightclub after nightclub, only to be told we could not be admitted. To observers, she said, we appeared to be two interracial couples.

"That's how we saw New Orleans, by getting kicked out of all these famous places," Judy said. "One or two o'clock in the morning, we found someplace that would let us come in and sit down. That was my first exposure to New Orleans."

I don't have the same memory of having to go from place to place, although it may be possible. My recollection is that we knew which places would admit us, and a group of us simply congregated there. I also thought the white activist's wife had been with us, although Judy said she was not. What I know for certain is that the white man we spent time with that evening was very talkative, and he was obviously a dedicated worker. His name was Michael Schwerner. He called himself "Mickey."

Mickey Schwerner was based at the CORE-VEP office in Meridian, Mississippi, and I met him for the first and last time at that gathering in New Orleans as we were all preparing to go back out to our respective bases to fortify our voter registration campaigns. Three months later, on June 21, word came across the CORE grapevine that Mickey and two other workers in Mississippi—a Negro resident named James Chaney and a new summer volunteer named Andrew Goodman—were missing. Given the hostile climate, and despite the skepticism of local law enforcement (who said their disappearance was a hoax), the community of activists had no choice but to assume the worst. We learned that the three activists had driven from Meridian to the small Mississippi farming community of Longdale, near a town called Philadelphia, to investigate several beatings and the burning of a church where Chaney and Schwerner had convinced church leaders to host a Freedom School. The three were driving back to Meridian when they were arrested by local deputies who held them in jail until nightfall and then released them.

Then they vanished.[2]

Before the three Mississippi workers vanished, many civil rights leaders and CORE staff members, including former FAMU professor Richard Haley, had been pressing the U.S. Justice Department for protection for voter registration workers. A month and a half later, after an extensive search, the bodies of the three workers were found. They had been murdered, it was discovered—handed over to their killers by the police.[3] (Unfortunately, many younger Americans' only exposure to this important case came from the film *Mississippi Burning*, which is so full of distortions that the events are unrecognizable to many of us who were involved in the Movement. In order to be more commercial, the film tells the story from a white point of view, while blacks stand helplessly on the sidelines. This is common in Hollywood films about the civil rights movement. We are so often written out of our own history.)

"That had a very profound effect on me. It scared me," Judy said, recalling how she spent that night in New Orleans staring at the back and side of Mickey Schwerner's head, not realizing how soon he would be murdered. "He was a very real person to me, and to think he was *dead*. He might have been the first person I ever knew who died."

Many years later, I interviewed Marvin Rich, a longtime member of CORE who served as the organization's publicity director for many years and, by many accounts, was the man who really kept CORE functioning during trying times. Marvin was in constant contact with me during that era. "When Chaney, Goodman, and Schwerner were killed, that was very, very hard on me, because I had been in Meridian, Mississippi, the week before, with Chaney and Schwerner," recalls seventy-one-year-old Marvin, who is now the program director for the National Coalition Against Censorship in New York. "I remember sitting on the street curb, eating half a sandwich with Jim Chaney—in the black section of town, obviously. The following week I was back in New York, and on Sunday morning I picked up the *New York Times*, and there's a little paragraph about a church being burned in Philadelphia, Mississippi. And I picked up the phone, I called the office in Meridian, and I suggested they go over there. For my sanity, they told me they were already there. Well, that's where they got killed, you know. And I was going to ask them to do something which I would have had to live with the rest of my life."[4]

I remember feeling saddened by their disappearance, but I was not surprised. After hearing so many threats myself, it was not difficult to believe that the hatred ran so deeply that civil rights workers would be killed. Not only were the men's deaths disturbing because we were in the same organization, but also because all civil rights activists were still in the thick of the violent resistance to our cause. Mickey Schwerner, James Chaney, and Andrew Goodman disappeared in June, when Freedom Summer was barely underway. In Mississippi, training sessions for the new college-age summer volunteers from all over the country were still being held, hanging under the cloud of missing workers while horrified parents called and begged their children to come home.

We all knew, without a doubt, it would be a long, hot summer indeed.

Not only had I met Mickey Schwerner myself, but John had represented James Chaney as one of seventy civil rights workers arrested in Meridian, doing petitions of removal for them. In early June, John had also driven Mickey's wife, Rita Schwerner, from Meridian to a Council of Federated Organizations (COFO) office in Jackson, Mississippi. She needed a ride with John because, John says, at the moment her husband was driving to Ohio to pick up new summer recruits, including a white college student named Andrew Goodman, who had taken part in demonstrations at the World's Fair. After John left Rita Schwerner in Jackson, he headed to Atlanta to meet me so we could enjoy one of those rare occasions when we could actually spend time together. I had brought Scout with me to John's apartment in Atlanta, where I was waiting for him with anticipation. John and I hadn't seen each other in two weeks, and we planned to spend a few quiet days with no interruptions.

Of course, that didn't last long. It never did. Right away, John got a telephone call from Wiley Branton and was asked to go to St. Augustine because civil rights workers there were in dire need of a lawyer. John was needed to assist the Southern Christian Leadership Conference, Dr. Martin Luther King, and 200 other protesters arrested in demonstrations. Dr. King was flying in and out of St. Augustine to help spur ongoing protests, and the tiny Florida tourist town was boiling over with racial problems.

We decided to take Scout with us to St. Augustine in John's car, and I planned to go back to my base in Gadsden County from there. Soon, the new CORE workers would arrive for our own voter registration campaign, and I needed to prepare.

The saga of the missing civil rights workers in Mississippi has always overshadowed events in St. Augustine during that summer, which were among some of the most violent in the civil rights movement. The crises in Mississippi and St. Augustine developed nearly simultaneously, and everyone from President Johnson to Attorney General Robert Kennedy to FBI Director J. Edgar Hoover to Dr. Martin Luther King had their hands full trying to juggle responses to both problems. John was there on behalf of the NAACP Legal Defense Fund in St. Augustine at ground zero, so to speak, working with a Jacksonville attorney named Earl Johnson to free protesters, between visits from lawyers from New York and elsewhere. (In an auxiliary capacity, John helped the NAACP Legal Defense Fund win a case without precedent, *Andrew Young v. Farris Bryant*, where the United States District Court ordered the state to protect nonviolent protestors. Young later went on to have a career as a statesman; he became a U.S. representative, the ambassador to the United Nations under President Carter, and then the mayor of Atlanta.)

They had their hands full. St. Augustine was ready to explode.

In 1963, there already had been several racially motivated bombings and shootings. Segregationists' terror campaign had resulted in the self-defense shooting death of an armed white night rider trying to terrorize a Negro neighborhood. Although they had only been trying to defend their homes, four Negro activists were convicted of murder. John had represented those men, but unfortunately they were found guilty, which had been a major disappointment to him. In the wake of that, Dr. Robert Hayling's house had been riddled with shotgun blasts, and terrorists had set one Negro family's home afire and another Negro family's car afire.[5] Meanwhile, for months, Dr. Hayling and others had been begging for more support and protection from the NAACP, the SCLC, and state and federal authorities. Instead of helping Dr. Hayling, the NAACP had deemed him too radical and cut him loose. (The NAACP Legal Defense Fund, which was under separate leadership, continued to provide legal aid to Dr. Hayling and others.)

Dr. King's SCLC stepped in instead. The SCLC was looking for its next big front after the mass marches in Birmingham and the March on Washington, and Dr. King and his forces believed the city held symbolic value. After all, founded in 1565, St. Augustine was the oldest European settlement in the country, and it was planning a widely publicized celebration of its 400th birthday the next year, in 1965.

On the surface, St. Augustine didn't seem like the sort of place you would expect to erupt in racial violence, but King would later complain to city officials that his organization had never worked in a city "as lawless" as St. Augustine.[6] The oceanfront resort town relied heavily on the spending of Northern tourists, who walked the streets in shorts and casual beach clothes, seemingly without a care in the world. Many whites who lived there, as in countless small Southern towns, believed the Negroes in St. Augustine were happy, even though Negroes were segregated, shut out of city jobs, and without government allies or a biracial commission to take their concerns seriously. A central tourist spot and gathering place in St. Augustine's historic district was the old slave market.

Thanks to Dr. Hayling and his colleagues, who had sought out the SCLC, the city's segregated policies came under the national spotlight in 1964. In March, answering the SCLC's call, 200 protesters, including visiting activists like Mrs. Malcolm Peabody (a well-known socialite who was the mother of the governor of Massachussetts), were arrested in various demonstrations. Because of Mrs. Peabody's presence, the events in St. Augustine received coverage on the *Today Show.* By May, Dr. Martin Luther King appeared at a mass meeting to give notice that large-scale demonstrations were about to begin in the city, which he called a "small Birmingham."[7]

The presence of Dr. King and the out-of-town demonstrators not only enraged the local segregationists in St. Augustine, but they also drew Klan leader J. B. Stoner and other racists from cities outside of Florida. Both sides were gathering troops, and St. Augustine was the battleground. St. Augustine was a miniature stage for the momentum of the national civil rights movement and the violent tactics of its opponents, who were more and more desperate, especially with the imminent passage of the Public Accommodations Act, which would make the integration of restaurants, hotels, and other public facilities the law of the land. Desperation breeds danger.

Because the Klan influence reached so deep in St. Augustine, the city was in turmoil. There were brutal attacks there. By the end of the summer, police officers would attack other police officers they believed were being too hard on white toughs attacking peaceful Negro swimmers at a beach protest; Klan members would riot with the police; a motel proprietor would pour acidic pool solution into his swimming pool to drive away Negro swimmers trying to integrate it; more bombs would be set off; reporters from national news media would be chased and beaten by racist mobs. The sheriff himself, through his bullhorn, would encourage unruly whites to take part in a "march through niggertown." Even the Florida governor, C. Farris Bryant, would dare a U.S. District Court judge to send him to jail after the governor banned Negroes' peaceful night marches in St. Augustine, despite the judge's ruling that Negroes had the right to march and deserved police protection. (In the end, the judge chose not to exercise his right to jail the governor for contempt.) Governor Bryant would also lie outright to Negro leadership and President Johnson, claiming he had formed a biracial commission in St. Augustine when he not only had not done it, but had no intention of doing it.[8]

Yes, St. Augustine was terrible. The only consolation, as Ralph Abernathy pointed out in his autobiography, *And the Walls Came Tumbling Down*, is that the timing of the violence in St. Augustine probably helped change the minds of some U.S. congressmen who had been on the fence about the Public Accommodations Act. Even so, businessmen in St. Augustine who agreed to abide by the new integration law soon buckled because of Klan threats and violence.

John gave St. Augustine almost constant attention throughout June and July, living in Jacksonville and driving the thirty miles back and forth each day. Even if he had found acceptable accommodations in St. Augustine, he did not believe it would be safe for him to live there.

It was not safe for Dr. King, either.

In St. Augustine that June, while John and I both happened to be there, Dr. King had a moment of truth. Although he rarely spent the night in the tense city, one day he learned that a Negro hotel had been bombed, and that the bomb had been intended for him. Shakily, Dr. King assembled his SCLC colleagues around him for a press conference in reaction to the assassination attempt. We were standing in the blazing summer sun under the shade of a tree outside Dr. Hayling's office, all of our faces grim.

Recently, when Tananarive asked John to remember that day, his voice became thin and he had to pause several times because of his tears. "All of the lieutenants were there, Andrew Young and C. T. Vivian, and Hosea Williams, and they were in a protective circle around Dr. King," John said. "And I could look at Dr. King's eyes. It was different from being scared. It was like his eyes were saying *I'm a dead man.* It wasn't just him; the rest of the people, too. They seemed to say, *You're dead, King. We love you.* We all knew he was going to the hill with the cross. You could feel that his destiny was clear, and that he might as well be dead."

At that same press conference, I was standing behind Dr. King with Scout on a very short leash, and Dr. King made a sudden movement backward. Scout had always been a mean dog, which is why I kept his leash so short, but Scout was in an especially bad mood that day because of the heat, and Dr. King had come too close. Suddenly, Scout lunged and snapped his sharp teeth, missing Dr. King by an inch. A few people gasped as Dr. King jerked out of Scout's reach.

To Dr. King, I'm sure, my German shepherd looked exactly like countless other vicious police dogs he and other marchers had faced in Birmingham. After Scout lunged at him, Dr. King did not laugh it off. He hardly composed himself.

I'll always remember that look on his face.

---

At the beginning of July, I rushed off to attend a conference in Kansas City. Once again, luckily, I had the chance to see John, who was there on behalf of the Voter Education Project of the Southern Regional Council. By then, it had been a month since we had seen each other in St. Augustine. Believe it or not, because our finances were so limited, for the first nights we stayed in Kansas City I slept in the room with other women activists while John stayed in a room with male activists. After the conference ended, John and I spent an extra day there and shared a room so we could be together on July 5, 1964. We knew it would be a long time before we would be together again, so we enjoyed at least one night as man and wife. Later, our night together would take on much greater significance.

As soon as the meeting ended in Kansas City, I was back in Gadsden County to begin the arduous task of welcoming and training new workers we had hired from around the country to help us with the expanded voter project, which we now called the North Florida Citizen Education Project. The newcomers were all college students, half of them were white, and most of them had at least some previous civil rights experience. These were idealistic college students answering the call for civil rights workers in the massive voter registration campaigns underway in the South, and they had applied to work with CORE. The arrival of new workers brought my staff to fifteen, and between them they would cover ten counties that summer. For pay, each of them would earn $25 a week. As project director, I was paid all of $70 a week.

As difficult a time as I'd had finding a place to stay when I was virtually alone in Gadsden County, I now had a much larger challenge ahead of me: Workers would need families to house them in every single county we had targeted, and the workers were to be assigned in interracial pairs, which would make people more reluctant to accept them as houseguests. We also needed a larger space for our regular staff meetings, to prepare meals, and to house the workers. I'd been at my wits' end trying to locate a space for us.

As luck would have it, I had met Vivian Kelly, an elementary-school teacher in Quincy, who came to hear me speak about voter registration during one of my early appearances at Arnett Chapel AME Church. One of her neighbors had complained that the church was involved in "some mess," vowing not to go. But Mrs. Kelly wanted to know what "mess" her friend was talking about, so she went to hear me speak, and she says she was struck by my sense of resolve. She also liked the fact that I was from Gadsden County and had come home to make a difference in my own community. Mrs. Kelly is a tall, queenly woman with rich, mahogany-colored skin, and although I did not know her at the time, she knew of me; she'd been one of Mother's classmates as a child, and my biological father was her cousin, so we were related.

Like many people who had grown up in Gadsden County, Mrs. Kelly had worked in the tobacco fields as a child, making fifty cents a day toting and stringing tobacco leaves. She'd attended school in Midway through the ninth grade, then come to Quincy to finish her high school education, scrubbing floors to earn her room and board at a woman's home because her parents were too poor to pay for it. Her father borrowed fifty dollars from a farmer, enabling her to go to Florida A&M, and she didn't stop there. She completed her master's degree when she was in her late twenties, even though she was the mother of four sons and had been widowed in 1955 when her husband was killed in a car accident.

Despite being a single mother, and despite the pervasive fear that drove many Negroes away from activism, Mrs. Kelly decided to get involved. Her personal problems with whites had been limited to having white children in school buses throw orange peels at her and the other Negro students who were forced to walk to school when she was a girl, but she'd grown up hearing many of the same horrific stories my mother had heard in Gadsden County. She knew about the physician, Dr. W. S. Stevens, who had been beaten and tied to a tree in the 1940s because he tried to register people to vote. (He was the same physician who'd built a small hospital for Negroes, although the white establishment never allowed it to operate. His son, Charles Stevens, also became a physician.) When she was eleven or twelve, Mrs. Kelly had met a woman named Miss Bowie, who traveled from home to home to demonstrate how to preserve vegetables and meat. Miss Bowie had also found a man willing to donate an acre of his land to build a sorely needed park for Negro children. Miss Bowie had also talked about voter registration, and when word of that spread, racists burned the woman's house down. After constant harassment, Miss Bowie left town, like so many other Negroes who tried to make a difference. In fact, Mrs. Kelly remembers a succession of Negro physicians who tried to set up practices in Gadsden County, but always left after four or five months. "They told me that the white people would tell them that they had to leave. They never could stay here," she says.[9]

By the time our voter registration drive came to Quincy, Mrs. Kelly was fed up. She was ready to help us despite her friends' warnings, no matter what the consequences. She'd bought her house in 1956, a few years earlier, Mrs. Kelly recalled at the age of seventy-seven during an interview in 1996, and a friend told her, " 'Child, you going to be bothered with that mess? And then how're you going to pay for your house?' But something within me said, 'How can they take your house or your job?' "

Although Mrs. Kelly didn't have much room in her home because of her sons, she offered space to civil rights workers when it was needed. She also suggested we should speak to another educator, Witt Campbell, who was part of the Good Shepherds, a civic organization that originally had been founded as a group of pallbearers right after the turn of the century. Mrs. Kelly was the group's secretary.

Witt Campbell, too, was a godsend. He was the principal at Stevens Elementary School, and he shared Mrs. Kelly's bold sensibility. He was eager to assist us. As it happened, the Good Shepherds had recently purchased a property that had formerly been a little store, which they used as their meeting hall. Nestled right behind it, only visible at a certain angle from the street, was a tiny house that was not currently in use. With a kitchen and several bedrooms, the house was perfect for us. A few members of the Good Shepherds objected when Mr. Campbell suggested allowing us to use the house, much to his disappointment, but he stood his ground.

"We always said if we're *not* going to do it and they *are* going to do it, at least we can support them. That is the philosophy we had behind it. That's the way I thought about it, and many of the others, too," said Mr. Campbell, who became a pastor in later years.

The little house on Fourth Street became ours, and we dubbed it the "Freedom House."

Now we were ready for the trainees. Preparing for the larger campaign was very much like having troops in boot camp. Several local workers and attorneys participated with me in the orientation session, which was held at the Freedom House. If anyone had thought arriving in the South for the voter registration project would be like a summer camp, they were dispelled of that notion right from the start. The mood we set was businesslike and very serious. We began with the history of CORE and the basics of nonviolent philosophy: *No matter what,* the new workers were told, we were to be nonviolent. I knew it would take only one case of a CORE worker involved in a violent incident to unravel years of hard work and undermine the civil rights effort. Our foes could not wait to discredit us.

I also told the newcomers that they had come to work, not to socialize. I heard later that some of the workers did not take me seriously on this point, because they apparently had sexual relationships with other CORE workers or community members without my knowledge. Some of them were enjoying the novelty of meeting men or women of another race, but since interracial socializing was such an explosive taboo in the South, I warned them that this kind of behavior would not be tolerated. I also said I would not tolerate people who randomly broke certain laws, such as those against speeding and smoking marijuana. Once, I was riding in a car with a white worker who lit up a marijuana cigarette right in front of me! I told her she'd better get rid of it and never do that again. Even while I was working so hard to change laws that I considered unjust, I have always believed that laws are very important, and I never broke any laws lightly. If we ignored drug and traffic laws like common criminals, it would greatly undermine our effectiveness. Later, I sent some volunteers home when they broke the rules.

Rubin Kenon later told me he considered me "bossy," but I can only emphasize that I knew these young people's lives were my responsibility. I hadn't needed the disappearance of Goodman, Chaney, and Schwerner to tell me that we were in a life or death situation, and we had to behave that way.

The CORE staff had to follow very strict guidelines about procedure as they worked. I didn't want anyone to have to work alone; where possible, they worked in same-sex interracial pairs, with two people per county. Lawyers instructed them that if they were arrested, they should not resist, but they should let the police know that they understood there was a new law stating that an attorney should be present during questioning. We gave them telephone numbers for CORE's general counsel in New York, Carl Rachlin; for NAACP Defense Fund lawyers Earl Johnson and Charles Wilson; and for the Lawyer's Constitutional Defense Committee in St. Augustine. If workers were leaving one location to go to another, they had to call headquarters to report their whereabouts. We also supplied numbers for offices of the FBI, because if anyone took longer than expected to reach their destination, or we did not receive a call, we would immediately report them missing to the FBI.

I regret that I can't remember the names of all the courageous young people who came to Florida to work that summer, but some of the people in our group were FAMU students Doris Rutledge, Sidney Daniels, and Ira Simmons (all of whom had been involved in previous civil rights activities). The white workers included Judy Benninger, a former military man named Scott McVoy from Gainesville, a student named Stu Wechsler, a student from the Northeast named Eleanor Lerner, and a University of Florida student named Mike Geison. Later in the summer and fall, other volunteers would arrive to help us out. One was James "Jim"

Harmeling (the twin brother of Dan Harmeling, the white student from the University of Florida who had been arrested with Judy at the Tallahassee theater demonstration), and others included FAMU students Johnny Watson (who would one day teach math at my daughters' high school in Miami) and Linda Dixie from Quincy, as well as a high school student from Madison County named David Dukes.

Of course, we expected to be arrested, so we needed lawyers. Our lawyers came to Quincy to work in shifts, depending on how much time they had to volunteer. John coordinated the paper trail for the next attorneys' shifts, so they could hit the ground running. Our lawyers that summer included Jeff Greenup and James W. Lamberton from New York and Dave Halperin from Chicago.

After the orientation, some of the workers admitted that our warnings frightened them. Still others were frightened by experiences they had already had in the field and shocked at the level of hostility directed toward them. My attitude was *It's better for them if they're frightened.* The more careful they were, I reasoned, the less likely we were to suffer any tragedies like the one that was playing out in Neshoba County, Mississippi, where the three workers were missing.

If any of my workers thought I was being paranoid, they learned better by our next staff meeting, on an afternoon in mid-July. While we were all gathered at the Freedom House, trading stories and making plans, we suddenly heard a loud popping sound right outside. A front window shattered, and Scout began barking in the backyard. "Get down!" I shouted, and we all lunged to crouch behind the sofa and under the table. There were several more gunshots, and then we heard the sound of a car speeding off.

Freedom Summer was officially underway in Gadsden County.

Judy Benninger was very much affected by the violent environment that summer and described her feelings in an essay she wrote later that year:

> *Night has begun in Quincy, Florida. A car drives down the street. Is it really possible that I can tell the difference between a car driven by a white man and a car driven by a Negro? At night in Quincy, many learn to do this. If it is a Negro car, ears return to television. If white and slowing down, those sitting in front of the curtained window cringe within. . . . 3 A.M. and I hear a shot. Sleep and I struggle, and Pat hears, "My God, Pat, they are shooting at us*

*now." And she, "Child, how can I sleep if you're going to be talking all night?" In the morning we will look for the holes in the screen.*[10]

Police responses to attacks at the Freedom House were slow, or nonexistent. I read a newspaper story where the police chief, J. W. Haire, smiled and told a reporter that the police followed us so much for our "protection,"[11] and yet when we truly needed protection, police were hard to find. Once, we were literally pinned inside the Freedom House for nearly twenty-four hours, and Judy Benninger recalled that ordeal in beautiful detail during our 1990 interview: "As the sun went down, I could hear some black teenagers walking down the street, humming 'We Shall Overcome.' Then, as it got really dark, these people in pickup trucks were circling more than usual. I remember Jim Harmeling went out and hid behind a bush by the road, armed with a flashlight and pencil and paper, and his job was to take their license plate numbers. And Scott McVoy was out there, too, and the night riders must have seen the flashlight, so they stopped. Scott was an ex-Marine. These guys were both white. They were pretty good about their nonviolence. Anyway, these guys with rifles came toward Scott and Jim. And Scott had been trained to take the rifle away from someone in hand-to-hand combat. He just could have grabbed his rifle and hit that guy, but he didn't. Finally, one of the guys just took his rifle and hit Scott across the head so badly that his face was just laid all open. He had to have stitches. That was the first thing. I got on the phone immediately. I called the mayor, I called the city police, I called the FBI. About an hour later, someone came by and started shooting into the Freedom House. And nobody came. The police didn't come. The FBI didn't come. No one came. And there we were.

"That night, we slept in the back of the house. We took all of our mattresses—the men were all sleeping on the floor in the living room—and their suitcases, and they piled them up as high as they could across the front of the house, and went to sleep on the floor. The next morning we got up and saw two things that, to me, were so typical of what was so meaningful about the civil rights movement: We found bullet holes all across the front of the house. We also found two huge pots of collard greens. And that couple next door came out of their house, a man and a wife, and the man stood there with a shotgun. It was such a wonderful feeling, not only the physical protection and the terrible danger they were putting themselves in, but also that support in bringing us food. We had really brought this down on their community."

The Negro man who lived next door to the Freedom House, a distant relative of mine through marriage named Arthur Jones, often appeared on his porch with his shotgun, looking for our attackers. "You all may be nonviolent, but I'm not. I have a family to protect," Mr. Jones told us. To his credit, despite his worries for his wife, Modieste, and their six children, Mr. Jones never complained about our presence next door to him. He was another unsung soldier, and he and his wife live in the same house to this day.

Can you imagine having no police response to an ongoing shooting attack in an otherwise quiet residential neighborhood? That's why it's so hypocritical for police to claim they were trying to "protect" us during those days, and I think even some of our own out-of-town attorneys thought we were exaggerating about the threat, until they happened to be present during an attack. Like any foot soldiers in battle, we grew accustomed to working while under seige. The words to one of the freedom songs we distributed to our workers described it very well: "We are Soldiers in the Army. / We've got to fight although we have to cry. / We've got to hold up the freedom banner. / We've got to hold it up until we die."

Someone might get killed, but no one's bullets were going to stop us.

---

Voter registration in the rural South wasn't as simple as going to churches, homes, bars, and fishing holes to encourage people to vote. Especially since our workers were sometimes sent out in interracial pairs, many prospective voters were nervous about being seen talking to us. Many doors were slammed in our faces, and we had to learn patience. Sometimes, the same person who slammed the door in your face today might welcome you tomorrow if you came by yourself, without a white companion.

Another obstacle was the living arrangements of the poorer Negroes. These were tenant farmers who lived in virtual shacks set far back on much larger, white-owned farms. We usually had to wait until sundown to talk to them, since they were working in the fields during daylight hours. Then we had to tread carefully, because most white farmers did not welcome us.

Vivian Kelly recalls that she and a white worker, Stu Wechsler—on a rare occasion when a black woman and a white man were paired, or vice versa—were approaching the homes of some Negro tenant farmers on a farm in Midway when suddenly she saw the white owner set his two large dogs on them. Barking angrily, the dogs charged. Mrs. Kelly and Stu turned and began to run. "Stu ran and lost his shoe. He had some tennis shoes on," Mrs. Kelly recalls. "That was one of my most frightening experiences, because, see, I'm afraid of dogs." (Luckily, the dogs didn't catch them.) Stu wasn't so lucky another time, when he arrived on the farm property of a Gadsden County commissioner with several other male civil rights workers to approach field hands. Stu was badly beaten that day, charged with trespassing, and sent to jail.[12]

Reaching the voters was only the first problem. Because daily survival was more crucial than book learning for the poor, many of the Negroes were illiterate. They could not read the ballots, and we had workshops to show people sample ballots, illustrating where the candidates' name would be placed. We never encouraged anyone to vote for a Democrat or a Republican, but we wanted them to know where to find their party's box.

Then, after all of that, if someone finally did decide they would take the step of registering to vote, we often had to provide transportation. We rented cars for our project, but we suffered so much vandalism and so many acts of violence in those cars that the rental companies stopped renting to us. Because registrar J. Love Hutchinson also ran the *Gadsden County Times* newspaper, voter registration in Gadsden County was at the *Times* office, a part of the white establishment most Negroes would never consider venturing to on their own. It was open only one day a week, on Mondays, and then, of course, the potential Negro voters faced the surveillance of nearby police or other intimidation. Mrs. Kelly recalls being so afraid that she was shaking the day she registered to vote there. She tried to put her hand on her hip, but it slipped because she was trembling so much. One county literally tried to close its books rather than register the growing number of Negro voters.

Every day brought a new struggle.

To Doris Rutledge, working in Florida was a compromise, because she'd originally hoped to do voter registration work that summer in Mississippi. Her mother was very relieved when she ended up in Florida, Doris says, but she was still far from safe. Doris was paired with a white woman named Eleanor Lerner, and they were both assigned to the small Florida town of Live Oak, in Suwannee County. Doris and Eleanor ran into a problem after their first day together. Residents from various counties had written to us to express interest in housing registration workers, and a local Negro schoolteacher had volunteered his home to Doris and Eleanor. They spent only one night there. In the morning, as they were dressing and preparing for another day in the field, they heard a knock at their door. Sheepishly, their host told them that he was getting harassed because Eleanor was white, so he asked them to leave.

He helped them find another candidate, a woman from his church. She agreed that Doris and Eleanor could move in with her. For the first couple of days, everything was fine. Then, another problem arose. "We noticed that she didn't go to work one day, and so we said, 'Well, that's her day off,' " Doris recalls. But by the next day, when the woman stayed at home again, they realized something was wrong. "The lady tried not to tell us she had been fired."

After that, a local eighty-five-year-old minister, Rev. Jenkins (Doris cannot remember his first name), offered his house instead. Rev. Jenkins was very strong-minded, and he not only owned his home, but also much of the property on that particular street, so he felt he could offer the workers more protection. After some time, someone actually posted a "Wanted: Dead or Alive" poster in Live Oak, bearing Doris's name and photo. Sure enough, at one point, someone fired a gun at Doris while she was standing in front of Rev. Jenkins's house. She recognized the man who'd fired the shot, so she called the FBI and reported him. She remembers a dismissive FBI agent telling her, "Well, it might have been blanks, you know."

"Yeah, and we might have been dead," Doris said.

The dangers and indignities were clear, but the rewards were much greater for us. On July 27, registration fever swept through Gadsden County on an unplanned Freedom Day. When the registrar's office opened at 9:00 A.M., twenty Negroes had already lined up to register, and there was a constant line all day long. In one day, 350 Negroes registered, which was more than during the entire month of January, when our project was new. Because the sun was so hot, we provided beach umbrellas, cold water, and soft drinks to cool people off as they waited. The line was quite a sight. Even when the office closed, there were still seventy-five Negroes waiting. The growing crowds of registering Negroes in Gadsden County brought our total countrywide number to 1,900.[13]

The greatest joy came for us at 2:45 P.M., when two CORE workers arrived in a car from Chattahoochee, which was twenty-six miles away. The workers opened the passenger-side door and carried out a very elderly

Negro woman, who told us she was 109 years old. "I was born a slave," she announced. "It's 'bout time I registered to vote."

The woman's name was Mrs. Pearlie Williams, and she had allowed herself to be driven into Quincy with strangers because she wanted to vote in her first election. When she arrived in her black Sunday dress with her hair pinned up, wearing a CORE button on her lapel, she buoyed all of our spirits. Mrs. Williams could *remember* slavery, and she had come to register. We had reached her.

Mrs. Williams told us there were other people in Chattahoochee who wanted to register, including her ninety-year-old daughter, but they were afraid.

"They say if I come back alive, they'll come register too," she said.

Frail Pearlie Williams was like Harriet Tubman that day, leading her people to freedom.

## Twenty-Two

# Tananarive Due

**"If I die or am killed . . . you may rest assured that what I've already set in motion will never be stopped."**
***—Malcolm X***

By August of 1996, not long after my mother and I began our work on the civil rights book in earnest, we learned that another quiet hero had died.

Witt Campbell, who had provided much-needed shelter for my mother and other civil rights workers during Freedom Summer, passed away at the age of eighty-five. When we learned of Mr. Campbell's death, Mom and I decided to go to the funeral in Quincy and conduct research while we were there, by searching the archives of FAMU, Florida State University, and the newspaper morgue at the *Tallahassee Democrat.* Mr. Campbell's death only emphasized for Mom, perhaps for both of us, how these strands of history are yanked so easily out of reach, giving us a sense of an urgent deadline.

That might explain why, even though there was no rhyme or reason to the timing, we decided we had to interview Dad at 8:00 P.M. on Thursday, the night before our departure, when both of us should have been making preparations for the trip. All of us were heading in different directions. Dad was on his way to Washington, D.C., to appear with other attorneys and advocates before the Justice Department on behalf of Haitians being deported from Miami. With the recent crash of TWA flight 800 and the bombing at the Olympics in Atlanta a week and a half later, we were all living with the sense that we didn't know what would happen next. Dad answered questions for two hours on videotape, under the hot light in Mom's home office.

I don't think I had ever seen my father shed a tear before, unless it was at his mother's funeral; and, in any case, I don't remember it. But that night, he shed tears. We asked him to recall any situations in which he'd believed his life was in danger, and he began discussing his field work not in Tallahassee or other points in Florida, but in Mississippi during Freedom

Summer in 1964. "I can remember today like it was yesterday when I was picked up by the field secretary for SNCC, by the name of Bob Moses," Dad said. "I had read about him, and I knew all about him. I thought he was one of these courageous soldiers. He was older than most young kids. He was about twenty-nine years old. That was old for an SNCC worker. He picked me up, and I remember going to Mississippi after leaving New Orleans, and I could see his eyes in the rearview mirror. He was not looking ahead, but just looking behind to see if he was being followed. And I began to realize *This is dangerous, what we're doing.* Until then, I just thought of the excitement. Then I began to realize *This man is afraid.* He's afraid for his life. And I began to think *If he's afraid, I'd better be afraid.* Then I began to realize we had young people working here in these dangerous situations, not for the excitement, because they were afraid, but somehow they felt they had to do what they had to do."

But that wasn't what made him cry. Rather, it was recalling the people who did not have the notoriety of Bob Moses or James Farmer, those who were the residents of Mississippi towns who were sacrificing their jobs and risking their lives. "They didn't have anything to gain from it," he said. "It was so hopeless."

His meaning, of course, was that these people, in the short term, could expect no personal gain from what they were doing. And it was "hopeless" because there would be no overnight changes, no changes that any of them might reasonably expect to see within their lifetimes. And yet they still worked, they still dreamed, they still sacrificed.

And for them I saw my father cry for the first time.

In my mind, that interview set the tone for our trip to Quincy. Mom and I left about 9:00 P.M., and I drove straight until four in the morning. We slept four and a half hours, ate a hurried fast-food breakfast, and made it to Quincy shortly before the funeral.

I didn't know Witt Campbell at all except what I'd seen of him in an interview Mom taped with him in 1989, when he sat with her and matter-of-factly discussed how he allowed her to set up a CORE office in the house he rented to her in Quincy, the Freedom House. He did this, of course, above the objections of some members of the Good Shepherds, the organization he led at the time. Mom had a warm spot for him, and she'd promised the last time she'd seen him, about a year before his death, that we were going to write a book about what had happened.

Blacks in Gadsden County had considered Mr. Campbell the unofficial "school superintendent" because of the breadth of his knowledge, and he later became one of the county's first black school board members. When he was demoted from his position as a principal in the wake of integration—like every black principal in Florida—he and fellow educators Vivian Kelly and James Palmer sued for promotions in the school system, citing discrimination. They joined dozens of other educators in two successful suits filed by white civil rights lawyer Kent Spriggs, who still practices in Tallahassee. Afterward, Mr. Campbell was again named a principal, and Mrs. Kelly became the first black woman in the county to gain that position. Mr. Campbell and Mrs. Kelly both retired after serving as school principals in a county that was mostly black, but which had few black principals.[1]

Mom had told me from the start that she planned to distance herself emotionally from the funeral, but it was difficult at the beginning. Gospel music, spirituals, and hymns almost always have the power to make me cry under any circumstances, but especially at an occasion as somber as a funeral. This one was particularly solemn, since the faces of the clergy and elders at the front of the church were as glum as those seated in the pews. Witt Campbell was a man who would be sorely missed, I could see, probably the kind of man no one believed would ever die.

The choir sang "Soon and Very Soon" during the processional: *Soon and very soon / I am going to see my King.* The sentiment was one intended as celebration, but it sounded more like resignation. The family members filed by, with a couple of girls (grandchildren, I'd presumed) walking with the physical support of older family members. One in particular was crying, and I believe it was her wretched face that made Mom start tearing up, too. There's something especially moving about watching a young person grieve for a much older person, since so many of us end up far removed from our elders, barely knowing them. But these girls knew Mr. Campbell, loved him, and grieved for him, and the fact that he'd lived a full life, to the age of eighty-five, serving on the school board until he died, was of little comfort to them.

"This is going to be hard," Mom said.

She was the first person on the program to give reflections.

"I'm so proud to be from Quincy," she began in her striking timbre. I believe Mom was the one who first began to awaken the church from its stupor.

She talked about how he supported her presence in Quincy, gave her a place to stay, didn't buckle even after the White Citizens' Council fired gunshots into the Freedom House. Some people in the room, I'm sure, knew nothing of that time. Mom was the chronicler.

The eulogy, delivered by Tallahassee's presiding elder, Rev. Ralph L.

Wilson, was very stirring to me because it painted an accurate picture of this man. He went just a little bit further, Rev. Wilson said, comparing Mr. Campbell's actions to those of Jesus as he slowly left his disciples, even his closest ones, behind. In the eulogy, he discussed Mr. Campbell's courage during the civil rights era, and his dogged tenacity throughout the rest of his life. Mr. Campbell personified the kind of person Dad was talking about when he was moved to tears Thursday night: the people who sacrifice for change, and who are often little remembered for what they do.

Not long afterward, Mom told me that she heard from a friend that Mr. Campbell's obituary in the newspaper was so spare that there was no indication of how important he had been in his community. "If I hadn't known him," her friend said, "I wouldn't have even known who they were talking about."

The forgetting begins as soon as we die.

After the funeral was over, a common remark could be heard outside in the blazing afternoon sun as school board candidates mingled with friends and devotees: *Who will take his place?* As for the school board, the question was left for the ballot. But an election only ensures a seat, not a voice. As Mr. Campbell himself said in that interview with Mom, he'd learned that a black face is no guarantee of a righteous voice. "The problem we are having is the very same—it is us," he said.

*Who will take his place?* The question was almost wholly rhetorical. The mourners seemed to take for granted, wistfully but with certainty, that there was, in fact, no one to take his place. Instead of bolstering itself to fight on, the community seemed to be preparing for its permanent losses.

Of course, these were only the impressions of an outsider visiting on a very sad day. It was heartening, I suppose, that so many people took comfort in the idea that Mom and I were writing a book to remember Witt Campbell and others like him. But knowing history, as imperative as it is, it is only the beginning of the process: The most important thing is to use it.

Sitting in the church basement, as we ate roasted chicken, collard greens, potato salad, and pound cake with the family members and closest mourners, one woman recalled how Thurgood Marshall came quietly into town during the 1950s on a fact-finding mission and stayed in the home of a woman she knew. Few people knew he'd been there until he was gone.

I imagined Thurgood Marshall as the young man, full of fire for change, about to spearhead one of the most important court cases in this nation's history. Then I thought of Marshall as I'd seen him when I was a young person: the staid, wise voice on the Supreme Court.

It's impossible for me to think about Thurgood Marshall without being stung by the biggest irony of all, that the Supreme Court's "black seat"—which was a foreign concept at the time he visited Quincy for that fact-finding mission—was so immediately filled by Clarence Thomas, one of the beneficiaries of the civil rights movement and yet a man whose conservative views are painful to so many of the very people who hoisted him upon their tired, sagging shoulders. How likely are we to have another black voice on the Supreme Court so long as Justice Thomas sits there? To understand the most recent history of blacks in America, one must look no further than this.

"Who will take his place?" they asked of Witt Campbell.

Who, indeed?

## Twenty-Three

# Patricia Stephens Due

**I swear to the Lord,**
**I still can't see**
**Why Democracy means**
**Everybody but me.**
***—Langston Hughes***

By August 1964, I had not seen my husband for a full month. This was nothing new to me. Soon after he'd passed the bar in November 1963, even before he began monitoring voter registration, John had actually moved to Miami for a while to find work, accepting a job at the state's first integrated law firm, Heiken & Marger, on Miami Beach. We both thought his career was on its way, but the experience had been very disappointing. John could not attract Negro clients because Negroes were not welcome on Miami Beach. John was tailed by Miami Beach police wherever he went. Because he had trouble building a client base, John couldn't produce an income and was forced to live with Mother during that time. As you can imagine, John felt very uncomfortable being forced to live with his mother-in-law. Our only earnings were the meager $70 a week I made as the voting project director, and John did not like being supported by his wife.

John's circumstances really worked against him as a Negro. Even people who professed to be "liberal" did not want to hire him. When he sought a new job at the American Civil Liberties Union in Miami, he was told he wasn't a good candidate because the ACLU was not a civil rights organization—then they hired a white civil rights activist, one who didn't even have a law degree! Both white and Negro students took the same bar examination, and although John had passed it, his degree from FAMU was considered inferior because it was from a Negro school that received inferior state support. In fact, in 1963, ACLU attorney Tobias Simon—who had been subjected to a malicious campaign to disbar him because of his activism—recruited one of our civil rights allies, Dr. John O. Brown, to file a lawsuit to close FAMU's law school by arguing that a low percentage of FAMU's graduates passed the Florida bar. John challenged the suit in a letter to the *St. Petersburg Times,* arguing that admissions tests for the University of Florida's law school were culturally biased and had excluded Negroes who later successfully practiced law, and that FAMU's law school should instead be opened to students of all races. Simon's case was dismissed, but within a few years, state funding for FAMU's law school stopped and Florida State University was awarded a law school. (Fights to reinstate FAMU's law school continued for years; a law school for FAMU finally reopened in Orlando in 2002, a hard-fought compromise that still leaves the law school isolated from the Tallahassee campus and community.)

In early 1964, we had been very relieved when John won his position as an Eleanor Roosevelt Fellow, but the separations were difficult for us. The only bright side was that we were always so happy to see each other when we had been apart for a long time.

When John finally came to see me in August of 1964, I was so excited! After weeks of tension, some intimate time with my husband was exactly what I craved. But when John and I were alone, making love, I felt the sharpest pain I've ever experienced in my life. I cried out. For thirty minutes, I was paralyzed with pain.

"What's wrong, Patricia?" John kept asking me, concerned. I had to tell him I didn't know. Maybe I thought the pain in my insides had been brought on by stress. I have always had a very strong pain threshold, so I hoped the wave would soon pass. I told John I just wanted to lie still. After a half hour, I very carefully made my way toward the bathroom.

That's the last thing I remember. On my way to the bathroom, I fainted.

My regular doctor was out of town, so John and I visited another doctor. He examined me and told me I had lost a lot of blood, so he ordered a blood transfusion for me, but he did not speculate *why* or *how* I might be bleeding internally. Sure enough, after the transfusion, I felt much better, so I decided to carry on with my life. Since everything seemed fine, John left to go back to his work and I went back to my old pace. It may seem silly now, but I didn't follow up on that doctor's visit to find out why I had been bleeding internally, even though Judy begged me to. "I feel fine, I feel fine," I kept telling her. "I have too much to do, and it has to get done."

One day, I finally had no choice. I found my panties covered in blood.

Alarmed when I told her, Judy insisted that I see my doctor this time. Grudgingly, I agreed.

I visited my regular doctor, a Negro doctor named Alexander Brickler II who had been very supportive during my forty-nine days in jail in 1960, visiting me often with his wife. I got a thorough exam at his office. "Mrs. Due, you're pregnant," he told me. Before I could rejoice or react in any way, he said in a very grave tone, while staring me in the eye, "But I'm afraid it's not a normal pregnancy. You have an ectopic pregnancy, which means that the embryo was growing outside of your womb, in the fallopian tube. Now that fallopian tube has burst inside your body. I'm not trying to alarm you unnecessarily, but you are literally dying. You need to have surgery right away. I have to admit you to the hospital now."

I cut him off right there. His words had not completely sunk in, but I felt an immediate reaction to his last instructions. "I can't go to a hospital now."

Dr. Brickler gave me a questioning look, then he added patiently, "If you don't have the surgery right away, you'll hemorrhage, and the bleeding will be much more severe. You will bleed to death, Mrs. Due."

Looking back on it now, I must not have been completely in my right mind during this time. I listened to everything the doctor said, and I understood it all. I had a serious problem. I needed surgery. I was dying. Perhaps I thought he was only exaggerating, since his language was so dramatic. All I could think about was a voter registration campaign and the endless details I felt I needed to supervise. I was the project director, and Judy and I couldn't simply disappear for the rest of the day. We had to talk to the workers in various counties who might call the Freedom House, whose lives might be in jeopardy. On August 7, seven more workers had been arrested in Mount Pleasant, a small town in Gadsden County: Betty Green, Cleola Goodson, Jesse McMillan, and Miles McCray, who were all minors; and Stu Wechsler, Scott McVoy, and Barbara Preston.[1] The workers needed us. Our staff was small, so our absence would be marked.

"I can't go to a hospital now," I said again.

Imagine the look he gave me. The poor man was exasperated! Thank goodness he told me I needed to stay somewhere close to a hospital. If I stayed in Quincy, which was more remote, he said I would be dead before I could get help. (Dr. Brickler, incidentally, later became the first Negro doctor admitted to practice at formerly segregated Tallahassee Memorial Hospital.)[2]

After the visit, Judy begged me to admit myself to the hospital as Dr.

Brickler had advised. Again, I refused. But Judy won one concession from me, and it no doubt saved my life: Instead of staying in Quincy that night, we would bring our work with us, tell people where to reach us, and get a room in a Tallahassee hotel. The Public Accommodations Act had just passed, so legally I was now permitted to stay wherever I chose. In Tallahassee, a Holiday Inn gave us a room, and we took a room together. Perhaps registering at the hotel that had recently been integrated should have felt like a victorious moment, but to me it was an inconvenience. My mind was still on the CORE workers.

I barely made it to the hotel room. As I climbed the stairs, I felt weaker and weaker. Something really was terribly wrong, I realized. As my doctor's words came back to me, I began to feel concerned. All I remember is that I wanted to get to the bathroom.

There I discovered yet more blood. Much more. Again, I fainted. Medically, I was in a state of shock. Judy called for an ambulance. I drifted in and out of consciousness, but I was lucid enough to try to keep my dress positioned modestly over me while they brought me down the stairs. After that, I lost consciousness again.

Since John was away and I was unconscious, I really believe Judy forged my name on the medical papers to authorize the surgery that saved my life. The next thing I realized, it was all over, and John was standing over my hospital bed with a worried look on his face.

"How did you . . . " I mumbled. "What happened?"

"I got brought in by the Florida Highway Patrol," John said.

Sure enough, when word of my dire illness had reached the police radios, the Highway Patrol had sent troopers to find John after being told he was on his way to Gadsden County, and they escorted him all the way to FAMU's hospital. The police had given us nothing but grief all summer, but they brought my husband to me when it really mattered. Usually civil rights workers and the police felt as if they were on opposing sides, and some police officers, particularly in St. Augustine, were Klan sympathizers who would have cheered to see a troublemaker like me die. Yet sometimes life's circumstances can bring both sides together. Sometimes we are just people after all. I am grateful to those officers.

Because I had lost my left fallopian tube, Dr. Brickler told me he didn't think I would be able to conceive a child without great difficulty, if at all. That made me sad. What made me sadder was when he told me I would need to rest for several weeks, and that it would be out of the question for me to return to the voter registration project I had been shepherding for months.

While I was recovering, I remembered a conversation John had had with our lawyer, Howard Dixon, soon after John and I decided to get married. He worried that once we were married and started our family, we would no longer be of use to the Movement. "Let all children be your children," he said. At the time, I thought his concern was unfounded. I never could have imagined that a pregnancy would sideline me from the civil rights movement. My commitment was far too strong. Now, without warning, a pregnancy *had* sidelined me. Yet there would be no child, and if my doctor's fears were right, there might never be any children. For all I knew, I had just lost my present and a part of my future. I felt useless. That was a terrible time for me.

Judy left the project soon after I did to become more involved in Gainesville, and CORE put a field secretary named Spiver Gordon in charge of the North Florida Citizen Education Project. He did a fine job. I moved into John's apartment in Atlanta. After years with virtually no breaks, I had no choice but to take some time off to care for myself. Only nearly dying could have kept me away.

---

I am so proud of Gadsden County!

Although I was in Atlanta with John for the rest of the summer, I moved on to Jacksonville in the fall after I received good news: I was permitted to re-enroll for classes at FAMU! I was finally able to complete the student teaching that had been interrupted by my suspension. I continued to get regular updates from the others still involved with the voting project.

It's important to remember that our project in Gadsden County was never limited to voter education and registration. Area churches, like Arnett Chapel AME and Mount Moriah, hosted meetings and workshops on community involvement and direct action protests. We also started Freedom Schools to teach young people new skills, such as typing. Many years later, I met a young woman who said she'd attended a Freedom School I taught in Quincy, and she credited the experience with eventually setting her on a path toward law school. With only a little initial leadership, the people of Gadsden County really came together to devise solutions to their own problems—unlike some Southern communities, whose grass-roots coalitions fell apart as soon as the civil rights organizers left town. Led by Rev. James Crutcher and others, Gadsden County developed a civic organization, C.I.G. (Citizens Interest Group), which remained quite active in community improvement projects.

Of course, segregation in northern Florida didn't end with the passage of the Civil Rights Act of 1964, and civil rights workers met continued harassment throughout the year. The *Florida Free Press,* a weekly newsletter, kept workers and the community informed of troubling incidents, such as the time four Negroes—Johnny Watson, Charlie Hall, Steve Hendley, and Vencille Gibson—were threatened with a shotgun when they tried to eat at the Havana Terminal diner in a small town right outside Quincy. A white CORE observer, Arlene Bock, was thrown to the pavement as she watched, her camera yanked roughly from around her neck. A crowd grew, chanting "Kill them! Kill them!" Another white CORE volunteer, Richard Williams, was arrested as he tried to drive the group that had been attacked to the FBI office to complain. Williams was charged with driving without a license, even though his license was perfectly valid. He was taken to jail, where he was beaten and released after two days.

That same week, six fires were set in the North Florida Citizen Education Project's office in downtown Quincy, damaging half the rooms in the six-room suite. Luckily, no one was there at the time, and many of the papers destroyed had duplicates stored elsewhere. As he viewed the damage from kerosene-soaked rags, Spiver Gordon told a reporter, "Florida at one time had the reputation of being one of the better Southern states, but this proves that the haters in Florida have come out of the same rotten barrel as those in Mississippi and Alabama. . . . He did not scare us, and he did not inconvenience us."[3]

There were many other incidents, probably too numerous to name, but none of that could diminish the sense of accomplishment the entire community felt on election day, November 3, when a record number of more than 3,500 Negroes in Gadsden County went to the polls to vote. In the previous presidential election, only 300 Gadsden County Negroes had been registered to vote; now 4,300 were reportedly registered, and about 90 percent of them voted. In fact, according to *The Pain and the Promise,* North Florida had registered more Negroes than any other region of the South.[4]

On election day, CORE workers amassed a fleet of eighty-five cars to help transport voters to the polls, and the ferry service ran all day. Those who couldn't get rides walked. People who could barely see struggled to choose the right lines on the ballots as CORE workers gave last-minute instructions on how to mark their candidates. When a CORE worker pointed out to five women he had brought that they should mark the ballot's second line if they wanted to vote for Barry Goldwater, the women all "whooped with laughter," a *St. Petersburg Times* reporter noted.[5]

It was a celebration. Everyone knew what a momentous occasion it was. Among the voters was Mrs. Pearlie Williams, the 109-year-old woman we had registered that summer. She turned up to have her say, too, although she admitted to a reporter that she had trouble seeing which candidate she had voted for. "I hope it was for Johnson," she said.[6]

The day did not go entirely smoothly. One Negro woman was physically removed from a polling place and her ballot destroyed because she was wearing a button that said "I Am Registered." (Polling places ban political literature, but it's ridiculous that a button proclaiming one's registration status would be considered "political" at election time.) Several other ballots were also impounded because the voters were carrying matchbooks with their candidates' names printed on them.

In the end, President Johnson won the state of Florida, but he did not win Gadsden County. Whites in the fairly affluent tobacco county gave the election to Barry Goldwater by a slim 190 votes.[7] If only a few more registered Negroes had turned up to vote, the county's election undoubtedly would have gone to Johnson, very much the same story that Floridians faced in the 2000 presidential election. I have always known that every vote counts!

Jewel Jerome Dixie, a Negro man who had written himself in as a candidate for Gadsden County sheriff, got more than 1,500 votes,[8] which was unheard of in that area, although he did not get nearly enough votes to win. Negroes' preferred candidates did not win the Gadsden County election in pure numbers, but we had all won something far, far greater.

Pride. Courage. Belief in our future as full American citizens.

I am so very proud of Gadsden County.

---

In the fall of 1964, I still had to contend with visits to New York based on my arrest at the World's Fair. During one of my absences, I had to leave Scout and Freedom, our two dogs, with John in his Atlanta apartment. That might have worked out fine, except that John was sent to Mississippi to help evaluate the results of the Freedom Summer voter education campaign. With no one to look after Scout and Freedom, John had to take them with him.

What happened next is one of those stories from the Movement that is both funny and sad.

John and I had a blue Volkswagen Beetle, and John drove the dogs to Mississippi in the backseat, as we often did. John stopped at the national SNCC office in Atlanta because he'd been asked to pick up Bob Moses. "Why are those dogs back there?" Moses said when John arrived, eyeing the two German shepherds suspiciously.

"Sorry, man, my wife's in court in New York," John had to explain.

The two men drove to Mississippi with the dogs in tow. John dropped Bob Moses off at the Council of Federated Organizations (COFO) office in Jackson, then drove to his final destination of Greenwood, Mississippi, where Stokely Carmichael and an activist named Art Cobb had an office under the auspices of SNCC. John met with the activists, and at about 2:00 A.M., he realized he needed to let the dogs out. He didn't have leashes for them—and he wouldn't have been eager to walk around Greenwood at night anyway—so he opened the door to the office to let the dogs run out.

"Scout didn't go very far, but Freedom took off," John recalls. She ran out of sight.

So John ran outside bellowing, "Freedom! Freeeeee-dom!"

I can only imagine how far his voice must have carried. The windows to the office were open, so John's fellow activists heard the fuss he was making outside as he cried for Freedom. By the time he came back inside with the dog, Art Cobb and some others gave him an earful. "What's the matter with you? Are you trying to get us shot?"

Somehow, John survived his trip to Greenwood, Mississippi.

During the 1964–65 school year, I threw myself into my studies. I had decided that nothing was going to come between me and my degree. I had been attending Florida A&M University, on and off, since 1957—for seven years!—and I was ready to move to the next phase of my life.

During my student teaching in Jacksonville, I taught five civics classes a day, and I was asked to conduct the program for what was then called "Negro History Week." I taught the students about Florida's most recent civil rights history, discussing the sit-ins and our subsequent projects. I already felt a need to begin passing on the story. I knew how short people's memories are. After I completed my student teaching and returned to FAMU's campus in early 1965, John joined me in Tallahassee because he'd been hired as Southern Regional Counsel for CORE.

I was finally doing what I wanted to do for myself, and John was doing what he wanted to do. As I wrote to Mother on February 8, *I am just happy to be together again.*

But happiness always seemed fleeting in the 1960s. Two weeks after my letter to Mother, on February 21, 1965, yet another horrible event took place: Malcolm X was assassinated. In many ways, the death of Malcolm X was more upsetting to me than the death of President Kennedy. Although I had never been a follower of the Nation of Islam, I always realized Malcolm X was a very necessary component of the struggle. He was the only one really talking about economic development, which I thought was crucial to the survival of our people, and because the black nationalist was perceived as so militant, more people in power were willing to listen to those of us who followed a philosophy perceived to be more moderate, like Dr. King. With Malcolm X gone, it seemed that the struggle was in the midst of a nightmare that would never end. Who would be next?

A month after Malcolm X's death, Priscilla, who was teaching in Ghana by then, wrote us with some news: She had gotten married! During her ship's passage, she'd met a Dutch radio operator named Muncko Derk Kruize, whom she called "Mun" for short. They married in Sekondi, Ghana. Like me, Priscilla had a civil ceremony, but unlike me, she had a honeymoon, in Israel, courtesy of some of her friends. I was happy for Priscilla, but I had never met the man she married, so now my sister's life was even further removed from mine. Since she had married a foreigner, it seemed less likely that she would return to the States anytime soon. Mother, for one, was very upset not to be included in the wedding, but it would have been too expensive. Mother couldn't afford to fly to Africa, and Priscilla and Mun couldn't yet afford to bring her.

Still, this was an exciting time for the Stephens sisters. Soon after Priscilla got married, despite my doctor's pessimistic prediction, I discovered that John and I had conceived a child. We were thrilled! This time, there was no confusion about whether I was pregnant because I suffered from terrible morning sickness. I felt sick all the time, to the point where sometimes I could hardly move. Everyone told me my morning sickness would pass after three months, and I looked forward to that milestone, but unfortunately it lingered. I was sick all nine months. We had to hire a housekeeper because all I could do was lie on the sofa, or on the floor. The floor was my favorite resting spot, really.

By then, John and I had a house on the other side of town, on Fourth Avenue, so I had to drive myself to classes each day. I still remember how I would drive a little, then pull over to vomit. Start, stop. Start, stop. But I always made it to my classes. Once I arrived on the campus, my professors were understanding, allowing me to eat crackers in class to soothe my nausea. I also signed up for a golf class during my pregnancy because it entailed a lot of walking, and walking was what I craved. I haven't played golf since.

I honestly don't know how I passed my classes during my last term at FAMU. When I was in class, it took virtually all of my concentration not to feel sick. I took notes, but I could tell I was not absorbing the information. I often panicked, thinking, "Oh my goodness, I'm going to have to actually recall this information!" I had no idea how I would manage, but somehow I did. By way of a miracle, right before exam time, I had one good day—and I mean *one* day—when I did not feel sick at all. Relieved, I gathered my notes and textbooks and studied as hard as I could, forcing myself to retain as much as I could. That was the only way I was able to make it.

I wrote Mother that I wanted to leave a trophy to FAMU that meant a lot to me. During our summer tour after the jail-in, I had received a trophy "for convictions above and beyond the call of duty" at a Freedom Jubilee at Forbes Field in Pittsburgh, soon before receiving the Gandhi Award from CORE. By the time I was finally about to graduate, I really wanted to begin mending the bad feelings that had brewed over the years between activists and Dr. Gore. *What has happened in Tallahassee should become a part of the history of the city and school, and as I see it, the only way for this to happen is for me to practice what I preach—nonviolence—forgiving and trying to bring all sides together.*

As I was approaching my own milestone in August, John had reached his earlier that year: He opened his own law office in Tallahassee. We have a photograph of John wearing a suit and bow tie while polishing the smoky glass on the door of his office—JOHN D. DUE, JR., ATTORNEY AT LAW, the sign reads. The dean of FAMU's law school, Thomas Miller Jenkins, who had just been selected president of Albany State College in Georgia, stands proudly beside John, watching his former student set out on his own. That photo ran in the *Indianapolis Recorder*, a Negro newspaper.

Graduation day was one of the proudest days of my life. There I was, twenty-five years old, finally graduating from a four-year college after so many setbacks! The only painful aspect of the day was that John and my brother, Walter, were the only family members who attended the ceremony. Priscilla was out of the country, and Mother had finally received a ticket to Ghana from Priscilla, so she had left for a trip we all knew she would remember the rest of her life. Priscilla sent me a letter of congratulations instead: *I am extremely grateful, proud, and overwhelmed that you have finished the beginning of a long educational journey,* she said.

It was good to see Walter, though, so the absence of Mother and Priscilla did not dampen my spirits. In fact, the night of my graduation party was one of the few nights I wasn't sick from the pregnancy. John and I invited all of our friends from the Movement to the house, and we had the party to end all parties. I danced myself nearly to exhaustion! People kept asking me, "Pat, how can you keep dancing like that when you've been so sick?" But it was as if I'd tapped into a source of energy I'd forgotten about, because I felt more happy and free than I had in a long time. Losing myself in the music reminded me of my days as a freshman on FAMU's campus, absorbed in my own world in those rehearsal rooms, not realizing how quickly my life would no longer be my own. I can't remember the last time I'd had a chance to dance before graduation night! That party is one of my happiest memories from the 1960s.

I had done it. I had been involved in civil rights *and* I had gotten my degree. That night, as I danced, nothing else in the world mattered.

---

Our first child was born at FAMU's hospital a month prematurely, on January 5, 1966, the same day as our wedding anniversary. Maybe I'm wired differently than other people, but I didn't experience the kind of immediate joy and bonding most mothers describe when I first looked at my new baby girl. Her little face was the spitting image of John's, but I have to admit that I thought the baby looked strange, with all those folds of wrinkled skin. Since I'd had an emergency cesarean section, however, I was probably in a daze. It took me some time to gather my thoughts and feelings.

Priscilla and I had vowed to name our daughters after each other whenever we had children, but I decided to use "Priscilla" as the middle name. I'd picked out a first name already. A couple of years earlier, while I'd studied contemporary Africa in a course taught by FAMU professor Dr. William Howard, I learned about the nation of Madagascar and its capital city, Tananarive. (Madagascar is the island near the southeast coast of mainland Africa.) The name sounded like music to me, and I'd vowed I would name my firstborn daughter after the city. The only problem was, by the time I finally had a child, I had forgotten how to spell the name. I took a guess on the birth certificate, spelling it T-A-N-N-A-R-I-V-E, but since I wasn't certain, I called Professor Howard to check. "No, no," he said, hearing how I'd spelled it. "You've left out an A. It has ten letters." Somewhere, there is an original copy of Tananarive's birth certificate with the original misspelling crossed out and a correction hurriedly added above it, thanks to Dr. Howard. We chuckled over that for many years.

I'd coordinated demonstrations and registration drives, but I was at a loss when it came to caring for a baby. I hadn't been around many people with young children, so having a baby in my life was a very new experience for me. Whereas most of my relatives in Quincy had kept their distance while I was there with the North Florida Citizenship Education Project, I found that they were eager to assist me with my new baby. It's not that they had ever stopped caring about me; they had only been afraid before. I have never been one to expect people to do more than they feel comfortable doing, in most cases, so I did not hold a grudge. Believe me, I was grateful for their help. Mother also came to spend a week with me. For the first few weeks, while I recuperated from my surgery, my new baby and I were waited on hand and foot.

When John and I needed a babysitter, Mrs. Augustine Hudson, the wife of FAMU chaplain Dr. James Hudson, was happy to look after her. There were so many people who were important to me that I named several godparents for Tananarive, all of them from the Movement—Judy Benninger, James and Lillian Shaw, and Mrs. Dorothy Jones. Later, I would name a Miami lawmaker, Rep. Gwendolyn Cherry, as another godmother. Tananarive was dedicated at the Unitarian Church in Tallahassee. Dr. Irene Johnson, a geography professor from FAMU, came to Tananarive's dedication, as did other friends and family. Walter, my brother, who lived five hours away in Atlanta, also attended the dedication, and he frequently visited us for holidays, including Tananarive's first Christmas. Our families were very close. (When Tananarive was a little older than two, she was the flower girl in Walter's wedding to educator Rita Willis.)

John and I did not slow down after becoming new parents. Although a rift would grow between us in later years regarding the demands of family versus the demands of activism, in 1966 we were still very much of the same mind. When Tananarive was only three months old, we took her to Miami to live with Mother for a while because John and I were busy on the campaign trail for state and local elections. We were supporting candidates we believed were sensitive to the needs of Negroes and the poor. With record numbers of Negroes in Florida registered to vote, we wanted to start capitalizing on the community's newfound voting power.

The previous year, we'd seen the passage of the 1965 Voting Rights Act, which President Johnson had supported, in large part in response to the travails of those of us who had worked in voter registration drives in 1964, and especially in response to the violence in Selma in 1965, where marchers supporting voting rights had been subjected to arrests and brutal beatings at the hands of police and racists. Again, it had taken suffering and bloodshed to prick the nation's conscience. It was so ridiculous that we needed new, special laws to guarantee rights Negroes should have been able to take for granted just like any other U.S. citizens.

John decided he would run for the state senate in Florida's Sixth District. At that time, there had been no Negro state legislators since the days of Reconstruction. John felt very strongly that all of Florida's citizens were not being properly represented. We were very hopeful that political empowerment could lead to rapid, sweeping changes. John thought he might actually have a chance to win.

John had an official campaign manager, but believe me, I had to do most of the work. And it was work! We knew it was going to be a very tough race, and not just because John was Negro. The Sixth District was drawn so that it included twenty-four counties, including Leon and Gadsden Counties. Our first challenge would be to reach all of the voters; the next challenge was the racist Democratic machinery, which saw John as an outsider. Armed with eye-catching campaign cards with green print reading "DO IT WITH DUE," we got a convertible and began the difficult task of driving from county to county to introduce ourselves to the voters. We brought Tananarive with us as much as we could, but for the longer trips we left her with babysitters like Augustine Hudson, the wife of Dr. James Hudson, FAMU's chaplain, who was so supportive of civil rights.

My skin was burned to a crisp and peeling as we traveled through those hot Florida counties in our convertible. We arrived, uninvited, at every official Democratic party function we heard about. Most of the events were picnics, and we would stroll in and look for John's rightful place among the candidates. You should have seen the looks we got! If John appeared to be approaching the vicinity of a white woman, the white men gathered around her as if John were some kind of beast who would attack her. Some candidates actually got up and left the table when John sat down. You could almost read their minds: *Look at the audacity of this nigger coming here into our territory.*

Though we were encountering hostility from racist whites, the Negro voters we met were overjoyed to see a Negro running for the Florida senate. When we had the baby with us, they cooed over her. I'm sure people were very pleased to see a family working together to make changes. When it was time for the election, John got enough votes to carry both Leon and Gadsden Counties, which even President Johnson had not done in 1964. Unfortunately, the other counties voted for his opponent, so John lost the election by a wide margin.

But the race had been a family affair, and even baby Tananarive had been in on the act.

---

After being a CORE activist for so many years, the philosophy of nonviolence was deeply ingrained in me. I never owned a gun, even during the worst times in Gadsden County, but when Tananarive was nearly nine months old, I realized how much motherhood had changed my perspective in some vital areas in my life. In the summer of 1966, I lost my belief in nonviolence, at least for a day. I was not launching a protest or looking for trouble, but somehow trouble found me, as my family tells me often seems to be the case.

Priscilla had told me in her letters that she planned to wait a few years before starting her family, but she got pregnant right before I gave birth to Tananarive. I know she agonized over her pregnancy, because her true desire was to have the baby in Ghana, but she considered the medical system there too unreliable at that time. Her baby was due August 25, so she had written to tell me she would be coming home for the first time since her departure. I begged her to come back to live in the States, where we could see each other more often and our children could grow up near each other. This was my dream, of course, but Priscilla's attitude had not changed, as reflected in a letter she'd sent me in February: *As for me coming to live in America again, Never!* she wrote emphatically. She also noted that since I had my own baby, it was less likely that I would travel to visit her in Africa. We seemed to be in a no-win situation.

When Priscilla returned to the States that summer, I wanted to show her that things had changed since she'd left. After all, we had the Public Accommodations Act and the Voting Rights Act. Although Tallahassee's municipal pools were still closed since Priscilla's kick from a police officer at the 1963 "wade-in" and a subsequent protest in the summer of 1964—sadly, the city fathers preferred to have *no* swimming pools rather than integrate—great progress had been made in other areas in a very short time. If we could only have a pleasant visit, I thought, Priscilla would change her mind about living in Ghana.

It was so good to see my sister again! She came home bubbling with stories about her travels, her admiration for Ghanaian reform president Kwame Nkrumah, and the University College of Science Education in Cape Coast in Ghana, where she worked. It really seemed that Priscilla had managed to cram several lifetimes worth of travel into only two short years, and I could live vicariously through her stories. As she liked to tell me, I shouldn't just think of the fact that she had left. I should think of all the places I might see through her, as Mother had done. To this day, Priscilla is the most well-traveled person I know.

I left Quincy for Priscilla's visit, bringing Tananarive with me to live with Mother in Miami for a month, until Priscilla's baby was born. By that time, Mother had left Leo Sears, the man she'd married after her divorce from Daddy Marion. Their relationship had been rocky from the beginning, and it simply never worked out. Mother had a job at Gulf American Land Corporation on Biscayne Boulevard in northeast Miami, so she left Priscilla and me at home with a list of chores each day when she went to work. I tell you, Priscilla and I behaved like we were children again. From the time Mother left the house each morning, we sat in the living room eating snacks, watching movies on television, and laughing as we talked about our days as young people. I purposely avoided some of the more painful subjects of the civil rights movement, not wanting to remind Priscilla of all the reasons she had left. Each day, as we realized it was almost time for Mother to get home from work, we'd scramble to do the chores she had asked of us. Those were carefree days, and we spent a lot of time laughing.

When Priscilla was nine months pregnant and as big as a house—actually, I believe she may have been overdue by then—she decided she wanted to drive up to Belle Glade to see some of our childhood friends. Belle Glade was about a ninety-minute drive from Miami, and we packed up baby Tananarive and left in the morning, planning to return home by late afternoon.

Priscilla and I had a good day visiting people we'd known in Belle Glade, but as the afternoon wore on and the summer sun grew hotter during the drive home, Priscilla began to feel sick. I knew that feeling well, and since she was pregnant we both understood what it meant: She needed to eat something right away to overcome the nausea. We had only made it to the town of South Bay about five miles outside of Belle Glade on Highway 27. We saw a sign for Roy's Pit Barbeque, so we stopped to get Priscilla a sandwich to keep her from being sick.

Imagine us as we were: Priscilla was very, very pregnant, and I walked in carrying a nine-month-old child. There were plenty of empty seats in the restaurant, so we took the first table we saw. Like any other customers, we sat and waited to be served. Yes, we got some stares from whites in the restaurant. Maybe I was being naive again, but since two years had passed since the federal law outlawing racial discrimination at public facilities, I did not expect to have a problem that day. If I had, I never would have exposed my baby and pregnant sister.

The waitress was very excitable, and when she saw us there, she flew to our table, her face red with anger. "You can't sit there!" she said. "Go on, *git*. I said you can't sit there."

Instead of pointing out that the law was on my side, I tried to explain what the problem was. "Miss, we just want to get a sandwich. As you can see, my sister is pregnant, and she isn't feeling well. We just need a sandwich and a drink, and we'll be on our way home."

"You *get up* from there!" the waitress said, as if I hadn't spoken.

"If you would just listen to—"

I never finished my last sentence, because I saw something I could barely believe even though it was happening before my own eyes: That waitress picked up a steel chair and began raising it as high as she could, heaving it over her head, as if she were going to hit us with it. Priscilla and I were shocked. We were a pregnant woman and a mother with a *baby*, and this woman was about to throw a chair at us.

"You listen to me," I said in a deep, solemn voice that I barely recognized, because my voice was filled with something that had never been awakened in me until that moment. "If you make one more move, I will *wipe up this floor with you.*"

I saw the waitress freeze. She knew I meant it. She had no doubt that if she hurt my pregnant sister or my child, she would be lucky if I didn't kill her.

Priscilla had such a bewildered, pained look in her eyes. To think that another woman could behave with such poison, with such mindless hatred! Priscilla glanced at me, and I knew what she was thinking: *How could you say things have changed? Pat, things are worse than before!* There was nothing else I could say to her about moving back to the States. As soon as she could leave after the September 6 birth of her son, Muncko Derk Kruize III, Priscilla went back to Ghana to live, and I couldn't blame her. Maybe, deep down, I wondered if John and I were the crazy ones for staying here to raise our own child.

That incident wouldn't still be so painful in my memory if it had somehow been resolved, if authorities had reprimanded the owner, who was responsible for the behavior of the employees. I called John to let him know what had happened, and he called the FBI to report the incident as a violation of federal law, but Priscilla and I were treated as if the whole thing was our fault. While we were researching this book, Tananarive and I put in a request for my FBI file under the Freedom of Information Act, and my file includes extensive interviews from the incident at Roy's Pit Barbeque. All of the witnesses interviewed by the FBI contended that Priscilla and I were the ones who had been belligerent, that I had threatened the waitress first! I don't think a single person told the truth, the way it had really happened.

I'm so puzzled when I read those varying accounts in the FBI report, which is riddled with inaccuracies. Were those the real witnesses the FBI spoke to? Did those people invent different accounts because they were trying to protect the restaurant? Did someone else tell them what to say? Or did they somehow see an event that looked wholly different in their eyes simply because Priscilla and I had darker skin?

"The owner was sick that day, you know," an FBI agent in Miami told me in a scolding tone. "Why would you go in there bothering the owner with a protest? They had to pull the owner out of bed." He completely missed the point. Priscilla was feeling sick, too, and I never asked anyone to call the owner, I said.

When Priscilla and I walked into that diner, we never expected to become part of a controversy. No one could understand that we had only wanted to order a sandwich.

Twenty-Four

# Tananarive Due

**"People are trapped in history, and history is trapped in them."**
***—James Baldwin***

"It's time to have a civil rights reunion," my mother said in the summer of 1997, after months of work sessions at her home, where we'd culled through the newspaper articles, letters, and photographs from the 1960s in her personal archive. "It's time for all of us to get together. Before long, it'll be too late."

She and a few activists had always talked about having a reunion someday, maybe in Tallahassee, which had been a hotbed of protest, or maybe closer to South Florida, where so many of them had settled later. But the plans always got swallowed by intricacies and logistics and busy schedules and, in particular, the devastation wreaked by Hurricane Andrew in 1992. A committee had been meeting regularly until Andrew hit, but even five years later, the effort had never picked up the same steam. Maybe, deep down, there was a little unwillingness to go back down that road as a group. Maybe the activists feared collective memories would be harder to stomach than the individual ones.

I'd had a taste of what that reunion might feel like in 1994, after the state teachers' union, Florida Education Association/United, bought a building in Tallahassee that had once been a site of many protests and hundreds of arrests while it was the Florida Theatre. A former University of Florida white student activist who'd been arrested outside that theater, Daniel Harmeling, now an educator and union representative, suggested that a plaque be erected in honor of the students who had made such a courageous stand at that building. After a two-year battle, the union finally agreed. I attended the dedication ceremony with my parents and about a dozen other activists, and the state's commissioner of education, the Tallahassee NAACP president, and a Tallahassee city commissioner, joined by Governor Lawton Chiles, thanked them for their efforts years earlier (an ironic contrast to the past, when my mother and other student activists were referred to in court as "niggers"). There, I met George and Clifton Lewis, two white Tallahassee residents who had been so helpful. Rev. Herbert Alexander, a black activist, had died only the night before, but his three daughters bravely came in his place, saying they would not have missed it. The activists exchanged hugs, posed for photographs, and reminisced briefly about the events that had brought them there, but they hadn't had time to sit and really talk to each other.

My mother envisioned a reunion where they could share the stories behind the stories: What had the personal price of their activism been? What did their children and grandchildren know about what they had done during the civil rights movement? What had the impact of activism been on their families? What did they think of present-day race relations? She wanted to follow through, even if it meant she and my father had to host it in their home.

As she planned the reunion, and I printed up colorful invitational brochures quoting Frederick Douglass's reminder that "There is no progress without struggle," my mother began to call it "The Gathering." There was little joy in this work. She simply felt a strong sense of duty and necessity. Time was running out, and organizing it nearly wore her out.

My mother was in college when she got involved in civil rights, which meant that the older activists were nearing their eighties. Even some of the younger activists had already died, and more were dying. Mrs. Mary Ola Gaines, who'd been fired from her job as a maid after joining the sit-in in 1960, had died practically penniless only two months earlier. James Van Matre, who'd been a crusader and the first white student to enroll at all-black FAMU, wasn't doing well at all, my mother found out when she spoke to his wife, Julia. And he was still a relatively young man, barely past fifty! Julia Van Matre, who'd been thrilled to hear a friendly voice from the past, said her husband had just gotten out of the hospital and was having problems finding work, and she hoped a meeting like The Gathering would give him a spark, maybe cheer him up. But he never made it, probably because of his health. Two months after The Gathering, he was dead.

Some activists were vanishing in other ways. My mother had reached Augustine Hudson, the widow of a now-deceased minister, Dr. James Hudson, the former chaplain at FAMU who had been active in Tallahassee's civil rights struggle. My mother had heard Mrs. Hudson was sick, so she didn't expect her to be well enough to fly to Miami for the reunion, but Mom called her because we were thinking about flying to Louisiana to interview her for our book, to ask her how the civil rights movement had affected her husband and family.

"Who?" the woman's frail voice had fluttered across the phone line.

"Patricia Stephens Due, from Tallahassee," my mother said, repeating herself because she thought maybe Mrs. Hudson's hearing was failing. "You remember, I worked very closely with your husband in Tallahassee. Pat and John Due. We had a daughter, Tananarive, and you were her first babysitter. I spent forty-nine days in jail in 1960 for sitting-in at a Woolworth."

"You *did?"* She sounded impressed, but there was no recognition in her voice.

Mrs. Hudson didn't remember her. She didn't remember Tallahassee, where she had spent so many years of her life. She didn't remember her own part in the civil rights movement at all, as if it had never happened.

Those were painful setbacks for my mother, which is why planning The Gathering was so much more to her than addressing envelopes or hunting down telephone numbers. Sometimes she would get a lead on the whereabouts of someone she had lost touch with—for example, the family members of long-deceased William Larkins, FAMU's former student government president who also had spent those forty-nine days in jail—and then end up disappointed by a cool trail or a disconnected telephone number. Even when she was able to reach people, the conversations meant catching up on years of changes and developments. Children. Families. The Movement. To her, it was an exhausting exercise.

And there were those who didn't seem to want to remember those times at all.

My mother has not been able to reach one woman on her list in several tries over the years, although the woman is very much alive. This woman was among those who served time in jail with my mother and aunt during the 1960 Tallahassee jail-in. Now she refused to take part in any conversation to recollect those times. When my mother finally reached her on the telephone to invite her to The Gathering, her tone was clipped and tight, on the edge of politeness. "You can just leave me out of it," she told her. She wanted nothing to do with those memories. My mother never did find out what happened to make her feel the way she did.

For many civil rights activists, the only true sense of community during the Movement was at meetings and protests. After that, when the battles had been lost or won together and the last freedom songs had been sung, they'd all simply faced the world alone. My mother knew from her own experiences that everyone paid their price in their own way.

Over the years, my sisters and I have seen the toll civil rights has had on our parents, too. To this day, both my father and mother have a distrust of the telephone. Important names and information like bank account numbers are never revealed on the phone, and during any given conversation my mother is likely to lapse into incomprehensible code, to the point where my sisters and I honestly think she's paranoid. But then again, why shouldn't they be paranoid? Our family discovered that my mother and father each have FBI files 400 pages long, presumably from the civil rights era, when they could hear the clicking of wiretaps on their telephones. From their perspective, wiretapping by government agencies isn't far-fetched.

There are other impacts, too. My father is a voracious reader, and the surefire gift for him at holiday time was usually a book about the struggle, such as *Race Matters* by Cornel West, *Rage of a Privileged Class* by Ellis Cose, or *Parting the Waters* by Taylor Branch. He's always been able to draw resolve and purpose from those books. But in the past few years, as he just *looks* more tired, he's told us no more books. His plate is full. No more.

When a *Miami Herald* reporter interviewed my parents separately for a newspaper story on the thirty-year anniversary of Dr. Martin Luther King's assassination in April 1998, they each broke into sobs in separate interviews, surprising themselves. "I guess I'm still in agony," my mother told the reporter, explaining her sudden tears. "Dr. King knew as we all did when we participated in the movement what the consequences could be. I felt badly for him and for his family, but I was in agony more for the country." My father was quoted as saying, "I'm mourning more now than then. I guess it's like what they call Vietnam syndrome. It's only twenty or thirty years later that they begin to mourn the people who died."[1]

I hadn't thought it would be easy for my mother to watch *Mississippi Burning,* the movie that fictionalized the FBI's search for murdered civil rights activists Michael Schwerner, James Chaney, and Andrew Goodman. Our family went to see it together years ago, and sure enough, not long after the movie was underway, my mother began coughing in response. As she watched the movie, I think she was probably as disturbed by the historical distortions as she was by its depictions of white Southerners' antipathy toward the civil rights workers. Eventually, she had to leave the theater altogether. A year later, I hadn't expected her to have that same reaction to Spike Lee's *Do the Right Thing,* a film by a black director, but in a scene where police turned fire hoses on protesting blacks, my mother suddenly began choking and coughing, feeling like she couldn't breathe, and she hurried out of the theater. It was too much for her.

I saw that same physical reaction to the stress more and more in the year leading to The Gathering, while we traveled throughout the state to research this book. She's been determined to tell the story—probably as much as she's been determined to do anything—but reliving those events extracted a price. Billie Holiday once said, "Sometimes it's worse to win a fight than to lose." I don't know if that's true. But I do know that, win or lose, fights always leave scars.

---

On August 23, 1997, the sun was shining full of summer, making it the sort of day when my mother is always careful to wear her dark glasses. My mother's glasses have large lenses as dark as midnight that hide her eyes and parts of her face, so it's easy for me and my sisters to forget what she looks like behind them. Sometimes, she says, she catches a glimpse of herself in the mirror, without her glasses, and is startled by her own appearance. One day, she was surprised to notice that the color of her eyes had changed from coffee to a lighter shade, closer to her mother's.

The dark glasses are a necessity. Sunshine and bright indoor light always mean pain to her—as if she needed a reminder of what The Gathering was all about. Just as her eyes were injured by tear gas in 1960, every single person my mother had invited to The Gathering had scars of their own, whether visible or not.

Almost all of my immediate family members were there: both my parents; my maternal grandmother, Lottie Sears Houston; my Aunt Priscilla; and one of my two sisters, Johnita, a New York attorney who is two years younger than I am. The other people who came weren't family in flesh and blood, but they were names I knew well: Doris Rutledge Hart was a longtime family friend who lived in North Dade County, and others came from farther away, like attorney Jeff Greenup from New York, whom I'd never met, and who had not seen my mother in more than thirty years.

By late morning, curtains drawn across the windows to keep out the light, my mother, by now a woman of fifty-seven with generous streaks of silver hair, surveyed the group of men and women assembled in a loose circle in her living room. All of the activists there were black except one, Daniel Harmeling, who had been arrested at a demonstration outside a segregated Tallahassee movie theater. Like Harmeling, some had been barely past adolescence in the 1960s; now, they all had their share of gray hair. Time had changed their appearance in many ways, but in other ways, at least for now, time was frozen. The freedom songs that had been playing on the cassette player—the near-mournful "Keep Your Eyes on the Prize" and the more bouncy "Freedom"—still hung in the air, fresh as yesterday.

"It really is such a pleasure to see everyone," my mother said, her voice tinged with emotion beneath the formality. I could also hear a hint of her exhaustion. I noticed her wipe perspiration from her brow, a sign of a fever. I'd come down with a cold myself within the past day, and the entire event, so long-awaited, seemed surreal. Stress and illness are surely related.

"All of you, I'm sure, don't know each other, but all of you had something to do with me and John in the Movement," she said. "I know you all have done so much. I would just like you to tell us where you're from, and your first experience in the nineteen sixties. You probably can't tell it all in one time, but we can begin."

Then it was time for the stories. My parents have never been given to much socializing, being very protective of their private lives to compensate for their very public presence. But despite the food and soft drinks offered, The Gathering wasn't a party; it was an opportunity for the activists to unburden, to share, and to understand that what they had done *mattered*.

Mom encouraged my grandmother, who was seventy-seven at the time, to speak first. Lottie Sears Houston was an elegant woman who had recently spent months recuperating in a nursing home from surgery to treat complications of diabetes. Considering that we'd spent Christmas of 1996 at her hospital bedside, and her frail appearance had made us all fear she might not live long past the new year, her presence at The Gathering was significant in more ways than one. (She died three years later on Christmas Day, literally weeks after learning that this much-discussed book about her children's civil rights involvement had finally found a publisher.)

My grandmother began to speak with the precision of her well-bred upbringing in Quincy, Florida. "This isn't pleasant for me, because during that time, my heart was very heavy, when you all were so involved in all this stuff," she began, squirming as though the words themselves caused her physical discomfort. "I didn't know half the time where you were, or where you were going, or where you were coming from. And it was very dangerous."

She admitted in a tiny, pained voice that even all these years later, if her telephone rang late at night, she still felt a quickening of her heart, leftover anxiety from the era when a phone call at such an hour was likely to bring tragic news about her two daughters. All over the South, parents regularly received heartbreaking calls that their children had been jailed, beaten, killed, or that they'd simply vanished. Being the parent of civil rights activists meant fearing the worst on a regular basis. "I just learned to live with it and support them. I didn't get out there and march with them, but I did give them support," she said.

Aunt Priscilla, who'd come to The Gathering in a bright-red African-print dress and matching head wrap—her trademark style of dress after living for several years in Ghana in self-imposed exile—flashed her smile and beautiful teeth toward her mother. "I didn't know it was going to be so serious. I was trying to get a steak dinner from Wolfie's," she joked, recalling her first introduction to the civil rights organization CORE.

"I thought you all were down here visiting your father, having a good time, and you're here at these workshops and getting all involved in this thing that's going to last for years and years," my grandmother said.

"A whole lifetime," Aunt Priscilla said, as if awed herself, and the room murmured in agreement. Everyone present knew that all too well. For many of them, civil rights involvement had simply taken over their lives after they'd chanced upon a demonstration, or heard a speech, and something inside them had been ignited forever. Each, in his or her own way, had always wanted to work toward change, but none could have anticipated to what extent the Movement would impact their safety, their futures, and their lives.

For Dr. Robert Hayling, who came with his wife, Athea, it was not easy to talk about his severe beating at a Ku Klux Klan rally in St. Augustine, even among kindred spirits. The sight of black-and-white photographs from the civil rights era, which my mother was passing around the living room, made tears spring to his eyes.

Familiar faces, immortalized in youth. Old hurts. Old outrage. Old fear.

Of the people we had contacted about attending, my mother had been the most excited when Dr. Hayling agreed to come. Dr. Hayling was in his early sixties and still very active in the black community of Ft. Lauderdale, about a forty-minute drive from Miami. As usual, the name sounded familiar to me because it had been repeated many times in my parents' anecdotes over the years. "John represented him in St. Augustine, one of his first civil rights cases," she always said. "St. Augustine was *vicious.* Dr. King said it was one of the most vicious cities he'd ever visited. And everybody knew Dr. Hayling. He was right in the middle of it."

Thirty-four years had passed since Dr. Hayling nearly lost his life in a beating at a Ku Klux Klan rally in 1963, but when he tried to talk about his experiences, he was smothered by his memories.

"So much has happened to us, and so many other people who were involved with us are not with us anymore," Dr. Hayling said after breaking down while trying to tell his story. "There's so much we're talking about, years and years and years, and to compress all of that, what I went through. . . . I apologize to everyone, because most people who know me would know this is very unusual, but this is a very unusual moment."

The activists made empathetic sounds, nodding. They all had their own hurts.

It has always been hard for me and my sisters to imagine the world these activists grew up in, the one they confronted. As the day passed, it was clearer and clearer that these activists had lived in the midst of a time when, in the South, tolerance was the exception rather than the rule. Blacks were considered less than fully human, and whites who recognized their humanity were considered freaks, at almost every level. Fear of change was so rampant that normally law-abiding citizens could justify violence to preserve the status quo. It's painful for me to think that my mother was a young woman trying to envision her future in an atmosphere of so much oppression and psychological poisoning.

Although Johnita and I had not experienced what Harmeling, Hayling, the other activists, and my family members were recalling that day, we knew full well that their experiences would have traumatized us, too. In a very real sense, they had all suffered what they did exactly so the world we inherited would be a different one.

Jeff Greenup, the New York attorney who had represented activists participating in a voter education project directed by my mother in Quincy, said that his children were his main inspiration for taking time away from his legal practice to volunteer as a civil rights lawyer in the South, and risk his life. "I confess I was somewhat of a coward," he began, "because I had two young daughters, and I looked on the TV screen up in New York and I saw those youngsters bucking those dogs and I saw white bigots spitting on them, and I just said I couldn't send my kids to do that. But I also couldn't just stand idly by. So, I went South."

It was children, he said, who made the biggest impact on him, especially as he observed the fearless high-school and college-age youngsters for whom the South was home. He recalled being picked up at the train station by interracial student pairs boldly singing freedom songs, and, later, how a football team from an all-black high school in Quincy served as his bodyguards when he was being followed.

"One of the things that always troubled me was what happened to those dedicated folk when we left and they were stuck there," Greenup said. He said he'd always wished he'd remembered the names of the people he came into contact with during that time. All he can recall most of the time is a string of nameless, faceless heroes. One, he said, was a young man who allowed him to live in his brick house in Quincy when he needed a place to stay. He'd heard later that the man had lost his job because of that courage and kindness.

"Oh, my cousin, Velton Banks!" my mother exclaimed. Vivian Kelly, still a Quincy resident and still active at age seventy-eight as the first black chair of the Democratic Executive Committee of Gadsden County, told him she knew of Banks and his involvement. She, too, had worked to find activists hot meals and a place to live during that time, becoming almost a surrogate parent to my mother. As a result of her own voter registration activities, Mrs. Kelly said, for years one of her sons had suffered difficulty finding a job in Quincy's school system. And Banks came under extra scrutiny because of his involvement, she said, particularly from the IRS (which, unfortunately, was not uncommon).

Another hero, Greenup recalled, was a little white boy in St. Augustine when Dr. King was in town in 1964 to support local civil rights activities. Since Dr. King received so many death threats, civil rights organizers established elaborate decoys to disguise his sleeping arrangements. That night, Dr. King was scheduled to sleep in a tent.

"There was a young white kid, no more than eleven or twelve years old," Greenup said. "One day he ran through our office while we were at a strategy meeting. He said, 'Look out for twelve o'clock.' We didn't pay too much attention to him. Then he came back about a half hour later and said, 'Dr. King shouldn't sleep in the tent tonight.' " Somehow, Greenup said, there had been a security breach, and outsiders had learned about Dr. King's sleeping arrangements.

Someone, somewhere, was plotting violence within earshot of that child.

"Nighttime came, and Dr. King was standing around talking, and then he walked over to the tent where he was supposed to sleep. And then I crawled back with him to the office and took him somewhere else," Greenup said. "I don't know if you remember or not, but that night they threw a stick of dynamite at the tent. I often wonder who that kid was. To me, he's definitely one of the unsung heroes."

Listening, we all nodded and muttered in agreement. "Unsung heroes" is a term my mother uses often, and was most of the reason she'd planned The Gathering in the first place. Telling and retelling the stories of heroes, she must have reasoned, would help ensure that the next generations would not forget. I heard her fear echoed time and again that day. In fact, many of the activists said they could already see their fears coming to pass.

"We allow people to hit us and we turn the other cheek, and that's the way we have survived," my Aunt Priscilla said, "but we have to leave a legacy for our children that is stronger than we are, because most of our children don't know anything about the struggle. Our grandchildren will know nothing. We may not even be around to tell our grandchildren how they have to fight, how they have to survive. They will have to have new strategies to survive."

Dan Harmeling sounded hopeful, mentioning that one of his white middle-school students had expressed her admiration for a poster he'd put up in his classroom quoting Frederick Douglass's words, the same words about power and struggle my mother had excerpted on her invitations for The Gathering. "My feeling is that young people are ready to hear these things," Harmeling said. "It's up to us. Part of our work now is just to get the younger generation ready to go on. But they're ready to know this stuff. I just think we have to be there to teach it to them."

But others in the room sounded less hopeful. Clarence Edwards reminded the group that black children were being lost inside the traps of poverty and violence at an alarming rate. He said he's run out of patience for the song-singing, nonviolent tactics of the past in the fight against racism. Instead, he said, he's making sure all of his grandchildren get target practice with BB guns.

Greenup, a friend of Mr. Edwards since the 1960s, admonished him. "I hear what you're saying, Clarence, but I've known you long enough to know guns are not your thing. You have made some of your greatest contributions through the power of the vote and getting the people out there to vote. Don't lose sight of the contributions you've made. That's why I'm glad you're here, and that's why I say you've got to tell your story to the youngsters. I know you're tired."

Yes, Mr. Edwards was tired, and he sounded like it. In fact, at given moments, I couldn't ignore the deep weariness that enveloped the people in the room. What they seemed to be saying, at times, was that they had suffered all they had and there *still* was a lot to be done. Although no one in the room regretted their actions or would not do it all again, they were disheartened because they didn't think enough young people were sensitive or involved enough to carry the work into the next century.

I knew what they meant, of course. The black community is still plagued by disproportionate representation in poverty, drug abuse, poor educational systems, the criminal justice system, and AIDS statistics. Too many young blacks have ended up in prison as our national incarceration statistics have grown obscene, shaking black neighborhoods at their foundations. There are still hate crimes. There is still police brutality. The word "nigger" is still ugly, despite attempts by the hip-hop generation to reclaim and redefine it. All over this country, communities are still as segregated as ever, and white children and black children never even meet to form opinions about each other for themselves, strangers for yet another generation.

In some ways, as Mom often says, the clock is turning back. According to a study published by Harvard University's Civil Rights Project in 2001, schools today are resegregating, with 70 percent of black children nationwide attending predominantly minority schools in the 1998–99 school year, when that was true of only 63 percent of black children during the 1980–81 school year.[2] Many schools in my home county of Miami-Dade are still in ethnically isolated pockets; in 1999, thirty-nine schools had a black enrollment of more than 85 percent. Meanwhile, the thirty-four-year-old desegregation suit my father has been spearheading against Miami-Dade County's school system was dismissed by a federal judge in 2001 after he insisted that enough had already been done.

Still, at The Gathering, time and again, all I could think was how vastly different life for blacks is now compared to the world my parents and their fellow activists described. They had literally fought a war in their own homeland, with no weapon except determination. I have never been forced to fight for my own survival and humanity in that way. I was called names and experienced feelings of inferiority as a child, but my sisters and I have always believed we could do almost anything we chose, that it was our *responsibility* to thrive. No one told us we could not attend the colleges of our choosing, that we could not apply for the jobs of our choosing, that we could not live where we chose. Some roads have been more difficult than others—as is always the case—but my dreams have run unfettered. My parents, and the others at The Gathering, dreamed the future I now live day by day. They dreamed the future my unborn children, Johnita's unborn children, and my younger sister Lydia's two sons will enjoy.

But could they really see life through my eyes any more than I could see it through theirs?

My mother had hoped Johnita and I might be able to have our own say at The Gathering, to describe how growing up as the children of activists had affected us, but we ran out of time before we had that chance. As dusk approached, everyone was tired of talking, tired to death of remembering, and it was time for The Gathering to end. My cold had gotten worse, and I only wanted to sleep. Even if I hadn't been sick that day, I don't know how clearly I could have expressed my wordless feelings of pride and more than a little anguish roiling deep in my chest as I heard the activists' disappointment:

*But don't you all know? Can't you see how much better you've made the world?*

# Twenty-Five

## Patricia Stephens Due

**"I had reasoned this out in my mind,
there was two things I had a right to:
Liberty and death. If I could not have one,
I would have the other, for no man
should take me alive."**
***—Harriet Tubman***

Life was not kind to many of the people I knew from the Movement, and it wasn't long after we scattered and began to fall out of touch that many of us met harsh times. I've come to think that when we were all together we had given each other a kind of strength that we did not possess as much on our own. Whatever the reason, the end of the 1960s was a bitter, unhappy time for many of us.

In January 1967, James "Jim" Harmeling a white activist whose twin brother Dan had been arrested with me in Tallahassee, shot himself to death at a Florida mental institution. Jim had worked with John doing voter registration and community organizing in Gainesville, and was a very close friend of Judy's. He'd had a nervous breakdown, and while he was being treated for depression, he somehow had smuggled a gun into his room in the psychiatric ward. One day, he turned it on himself and pulled the trigger. Two days earlier, he had tried to commit suicide with pills, and his stomach had been pumped. John and I were still living in Quincy and still in touch with our civil rights friends, but somehow we did not hear about Jim's death until long after it happened. When I heard, I was shocked.

Jim Harmeling's family blamed his death on the civil rights movement. Dan, Jim's identical twin brother, had to suffer the loss of his twin alone because his father forbade him to invite any of the friends he and Jim had made in the civil rights movement to the funeral. Hundreds of Movement supporters had planned a caravan in Jim's honor, but his father told them he wanted the funeral to be private. Like me, almost everyone Dan knew was from the Movement. It had consumed us, and we didn't have time for friendships with people who weren't consumed in the same way. Because of his father's anger at the Movement, Dan could not reach out to us, and he was left to wrestle with all those questions of "why" without the comfort of friends who understood the ordeals that Dan and Jim had faced together.

Threats. Violence. Lies. Betrayals.

I had never been "buddies" with the Harmeling twins in the 1960s because we were all so busy, yet we were more than mere friends. All of us cared about each other deeply, and the civil rights cause bonded us. Even though we were not overly involved in each other's personal lives, the news of Jim's suicide hit me hard. We had fought in a war together. What had happened to make him believe he could no longer face life? (Today Dan is a very good friend, and my heart went out to him when his adult son, Lance, died suddenly in 2002, another horrible loss.)

In many ways, it feels to me that the impact of the civil rights movement was psychologically more difficult on some of the whites involved than on the Negroes. There were many exceptions to this, of course, because whites could choose to walk away from the Movement at any time and blend into the larger society, whereas Negroes would always be Negro. But for those whites who were truly committed and very sensitive, the agony of their disillusionment was sometimes too much to handle. Most Negroes had a better idea of how things really were, and some of the whites had been too sheltered from reality. I think that's what happened to Jim Harmeling.

Dan and Jim were two of five children who'd been born in Sheboygan, Wisconsin, to the late Carl and Ruth Harmeling. In Wisconsin, of course, their encounters with Negroes were limited, although Dan remembers incidents when he and Jim were very young, not yet ten years old, when their father offered a ride to two Negro professional baseball players when he saw them walking along the street. Grateful, the men climbed into their car—real baseball players! To the boys, these were the two most important people in the world. At the time, the boys didn't realize that even though the Negro men played baseball for their city's team, they were walking because they were not permitted to ride the city's buses. They learned that only later.

When the twins were fourteen, their family moved from Wisconsin to Florida. There, in Winter Park, a Negro woman cleaned their house, and

Dan recalls that his mother felt uncomfortable because the woman always insisted on sitting in the backseat, saving the front seat for the children. "My mother felt very bad about that, that this lady should be in the front seat and the children should sit in the back—and she didn't want to do that. To us, it meant that there was something wrong with that," Dan said when Tananarive and I interviewed him in 1997. "And yet, her grandson would come, and he was a little younger than we were, but we'd play with him during the day—and then it started to occur to me that black people were living in a separate part of town, and there was something going on that was wrong. But I really didn't have my parents sitting down and saying, 'There's racial segregation, and there are laws. There are organizations working to change it, like the NAACP.' I knew none of that," he said.

The turning point for Dan and Jim came through involvement with a youth group at their Methodist church, which happened to be headed by a man named Rev. Caxton Doggett, who served on the Florida Civil Rights Commission. Rev. Doggett and his wife, Becky, arranged for members of their youth group to meet with a group of Negro students, then Jewish students, to expose them to other kinds of people. That was where he got his first seeds of consciousness, Dan says. He first began to see through those walls of separation.

Although they were twins, Dan and Jim were very different. Jim was more academically oriented, whereas Dan was more drawn to athletics. Originally, the boys chose two separate colleges because they wanted to learn who they were apart from each other. Jim went to the University of Florida, and Dan started his college education at Hope College in Michigan. Independently, without consulting with each other, they both declared psychology as their majors.

In 1962, Dan was ready to return to Florida and be closer to Jim. He transferred to the University of Florida, and within a year, they met Judy Benninger and began to get active in civil rights, primarily through CORE and the NAACP. They also both joined the Student Group for Equal Rights, an on-campus organization, where they first picketed a segregated restaurant in Gainesville, the College Inn. They didn't hide their involvement from their parents, Dan says. Their father, noting the danger, vowed he would take revenge on anyone who might harm his sons, but aside from that his main concern was that they would get so caught up in civil rights that they wouldn't be able to finish their degrees or begin their careers; which was not a foolish concern, as I knew well. Their mother was worried that the work was dangerous, but not so much that she tried to convince them to stop. "My mother told me later—and I always had the feeling—that she was very proud we were doing this. I don't think my mother in any way wanted to discourage us. She'd worry, but she also knew what we were doing was right."[1]

Mrs. Harmeling only understood enough to worry about the physical harm that might come to her sons if they got involved. As it turned out, in Jim's case, her son died without ever sustaining a serious physical injury from another person. Instead, he'd lost his mental health, drifting away from himself. His mind and heart had not been prepared to face the things he had seen and experienced in the Movement.

Rubin Kenon had already been through it when he committed himself for a short time. In 1969, Judy Benninger would also feel a need to commit herself for two months. She wrote me that she had been afraid she might commit suicide. *Part of it, I know, is that I found that none of the dreams of youth were coming true,* she wrote.[2] I never thought less of anyone who felt they couldn't cope, because sometimes I felt so much like that myself. I understood what they had been through. At one point, my friend Nancy Adams referred me to a psychiatrist because I felt so overwhelmed.

Dan believes his brother's depression was fanned by his role as a behind-the-scenes negotiator in the civil rights movement, trying to work with whites to bring about change through dialogue and persistence. Jim, unlike Dan, believed people in the establishment could change without being forced to. Jim believed in the power of reasoning.

"It bothered him a lot that people weren't responding. I didn't see that because I wasn't looking for a change of heart by the whites. I was more a part of the group that said, 'We're going to make trouble for you unless you drop your racist policies, your segregation,' " Dan says. "I think what he experienced was a lot of promises that were broken, a lot of sweet talk that essentially was poison, a lot of administrators at the University of Florida who could say, 'Jim, you're going to have an outstanding career' at the same time they were plotting to do him in. While he was running for president of the student body, part of our platform was sharp criticisms of the administration. And after the election was over, he was arbitrarily dropped from a master's degree in psychology that he had been a part of at the University of Florida, and had to fight very hard to be reinstated in that program."

Jim wasn't the only one punished for his activism. Marshall Jones, a

University of Florida professor who worked closely with student civil rights activists, became a professional casualty of the Movement. Shortly before Dan's mother died in 1996, she told him something he'd never known: About a year after Jim's death, a high-ranking university administrator came to see his parents in Orlando and asked his father to meet him in a motel. There, the administrator coaxed Dan's father to draft a letter claiming that University of Florida professor Marshall Jones had caused their family enormous harm because one son, Dan, had married a Negro woman; their other son, Jim, had committed suicide; and their daughter, Jane, had married a white campus radical. That letter helped fuel the professor's firing in 1968, when his tenure was denied. (Another active professor, Ed Richer, had been fired earlier.) When Marshall Jones was denied tenure, Dan was furious. In retrospect, he is even more furious about how his father was manipulated during his time of grief. That bitterness has not left him. "In terms of the people you would call the decision makers, I have absolutely no respect, no sense of trust, no sense that they act on behalf of people," he says. "[University officials] had absolutely no remorse over my brother's death."

I knew about none of this at the time. Nor did I know about John Parrott, a former Florida State University student who'd been a friend in Tallahassee in the 1960s. I remember how he was always so concerned about my safety when I was walking between the FAMU and FSU campuses, mostly at night. I was told that John, too, committed suicide after he became involved in civil rights. Again, I did not hear about his death until much later.

One reason I didn't learn about Jim Harmeling's death was that I was pregnant again, and once again my pregnancy had been a difficult one. John and I were living in Quincy. I struggled, doing what I could to remain active. Mary-Booney was a children's clothing store in Quincy whose employees treated Negroes badly, ignoring them to wait on white customers who came in after them, refusing to address Negroes with the same courtesy titles used for whites, and disrespecting Negroes in other ways. After I'd heard a number of complaints, I typed up a notice that I copied to distribute to as many people as I could: URGENT!!! REFUSE TO SHOP AT MARY-BOONEY, INC. UNTIL NEGRO CUSTOMERS ARE TREATED WITH DIGNITY AND RESPECT! REFUSE TO SUPPORT BIGOTRY AND DISCRIMINATION!

Even if I couldn't get around as I once had, I could still have a voice.

On March 1, 1967, I was admitted to FAMU's hospital and gave birth to a full-term baby. Again, I'd had a cesarean section, so I was not conscious during the birth. I woke up groggy, expecting the nurse to bring my baby girl to me so I could see Tananarive's new little sibling. If it was another girl, I had already decided to name the baby Lydia Johnita Due—Lydia after John's grandmother, and Johnita after John.

When I opened my eyes the morning after the baby was born, I was alone in my hospital room. Nurses were coming in and out of my room, so I asked to see the baby. I was told time and again that I had to wait until the doctor arrived.

"But why? Just bring me my baby."

"The doctor will be here soon, Mrs. Due," the nurse said.

Soon the doctor arrived and told me that my baby had died. I was not prepared to hear such shocking news. "What do you mean, the baby died?"

Dr. Brickler explained that the baby had been born alive but suffered from a disorder in which the lungs had not fully developed. He tried to comfort me by telling me that the same disorder had killed President Kennedy's baby, as if that would somehow make me feel better. But I was inconsolable, and I could not be comforted by anything as meaningless as that. This had been *our* child. "Bring me my baby," I said through my tears.

"But the baby is dead," the nurse said.

I kept insisting, and finally Dr. Brickler relented. "Let her see the baby."

She was a little girl. She looked exactly like John, just as Tananarive had. She looked much more well-developed than even Tananarive had been at birth, so how could she be dead? She was flawless. She was beautiful. Somehow, although I didn't understand it, she had died only twenty-four hours after her birth.

Immediately, my old CORE colleague Marvin Rich sent me and John a letter. By then, Marvin had left CORE and was executive director of the Scholarship, Education, and Defense Fund in New York, but he had heard about the baby's death through the civil rights grapevine. *What can I say about the loss of a daughter? Lucretius once said, "No single thing abides, but all things float. Fragment to fragment clings." Truly, we are all fragments and I see the changes from stormy to peaceful without rhyme or reason,* Marvin wrote, doing his best to console us.[3]

I'd had endless energy when it came to organizing, planning, and protesting, but I felt completely drained when it came to losing my child. I was so upset during that time, the days passed in a complete daze. I was not even well enough to attend my own baby's funeral, so Mother must have planned it with help from a family friend, Rosa Burns. The only remnants of the funeral I have are photographs of that day: John in his suit, and little Tananarive in a beautiful yellow dress, near her sister's grave, although she was only fourteen months old and far too young to understand the significance of the event. Believe it or not, I never visited the grave site, not even once I was able to leave the hospital. It was too difficult for me. Until more than thirty years later.

In March 2001, Tananarive and I visited St. Hebron and Quincy so I could show her the sites that were significant for this book: the house where my family lived when I was very young; the property where the Freedom House had once stood; Mount Moriah Missionary Baptist Church, where we held mass meetings; Arnett Chapel AME Church, where James Farmer spoke; the former *Gadsden County Times* office, where Negroes registered to vote in record numbers; and St. Hebron AME church, the church my mother brought us to each Sunday when we lived there, and which awarded me a plaque in 1964, when I returned to work with the voter registration campaign.

St. Hebron AME has a graveyard on its property, and I knew our baby had been buried there all those years ago. I did not know if she had a proper marker on her grave, or if it had been entirely overgrown with grass or weeds, but I wanted to find her.

What had drawn me to that cemetery so many years later for the first time? I'm still not sure, but something had been pulling me back to Gadsden County for many years. John and I had recently finalized the purchase of a home near Quincy, since it had been my dream for some time to retire there, in the county of my birth, and we'd bought a home large enough for Mother to live with us, since she had grown frail and it was clear she would not be able to live on her own much longer. Only days before we were scheduled to close on the new house—on Christmas morning—Mother died in her bed at home in Richmond Heights. (Across the ocean in Holland, Priscilla's husband, my brother-in-law, died the very same day, multiplying our family's loss.)

Mother had said often she didn't want to leave her house to move back to Quincy, and sometimes I believe she knew she never would. I had spoken to her only the night before on the telephone, making our Christmas plans for her to visit with us at our Miami home, ten minutes from hers, because she was no longer able to host the Christmas Eve celebrations that had been our family tradition for decades. My youngest daughter, Lydia (who would later be my dead baby's namesake), had spoken to Mother the night before, asking questions about Priscilla. "I asked if she thought Aunt Priscilla had been affected by the civil rights movement. She said yes, that she had never been the same," Lydia recalls. The next morning, Mother was talking to Priscilla on the telephone when she died.

So only a few months before, all of us had attended Mother's funeral and stood at another grave site at the same funeral park where Grandmother was buried, and which Mother had visited faithfully at holiday time for years. Her three children, six grandchildren, and one of her four great-grandchildren had all been there, as well as cousins, friends, church members, and admirers. We had all watched her casket lowered beneath two palm trees at Dade South Memorial Park, hardly able to believe a woman who'd always been so spirited and clear-minded was really gone.

Only weeks before Mother's death, at the beginning of December, Tananarive and I learned that our book of family history would be published, and Mother had been thrilled at the news. She knew we had been searching for a home for this book for years. "I'm so happy for you, Pat," Mother had said. "Once your book is published, you can put this behind you and enjoy the rest of your life." Mother had always felt that all of the energy I'd put into documenting the Movement took away from my ability to do things for myself and enjoy my life. Although it saddened me greatly that my mother would not live to see the publication of this book, I took solace in the fact that she had heard the good news. She knew her story, too, would be told.

I was also glad Mother had lived long enough to know that Tananarive was pregnant with her first child, news that had coincided with our book sale. But only two weeks after Mother died, while Tananarive was in the middle of a book tour for her novel *The Black Rose,* she miscarried. My daughter relived her own version of the losses I had known while I lived in Gadsden County. (Tananarive was as hard-headed as her mother; she kept touring even after she learned the eight-week-old embryo had died, and she was on the road again two days after her surgery.)

Mother had died in December, so her death was very fresh on that day in March. I was still not myself, and it was hard to imagine a time when I would feel like myself ever again. Mother had not only been my mother, but truly my best friend, someone I talked to on the telephone several times each day, and one of the few people I could say anything to. She lived to be eighty years old, and perhaps that sounds like we'd had a lot of time together, but all I could think about after she died was that I had wanted more time. I had been robbed of a part of my life that could never be replaced. Now that I was back in St. Hebron, I was remembering the old days clearly, when Mother had been much younger and the times had been very difficult.

Given how emotionally fragile Tananarive and I both were at the time, I did not know how it would feel to go to the little cemetery in St. Hebron where Mother's lost granddaughter had been buried since 1967. "I don't think we'll find her," I kept saying as Tananarive and I scanned the grave markers with one of my childhood friends, Ethelyn "Jay Baby" Cunningham, who had directed us to the cemetery. Perhaps a part of me was hoping I wouldn't.

Would I be able to bear seeing my daughter's grave for the first time?

"Look!" Tananarive cried suddenly from a distance in the graveyard. "Richard Allen Powell! Your grandfather, Mom!"

There it was: the gravestone for Richard Allen Powell—and beside it, neatly lettered on a marker small enough to be easily overlooked, we saw the name DUE. *Lydia J. Due,* the marker said. *March 1, 1967–March 2, 1967.* The baby I had never even met had been beside her great-grandfather all these years. She had never been alone.

Later I described the day in my computer diary as my eyes overflowed with tears:

> *I was overcome with joy and sadness all at the same time. I could hardly speak. I had to breathe deeply to make sure that I could catch my breath. I found my baby at last. We must have a proper tombstone made for her, documenting her Powell roots. I pulled the grass with my bare hands around her small headstone to be certain that she is forever visible to me. Now, she can rest in peace. Her mother is back and will take care of everything.*

"Maybe this is why I was supposed to come back to Quincy," I told Tananarive later. "Maybe I was supposed to be closer to the baby."

The losses in 1967 did not end with little Lydia Johnita.

In August 1967, five months after my baby died, there was more terrible news: Calvin Bess, the Tallahassee student who had been in high school when he first grew interested in civil rights as a member of my Young People's Progressive Club, had been killed under suspicious circumstances while registering voters in Mississippi. In my memory, Calvin was a child. As far as I knew, he had gotten involved in civil rights because of me.

I was not at home at the time, but John tells me Calvin's mother came to our house in grief, saying her son's death was my fault.

Those were very painful days. For all of us, it seems, death was in the air.

Twenty-Six

# TANANARIVE DUE

**"One does not fight to influence change**
**and then leave the change**
**to someone else to bring about."**
***—Stokely Carmichael***

George Calvin Bess's family could not make it to The Gathering, and neither could he. His father was too sick from kidney problems to travel. His sister had a prior obligation with neighborhood schoolchildren. George Calvin Bess himself had been dead for thirty years.

His name had come up many times over the years as one that stuck particularly in my mother's memory, and she had been afraid his family members might react coldly if she called to interview his family for our book. Mom has always felt that his family blamed her for his death, and deep down, I think she always blamed herself, too.

But when we tracked down his family in Tallahassee and Mom was brave enough to make the call, the family was happy to hear from her. "Patricia *Due?*" his father kept exclaiming with happy recognition. They were eager to take part in interviews about the impact of the civil rights movement on their family.

Calvin's mother was in a nursing home and could not speak to us. Nor would she have agreed to it, her husband said; she'd never recovered from the loss of her only son. But we did speak to Calvin's father and his sister, Cherrye, who'd been only six in the summer of 1967, when the older brother she'd simply called Brother never came home. (Mrs. Cherrye Bess, Calvin's mother, died in 1997, the year after we interviewed her family; and Calvin's father, also named George Calvin Bess, died in 2000.)

Most people know about Mickey Schwerner, James Chaney, and Andrew Goodman, the three civil rights workers who died during Freedom Summer in 1964. I remember seeing Mickey Schwerner's mother years ago on *Donahue* and thinking that, no matter how painful it was to lose her son, she might have won some small consolation in the fact that her loss, and his sacrifice, were known. Hollywood fictionalized it and made the movie *Mississippi Burning* about it. But Calvin Bess had died, too, and almost no one knew. He did not make national newspaper headlines. His name does not appear in history books. His family has not been on *Donahue*, nor on *Oprah*, nor have they had to watch the horror of their son's final days Hollywoodized for the careful consumption of the general public. Hollywoodized, perhaps, but at least remembered.

Mom's spark was able to light a durable flame in Calvin for a variety of reasons, not the least of which, we know now, was the influence of his father, also named George Calvin Bess. Mr. Bess and Mom hugged upon meeting each other. George Bess was tall, at least six-foot-two, with thick arms and a handsome face, despite his seventy-one years. Mom and I were both struck by how attractive he was. His nature matched.

At the beginning of the interview, he chuckled good-heartedly over stories of his exploits as a young man, like getting into a brawl with a Tallahassee store clerk who called him "nigger," and not getting arrested because someone intervened and argued that he didn't know local customs since he was from New York. He also took part in an on-base riot at an Army camp in Florida, when the black soldiers weren't permitted to watch a Noble Sissle concert with the white soldiers. "We broke into the main post warehouse and we took all the guns we could find, and all the ammo, and we shot the place up. And we burnt the post headquarters down," he said. "This was in 1942. Shortly thereafter, they shipped us out of there. They shipped us overseas."[1]

Mom and I could instantly see where Calvin got his determination.

Calvin's mother, predictably, was worried about his involvement in the civil rights movement, especially once he was arrested, but she gradually had to accept it. There was no convincing a Bess man not to do something he wanted to do.

There were no classes at Harvard that Calvin was interested in that summer term in 1967, nor at FAMU, so he decided to do some voter registration work in Selma. Before he left, his father took him to a nearby auto shop to buy a blue Triumph convertible. After he'd packed up his car, his father noticed he had a taillight out, so he warned him and fixed it for him.

At the time Calvin died, his kid sister, Cherrye, who rode with him everywhere he went, was six years old. Cherrye called him "Brother," and he called her "Q" ("Because he said I was cute," Cherrye said). Cherrye told us that she remembered riding in the convertible with her brother to civil rights meetings when she was very young, and how much she'd loved singing the freedom songs even though she hadn't understood what they meant. Cherrye remembers him studying and writing a great deal before he left.

Neither of his parents had really wanted him to make the trip because of the danger. But at least it was Selma, his father told him. Selma wasn't so bad. Cherrye wondered why she couldn't go on this trip with her brother—she went to all of his other meetings with him, she sang freedom songs with him. But he was very insistent, she says. She could not go. She would have to wait. And wait she did. She waited by the front door's jalousie window for her brother to come home.

Soon after he left, Calvin called home and said he wasn't in Selma, after all. There wasn't anything for him to do there. He'd gone on to Mississippi. His father recalls how, when his son called him and told him he'd decided to move his voter registration work that summer from Selma to Mississippi, he'd told his son, "Well, you're in no-man's land now." But Calvin always told his parents he was all right. He was safe. He talked to them a few days before he died.

The other call came the first Sunday in August. The sheriff's office in Mississippi and one of Calvin's civil rights coworkers, a man Calvin had nicknamed "Tex," had tried to call the Bess family several times that day. George Bess remembers getting the call after church. Cherrye Bess remembers she answered the phone first, that they'd come back from getting groceries. Her mother took the phone from her, then shrieked and sank to her knees, sobbing. "And then Daddy ran to the phone," Cherrye recalls, "so I knew it had to be something pretty bad. Nobody was speaking to me, though." Even after she was told what had happened, she did not fully comprehend it. She still waited for her brother by the window, she remembers. "I told Mama, 'God gon' put a Band-Aid on him and send him back,' " Cherrye recalls.[2]

People who visited the house, like Stokely Carmichael and others, kept telling Cherrye about the Movement. "They asked, 'Do you understand the *Move*-ment and Civil Rights and why they were fighting for *my* rights? They made it very personal," she said. She did not understand until much later, but she remembers that when she was a child, people thought it was very important that she should know.

No one ever fully believed the police account of what happened to Calvin. Calvin died of a blow to his head that made a large gash at his temple. Mississippi locals always thought the car had been hauled to that creek by racist murderers, that they had not really driven into the creek. But Calvin's parents were too distraught, and too frightened, to go to Mississippi to investigate, even when the NAACP offered assistance. They did not think they would find the truth, and they were afraid the same fate might befall them.

Calvin's father had the water-damaged car towed back to Florida. For six months, it sat in front of their house. Every time Calvin's mother saw it, she was overcome with grief. He put it in storage eventually, but it was eating away at him, too, so he finally got rid of it.

Along the way, though, the family experienced tiny miracles. The biggest was that soon after Calvin died, they discovered he'd fathered a child they didn't know about. The mother lived in Ocala, and the boy was about a year old. They intervened just as he was about to be adopted by a family in Daytona, proved they were related from the similarity of photographs, took the boy home, and named him Calvin. Everyone, even little Cherrye, felt the baby was solace. Now there was a Calvin, Cherrye says, and she could stop waiting. Calvin had come back.

The day we spent with Calvin's father and sister was very moving. Listening to Calvin's father tell his story, recalling the awful day the telephone call shattered their lives, my mother began to choke and had to excuse herself from the room. Later, I took pictures of Calvin's father hugging my mother, and I hoped that the book we wanted to write would give him and his family a sense that his son has been properly honored.

The tragic footnote is that George Calvin Bess IV became one of a long line of Bess men who fathered children shortly before being separated because of traumatic events—George Calvin II was overseas during World War II, with no expectation of returning, and didn't see his child until he was two; George Calvin III died in Mississippi, never seeing his child at all; and George Calvin IV was incarcerated, leaving a young daughter outside. At nearly the same age his father had been when he died, Calvin's son was sent to prison on drug charges, sentenced to thirteen years for his first offense, a nonviolent crime. He is almost thirty at this writing, and he has spent most of his adult life in jail. Truly, the criminal justice system in this country is the next great frontier in the civil rights struggle.

How did we leapfrog from the painful gains of the civil rights movement to seeing so many of our young men end up in jail? It's a question of economics, in part. For so many misguided young people, even the brightest ones, drugs are a trade, an attainable means of support. Too many of us are still outside the system, haven't learned to thrive within the law. And the "War on Drugs," which is really a war on drug addicts and the poor, a war on inner cities, has filled our prisons with obscene numbers of nonviolent offenders.

Calvin Bess always told his father that he was dedicating himself to civil rights work for Cherrye, so she could go to school anywhere she wanted. She chose Bethune-Cookman College and FAMU, historically black schools, but she *chose* them. Today, Cherrye says she cherishes the memory of singing with Calvin when she was young, her first memories of singing. Today, she is active in Tallahassee's black community, giving of herself to make the city better for everyone, often through song, gracing audiences with her lovely singing voice every chance she gets. Her brother would be proud.

I've had many occasions to reflect upon that young man's sacrifice. One election day more than a year after the interview, my telephone rang early, waking me. "Good morning, darling. I hope you weren't asleep, but I wanted to catch you before you left for work. It's election day. Don't forget." It was my mother's voice.

"Election day? For what?" I mumbled.

"Don't you read your own paper? For one thing, the mayor is trying to change the name of the county. There are a couple of other items, too."

Still only half awake, my mind was on anything *but* an election. By then, I'd returned to my job as a newspaper reporter because I needed an income, and I had a deadline that day. "Mom, I don't have time to vote today. I have an assignment this morning, and then—"

I didn't finish, but I didn't have to. "I don't believe you," my mother said. She couldn't have sounded more hurt and angry if I'd slapped her.

"I don't have an opinion about that name-change thing. And I don't even know what else is on the ballot."

"That's why you *read,*" my mother said, then she was silent. She is not an inarticulate woman, but it seemed she had to search for words because she was shocked by my response. To her, the question *Why should I vote?* was like *Why should I breathe?* On that day, though, I was pretty sure my sisters in Dallas and New York weren't headed for the polls, either. We all vote religiously in presidential or mayoral elections, but the occasional local election goes unnoticed because of busy schedules.

"Of course you *vote,*" my mother said. "I really can't believe this, from you of all people. I thought you understood by now how important this is."

I was waking up. I sighed. "Mom, of course I understand how important my choice to vote is. That choice is sacred to me." *Choice?* I could almost read my mother's mind, her silence was so loud. "And I understand that people sacrificed their lives so I could voice my opinion. In this case, I don't have one. This is just a little local thing. Most people haven't even heard about it."

"Yes, the newspaper is expecting a five percent turnout, and that's all the more reason for you to vote. That's all I have to say about this. I have to go."

We both hung up the phone feeling frustrated, at an impasse. I knew my mother was profoundly disappointed to hear her daughter sound like some insensitive person who didn't understand where she had come from. I hated to prick my mother's pain, but I'd longed to be honest about my feelings, too. I wasn't a deadbeat. I voted and I voted often. Was it really shirking the responsibility of my race to miss one election?

Regardless, I got up earlier than planned, dug through my wallet for my voter registration card, and drove to the nearly deserted polling place about two miles from my home. It was a ghost town. The staff members were so glad to see me, they smiled as if I'd just brought them breakfast. At that moment, I was glad I was there.

I hadn't gone just to avoid another argument with my mother. I hadn't gone even because I had any opinion whatsoever on whether Dade County changed its name to Miami-Dade County.

In the end, maybe I'd gone because of the interview with Calvin Bess's father. I thought about that visit, when he was forced to recall the death of a bright young man who never had the opportunity to grow up, meet his own son, finish his promising college education, or live the life his parents had dreamed for him.

Calvin's father had told us how he felt on election days when neighbors who had known his child since he was a boy, and knew how he had died, still refused to walk the simple distance to a nearby church to cast their votes, even when it was time to choose a president. He said he had one neighbor who was barely literate and yet voted every single time, but unfortunately he was the exception: *There's other guys sitting around there saying, "Ain't gon' do no good." It makes me feel bad, angry. I say, "Hey, I had a son who gave his life just for this purpose, to get people like you involved in voting." It goes in one ear and out the other. I hate to call them ignorant, but what more can you say?*

I couldn't remember Calvin Bess and neglect to vote that day.

In November 1996, two weeks after our interview with Calvin Bess's family, an unforgettable opportunity came to Mom and me: a chance to interview Stokely Carmichael, the influential black nationalist and former Black Panther who popularized the phrase "Black Power." Since Calvin Bess had been working for Stokely Carmichael's SNCC at the time of his death, the well-known activist had visited Calvin's family often at their modest Tallahassee home in the following years. We'd hoped to have the chance to talk to him about Calvin, and now we did. He was in Miami to visit his mother, Mabel Carmichael, and to take part in a public tribute, and he was gracious enough to agree to an interview when my mother called.

It was November 5. Election day. I drove to South Dade to interview Kwame Turé, a.k.a. Stokely Carmichael.

Mom had heard that he was ill. His sickness, we learned, was prostate cancer. He walked and sat very gingerly, and I couldn't help noticing how swollen his bare ankles and feet were. Yet he had a beautiful smile that enlivened his entire face, showcasing a row of bright teeth against his clay-brown skin. He spoke very properly, in a careful West Indian manner, and he was not nearly as intimidating as I had expected from a revolutionary. He seemed, in fact, like a man who could sit and listen very patiently to the arguments of someone with whom he disagreed vehemently.

On that day, even more than other days, I felt the very strong sense of recording a fleeting bit of history. I didn't know how much longer Kwame Turé had left to live, but I did know how serious prostate cancer is, I knew it was undetected for some time, and I knew his feet were swollen. I did not believe he would live to see this book published.

I was every bit the journalist that day, helping Mom set up the video cameras, testing the microphone on our tape recorder, interviewing him in very much the same way I've interviewed countless other people. I listened with interest, not sorrow or mortification, as he described being in a Montgomery, Alabama, hotel on the day of an SNCC march in Montgomery in 1965, when he could see the horse-mounted police with their batons waiting for marchers. The marchers could not see the police, but Turé could see them from his fifth-floor vantage point. When he tried to run downstairs to warn the marchers, he found he'd been locked inside the hotel.

He told the story best in his own words: "Julian Bond was then our communicating secretary in Atlanta, so I had to call him, and I was giving Julian a blow-by-blow description of the brutality I was seeing before my very eyes. I mean, they were brutal. I've seen a lot of brutality in my life, but they trampled kids on horses, they had bullwhips, they had batons, they rode into the crowd and smashed them down. I mean, the horses were coming fast, at galloping speeds. So I was giving a blow-by-blow description. They sent a man from the telephone company, directly opposite me, and he began to climb the telephone pole. I told Julian, 'OK, I'd better give it to you fast, because they're getting ready to disconnect the phone, you know.' And of course, the man did disconnect the phone. Since I couldn't get out because they had locked the door, I had to stay by the window and see all this brutality, and there's nothing worse than witnessing it when you yourself cannot participate in it. . . . That evening, I went off and they had to send me out of Montgomery. I went off. I went off."[3]

After Turé described this scene, Mom began to cough and ended up needing a glass of water and excusing herself to go to the bathroom. When Mom returned, she said she'd been more caught up in his story of brutality than she thought. "The flashbacks," she said. There were tears in her eyes, and it was only then that I understood that her emotions had provoked the coughing bout, not simply her allergies or her asthma. She had been drawn in. She told me later she felt as though she'd been *in* that hotel room with him, seeing everything he was seeing through his eyes.

We asked Turé why he visited the Bess family for so many years after Calvin died. He explained that SNCC, which Calvin was working for at the time he died (and which Turé headed), was a poor organization. There were many others who died like Calvin, he said, and the visits were the least he could do. "There were many. We lost many people, so it wasn't unusual at all," he said with his gentle, plainspoken eloquence. "He was a comrade who had died, so we had a responsibility. Of course, we were poor, and we were so poor we couldn't even feed the families of our dead comrades, you know. So, we couldn't do anything for them, but at least we had a responsibility to visit them to let them know that, if nobody else knew, *we* knew the death was not in vain. We were aware of the sacrifices made, and grateful for those sacrifices made. And thankful to the family for having produced him."

Simply put, he was a man who believed in doing what should be done. That, I think, was the quiet mark of his life. After the interview, I presented Turé with a copy of my first novel, *The Between*. Exactly two years later, to the month, he was dead.

"Keep writing that history," he said to me that day.

I will, I told him. Oh yes, I will.

Twenty-Seven

# Patricia Stephens Due

**"An elephant doesn't die because of one broken rib."**
***—Tsonga proverb***

A month after our baby died in 1967, while I was still recovering both emotionally and physically, I was contacted by a white woman in Miami, Nancy Adams. She asked me to get involved with the NAACP Legal Defense Fund, which was at the forefront of the school desegregation movement in Leon County, under a plan called "Freedom of Choice." It was just the thing I needed to help pull myself out of my grief after such a sudden, unexpected loss. Under the new Freedom of Choice plan, Negro students could choose to attend white schools that had formerly been segregated, and we wanted to get the word out. Thirteen years after the *Brown v. Board of Education* Supreme Court ruling, students in northern Florida could finally attend integrated schools. But students had only thirty days to submit their choices to their school system.

I volunteered to help, but I had a great deal of difficulty setting up any kind of organized movement. In some ways, what happened during that period was a microcosm of what was going on in the civil rights movement around the country by 1967. The problems were clear in a frustrated letter I wrote to the NAACP Legal Defense and Education Fund on May 16, 1967:

> *The Leon County Community is very difficult to organize for several reasons. The major reason is that many potential leaders are employed by the state and others are dependent on whites in one way or another. Secondly, there is and has been for the past ten years a lack of communication among Negro groups in the community. Also, there is considerable rivalry and jealousy within groups, making it difficult for them to function effectively. . . . The lack of cooperation between the*

> *NAACP and the Educational Improvement Committee of the NAACP made it twice as difficult to operate; one would think they were separate groups.*[1]

I did my best. Working out of John's office because I had trouble obtaining an office of my own, I contacted volunteers and we scheduled meetings in twenty sections of Leon County. We handed out kits with fact sheets, leaders' guides, booklets, and extra Freedom of Choice forms. After the meetings, we canvassed door to door. Most of our volunteers were high school and junior high school students. We were effective, but I hated the feeling that we were working against ourselves. All over the country, to tell the truth, the Movement seemed to be falling apart.

The strings that had bound us together in the first place had not always been strong. I thought too many leaders were blinded by their allegiance to their organizations instead of really keeping their "eyes on the prize." I met the great NAACP leader Ruby Hurley once. I'd heard rumors that she couldn't stand me, and that she had said so to others. When I met her in person, however, much to her apparent amazement, we liked each other. Hurley represented the NAACP and I represented CORE, so I guess she had considered me an upstart and a rival. I never felt that kind of rivalry.

I was an NAACP Youth Council adviser myself in Tallahassee at one point, and I had to try to learn to maneuver around organizational politics. I remember being involved in an activity that was not very successful once—I honestly can't remember what it was—and I was quoted in the newspaper as an NAACP Youth Council Advisor. Soon afterward, the NAACP national director, who was very irate, contacted me. Roy Wilkins told me that there were very specific guidelines on approval for any event to be sanctioned by the NAACP, and I should never use that organization's name without prior approval. Okay, I said. Perhaps I've never been very good at following rules, and I could understand his concern. So the next time I was involved in a big event, since I didn't have time to go through all of the NAACP channels, I said I was representing CORE. This time, the event was a huge success, and once again I was contacted by Roy Wilkins. This time he wanted to know why I hadn't given the NAACP credit.

As for me, I didn't care who got credit, as long as the job got done. But more and more, it seemed to me it did not.

CORE had been in disarray since the departure of James Farmer in 1966, with much of the membership drifting away because of budget problems and infighting over racial and political ideology.[2] The Black Panther Party had also been founded in 1966 by Huey Newton in Oakland, California, and there was growing strife among Negroes—or "blacks," as we had begun calling ourselves—in the civil rights movement. By 1968, the Movement had firmly splintered off behind the "Black Power" slogan popularized by Stokely Carmichael in 1966, espousing black nationalism. Whites had held prominent positions in earlier stages of the Movement, and many Negro leaders had grown to resent white involvement. By 1968, CORE's new director, Roy Innis, announced that black separatism was his organization's goal. "Separatism is a necessary and pragmatic way of organizing two distinct and separate races of people," Innis said in a press release. "When we have control of our self-destiny, then we can talk about integration."[3]

I didn't realize everything that was going on inside CORE until after the fact. I met Roy Innis only once or twice, so I never got to know him or his ideology very well. Personally, I thought it was about time for blacks to begin to love themselves more, and I liked the idea of "Black is Beautiful." Some people may have misunderstood what the "Black Power" cry was all about. It had to be dramatized that way for black people to finally like themselves for who they were. We did not like ourselves, so "Black Power" and "Black is Beautiful" were a natural progression to raising our consciousness. On the other hand, I didn't feel the need to reject any whites who were working with me. "Black is Beautiful" did not mean white was bad, and "Black Power" meant it was time for us to take charge of our own destiny. I thought it was a good thing.

Some whites did not agree and felt threatened, and some whites were ousted, just as Jim Robinson had been ousted from CORE years earlier. I think because they were feeling rejected, a lot of white activists began to desert the Movement to protest the Vietnam War and to support the Women's Movement. I resented this, believing that if whites were truly dedicated to our cause, they should be willing to remain, even if there was some hostility toward them, just as blacks had been forced to tolerate hostility from white society for so long.

Now that the heyday of CORE and SNCC had passed, and black nationalism was gathering momentum, Dr. King and those in the more moderate SCLC found themselves pushed more and more to the side. Dr. King did not believe in black separatism, and he still firmly espoused nonviolence. He had also grown more committed to opposing the Vietnam War, even though some civil rights allies warned him that it would alienate him and the SCLC from President Johnson and the organization's donors.[4] Because of that war, Dr. King eventually opposed President Johnson's 1968 presidential candidacy, despite everything President Johnson had done for the cause of civil rights.[5] I thought Dr. King was putting too much emphasis on the Vietnam War. We had so much to worry about at home, I couldn't understand why Dr. King would focus so much of his energy on the war. I know many other activists at the time felt the same way.

On the surface, despite many changes, so much remained the same. There can be a big difference between laws on paper and laws in practice. Priscilla and I had already learned that the hard way—when we tried to order food in 1966 and the waitress threatened to hit us with a chair—but it was an ongoing lesson for me and John in the late 1960s.

We had a favorite seafood restaurant in Leon County near Tallahassee, St. Mark's, which had very good food. We would have eaten there often, except that we never knew how we would be treated and John decided he didn't want to bring his family there anymore. He couldn't feel relaxed with all of the stares and angry muttered comments from racist customers. It's one thing to face that kind of stress without a family, but it's different when a child is present. If someone had tried to act crazy then—either by trying to hurt me or Tananarive in John's presence—John knew he might not stay in control of himself. So we stayed away.

Despite our new civil rights laws, discrimination and violence against blacks was still very much a part of life.

---

For me, 1968 began with yet another trying pregnancy, very soon after losing my day-old daughter—perhaps too soon. We lived in Quincy, where John was a labor union organizer and had a law practice, although he was still traveling a great deal. I spent much of my time alone with two-year-old Tananarive, which was becoming an all-too-familiar story.

In late February of 1968, I left Quincy so that Tananarive and I could stay with Mother for a month in Miami. John was traveling so often that my doctor in Tallahassee worried about my isolation in Quincy, believing that if I went into labor when I was alone, I might not survive childbirth. The baby was scheduled to be born in April.

I was being treated by a new doctor in Miami, and he was not an honest man. Although I had a checkup the day before and the doctor told me everything was fine, this doctor lied to the hospital on Sunday, March 17, saying I had gone into premature labor. It may sound silly, but because my previous births had been through cesarean section and I was so involved in other things, I had no idea what labor was like. After I was admitted to the hospital, nurses kept coming into my room, asking "Did you have another one?" They wanted to time my contractions, but I really did not know what they were talking about. "Oh, you just missed it," I kept saying, feeling afraid and foolish.

My hospitalization was so sudden that I had a hard time contacting John. The Miami doctor suggested that I have my tubes tied in light of my difficult pregnancies, and my husband needed to sign papers for this to happen. I also wanted him with me during our child's birth. John arrived in Miami just as I was being taken into the operating room. Fortunately, we decided against having my tubes tied.

I had an emergency cesarean section at Baptist Hospital, and Johnita Patricia Due was born. This time, the baby was fine, despite the fact that the doctor had delivered her a month early! My blood pressure was very high before the surgery, and I experienced terrible vomiting, so after such a hard time, I was incredibly grateful to see my new baby girl, healthy and alive. I was told Johnita looked more like me than John, unlike our two previous children, but it was hard for me to tell. I was just happy she was alive.

As soon as I was well enough to leave Miami, Tananarive and I flew back home with two-week-old Johnita, where other family members were waiting to help take care of the baby. My aunt on my biological father's side, Hattie Martin, sent her nineteen-year-old daughter, Shilda, to stay at the house and help me, as she had with Tananarive in 1966. My great-aunt Amy, my father's aunt, also came from time to time to do my laundry and iron. Aunt Amy, like many other relatives, did not offer me much conversation, but in her own way she showed me she cared. I think my biological father's family saw me as an oddity, the way many people in my home county did in the 1960s, but many of them were there for me when it mattered. I was recovering slowly, but I was happy to be back in my own home.

Finally, I thought, life was turning brighter.

Johnita, the new baby, had more than one godmother: Hers were Mrs. Susan Ausley and Mrs. Vivian Kelly, both of whom had been helpful during the voter registration campaign.

While John and I were celebrating the new addition to our family, the world outside took some terrible turns that did not give us much faith in what the future might hold for our children. On April 4, only the day after one of Dr. King's most famous speeches—where he spoke of going to the "mountaintop" and seeing the "Promised Land"—one of our greatest fears was realized: Dr. Martin Luther King Jr. was shot to death on the balcony of the Lorraine Motel in Memphis. A white man named James Earl Ray was charged with his murder.

"Oh, my God. Oh, no. Oh, no," I kept saying, hardly believing my eyes as I watched the television reports. President Kennedy's assassination had been a shock in 1963, but Dr. King's senseless death in 1968 hit me and John on a much deeper level. His death was not only the death of one man, in my mind, but the death of the dream all of us had shared.

Our phone began ringing off the hook as activists I had worked with during the Movement began to call. All of them sounded so angry: *Is there any hope for this country?* In major cities, as blacks tried to grapple with their feelings of rage and grief, riots broke out and buildings burned. On the nightly news, the whole country appeared to be in flames. The riots went on for ten days in more than a hundred cities, costing forty-six people their lives.[6] I won't mention his name, but I remember one young man I'd worked with calling me from Detroit, where looting was rampant. "Do you want some jewelry?" he asked me.

"No. You get out of there," I told him quickly. "Just take care of yourself."

I understood why people were rioting. After so much frustration and so many sacrifices, sometimes you feel as if you're about to lose your mind, and it only takes one event to trigger violence. But I am not a believer in riots. As anguished as I felt, I knew that was not the answer.

What really made Dr. King's death so hard on me was feeling helpless. I'd just had a major operation two weeks earlier, when Johnita was born, and there was nothing I could do. Atlanta was a five-hour drive from Quincy, and Dr. King's funeral was going to be held there. I really wanted to attend the funeral out of respect for his family, to show them that I cared. I really agonized, because I wanted so much to be among the thousands of blacks I knew would be there to bury the great civil rights leader who had sacrificed his life trying to make the world better for others. But I was still too weak, and I could not go. John went to the funeral march and walked behind the mule-drawn casket in the endless sea of people that filled Atlanta's streets. He could not get inside the doors of Ebenezer Baptist Church for the service because the church overflowed with mourners.

To this day, I regret that I could not be there.

---

Dr. King's assassination made many activists feel more determined than ever to show this country's racists that the murder of one leader would not stop our people's fight for freedom. Even though I now had two young children, I was no exception.

The civil rights movement had taken many forms since I first got involved as a college student, from sit-ins to the jail-in to the Freedom Rides to voter registration to political empowerment, and now my focus was on economic empowerment. At the time of Dr. King's death, he'd been in Memphis trying to resolve an ongoing sanitation workers' strike and planning a Poor People's Campaign. He was in a pessimistic mood at the end of his life. He had announced to his church in Atlanta that his Sunday sermon would be entitled "Why America May Go to Hell."[7] He never got the chance to preach that sermon. The assassination of Robert Kennedy exactly two months later, on June 4, was surreal and devastating.

In Memphis, black sanitation workers had staged a strike and launched demonstrations because Mayor Henry Loeb refused to recognize their nearly all-black local. Black workers were tired of white sanitation workers receiving favorable treatment, so 1,300 of them had left the job. A community boycott of downtown stores was also happening.[8] Because Dr. King had died trying to help sanitation workers, the spotlight was on the problems of sanitation workers throughout the country.

In Florida, we had our own problem brewing with sanitation workers in St. Petersburg. The custom in St. Petersburg's sanitation department had been for the blacks to ride on the trucks and physically gather the garbage while whites drove the trucks. Obviously, it was more pleasant to be a driver than a garbage handler—not to mention that driving was less demanding work, but the white drivers were paid more than the black garbage handlers. That was just one of many problems of discrimination the black workers faced.

In addition to his law practice, John was working for the American Federation of State, County, and Municipal Employees, which had been supportive of CORE and had Dr. King's blessing, so they sent him to St. Petersburg to talk to the workers to convince them to join the union. John had been able to get a union representative from AFSCME to help him organize an integrated local union, but the city's history of racial problems made John's work an uphill battle. The public employees' union was all-white, so blacks were suspicious of the union.

I went with John, bringing Tananarive and little Johnita, who was only a few months old. The union put John up in a very nice hotel in nearby Tampa, so our family stayed there at first. My reputation had spread to St. Petersburg, and when blacks heard I was staying with John, they asked me to join their grassroots campaign. They wanted my help in organizing, speaking, and rallying the community for a sanitation workers' strike—just like in Memphis. I sympathized with their cause, so I agreed.

As a result, John and I ended up on opposing sides of the issue. This was the first time this had happened so dramatically in the course of our marriage.

John and I still chuckle about it today. He was being put up in a fancy hotel, and I was brought to a simpler hotel for Negroes in St. Petersburg that served as a gathering place for community activists. The girls and I traveled back and forth between the accommodations so we could spend time with John, but the people of St. Petersburg made us feel very much at home. I think they felt particularly warmly toward me because I had come with my children, which showed them that I truly believed in what they were doing. All my needs were seen to, especially those that counted most: those of my children.

The only way we could ensure that blacks' concerns would be listened to during the sanitation workers' strike was to keep the trucks from completing their routes. We decided that volunteers—me included—would go to the sanitation headquarters before the trucks left early in the morning to block their way. Tananarive was only two, Johnita was practically a newborn, and John was busy on union business, so I needed a baby-sitter.

At 4:00 or 4:30 in the morning on the first day of our protest, I heard a knock at my hotel room door. Someone from the community had volunteered to baby-sit for me, and she was there right on time to do her job. I wish I knew the names of the people who volunteered for babysitting, but I do not. I do know they were just as dedicated as I was, in their own way. No one job was more important to me than another, because to me, there was no job more important than taking care of my two babies.

I was ready to go, trying to be quiet so I wouldn't wake the children. As usual, I was neatly dressed, and I had already prepared contact numbers for the baby-sitter in case I was either killed or arrested. "Good luck, Mrs. Due," the baby-sitter whispered in the darkness, and I went on my way to stop the garbage trucks.

Unfortunately, we did not have large crowds of volunteers to block the trucks, so we could not form a human wall. Instead, the handful of us who came before dawn did the only thing we could: We sat down on the hard asphalt in front of the trucks so that the drivers would have to run over us if they wanted to leave. Then we waited to see what would happen next. I knew from experience that blacks were not treated as human beings, so I realized these drivers might feel justified running over us.

Those white drivers were very angry. They were already annoyed about the complaints of the black sanitation workers who, in their minds, were trying to unjustly steal their jobs, but now they had to contend with blacks trying to keep them from working. The drivers started their trucks and began rolling toward us. As the huge trucks came closer to us, instead of slowing down, we heard roars from the engines. They were accelerating.

I sat like a stone. I closed my eyes, accepting that I might be about to die. I had already decided *I'm doing this, and I may have to pay the consequences.* I never could have done it otherwise. I could not afford to think about the reactions of Mother, or of John, or of the daughters who might never get to know their mother. Just as I'd felt when I was a student, I was ready to give my life.

If the truck drivers weren't going to stop, I knew there was no way I could move in time. The drivers knew that, too. They wanted us to be *certain* we were about to be killed, because they raced right up to us—then stopped, their brakes screeching. Then they backed up and did it all over again, always racing and stopping on a dime. Eventually, feeling they had made their point, they drove around us and went to work.

The next day, another knock at my hotel room door came promptly at 4:00 A.M., and another baby-sitter came. Just like the day before, I went to sit in front of the garbage trucks.

This time, the police came, and I was arrested. This was my first arrest since the birth of my children. Although I knew they were in good hands, my thoughts were of them as I was taken to my jail cell. Still, while the other demonstrators were bonding out, I was firm: "No, no, no. I'm not going to bond out," I said.

The jailers looked at me like I was crazy, but I later heard that a police officer who had worked in Tallahassee was present, and he recognized me. "She's not joking," he told his fellow officers. "She's going to stay in jail." He must have started rumors about the jail-in in my past, because after only a day, the jailer said, "You're free to go."

"But I didn't pay the fine," I said.

"Never mind that. Just go."

At my trial, I was found guilty and charged $25. I guess they thought I wouldn't refuse to pay such a small fine, but they were wrong. "I'm not going to pay any fine," I said.

Once again, after I said I wouldn't pay, I was told I could leave without paying. My attorney was James Sanderlin—a black lawyer who later became a judge—and I think he was as happy to be rid of me as the police and the court were. I believe everyone's thinking was "Let's get her out of town."

No one wanted the publicity of a protestor's extended jail stay, especially a mother with two small children. That would have been a public relations nightmare. I remained in St. Petersburg a while longer, and I decided to help John. I convinced the residents to talk to him about the union just so they could hear what he had to say. Eventually, the black sanitation workers decided to join AFSCME. To show their gratitude, the sanitation workers sang a song for the civil rights workers to the tune of "How Sweet It Is to Be Loved by You": *Thank you for the sore feet that you have given us, / Thank you for the hours that you have walked with us, / Thank you for singing with us, / Thank you for clapping with us, and thank you for working for freedom with us.*[9] It was so good to see people happy. That time, John and I were the perfect team.

Our most difficult ordeals as a married civil rights couple were yet to come.

Twenty-Eight

# Tananarive Due

**"To give to thy friend is not to cast away,**
**it is to store for the future."**
***—Swahili proverb***

In the 1946 Frank Capra Christmas classic *It's a Wonderful Life,* a man played by Jimmy Stewart learns how much his presence has meant to his quaint little town of Bedford Falls: first because an angel allows him to see how the town would have deteriorated without his selfless presence, and then when all his friends and neighbors, rich and poor (even a black woman!), pour into his living room to give him money to pull him out of a financial mess, all of them singing "Hark the Herald Angels Sing." It's a favorite moment in film for Americans.

On a Monday night in October 1997, my father had a similar moment of enlightenment in the quaint little town of Miami, Florida, where his selfless presence was celebrated at a meeting at the Joseph Caleb Center in Miami's inner-city in northwest Dade County. Like the Jimmy Stewart character in *It's a Wonderful Life,* my father was feeling gloomy when he had his glimpse into the community's heart. He was not at the meeting by choice. Also like the movie character, an unexpected turn had left him feeling mounting desperation.

For seven years my father had served as director of the Office of Black Affairs, and for seventeen years as program officer of the Community Relations Board of Miami-Dade County. From that post—and in his years with Legal Services, the Economic Opportunity Program Inc. (EOPI), and the NAACP—he had traversed the county and state from end to end, forging the next phase of the civil rights work he'd begun as a young man in law school. He'd worked on tenants' rights, poverty programs, school desegregation, legal aid, Haitian amnesty, police accountability, and juvenile justice. In 1995, under the auspices of the Black Affairs Advisory Board, he'd helped mobilize community pressure to free more than 200

Haitian children being held at the Guantanamo Bay naval camp, one of the things he has told me he is most proud of. His office's community advisory committee included a vocal member—my mother—so my parents were doing what they have always done in more than thirty years of life together as civil rights activists and community advocates. They were working for change in the best ways they knew how.

In 1997, in the wake of budget problems, the mayor was cutting jobs. My parents worried in the weeks after the rumors of cutbacks began circulating, but I was never seriously concerned. My father was *John Due.* He'd been out on the streets trying to ease the lives of people in the county since I could remember, braving riots, frustration, and bureaucracy. Even if the county shuffled him to a new position, I was certain his bosses would take care of my father after he'd spent twenty-five years trying to keep a lid on such an emotionally volatile place.

I was wrong. Dad was among 158 people who received pink slips. No new job had been offered to him. Two years before retirement, it seemed, my father was being put out to pasture. The new mayor of Dade County, Alex Penelas, was in his thirties, one of *my* peers. Also, newer voices from different communities were vying for recognition, some of whom had not lived in Miami during the 1980 riots and had no memory of a time, some years earlier, when black people had to carry passes to work on Miami Beach—or, like my father, were constantly followed by police when they crossed the causeway. Miami is a city of newcomers who bring memories of their histories from other places, which gives the region both its amazing vitality and a kind of collective community amnesia. I realized my father was being forgotten by the county he and my mother had helped build.

Sometimes bad news dazes me, leaving me feeling paralyzed. That had happened in the wake of Hurricane Andrew in 1992, when it took me two full days to pull myself away from the *Herald*'s newsroom to visit my parents, aunt, and grandmother in the hurricane-torn area of Southwest Dade and bring them a hot meal. It happened again when I heard about my father's pink slip in 1997. I felt helpless to do anything. I was a reporter dancing that ambiguous line of trying to observe and report the news while my family was busily making news. I'd had to grow accustomed to this role at the newspaper, with coworkers on the news desk often asking me for my parents' telephone number when they needed comments for their stories. (Once, during my earliest days as an intern at one of the *Herald*'s suburban bureaus, I quoted my own father in a story about the NAACP, in a moment of supreme awkwardness and understaffing. It only happened once, and yet it seemed to be the story of my life.)

Through none of my own doing—I was too dazed to make a trip to my newspaper's editorial board offices, nor would I have considered it proper—the *Herald* did run an editorial chastising the county for its treatment of my father. "Florida's and Dade County's history record Mr. Due as a courageous and selfless champion in the struggle for equality. He risked everything—life, family, and future—to secure rights enjoyed today by so many."[1]

In some ways, Johnita is the most emotional person in our family, and she also has the most clearheaded ability to jump into the fray with both her mind and her claws sharp. From New York, she immediately dashed off letters to Mayor Penelas and every county commissioner to plead my father's case, squeezing in the time to do it while she worked sixty-hour weeks at a Wall Street law firm. She also sent copies of her letters to a black-owned radio station, WMBM–AM, owned by New Birth Baptist Church in Miami. Miami activist Bishop Victor T. Curry, pastor of that church, read Johnita's letter over the airwaves. Dad did his part, too. He took copies of his pink slip to the *Miami Times* and to Miami's black radio stations.

I hoped the situation would take care of itself right away, that someone at the county would slap his forehead like Homer Simpson and restore Dad's job with a letter of apology and a gift certificate for dinner for two to compensate for the stress to my parents. That did not happen.

This was also about the time I'd begun to notice that my parents were getting older. The first shock had come at my college graduation in 1987, when they'd both come out to Evanston. Mom's hair had gone completely silver since the last time I'd seen her. Dad, too, had much more gray than usual, and his posture was slightly stooped, his gait much less spry than it once had been. In every year thereafter, I'd witnessed their continued aging: Mom needing more and more prescriptions for growing problems with high blood pressure and diabetes, which runs in our family, and Dad having less and less energy for the sit-ups and morning jogs through the neighborhood he had once enjoyed. They weren't old to me, not by a long shot, but I was beginning to imagine with disturbing clarity what they would be like once they were. The older people get, the more tired they become. Even fighters get tired of fighting.

I wondered if Dad might fall victim to the biggest irony of all: that after he and Mom had spent their entire adult lives fighting for others, they would not have the energy left to fight for themselves. That scenario began to seem more and more like harsh reality in that October.

As hard as it is to accept that strangers do not know and appreciate us, it's harder to accept that often our own people do not know us either. It must be human nature to forget, a biological function of the brain that encourages old information to fade, enabling us to absorb new information more readily. Perhaps our forgetfulness is just a human tendency that enables us to avoid pain at every opportunity. Memories hurt sometimes. Dad told me that when he stopped in Meridian, Mississippi, in 1994 to commemorate his civil rights work with Michael Schwerner and James Chaney, he met a group of black ministers for breakfast. After he introduced himself and stated his purpose, they collectively told him, "There's nothing to remember. It's time to move on," a form of community amnesia. Bearing in mind that forgetful tendency, my deepest fear during the 1997 upheaval in Dade County's government was that even blacks in Miami would have forgotten my father, and that the people he had fought for would not be willing to fight for him.

I did not know what to expect when Mom, Dad, Mother, and I drove to a community meeting at the Joseph Caleb Center, the arts and meeting complex on Northwest 54th Street in Miami. I have seen plays and music concerts at the center, which is named for black labor leader Joseph Caleb. I once had the honor of introducing actress Alfre Woodard when she made an appearance there. The center also has a library, and it is a satellite government center. I had attended meetings there, mostly as a reporter. I'm sure my parents could not calculate how many meetings they had attended at the center and places like it. Sometimes meetings bear great fruit, and sometimes they're a waste of time and gasoline. That night, as we drove, none of us knew what kind of meeting this one would be.

Mother was not traveling nearly as much as she once did. She'd had surgery to remove two of her toes, and learning to walk again had been a struggle for her. She also grew fatigued much more easily. If I'd been watching Mom and Dad slowly grow older, I'd been watching my grandmother simply falling apart, and not nearly so slowly. Toward the end of her life, Mother was in almost constant discomfort, but that night she was with us. She was worried about Dad, but I'm sure she was even more worried about Mom. After her daughter had been forced to grapple with so many family and community emergencies over the years, I'm sure Mother was worried Mom might be at her breaking point. The future financial insecurity was bad enough, but the added disrespect made the situation that much harder to accept.

Dad didn't want Mom to speak at the meeting. He knew how emotional she'd been over the last few weeks, and he feared the worst if she stood in front of an audience that would probably include the mayor. Mayor Penelas, after all, held my father's future in his hands, and diplomacy might not be on Mom's mind, given her anger. "Patricia, this is a meeting about the county's budget cuts, not about me," he reminded her.

"I won't speak," Mom said. "I'm just there to show my support."

I've heard stories about the mass meetings of the 1960s that filled black churches throughout the South, but the closest I'd come to seeing one for myself was the night of October 27, 1997, at the Caleb Center. The meeting room was packed. Scanning the crowd, it seemed to me that every seat was filled. The newspaper estimated that 400 people were there, but in my mind there might as well have been a thousand. People were crowded in the back, hugging the walls. There was standing room only.

The crowd was in a bad mood, stirring restlessly. Bishop Victor T. Curry, serving as moderator, set the tone from the start. "We are in trouble in Metropolitan Dade County," the clergyman said, and the crowd *uhm hmmm*ed with recognition. "We are in *trouble.* This is not the same old Ku Klux Klan, Jim Crow trouble. This thing has taken on a whole new scenario."

"That's right. It sure has," Mother said quietly beside me. Because her eyes troubled her, she often allowed them to fall shut when she was in public, but she was listening.

"It's deeper than you and I can ever imagine," Bishop Curry continued. "This thing is so deep, it's not even black and white anymore. It has crossed all color lines. It has crossed all ethnicities. Now we have to make those persons who have been elected to public office accountable. They must be."

The crowd rippled with amens and applause.

The mayor was tardy for the meeting, and much was made of that. When Mayor Penelas arrived, he contended that he hadn't heard about the meeting, and a small debate ensued, claims and counterclaims. After that, the business of budget overruns and the mayor's proposed staff layoffs came to the fore.

Mrs. Eufaula Frazier, a Democratic committeewoman from Dade County with whom my parents have worked since I was very young, was one of the people who stood up to speak. She spoke up for Dad and the others whose jobs had been threatened. When she finished, the audience cheered her. Marlene Bastiene, president of the Haitian Women of Dade County, also spoke passionately on Dad's behalf. Black Miami was in a bad mood.

The community had also been in a bad mood in 1990, when a different set of mayors throughout the region denounced Nelson Mandela on the event of his first visit to the city after his release from prison. In that situation, the county's leadership clearly had embraced the feelings of the Cuban-American community toward Mandela, rendering the black community's feelings wholly inconsequential. The ensuing economic black boycott, spearheaded by black Miami lawyer H. T. Smith and others, ended after Dade County had lost millions in tourism dollars. The word "boycott" was being uttered at that meeting again.

Dade County's new mayor, feeling defensive after being booed soon after his arrival, was doing little to soothe hurt feelings. His answers were polite, but he captured none of the "I feel your pain" sincerity it takes to win over an angry audience, which Bill Clinton, for example, had mastered so well. There were times the freshman mayor seemed on the verge of losing his patience. His youthfulness only made matters worse, since several people at that meeting were many years his senior and there were moments when he sounded condescending.

When my mother stood up to speak, my heart froze with dread. What would she say?

After the ritual of welcoming the honored guests—who included the mayor, County Commissioners Barbara Carey and James Burke, and State Rep. James Bush—her voice trembled with barely suppressed emotion. "I want to get to the meat of some things," Mom said, and the crowd knew she was about to preach. She began slowly, asking some general questions about the mayor's proposed changes as it related to her appointed position on the Black Affairs Advisory Board, but then her voice swept into the same rhythms I imagine had inspired students in Tallahassee to go to jail. "I have several interests here tonight. I should say that I have a personal interest, and I have a *personal* interest. My husband is John Due, and this is my community."

The audience was hypnotized. Applause rained on my mother.

"And you know, Mayor Penelas, you may not understand where I'm coming from. You may feel, and some other people may feel, that I have audacity to be up here because my husband is involved. But this is my community. I am concerned about him personally and about this community. Because this is a man whose children sometimes felt that the community *was* his family." Again, her voice trembled. Listening, I had to fight tears. Yes, the truth hurts.

"That's right, that's right," Mother said beside me, patting my knee.

"I respect him," Mom went on. "He's my husband, and we are very different. He'll say, 'You're talking tonight. You said you weren't going to say anything.' But I have to." There was laughter and applause.

My mother told the story of Dr. Tee S. Greer, the Dade County Public Schools administrator who'd recently passed away after being continually overlooked for a permanent position as school superintendent even though he'd been designated several times to serve as an interim superintendent. (There had not been a black school superintendent in the Dade County school system since the removal of Dr. Johnny Jones in the 1980s.) "You know, Dr. Greer died recently," Mom said. "Some of us said over Dr. Greer's tenure that he was too conservative, that Dr. Greer always wanted to work within the system. And what happened? That system rooted him out—and, I feel, killed him prematurely. Why is this important? This is important because we tell our children that you must work within the system, and this is what we have to say happens to people who work within the system."

The audience applauded loudly. Then they waited to see how the mayor would respond.

Mayor Penelas addressed Mom's more general concerns in great detail, explaining how he wanted to organize the advisory boards dedicated to black, Hispanic, Asian, and women's affairs as subcommittees of the Community Relations Board, so members could sit at the table together. Then he addressed the question of Dad.

"As it relates to your husband. . . . We're working with him, and he's working with members of my staff, and we're doing everything we can to help him, but I don't think this should become a meeting about particular people, because—" At that point, the mayor was nearly drowned out by the restless, irritated stirring of the crowd. They did not boo him again, but they wanted to.

At that, Bishop Curry spoke up. His voice, too, was soaked with emotion. "Mr. Mayor, I think you miss the point of why it's personalized. This man, Mr. Due—" He stopped, frustrated, and began again. "See, this is part of the problem with many of our Hispanic brothers and sisters. You all don't know the history. You all don't know the history of the black community." Applause, a few shouts.

"You don't know and you don't care," Bishop Curry went on. "This man is on record as the attorney to help desegregate the school system. Sir, in our opinion, this man is a *hero.*"

At that, the crowd erupted with applause and hooting.

"And if this is how your government treats our heroes, if you can do it to John Due, the rest of us will catch *much* hell. If you do it to him, the rest of us don't have a chance. And Mr. Mayor, that's what's missing. That's what many of our wonderful Cuban brothers and sisters are missing. You have no respect. You've got to respect us, Mr. Mayor. That's disrespect right there. This man shouldn't have to be working with anybody in your office. Leave that man alone. It's wrong, Mr. Mayor. And that's what you're hearing today. People are upset because we're not being respected *as a people.*"

The roar of the crowd sounded to me like a powerful creature stirring to wakefulness. Their shouts were a combination of love and rage. The people were on their feet, venting decades of frustration. I think Dad and Mom were too tense that night to savor the community's love, as speaker after speaker stood up on Dad's behalf, but I'll never forget that meeting. I'll never forget the sound of that love. That night, I knew exactly where my father had been all those years my sisters and I were growing up, what he had been doing with those papers in his garage. I saw my father's other family.

Little more than a week later, Dad got a new job assignment within the county, as an executive with the Miami-Dade Community Action Agency, to help coordinate anti-poverty programs. He would no longer enjoy the freedom of running his own office, but he would have a job at the same salary. Sometimes communities are heard, if only they speak up.

Sometimes people don't forget.

# Twenty-Nine

## PATRICIA STEPHENS DUE

**"A man who won't die for something is not fit to live."**
***—Dr. Martin Luther King Jr.***

I was pregnant again by the spring of 1969, and John and I had made the decision to move from Quincy to Miami. This was my fifth pregnancy in five years, and I was exhausted. As usual, I was uncomfortable and sick all of the time. I loved my two daughters, and I wanted to have another healthy baby, but I knew this would have to be our last child.

In many ways, life had been going very well for us in Quincy as a married couple and growing family. I have always loved the relaxing, country feel of Quincy, and it reminded me of my childhood. There's no place like home, as they say. We had a house we loved, and we had a steady income from John's private practice and his work as a union organizer with AFSCME, so our friends kept asking us why we wanted to leave.

We wanted the best for our children, as all parents do. Tananarive was three years old, and we thought it was time she started school. We wanted her to have more exposure. From the time she'd started talking, my relatives and neighbors had come over just to hear the way Tananarive spoke, believing her diction was remarkable for such a young child. Tananarive was too young to register for kindergarten in Quincy, and the waiting list for what was called a "laboratory school" at one of the Tallahassee universities was simply too long, taking years. As parents, you have to make decisions where your children come first, so John and I had decided to move to a bigger city to find schools that would accept Tananarive.

We would soon have cause to wonder if we had made the right decision, but that was what we wanted at the time.

Mother was also living in Miami, which was a very comforting idea to me. Mother had a job at a land deal company on Biscayne Boulevard that required a long daily commute, so I knew she could not help me by babysitting, but I longed to see her more often. John was constantly traveling through the state because of his job, which meant I was still spending much of my time alone with the children. I was alone so much, we later learned that someone who was informing on John's activities to the FBI told agents that he thought John was living in St. Petersburg and that we had divorced.[1] Mother wanted to give me extra moral support. It's hard for any mother to feel that her daughter is spending too much time on her own, and Mother was no exception. I know she really wanted me to come to Miami.

At first, since we didn't have a home lined up in Miami, Mother gave us much more than moral support. For a few months, we lived with her, sleeping on a sofa bed in her living room while we searched for our own place. A few months before the baby was due, we found a duplex in Liberty City. The house would be small for three children, but it was our own, so we were glad to have it. Our home in Quincy sat empty with our remaining furniture, and I still missed being in Quincy, but Miami was our home now.

It was very difficult adjusting to a new place. I was very disappointed by my early attempts to find a Montessori school for Tananarive. Dade County is the biggest county in the state, but it had some of the same problems as Gadsden County. Even in 1969, as I drove from school to school with Tananarive and Johnita because I did not have a babysitter, the schools told me very flatly that they could not accept Tananarive because the schools were for "whites only." *"We don't accept colored children,"* they said.

Tananarive was present to hear these conversations, unfortunately. When we got home one day, she covered herself with white talcum powder and said, "Mommy, can I go to school now?" The sight of my daughter covered in powder like that brought tears to my eyes. That really, really hurt me. I had hoped Tananarive was too young to really understand what was happening during those school visits, but she had understood enough. Children know much more than we realize. Racism has always cut me like a knife, but never so much as when I observed how my daughter's feelings of self-worth were already being damaged, and she was only three-and-a-half!

It's a shame, but I had to look far and wide for a school in Miami that would accept a black child. Sometimes I felt so frustrated I wanted to scream. I eventually enrolled Tananarive in Miami Shores Montessori School, her first school.

In the meantime, John had become more and more involved with black militant organizations, especially one called the Junta of Militant Organizations (JOMO), serving as their Minister of Justice. JOMO had been founded in St. Petersburg in 1968. John didn't realize it at the time, but some of the same people he was trying to help were reporting regularly to the FBI with updates on his activities, verifying his address and tracking his appearances. One informant told an FBI agent that while John was serving as moderator at a JOMO conference in Louisville, Kentucky, John supposedly said "the time has come for Black militants to put their guns down and attempt to gain their goals by undercover, subversive, and infiltration methods." He said, however, they should keep their weapons handy and know how to use them in the event they are needed.[2]

John had lost his job with the union in the fall of 1968 because his bosses believed he was spending too much time involved in community activities and not enough time working for them. In truth, John did have a tendency to overcommit himself, so I do not think his firing was a direct response to his more militant associations. His bosses just wanted him to be more focused on organizing unions and less focused on everyone else.

Soon after we moved to Miami, John got a position with Legal Services of Greater Miami, which provided legal help and advice to the poor. He continued to travel and meet with black militants throughout the state, but he also had a full-time job again, so I thought everything would be fine. I was wrong.

In December 1969, it was time for new baby's arrival. Because this pregnancy had been another difficult one, I was scheduled for a cesarean section. But this time, I had a different doctor, not someone who tried to schedule the surgery prematurely, so I didn't have the same problems I'd had with high blood pressure and vomiting shortly before Johnita's birth. On December 12, 1969, we had another girl. We named her Lydia Charlotte Due, honoring John's grandmother, Lydia Graham, and my mother, whose first name was Lottie. Lydia was born completely healthy, and I was very grateful. I never took a new baby's health for granted, not after everything I had been through. While I recuperated at the hospital, John posed for Christmas pictures at a department store with Tananarive, Johnita, and Cynthia Barnes Hartfield, a relative who was the daughter of Mother's brother, my Uncle Guy. Cynthia came to help John with the children while I was in the hospital.

Lydia was dedicated at the First Unitarian Church of Greater Miami, and I named Nancy Adams—my friend in Miami who had enlisted me in the Freedom of Choice schools drive and would later pay private school expenses for Tananarive and Johnita—as her godmother.

In early January 1970, only a couple of months after Lydia was born, we received a devastating blow to our family's finances and future: The Florida Supreme Court suspended John from the Florida Bar, which meant he could not practice law.

This happened for many reasons, some of which were unjust and some of which John had to take responsibility for. The background leading to John's suspension stretched back to 1968, originating with his work organizing the sanitation workers in St. Petersburg. Although John had been spending much of his time as a labor organizer, in 1968 he still had a law office in Tallahassee. One of his clients was a woman who'd been charged with displaying a weapon when the deputy sheriff came to see her on a charge about her dog, as John recalls. Before John left for St. Petersburg to help organize the sanitation workers, we both stopped by the clerk's office to make sure the case was not on the schedule. It was not. We assumed he would be free to go. We were wrong. The case was called the very next day.

Unfortunately, John's civil rights activities meant he had many enemies in the legal and law enforcement arenas. Someone had quoted John in the newspaper as having said that the Florida Bar was racist. That statement had infuriated some white attorneys. So once John began making trips down to St. Petersburg to organize that union, his enemies saw a golden opportunity: They brought up on the court docket the case involving John's female client, and the case was called. Exactly as they'd expected, John was absent from the courtroom.

People tried to claim that they'd notified us, but they had not. Regardless, since John didn't appear in court, his client was encouraged to file a petition of negligence against him. That's a very serious matter. When John got the notice, he was expected to explain himself. He knew about the problem long before he was actually suspended.

I believe this is where John himself should have taken more responsibility. Today, he explains his refusal to try to fix the situation as a rebellion against the power structure. "All I needed to do was go up there and say, 'Yassuh, boss. I sho' do apologize. There wuz a mistake somehow,' " John said when Tananarive and I interviewed him, imitating the bowing and scraping persona blacks had been forced to use to placate whites for generations. "But I was in my full balloon of Black Power activism at that time, and I said, 'No way—to hell with these racists.' "

That's fine and well, but I think there was more to it than that. John had endless energy when it came to seeing after other people's affairs, but he seemed paralyzed when it came to some personal and family affairs. He had not done anything to avert the initial three-month suspension, and even after he was suspended, when the state's black lawyers and community activist Gwendolyn Sawyer Cherry offered their assistance, John just seemed to withdraw. All of the burden for trying to reinstate him to the bar fell on my shoulders, and I now had three young children I was trying to raise. To Gwen Cherry's credit, I must say that she labored long and hard on John's behalf, even when he seemed less interested in his reinstatement than she did. Many blacks saw his suspension as a racist act—and it had been sparked because of racism, I believe—so John was a symbol to them even if he himself seemed nonchalant.

Because he'd been suspended, John could no longer work at Legal Services, so money was very tight at a time when we had just had a baby. And John's failure to take part in trying to resolve the situation brought a great deal of tension into our home. This was the beginning of one of the most stressful times of our marriage. About two years after John's suspension, we suffered an episode I have heard John refer to as an eye-opening experience: He was gone for two weeks, and I did not know how to reach him. I had three children, I needed money, and my husband was nowhere to be found. Suddenly a situation that had already been stressful became almost unbearable for me.

Luckily, John came home and realized that his first responsibility was to his family, not to the people he was trying to help.

But for me, those were very long years.

---

John and I both worked with welfare mothers in some capacity, trying to help them improve their lives. By the end of 1970, we were involved with the SCLC in planning a Poor People's March from Miami to Tallahassee. The plan was not literally to march all of those hundreds of miles. Instead, marchers from throughout the state would congregate to march in major cities, then drive to the next city to march, and so on until we reached the state capital. The march in Florida was modeled after the SCLC's Poor People's Campaign in Washington, D.C., which Dr. King had been helping to plan at the time of his death. In 1968, led by Rev. Ralph Abernathy, the SCLC had carried out a Poor People's March from Mississippi to Washington, D.C., and then erected a makeshift Resurrection City for poor people of all races and ethnic backgrounds, pushing for legislation to ease the burden of the poor. When police dismantled the camp and arrested several protestors, including Rev. Abernathy, people rioted in some of Washington's poor black neighborhoods.[3]

As 1971 approached, all of us wanted to rekindle the spirit of the earlier 1960s. I believed then—as I still do today—that economic empowerment must be the next step if blacks are going to avoid the fate of being a permanent underclass in this country. I had gone to jail and been arrested many times to fight for access to public facilities and the right to vote, but now we had to address the long-term economic gaps that had grown because of our unfair treatment. The Civil Rights Act and Voting Rights Act had nothing to do with compensating for blacks' poverty after so many generations of second-class citizenship. Those new laws guaranteed us rights we should have had already as citizens, but now poor blacks had been left behind to cope with the mess. President Johnson's War on Poverty had been a good start, but to me it was not enough. Too many of us were poor simply because we were black. I was going to do my best to give my children the best opportunities, but what about other black families and other black children? Who was going to speak up for them?

I was excited about Florida's Poor People's March. I knew how powerful marches could be. I remembered the feelings inspired when all of us had been assembled en masse, singing freedom songs, sharing heart and soul the way we had during the theater demonstrations in Tallahassee and on the Freedom Train to the March on Washington. The Movement had become very divided and ineffective in the late 1960s, a situation that had worsened when Dr. King was killed. As the Rev. Ralph Abernathy, Dr. King's best friend and advisor, wrote in his autobiography, *And the Walls Came Tumbling Down*, "Just as we were getting to the point where we could address the most basic needs of our people for the first time, our soldiers wanted to go back home and live in peace and poverty."[4]

I did not want to see that happen. I knew from experience that making changes is never easy, but the first step is to believe you can make changes. We had to love ourselves and believe in ourselves first, and I hoped our march could help us do that. Marches had unified us in the past, and I wanted Florida's march to unify us again.

Since Tananarive was attending school, and I had no idea how long we would be gone (if we were arrested somewhere along the way, the trip might take much longer than planned), I left her in the care of some members of our Unitarian church. Mother was also there to look in on her from time to time, so I felt confident leaving her. I knew my daughter would be in good hands. As for my younger daughters, however, John and I bought a double stroller and brought them with us. Pudgy-cheeked Johnita was about two-and-a-half, wearing pigtails, and Lydia was about a year old, sporting a very cute little Afro. Johnita and Lydia were about to take part in their first major civil rights demonstration.

The march began in Miami, where about forty of us gathered to begin, the most die-hard activists. We knew we would gain marchers as we traveled north. John began with us, but he had to go back to Miami because he had a job with Legal Services and could not afford to take the days off. With us were a Miami activist named Gladys Taylor and another activist, Johnnie Parris, who, like me, had come with two young children. Johnnie was always one of the first people to respond when there was a march; she and her husband would load their eight children into their station wagon and go at the drop of a hat. (Johnnie had taken five busloads of people from Miami to Washington, D.C., for the Poor People's March in 1968.)

Since the SCLC was the major supporter of the march, both Rev. Abernathy and another SCLC representative, James Orange, joined us in Miami. I owe both James Orange and Gladys Taylor a great debt for helping me push the stroller and carrying Johnita and Lydia when they were tired of being pushed. I really do not know how I could have participated without them. The saying "It takes a village to raise a child" was appropriate during that march.

Our first stop, fittingly, was in Palm Beach County, where Mother and Daddy Marion had raised me, Priscilla, and Walter. The marchers stopped in Riviera Beach, where members of a church were waiting to give us food and drinks. (Food stops were planned all along the route, staffed by volunteers.) We were hot and hungry by the time we reached Palm Beach County, so we were grateful for the meal. As I entered the church with Johnita and Lydia in tow, I felt the warmth of the volunteers and their encouraging smiles. I was looking forward to a meal and a rest. Then I realized one of the church volunteers was someone I actually knew. I stared for a moment: It was my high-school home economics teacher, Mrs. Ernestine B. Moore. She saw me, too, and came over to give me a big hug.

"Patricia, I'm so proud of you!" she said after she had admired Johnita and Lydia and asked about Mother. "I've been reading all about you in the newspapers. I read about the sit-ins and the jail-in and all those times you were arrested. I've wanted to tell you how proud I am for the longest time. Look at you now, with these two babies. And *still* marching." She laughed, hugging me again.

There were some glorious moments in that march. In the city of Monticello, twenty miles outside of Tallahassee in Jefferson County, hundreds of people stood waiting to join our march. There was so much comradery as we swept into town, I truly felt like I was surrounded by brothers and sisters. I don't drink from communal sources as a strict rule, but when we got to Monticello, I was grateful to sip water from a common dipper no matter how many people had used it before me. No matter how tired I was, my excitement kept me going.

Of all my memories of that Poor People's March, the most personally significant happened soon after we left our first stop in Palm Beach County. Mrs. Taylor was pushing the baby stroller, and James Orange was carrying Lydia, but Lydia was tired of being carried. She squirmed to be let down, so we allowed her to stand on the road where we were marching. Lydia stumbled forward, one step, then two steps. Then three. Then four.

During that march, for the first time, my youngest daughter walked.

Thirty

# Tananarive Due

**"Just don't give up trying to do<br>what you really want to do. . . .<br>Where there's love and inspiration,<br>I don't think you can go wrong."**<br>***—Ella Fitzgerald***

Atlanta, to me, is a city of pure magic.

I met my husband, science fiction novelist Steven Barnes, at a 1997 writers' conference sponsored by Clark Atlanta University on "The African-American Fantastic Imagination: Explorations in Science Fiction, Fantasy, and Horror." The city hummed with history and vibrancy. Our hosts in the college's English department, Phyllis Briggs-Emanuel and Mary Arnold Twining, took us to a restaurant at an upscale black shopping mall, and someone at our table pointed out that the singers from the sensational a capella singing group Sweet Honey in the Rock were sitting at a table behind us, near the wall. While we sat and ate, I saw lawyer Johnnie Cochran and an entourage pass before the restaurant's large picture window.

Sitting in the company of wonderful writers Octavia E. Butler, Samuel R. Delany, and Jewelle Gomez, Steve and I both felt as if we were at a family reunion in Chocolate City. We had both spent many years feeling isolated from other blacks, especially given that the kind of fiction we wrote had not been embraced traditionally by the black community. Horror? Science fiction? Please. But there we were in Atlanta, introduced to audiences of blacks who cared about our work. I felt as if I'd awakened in an alternative universe, just like the lead character in my novel *The Between,* who dreams himself to different planes of existence.

Steve felt the magic, too. Steve and I lived in opposite corners of the country—he lived in Washington State and I lived in Miami—but Atlanta had brought us together. Before we realized what was happening, we began to fall in love. "We could build an empire," I said to Steve as we sat in Atlanta's airport and stared into each other's eyes like two teenagers about to go home from summer camp. I felt foolish, but I also knew my words to be the absolute truth. It wasn't love at first sight, not exactly, but it was close enough that I now believe in those fairy-tale meetings I'd always believed were exaggerated. Steve and I had done enough hard soul-searching to take responsibility for our own faults and decide exactly what we needed in a partner, so we recognized each other virtually upon sight.

I will always love Atlanta for Steve alone. But at the start of 2001, in January, I needed Atlanta's magic again.

Life had been progressing beyond my dreams since the time I met Steve in 1997—a new marriage and stepdaughter, a full-time career as a novelist for the first time, my first pregnancy—but suddenly events had taken a horrible turn. Both my grandmother and Uncle Mun had died on Christmas day in 2000. My phone on the west coast rang at 7:00 A.M. Christmas morning, when my cousin Muncko called from Miami to tell me that both his father and our grandmother were gone. He'd gotten both calls himself in the space of a half hour, soon after opening Christmas presents with his wife, Carol, and their young daughter, Jojo.

No one in my family ever wants to relive another day like that one.

Mom was handling the loss of her mother with strength that amazed and inspired me the way she always has, but I didn't allow myself to be fooled by her outward display of what seemed like utter composure. I knew she had to feel like pieces of her were being torn to bits, that she was stumbling through a bad dream. My mother has spent almost her entire life taking care of others, and for once I wanted to try my best to take care of her. What could I do to help her?

Distraction, I decided.

Early January marked the start of my book tour for the paperback version of *The Black Rose.* The summer before, Mom and Dad had accompanied me during portions of my hardcover tour, going to appearances in both Chicago and Indianapolis. I always enjoy the chance to travel with my parents. In October 1999, I'd accompanied them to a CORE reunion in Des Plaines, Illinois, outside Chicago, where, for the first time, I'd met people like Marvin Rich and Jim Robinson, who had been on the national CORE staff, and former CORE field secretaries Gordon Carey, Dave Dennis, Rudy Lombard, and Mary Hamilton Wesley, whom my parents had known. (Lombard, who attended the 1960 Miami Action Institute with Mom and Aunt Priscilla, was arrested in sit-ins while leading the New Orleans CORE chapter. He later became CORE's national vice chairman. Dennis also led New Orleans CORE.)[1]

Since *The Between* was first published in 1995, my mother has been my (mostly unpaid) manager. My mother approached my book career with the same methodical energy she'd always tackled other projects with, studying literary and film law, helping me schedule appearances, videotaping my readings, guiding me through this new, untested phase of my life. Along the way, she has always delighted and motivated the booksellers, librarians, and readers we've come in contact with. And while she was with me during the *Black Rose* tour the summer of 2000, everyone had been excited to hear that we were writing a mother–daughter civil rights memoir.

Since the same publisher, One World/Ballantine, would be publishing *Freedom in the Family,* I wondered if my editor, Anita Diggs, would be willing to pick up the tab so that my mother could spend a couple of weeks on the road with me for the *Black Rose* tour. I was thrilled and relieved when Anita said yes. Since we were also promoting our book, she said my mother could accompany me on the East Coast portion of the tour. The trip would not erase the pain of Mother's death, but at least Mom and I would be together during that horrible period after the loss. Since I'd moved to Washington State after my wedding in 1998, Mom and I weren't spending nearly as much time together as we once had, so this would be a treat for us.

We enjoyed ourselves as much as we could. We saw everything in hues of gray during that time, but we snatched a few bright moments of laughter. We bickered, vowing never to share a hotel room again. We found ourselves wanting to call Mother to share things, only to be faced again and again by the incomprehensible fact that she was not at home where she usually was. We fought tears at unexpected moments, neither of us wanting to cry in front of the other.

Mostly we did our job. We interacted with readers and booksellers, trying to stoke the fires of enthusiasm for *The Black Rose* and *Freedom in the Family.* We stayed distracted. As she learned to do long ago, my mother swallowed her emotions and went to work.

Our first stop was Washington, D.C., then Baltimore. Next, we flew to Atlanta.

Atlanta had a gift waiting for us.

As soon as we stepped off the plane, I began scouting for my driver.

One of the real pleasures of touring, to me, is having a driver or escort waiting at the gate with a sign bearing my name, something that never happens to me in my "real life," away from book tours. Sure enough, I saw a chauffeur waiting with a sign: TANANARIVE DUE. Most people don't bother to spell out my first name, or they spell it wrong, but this driver had it right.

Waiting beside the chauffeur was a tall, smiling black man I had never seen before. When he saw us approaching the driver, the stranger said, "Excuse me, but are you Tananarive Due?" I said I was, so he said, "Tananarive, my name is Gregory Allen Howard. My uncle is William Howard, and he taught your mother at Florida A&M University."

"Dr. Howard!" my mother cried, overhearing him. "You're Dr. Howard's nephew?"

"Yes, Ma'am," the man said politely. "I'm here at the airport to pick him up. He's coming to Atlanta, and his flight gets in a little later tonight."

"That's wonderful!" my mother said. "I would love to see him."

"Uncle Bill has told me the story about how he had a student in his class in the nineteen sixties who named her daughter Tananarive, and she grew up to be a writer."

"Yes, Mom's told me that story," I said. "And she had to call Dr. Howard so he could tell her how to spell the name, because she'd forgotten." We all laughed, having heard the story many times before. My mind was swimming. What were the odds that one of my mother's old college professors would be arriving the same night we did? And on a trip she had not been originally scheduled to make?

The stranger gave me his business card. "My cell phone number is on here," he said. "Why don't you give me a call tomorrow? I know Uncle Bill will be tired when he gets in tonight, but I'm taking him to dinner tomorrow, and I'm sure he'd be thrilled to see you two. I'm in Atlanta because I'm being honored by the governor."

"Why are you being honored?" I asked him.

"I'm a screenwriter," he said. "I wrote the screenplay for *Remember the Titans,* and we shot most of that in Georgia."

I congratulated him heartily, my eyes shining with admiration. *Remember the Titans,* starring Denzel Washington, had been one of the biggest movies of the year. When I'd seen the movie, the screenwriter's name had passed in a blur. I hadn't known he was black, much less that he was the nephew of someone my mother knew.

The next night, we sat at a table in a restaurant with Gregory Allen

Howard, his uncle, and various representatives from the governor's office who'd taken part in the ceremony earlier that day. For my part, I was glad to be included in a celebration for *Remember the Titans,* one of the few successful mainstream movies to tackle a story about this nation's struggle to bring understanding between the races. More than that, I felt a warm satisfaction as I watched my mother sitting at the end of the table beside Dr. Howard, huddling close in their own private conversation about life, losses, and an era in Tallahassee, Florida, they alone could remember. Dr. Howard had known Mother long before I was born, and I was glad Mom had someone she could share her pain with. Dr. Howard knew the essence of who my mother was, and she didn't have to explain herself to him, nor he to her. There is so much comfort in unspoken familiarity.

Unfortunately, Dr. Howard did not have much longer to live; Greg Howard wrote me that his uncle had died in March 2002, only a year later. But that night, time had not yet marched on. That night, we created a timeless space for ourselves.

During that dinner, I told Greg Howard that I'd assumed *Remember the Titans* was based on a novel. Not so, he said. He told me he'd left Hollywood in frustration a few years back and ended up seeking a more quiet place and finding it in Alexandria, Virginia. One of the first things he noticed about the town was the unusual harmony between the races. He was in a barbershop one day, and asked somebody why blacks and whites in Alexandria got along so well.

"It all goes back to the Titans," someone told him, and he heard the story of the high-school football team that had been forced to integrate and gone on to an undefeated season. It was all there: The racial hatred. A tough-as-nails black coach. High school boys who had been forced to grow past prejudice and become men. Lifelong friendships between blacks and whites.

Stories are like that. They're always sitting there, waiting for someone to discover them.

I was in a state of calm awe that night, feeling a circle closing around me. Dr. William Howard was in Atlanta for an event to honor his nephew, and my mother was with me on my book tour, all of us celebrating family love, achievement, and pride rooted in the untold stories of our people's struggle. Dr. Howard had helped prepare my mother and her generation, and my mother's generation had sacrificed for mine. Gregory Allen Howard wrote *Remember the Titans* and a script for the movie that would become *Ali,* and I was about to write a book with my mother about the civil rights movement, honoring everyday heroes and heroines.

All of us sat there in the city of Dr. Martin Luther King Jr.'s birth in a space somewhere between the past and the future. We laughed. And remembered. And dreamed some more.

Thirty-One

# Patricia Stephens Due

**"Parents have become so convinced that educators know what is best for children that they forget that they themselves are really the experts."**
***—Marian Wright Edelman***

During the 1960s, I had always understood how difficult it was for activists to adhere to the principle of nonviolence, not arming themselves or striking back when they were attacked, but perhaps I hadn't truly understood what those people with families had suffered until my family came under attack in the 1970s.

Our family had done a lot of moving around by 1974. We'd lived in Liberty City, Opa-locka, and Richmond Heights, which were all predominantly black areas. Once John got a steady job with the county's Community Relations Board, we wanted to buy a house, and we had trouble finding a house for sale in those areas. Middle-class black families just did not want to let their homes go, we discovered. So John and I took our home search to the predominantly white suburbs of southwest Dade County, and we ended up moving into an area called Colonial Drive, where we rented a home with an option to buy it. Usually, moving into a new home is an occasion to celebrate, but it didn't feel that way to us.

Colonial Drive is a very ethnically mixed area today. In fact, Priscilla has lived there since she returned to the States in 1977, when she decided to see if she could emotionally reclaim this country, but a black family really stood out in 1974. Many of our neighbors were transplanted from other Southern states and considered themselves hard-core rednecks, so they were not happy to see us move onto their street. "You tell those nigger kids of yours if I ever see any of 'em in my yard, I'm gonna go get my shotgun and shoot 'em," one neighbor told me point-blank with a hateful stare. Other neighbors threw stones and eggs against the house, and since Tananarive and Johnita had bedrooms near the front of the house, I worried that one of them might be hurt by breaking glass.

Another issue was John's high visibility because of his job, which often entailed public statements to the media, so sometimes our neighbors took out their frustrations against him on our family. For the first time in my life, I considered buying a gun. John never liked the idea, but I felt very exposed in that house. Instead of arming ourselves, though, we tried community mediation. Representatives from John's office at the Community Relations Board came to our neighborhood to talk to our neighbors and to build goodwill, but that didn't work. We called the police, but there wasn't much the police could do. White members of the First Unitarian Church we attended grew so concerned after they heard us talking about our harassment that they volunteered to sit in front of our house at night to check on our safety. Feeling like we had no choice, we agreed.

For me, the hardest part of that whole ordeal was having children old enough to perceive the things going on around them. Tananarive was eight, Johnita was six, and Lydia was nearly four. Tananarive was a tomboy, making friends with some of the neighborhood boys (including the son of our neighbor who'd threatened to shoot them) and breaking her eyeglasses while she played tackle football. I did not want her to feel afraid, but I was also uneasy about exposing her to verbal attacks or violence. John and I never told the girls about the severity of the threats, or the church members sitting watch outside of our house, so we were able to shelter them somewhat, but I'm sure they sensed that something was not quite right.

Beyond that, I was happy during that time because I had a job I really enjoyed. After many years of staying with the children, working and volunteering only when I could find the time, I loved the stimulation of adults. James Burke, a black attorney, hired me to work for Community Lawyers, a government-funded program, which was designed to give legal assistance to people in the Liberty City area.

Preventive law was a major part of our program, and we taught people how to evaluate contracts carefully before signing. We also handled divorce cases, which could be quite traumatic. Sometimes people would come in threatening to kill us, blaming the lawyers who were helping a spouse get the divorce, but that was not the norm, and the occasional drama at work didn't dampen my enthusiasm for the job. I loved being part of a program helping people in the community do things for themselves. We also reached out to Haitian refugees, who were often denied jobs. As far as I was concerned, racism prevented many of the Haitians from entering the country at all, and then racism surfaced again when they tried to find work. Many of the Haitians didn't have clothes for their families, so we took part in what was called the Haitian Refugees' Concern Board, and we had a room at Community Lawyers where we piled the donations people brought in nearly to the ceiling. There was a real spirit of giving.

During this time, I also became involved with a grassroots organization, the Tenant Education Association of Miami (TEAM), which assisted people in affordable housing, public housing, and landlord disputes. The two women who really organized TEAM were Mrs. Eufaula Frazier and Mrs. Adell Dillard, but I served as the vice chairperson. I also became involved in a dispute centered around Miami Northwestern Senior High, an inner-city high school, because parents were organizing to secure better equipment and facilities for their students. The school was 99 percent black and needed many repairs and upgrades. My children were too young to attend high school, of course, but I saw the situation at Northwestern as a separate-but-equal question that is of concern to any parent. All children deserve good schools, no matter where they live, what color they are, or how much money their parents make. Unless parents speak up and organize, though, schools in affluent neighborhoods with more parental involvement will always have the advantage. Parental involvement in education and health care proved to be two of my strongest issues in the next few years, as they remain today.

I kept telling John parental involvement begins at home, and soon that became an issue for me. I began having problems with Lydia, the youngest, during the time I was working at Community Lawyers. All three girls were in school by then, and because I was working, they were in an after-school program until I could pick them up. Tananarive and Johnita were fine, but Lydia was in a classroom with younger students, and she was crying every day when I came to pick her up. Not only that, but day after day, I got telephone calls from the school asking me to pick her up early because of her crying. Parents might expect a young child to take some time to adapt to a new situation, but Lydia's crying never stopped.

I finally realized I could not do that to my child. As much as I hated to, I told my director, James Burke, that I would have to resign from Community Lawyers. Mr. Burke, who would later become a Miami-Dade

County commissioner, was very concerned. He asked me why I would resign from a job he knew I loved. I told him my problem.

"Patricia," he said, "why don't you just go pick up your kids from school every day and then take them home?" It had never occurred to me that he would permit me to do that. Mr. Burke was actually very progressive for his time. Excited to have a solution, I found a baby-sitter and tried it.

Unfortunately, I had already been driving fifty-two miles a day to work in the county's northwest section even though we lived in the southwest section. Since now I had to double back to pick up the girls, I was driving 104 miles a day. I also arranged for ballet lessons and drama lessons for the girls, which meant more driving. After fifteen months, I sadly told Mr. Burke I couldn't keep my job at Community Lawyers. There was too much driving and not enough time.

My girls were my first priority.

---

In 1975, we left Colonial Drive because the homeowner wouldn't stick to the original sale price he'd offered us. We found another house we liked on the bank of a canal in Point Royal, a Cutler Ridge neighborhood not far from the Colonial Drive area. Like our old house, the new one was also very close to Mother, which was nice for us. This was also the time I'd realized that Tananarive, Johnita, and Lydia needed to attend public schools. I liked the curriculum at the Horizon School for Gifted Children, but I was very worried about their racial isolation. Although the Point Royal area was not yet very integrated, its schools drew students from a wide area and all income levels and races. I knew that would be a better situation for them.

On the first day of school, I took all three girls to Bel-Aire Elementary School, within walking distance, expecting to register them. The front office told me that Johnita and Lydia could stay, but Tananarive was a fifth grader, and fifth graders attended R. R. Moton Elementary School, which was in another neighborhood entirely, West Perrine.

I had never heard of R. R. Moton Elementary School. The flyers our real estate agent had given us said that children attended Bel-Aire Elementary and Cutler Ridge Junior High. There had not been a word about R. R. Moton. Confused, Tananarive and I got into the car.

When I drove Tananarive to R. R. Moton, I understood why the school's name had conveniently been left out of the flyers: West Perrine was a poor black neighborhood across the highway. Sending my daughter to a school in a black neighborhood pleased me, but it would not have pleased the majority of families moving onto our street. The school system achieved school integration by busing the children in first through fourth grades from West Perrine to Bel-Aire Elementary School, and then busing the older white children to R. R. Moton. I am a believer in integration, and I knew that busing was the only way to introduce students from different backgrounds to each other so they could all attend schools side by side, but I saw that particular system as unfair. Why should the youngest black children have to be bused while the youngest white kids could walk to school? As usual, the situation favored the families with more money.

But R. R. Moton Elementary, named after black educator Robert Russa Moton, who worked with Booker T. Washington and became president of Tuskegee University, was everything I could have hoped for in a school for Tananarive. On the outside, the school needed paint and the fence needed repairing. Constructed in 1951, the building did not have air-conditioning like Bel-Aire Elementary, which was a much newer school, but inside the hallways were neat and colorfully decorated, and there were children and teachers of all races. Tananarive's assigned teacher, Mrs. Janelle Harris, was black, and so was the school principal, Maedon S. Bullard, a woman with a lovely personality. Mrs. Bullard's smile could light up a room, and she had a wonderful spirit.

I met Mrs. Bullard right away because it was my custom to introduce myself to my children's teachers and administrators, which is something I believe all parents should do as a matter of course. Not long after Tananarive started school at Moton, Mrs. Bullard came up to me and asked if I would run for president of the PTA.

I nearly laughed. Me? A PTA president?

"I'm sorry, but I don't know anything about baking cakes and cookies," I told her.

Mrs. Bullard shook her head, and I could see there was serious business in her eyes. "Mrs. Due," Mrs. Bullard said, "if I needed someone to bake cookies, I have plenty of other parents who can do that. I've heard about your civil rights and community involvement, and I need somebody who can fight for this school."

R. R. Moton's existence was very much in danger, Mrs. Bullard told me.

The school had been desegregated because of a court order, but a vocal group of white parents didn't like the situation, believing that the neighborhood was dangerous. White families tended to "get religion" when their children were old enough for Moton, sending them to private schools instead, so Moton's population was shrinking. Even while Moton was under-enrolled, white parents had lobbied the school system to build another elementary school in a nearby white area, with the hope that their children could go to the new school for fifth and sixth grades, instead of to Moton.[1]

Perrine's families were really almost at war with one another, I came to learn. Perrine's unofficial dividing line was South Dixie Highway. Tananarive was bused with the white children to Moton from the east side, but my sympathies lay with the school, which was located in a black neighborhood on the west side.

Moton tried very hard. I think its disadvantaged surroundings had forced the staff to raise the bar in terms of the school's programming. Quality was not the issue. R. R. Moton Elementary School had an excellent staff. While Tananarive was there, the school was one of only ten elementary schools in the state to win a prestigious "Little Red Schoolhouse" award, offering its students accelerated math and literature classes, modern dance, a macramé club, a creative writing club, an art club, a drama club, a school newspaper, Cub Scout pack, school band, and guitar ensemble.[2] Tananarive played trumpet in the band, and she won a part in the school production of *Mary Poppins,* which was only an amateur production, but students and teachers were so dedicated that I thought Moton's play nearly rivaled the version of *The Wizard of Oz* Tananarive had once starred in at the well-recognized Coconut Grove Children's Theater.

The stereotype of the substandard inner-city school did not match R. R. Moton Elementary. But I'm afraid many white parents saw the poverty surrounding the school and were afraid it was something that would reach out and harm their children, rather than simply serving as a lesson that some people in this world are less fortunate. For my part, I was glad Tananarive was forced to acknowledge the existence of poverty. I had always tried to take the girls to poorer neighborhoods so they could see how many black people lived. My children grew up with certain advantages, but I did not want them to develop a rose-colored view of the world.

Another thing Mrs. Bullard told me bears mentioning: She liked the fact that I visited the school so often, three or four times a week, because I served as an example to other neighborhood parents who were not accustomed to being participants in their children's education. Not every school will face a battle for existence, but all schools need parents.

I told Mrs. Bullard I would help her keep the school open.

I don't think I realized what I was stepping into, but the fight that ensued demanded as much of my energy as any civil rights campaign from the 1960s. The opposition to Moton was organized under a parents' group called PAGE, the Parents' Association for Good Education. That group definitely kept me running. I had to drive the twenty-one miles between my house and the Dade County School Board meetings twice a month just to keep up with the latest developments in that fight. It dragged on for several years. By the time Johnita arrived at Moton two years later, in the fall of 1977, the school's student body had been slashed from 436 to 230, and the number of teachers had been cut from 55 to 28. Many of the arts programs that had won it honors in the past were cut because of lack of staff.[3]

PAGE also made the fight personal, singling out three of Moton's black teachers with charges that they took long coffee breaks and paddled students. They raised charges with the Professional Practices Council, a state oversight agency. Those charges caused a good deal of stress to some excellent teachers, and although one of the teachers acknowledged "tapping" a student with a ruler, I believe to this day the charges were only raised in the effort to close the school.[4] As far as I'm concerned, PAGE launched a witch-hunt at R. R. Moton Elementary.

Not only did I have that to contend with, but at the same time, Neal Adams, a black Metro-Dade commissioner who was very involved with the NAACP, had appointed me to the Dade County Commission on the Status of Women. I had to go to those meetings, too, and they happened to fall on the same night as the school board meetings. Usually, I tried to go to the school board meeting first to keep pace with PAGE, which always had representatives there, and I knew school board politics well enough to understand that the school board members were often swayed by whichever group seemed to be the most dedicated and to carry the most clout. When my appearance at the school board was complete, I drove over a few blocks to the courthouse for the meetings for the Dade County Commission on the Status of Women, but I monitored the school board meeting on the radio while I drove. Occasionally I heard the school board about to reverse an action that had been made while I was there, so I had to turn around and go back. It got so bad that I would spend seven and eight hours at every school board meeting just so I could be certain they wouldn't change their minds and try to destroy Moton after I had left for another meeting.

Emotions were running high during that time. The parents from PAGE were very emotional, and of course the Moton staff felt under siege, with teachers' livelihoods at risk, so they were very emotional, too. I remember one school board member, Mrs. Ethel Beckham, telling me once, "With all that emotion and stress, it's just going to make you sick." I knew she was probably right, but I could not back down. I believed in my cause. This was a neighborhood institution—my own children's school—with a majority-black staff that needed an advocate, and I felt I had no real choice.

Mrs. Bullard knew how much she was asking of me. Just like those women who used to come to my hotel room in St. Petersburg at 4:00 A.M. so I could go sit in front of garbage trucks, Mrs. Bullard understood that my children needed to be looked after. She made certain there were people to stay with my daughters, that their homework was monitored, that they were given meals to eat when I was not at home. As important as the fight to save Moton became to me, I had learned from living with the Steeles and reading about others who were very involved that families could suffer in the cause of activism. I constantly prioritized what I could do, which meant there were times I did not go downtown. I felt torn, but my children came first.

I'm happy to say that R. R. Moton Elementary School is still open and is today a magnet school for the arts, with a program that attracts students of all races from all over the county. Rebuilt after Hurricane Andrew in 1992, it still stands in a poverty-stricken neighborhood as an example of excellence in a community badly in need of good news.

Integration, to me, never meant that we should give up everything *we* held dear. We have excellence to share, too.

When Mrs. Maedon S. Bullard died in 1996 at the age of sixty-eight, she instructed her family to ask Tananarive to write her obituary in the *Miami Herald*. Tananarive, who was a features writer and columnist twenty years after I first took her through the doors of R. R. Moton, agreed. Mrs. Bullard died so young! As I read her obituary, my memories of my days as a PTA president came back to me. I wonder sometimes if Mrs. Bullard's fight for her school in the mid-1970s helped cut her life short, combined with countless other battles blacks have been forced to fight.

I don't think I could ever calculate how many years all of us have lost.

---

Again and again over the years, I've realized that the lessons I learned during the mass struggles of the 1960s can be applied to other aspects of life.

Based on my experiences as a parent, I'd been involved with Title I, a federally funded education program signed into law in 1965 by President Lyndon B. Johnson that provides funds to school districts nationwide for disadvantaged children. In Dade County, we had a particular focus on math and reading. As a Bel-Aire Elementary School parent, I'd been asked to serve as chair of the Bel-aire Title I Parent Advisory Council, as mandated by the federal government in order for schools to receive their funding. I eventually became president of the Area and Dade County Parent Advisory Council, then the Florida Title I Parent Advisory Council. At one point, I was president of all three of these groups.

All of these parent groups were organized to monitor and participate in the education of their children, especially where Title I funds were concerned. Although this was no longer considered a part of the civil rights movement, I saw it as an extension of what we had been fighting for. Education, to me, was the most important thing I could be involved in, helping to build the foundation for the next generation, and parental involvement was the key ingredient to children getting a good education. If parents weren't there and didn't understand what their responsibilities were, the schools would do whatever they wanted.

The Florida Parent Advisory Council had been headed previously by a very good-natured man who allowed the state to run everything. The state made up the agenda, the state decided what would happen, and the state decided when it would happen. That is not the way I do things. I was urged to run for president because my experiences spanned the entire state. I'd been born in Quincy, I'd grown up in Palm Beach County, I'd interned in Jacksonville, I'd worked throughout North Florida, and now I lived in South Florida. I never ran based on my civil rights work because there were too many conservative whites among my constituency. I had the support of parents and school administrators as well, especially Johnnie McMillian, a very involved parent specialist in Dade County. She and other administrators and parents spent many hours assisting me as I finalized my platform. (Based on that experience, I later asked McMillian—who has since changed her name to Adora Obi Nweze and is now the president of the Florida State Conference of NAACP Branches—to chair a committee during the planning of the

1980 NAACP convention in Miami Beach.) I won that election because blacks *and* whites from throughout the state elected me on the basis of parental involvement and my deep belief in education.

At the same time, I was education chair for the Florida Conference of State NAACP Branches, and the NAACP had some of the same concerns as Title I, and vice versa. It was funny during that time to see all of these conservative whites sitting around the table hashing out a strategy with me, and they'd say, "Well, we don't want the NAACP riding on our coattails." They didn't know I was representing the NAACP, and I was using many of the same ideas in both venues. But as parents, we would all become much better trained and more sophisticated about having a voice when it came to spending and programs for our children.

Unfortunately, parents have to fight for representation, too. Nothing comes easily.

In Dade County, Title I was responsible for bringing millions of dollars into the school system, but parents had to sign off on all new proposals. That was the way it was set up. Sometimes the administration failed to give parents adequate time to review documents, and under my leadership we insisted on following the letter of the law—that is, having the opportunity to review and have input before signing off. That was one of the reasons I had a disagreement with Dr. Johnny L. Jones, Dade County's first black superintendent of schools.

I was out of town attending a national meeting, and Dr. Jones wanted to present something to the school board, saying the parents had approved it. Since the parent representatives were out of town, he had someone contact me because I was president and could poll the other parents. I realized I had been presented with a very long document, and I knew I could not approve it over the telephone. I had no idea what it was, so how could I properly explain it to the other parents and hope to reach an informed consensus? I thought they should have presented it to us in time to give us an opportunity to study it properly. I had learned even before my days at Community Lawyers never to sign my name to anything unless I knew *exactly* what I was signing. The way I see it, the schools system would say it wanted parental involvement but, to expedite things, sometimes the parents were rushed.

Regrettably, that situation caused a rift between me and Dr. Jones. Dr. Jones was a man of strong will who did not want to have to regularly butt heads with me because I have a strong will, too. During his time as school superintendent, he really did a lot for black children. For instance, he insisted that teachers include more minority children in gifted education. I would never try to take that away from him. He insisted that all children develop to their fullest potential, and his strong style of leadership caused much racism to surface among the teachers charged with carrying out his vision. I respected him for his efforts, but I would not lie down for anyone simply for the sake of political friendships. I am a real stickler in that way.

When he asked me to sign off on a document I had never seen, I told Dr. Jones to wait until the parents returned, and he did not like that one bit. He got very angry, and I believe he retaliated by having people close to him control the parent elections. In that way, through manipulation, he was able to have me ousted from my role as president in Dade County.

The other parents were very upset, and people encouraged me to take him to court, but I stopped and took stock of the entire situation, not only the situation as it affected me. Would suing Dr. Jones and having a nasty fight between the biggest black Parent Advisory Council and the black superintendent do the children any good? Honestly, if he had not been doing a good job otherwise, I would have fought him tooth and nail, race aside, but he was making a positive impact, so I decided to let it go. The other parents did not agree with me, but it was my decision alone. I have always acted according to my personal principles, whether or not other people have understood or appreciated my position. Whether it was a police officer, a judge, a school superintendent, or my own colleagues, that has never changed about me. I have lived my life trying to do what I think is right for everyone, not necessarily for myself.

Then Dr. Jones was accused of stealing money and equipment and having his home fitted with gold-plated plumbing fixtures, and the situation changed yet again. After the school board met on a *Sunday* to vote him out of his post, I was more convinced than ever that his political enemies had simply taken advantage of an opportunity to get rid of him. I organized mass meetings and protests over it. Some people who knew our history might have found that puzzling, but once again, this was a decision that had nothing to do with me personally. I wanted only what was right.

Although Dr. Jones eventually won an appeal of his conviction and there were not sufficient witnesses to try him a second time, that situation destroyed him, and some of what he'd tried to build was lost with him. I think a lot of people lost jobs and were shuffled around once he was gone. No one can tell me that racism didn't play a part in that situation. During this time, Mother was working as an occupational specialist at a middle school in South Dade, and she saw with her own eyes how people on staff at the school had written notes calling Dr. Jones a "nigger" and a "coon" on the school bulletin board long before the plumbing controversy. And some of these people were teachers responsible for the education of black children!

I'll never forget how excited I was about the *Brown v. Board of Education* decision in 1954, but many other activists and I have come to wonder if school integration was really the right thing for black children. Our black schools may have been poorly equipped compared to the white schools, but how do you fix a value on having teachers who love black children? The WHITE ONLY and COLORED signs came down in the 1960s because we worked to change the laws, but changing laws isn't the same as changing hearts and minds.

Changing hearts and minds is a battle all its own. And it will be the hardest one to win, especially since too many of our young people have been fooled into thinking the "old days" of fighting for their rights are over.

Or they don't know how to fight at all, unless they're fighting each other.

Thirty-Two

# TANANARIVE DUE

**"You can't be nobody but who you are . . .
that shadow isn't nothing but you growing
into yourself. You either got to grow into it
or cut it down to fit you. That's all you got
to measure yourself against that world out there."**
***—August Wilson***

*Why do you write horror?*

Since I have been best known for my horror novels, that's one of the most common questions posed to me during interviews or bookstore appearances. I've been making up my answer as I go. It could be because my mother is a die-hard horror movie fan, and my sisters and I were raised on weekend Creature Feature movies, *The Mummy* and *Dracula* and *The Fly.* Or, it could be because a high school friend gave me a copy of Stephen King's *The Shining* on my sixteenth birthday, and although I had never read King before, I was hooked from the first sentence. That book made my eyes widen, my heart pound, and my palms sweat. I wanted to recapture that feeling again and again, and by the time I started writing novels myself I'd figured out that the way to really tap into it would be to write about my own deepest fears.

Loss, for one. And death, for another.

I've always lived with a wary knowledge of death. I used to lie awake as a child and imagine what it would feel like to be *nothing.* I knew I was only here temporarily, and even as a child, time always passed too quickly for my liking. I hoped there was an afterlife, as the Bible taught, but even if the afterlife was waiting, I was not ready to say goodbye to this world, and I didn't think I ever would be. For all its problems, I have always loved life. I have always felt blessed, in part because my parents taught us to feel blessed, and in part because plain common sense told me so. My parents loved me. I had a roof over my head. I had my writing. I had two sisters who, for all our bickering, I knew would forever be my best friends. Death was the robber waiting to steal everything I held dear.

Yet in the midst of the hardest moments helping my mother write this book—those moments when I faced unexpected tears, spiritual fatigue, or stubborn memory blocks—I began to consider the possibility that my fascination with horror stories sprang from a very different source. What if it was my knowledge of real-life horror that drove me to the sanctuary of horrific fiction? What if it started when I read *Roots* at the age of eleven with the keen realization that my ancestors had faced the same fate as Kunta Kinte? Or when I put pen to paper that same year to imagine what it really would have felt like to be a confused African girl chained in the bowels of a ship as it rocked its way across an unknown sea to an unknown land? Or during those Martin Luther King Day commemorations with my family at Miami's Torch of Friendship, when I visualized Dr. King—a man who'd nearly been bitten by my parents' dog—suddenly felled by an assassin's bullet during a casual moment on the balcony of the Lorraine Motel? Or knowing that black men could be beaten to death by police officers in a way no sane person would beat a dog, and no one would go to jail for it?

Or, to bring it closer to home, did I begin to embrace imaginary monsters when I thought of my own mother, her eyes burning with teargas as a girl not much older than I? Maybe that's why my mother loves horror movies, too. Maybe they're infinitely preferable to dwelling on the real-life horrors people inflict upon one another. I realized without being directly told that there was hostility for my family outside of the solid walls of those suburban homes where we lived in racial isolation. And I knew very well, even if the knowledge wasn't conscious, that both of my parents carried war wounds I might one day carry myself. I wouldn't realize the larger cost imposed by their activism until I was an adult, but I have always known what happened to my mother's eyes.

In December 2001, my family had a Christmas and Kwanzaa gathering at my parents' new home in a rural development called The Farms at Quincy, in Gretna, our first Christmas together since Mother's death the previous year. The house has a parklike yard dotted with more than sixty pine trees and moss-hanging oaks, nestled in a community of very nice homes where the occasional dilapidated shack or immense tobacco barn had been left standing as a testament to the area's past. For several days, all of us lived together in our own rooms in the same house for the first time since we were in college, bringing spouses, children, and my stepdaughter with us. As we have since we were children, we celebrated Christmas and then Kwanzaa, reviewing the seven principles and reflecting on which one has meant the most to us in the past year. (My favorites are *Kuumba*, or creativity, and *Imani*, which means faith.) Mom brought old *Cosby* videotapes to recreate the times when we'd all huddle around the television to watch that program religiously, seeing our own family reflected back at us through a more humorous, stress-free looking glass. We also watched videotapes of Christmases past, family celebrations, and a party we recorded when Nelson Mandela was released from prison, enjoying the images of Mother and the rest of us at different ages and with different hairstyles. In one video, I played South African township music on my keyboard while Mom danced and shimmied, laughing about the United Nations parties she'd attended the year she lived in New York in the 1960s, and I could see a peek at the carefree young woman I wish I'd had a chance to know.

After Christmas dinner, our family made a pilgrimage to the grave site at St. Hebron AME Church, where Lydia Johnita is buried. Aunt Priscilla, who had arrived on Christmas Eve to stay at the house with us, joined us as Mom, Dad, and I took Johnita and Lydia, and their husbands, to see the grave of the sister who shares their names.

"Why do you think none of us has followed in Mom and Dad's footsteps as activists?" I asked my sisters during a moment of solitude during that Christmas gathering. I told them about a woman I'd interviewed weeks before, a Miami resident named Mrs. Johnnie Parris, who told me that none of her children had followed her activist path either. Why not? Why weren't any of us more like Jesse Jackson Jr., who is a United States congressman, or Florida Senator Kendrick Meek, whose mother, U.S. Rep. Carrie Meek, sponsored me as a high school messenger when she served in the Florida Senate before going to Congress? Why weren't we like the children of legendary SNCC activist Bob Moses, helping their father with his newest campaign, the Algebra Project, which is teaching black children the skills they need to succeed in math and in life?

Or are we like our parents in ways we don't even know?

Johnita and Lydia are both lawyers like our father, but neither of them practices civil rights law. Johnita's first job was on Wall Street. Now, originally based on her desire to help me navigate through confusing book and film contracts, she has specialized in media law at the McGraw-Hill Companies. She recently taught the subject for a semester at Cornell Law School, where she received her law degree. Still, our parents' imprint is evidenced by Johnita's interests: When she first went to law school, she wanted to do public-interest work. Like me, she went to England as a Rotary International Ambassadorial Scholar, and she wrote her master's dissertation at the University of Sussex on the leadership, structure, and strategies of Afro-Caribbean organizations that emerged in Britain's racial climate. During law school, she interned with the NAACP Legal Defense Fund and the United Nations Center for Human Rights. After law school, she spent a year working pro bono at a nonprofit antiracism organization in Rome, Italy. Today, she is still committed to public-interest work. She has tutored prisoners to improve literacy and advised incarcerated mothers in their desire to fulfill their responsibilities toward their children. At McGraw-Hill, she has become a mentor for disadvantaged youth and has been involved with the Lawyers' Committee for Civil Rights Under Law.

"We need to be everywhere," Johnita says. "We need to be in the corporations, the boardrooms, and the universities, in addition to the civil rights organizations, helping the civil rights cause and making a path for those who come after us."

And Lydia, who had initially proclaimed that she would depart from family tradition by practicing corporate law and getting paid, has found a job she loves, working for the United States Department of Health and Human Services Office of the General Counsel in Dallas as a lawyer who helps monitor the quality of care provided in nursing homes. After watching Mother's decline late in life, including her brief stay in a nursing home while she recovered from surgery, work on behalf of the elderly is more important than ever in Lydia's mind. "I have an overall sense of pride in what I do because I feel that ultimately my job does ensure that the elderly receive better care," says Lydia, who is the only one of us who has the full responsibilities of motherhood, at least for now. "It's important because in this society we tend to take our elders for granted."

As for me, I'm a writer. I write about history and race sporadically, but I am not a Randall Robinson, bell hooks, Derrick Bell, Jill Nelson, or Michael Eric Dyson. Most of the characters in my books are black, which is important to me because I've read too many books where I did not feel represented, but with the exception of *The Black Rose*, my characters' stories are not focused on questions of race and discrimination. I like to think I'm having an impact in my own way, but if I have an agenda, it's unclear even to me. I have no master plan. I only know how to write the stories that ask me to tell them.

When I was awarded a Rotary Foundation Scholarship, I had the pleasure of hearing Nobel prize–winning author Toni Morrison read from her work in 1988. I was a graduate student in English literature at the University of Leeds in England at the time, and I gathered enough nerve to stand up to ask Ms. Morrison a question. "When you write, do you ever write from anger?" I asked her. She thought for a moment, then she said she had never found anger to be a productive place from which to write. Listening, I felt the young writer in me loosening with relief. *No, anger is not a productive creative place for me either,* I thought. Maybe I'd believed I had to write from anger to be effective as a black writer, but I didn't think I would know how to do that. The larger unasked question that lingered in my mind: What *is* a black writer? What does a black writer do?

I think I was looking for permission to be myself, free of constraints imposed either from without or within. I'd always included black characters in my writing, but I'd also spent much of my adolescence writing about white characters because they were "generic," and in college, when I began depicting more black characters, I picked inner-city subjects whose experiences were very different from my own. Writing streetwise dialogue I had never mastered myself, I felt like a fraud. For whom was I writing? What should I be writing about?

Buried deep inside of me, I had a love for horror I'd never given myself permission to explore as a writer. When I interviewed vampire maven Anne Rice as a reporter for the *Miami Herald,* I got another vital blessing to be myself when I asked Ms. Rice how she responded to criticism that she was "wasting her talents" writing about vampires. She nearly laughed. "That used to bother me," she told me, "but my books are taught in universities. Writers don't have to choose between being 'literary' or 'commercial.' They can be both." Hearing those words, I shed my last vestiges of doubt. I'd always wanted to be respected as a writer more than anything, especially given that I grew up feeling a responsibility to achieve because I sensed the eyes of white society studying me, waiting for me to reinforce every negative stereotype. But without ever knowing why I'd asked her the question, Anne Rice gave me hope that perhaps I could write exactly what I pleased and still be respected, even if I didn't write what might be expected of me.

Within weeks of that interview, I started writing my first published novel, *The Between.* In that book, my protagonist, Hilton James, is caught between life and death after a childhood near-drowning incident, so death is chasing him in his dreams. Hilton also happens to be a black community activist who is often away from home, trying to save the world. His wife is a highly regarded judge. His family lives in a mostly white neighborhood and faces hostile neighbors. I specifically chose to write from a black male viewpoint because I did not believe there were enough strong, sympathetic black males in black commercial fiction. Some of the decisions I made in writing *The Between* were purely political, but it is not a political book. Neither is my second novel, *My Soul to Keep,* although I took great pleasure in writing a novel about an immortal African because it gave me opportunities to create a living eyewitness to important moments in black history. At one point, my immortal, Dawit, laments his experience as a slave in the American South: *I remember these events as well as I do eating breakfast this morning. It was a very short time ago. Yet, I have lived to see it buried. And Adele, and all of us, treated as though our pain was imaginary. It was not imaginary. It is with me every day.*

In other words, history is real, and its effects still live and breathe among us.

Then, there is my only historical novel, *The Black Rose,* about pioneering entrepreneur Madam C. J. Walker and her dogged quest for human dignity and success at the beginning of the twentieth century, but I would not have thought to write *The Black Rose* on my own. The Alex Haley estate approached me and asked me to write the novel Haley had been researching for years but died before he could write. Given my childhood fascination with *Roots,* I eagerly agreed. I often joke that I feel sorry for the traditional, history-conscious readers who discovered my writing through *The Black Rose,* then were confronted with the terrifying creature on the cover of *The Living Blood,* the novel that followed. My unpredictability as a writer is due to a kind of split personality, I suppose. I want to teach, and yet I want the freedom to explore my heart's whims.

So at that recent Christmas gathering, as my sisters and I found a quiet moment together in a house bustling with relatives, we pondered why we are not the modern-day equivalent of the radicals Mom and Dad were considered in the 1960s. We are our own people, living our lives with integrity the best we can, but with neither Mom's unswerving courage in the face of opposition nor Dad's single-minded quest for social change.

It was Lydia who first spoke what was uppermost in our minds. "I think it's because we were there, and we saw the cost. We don't want to have to live through what they lived through," Lydia said as she fed her seven-month-old baby, Jordan, trying to keep him clear of the reach of three-year-old Justin, his older brother.

Johnita and I nodded our agreement. If we learned the nobility of struggle from our parents, we had also learned that there is nobility in sacrificing to raise one's family. As Mom always said, charity begins at home.

There was something else, of course—the part that's harder for us to admit: The times are different now. Nowadays, affronts are usually more subtle, and sometimes even careful social observers overlook the full breadth of the challenges still facing the black community. I can only imagine that a lifetime of activism today must feel like boxing a shadow. Here one second. There the next. And it would be so easy for many of us—particularly those of us in the middle class who do not live in black neighborhoods—to close our eyes, pretending the challenges aren't there. But the seeds our parents planted in us will not allow any of us to overlook the work that remains to be done. My sisters and I are not naive. Just because today's world shakers and social pioneers aren't all carrying picket signs doesn't mean the struggle is over, and we know this. We know that there are horrible discrepancies in school resources and test scores between black and white children. And in arrests and jail time. And in the imposition of the death penalty. And income. And AIDS statistics. We know that police in New York shot Amadou Diallo forty-one times, fueled by a raving fear of black men. There's plenty left to do. But there is no single most obvious place to begin, and the avenues for bringing about change are infinite.

So what is our part, and how do we know if we're doing enough?

It's hard to believe we're ever doing enough. As much as my parents have done, I know they both wish they had been able to do more. There is no "Movement" in the early twenty-first century, so all of us have to pick our battles and hope we're making a difference. We have to reach out to each other across neighborhoods and income levels. We can't dismiss segments of black youth because we feel we no longer speak the same language. We have to teach each other and learn from each other. We have to take responsibility for raising our families.

We can't give up.

In 1996, I was able to donate $10,000 to Florida A&M University to inaugurate what I called the John D. Due Jr. and Patricia Stephens Due Freedom Scholarship, intended for students who need extra help to attend college. Mom and Dad were both with me when I presented the check to Florida A&M President Frederick S. Humphries on the Tallahassee campus where I was born. The money came from an unlikely source; I'd taken part in a book called *Naked Came the Manatee,* where thirteen writers with South Florida ties wrote a chapter apiece. Dave Barry, Elmore Leonard, Carl Hiaasen, and Edna Buchanan all took part, among others. In the coming years, I plan to continue to donate money to that fund and help administer the scholarship in my parents' names.

Aside from that, in many ways I am most proud of the seven years I spent as a volunteer with Big Brothers/Big Sisters of Greater Miami, an organization that attracted me because of my burning need to do something that felt concrete. I learned long ago that I'm not cut out for endless meetings or direct confrontations, but I could spend a few hours each Saturday with an inner-city girl, Penny Darien, whose mother had died of an asthma attack when she was five. Penny was seven when I met her, very shy and reserved. She needed me, so over the next years of her childhood, I was big sister. I took her to museums, to movies, to bookstores, to the beach. I took her trick-or-treating and to the park for pony rides. I brought her to my office at the *Miami Herald* and let her sit at my desk, typing on my computer. I tried not to overindulge her with gifts, but I bought her books readily because I wanted her to love reading. To my delight, she once told me that reading helped her escape the noise in her home. "Sometimes when I'm reading," she said, her soft little voice filled with awe, "it feels like I'm in the book!"

Today, Penny is a teenager who is taller than I am. I left Miami in 1998 after I got married and had to move to a small town in Washington State because my husband's daughter lives there with her mother, but Penny and I still call and write to each other, and I visit her when I can. She is in high school now. She wants to go to college. I have no doubt she will live out her childhood without having any children of her own, the fate that befalls so many other ill-prepared girls in her neighborhood. She told me not long ago that she doesn't have too many friends because, in her words, "Friends get you in trouble." Penny isn't looking for trouble. Instead, she spent a recent summer working in a shelter for battered women. I'm so proud of her. She is a lovely, self-directed young woman. I don't know who she will become in future years, but I pray my role in her life will help give her at least a fraction of the chance my parents gave me and my sisters.

Penny has also helped inspire me. Because of the historical component and the unusual situation of working from another writer's notes and research, *The Black Rose* was a very difficult book to write. But during my most frustrating moments, when I wrestled with the question of how best to convey the story of a nearly illiterate black woman who was born poor but whose tireless self-determination built a hair-care fortune and helped uplift thousands of other black women, I told myself that I was writing that book for Penny.

Of course, *Freedom in the Family* is the most special book of all, and not only because it's a family chronicle of one piece of the Struggle. It's special for reasons I didn't predict.

I am no longer the same person I was when I first began researching this book with Mom, when we went to the dude ranch to celebrate the beginning of our journey. To be honest, I began this work with an overwhelming sense of personal obligation, and I was full of self-doubt and trepidation, plowing ahead on faith because I knew how important this book was to Mom. I think I believed I owed it to her and that once it was finished I could proceed with my own life unfettered. That mind-set seems foreign to me now.

Mom and I have learned so much about each other while we have worked on this book, shaking some of our long-held impressions as a mother and child and discovering how to see each other as people—and friends. Each of us has surprised the other along the way, and it's an experience I will always cherish. I have grown up since Mom and I interviewed my ailing godmother Judy Benninger in 1990, when I was barely out of graduate school and full of anxiety about how I would carve my place in the world. In 1990, Mom and I never imagined that we would be sending each other text files thousands of miles over the Internet to finish this book. Or that Mother, who was so healthy and lively then, would be gone.

Over time, I have come to realize that this book is not a gift to my parents, but to me—a spiritual force bringing healing and enlightenment. No matter how many other books I write after this one, it's hard to imagine that any of them could make me feel so complete. Even if I had only written this book for our family's private library and no one else's eyes, I needed to write it. Every family needs to write its history.

I have a stepdaughter, Nicki, and my husband and I hope to have other children soon. I have felt great satisfaction in knowing that they will always be able to read *Freedom in the Family.* This book is also for my grandchildren who will arrive at some hazy point in my rapidly approaching future, when my parents will likely be gone and this book will be all my grandchildren will ever know of John D. Due Jr. and Patricia Stephens Due. Now I understand why Mom has always wanted to keep records of everything, and why my great-grandmother Lydia wrote me those letters about my Indiana ancestors even though her eyesight was poor and her hand was probably cramped with arthritis. They wanted me to know them and their stories, and through them I would better know myself and my stories.

Accidentally, I believe I may have discovered the remedy for my childhood fears of death and loss at last. Remembering is the one and only thing that can make time stand still.

## Thirty-Three

# Patricia Stephens Due

**"For, while the tale of how we suffer,**
**and how we are delighted, and how**
**we may triumph is never new,**
**it always must be heard.**
**There isn't any other tale to tell.**
**It's the only light we've got in all this darkness."**
***—James Baldwin***

I believe in reparations.

I believe black people in this country are owed a great debt for what we have gone through, and for what our children and grandchildren are continuing to go through. I'm still waiting for my forty acres and a mule. I'm waiting for the day when I'll be able to live my life without seeing how much racism is still a part of our society. Lydia has two sons, Tananarive has a stepdaughter, and both Tananarive and Johnita plan to have children of their own, and I am honestly afraid for my grandchildren. I know there have been improvements in this country, but I also see that there is so much more left to do, and there seem to be fewer people willing to do the work. Really, there seem to be so few people who are aware of how much work is left to do, which is even more troubling to me.

I didn't expect my children to have so many battles left to fight. When Johnita was much younger, I remember her agonizing to me one night, in tears because she didn't think she would be able to accomplish the kinds of things John and I have accomplished. I told her she shouldn't feel like she has to accomplish the same things. I never wanted my children to have to undergo the experiences John and I did, but at the same time I want their generation to understand that just because some of us appear to have made it over, that doesn't mean the war is won. Too many people have been left behind. I wanted to be able to see this fight through to the end, but the older I get, the more I realize that those of us who were fighting in the 1960s will not live to see the victory we wanted. I think some activists realized that truth a long time ago, which is why life was so difficult for them to bear. But I haven't given up.

Of course, there have been things along the way I didn't expect. I have some friends I discuss my children with, and sometimes we laugh to ourselves, saying, "Well, we taught them that everybody was the same, but we didn't expect them to believe it." Johnita married a white man from Ireland who works in finance, Mark Willoughby; and Lydia married a white computer programmer she met when she was in law school, Jonathan Greisz. Tananarive's husband, Steve, is black, but his first wife—his daughter Nicki's mother—is white, too. As a result, our family is all colors of the rainbow, and I have other black friends from the Movement who are in a similar situation. That's why we laugh sometimes, but in a good-natured way.

It's just one of those things we never predicted, like I'm sure Mother never predicted I would come home with a white man, John B., and announce in 1960 that we were engaged, or that Priscilla would marry a Dutchman. I have to admit, I had hoped all my daughters would go to college and find black men to marry like I did, but I love my sons-in-law. They are good to my daughters, which is all I ask of them. And I know Johnita, Lydia, and Tananarive well enough to feel confident that they will teach their children who they are. My biggest concern with interracial marriages is when parents do not raise those children with any knowledge of their black heritage, either from ignorance or shame. As far as I'm concerned, those parents are sending those children into the world completely unprepared. From the time they were born, I have given Justin and Jordan, Lydia's sons, children's books with African and African-American folktales. I want to teach them the freedom songs, too, just like I taught my children. I look forward to the day when they will be old enough to read this book, to learn their family history. I want them to have pride in themselves. I want them to know where they have come from.

This country may look different on the surface than it did forty years ago, but I know better. They should be ready.

In all honesty, I never set out to write a book about the Due family. I am a very private person, and there are many people who have known me for years, even my own sister, who have not been privy to some of the incidents I disclosed in this book. I had to think long and hard about exposing myself this way, but in the end I decided I would do whatever it took to tell the stories of the people I knew. In telling our family's story, I believed, I could also shed some light on the stories of other civil rights families. I had to go beyond myself to write something I thought would be beneficial to young people—older readers, too, but especially young people.

As I write this, I am sixty-two years old. I can barely believe it. When I go through my papers and see everything I've been through and everything my family has been through, it's amazing to me. This country really has not made it easy for us to exist here. Now, I feel as if it's flying in front of my eyes, all of the running around trying to right the wrongs in the community and country, being knocked down time and time again—and getting up. Whether we were knocked down physically or emotionally, we were knocked down, and it took its toll.

I have a half dozen different kinds of pills I have to take every single day. Even Mother used to tell me she didn't have to take as many kinds of pills as I do. As I look at all of these bottles of pills, I remember the collective toll all of this has had on me. It really is amazing I have lived to be sixty-two. I think about Stokely Carmichael, who has already died. He was younger than I am! A lot of fallen soldiers died so young. The system is still set up so that blacks do not live as long as whites in this country, and it's no wonder. Sometimes it's enough to knock you down for good. But no one has knocked me down.

I was inducted into the Florida A&M University Gallery of Distinction in 1987 in recognition of my civil rights work, and John and I were named "Living Legends" by the university in 1997, commemorating its 101st birthday. In 1998, FAMU awarded me and John the Dr. Martin Luther King Jr. Leadership Award. "Your alma mater is proud of the courage you displayed as a major force in the civil rights movement," my plaque reads.

Those awards were all very gratifying, especially in light of the problems I had with FAMU's administration as a young person, but I felt most excited when Tananarive established a scholarship at FAMU named for me and John in 1997. I feel it is so important for new generations of young people to learn about the events that have taken place on FAMU's campus, as well as all over this country. Through the years, I have given civil rights presentations to thousands of people at schools, colleges, churches, and civic organizations, sharing our history. Although sometimes it brings back painful memories, I think it is very important to have role-playing exercises with the students, giving them an opportunity to go back to an earlier time. Our youth are an immeasurable resource, and I want to give them as much as I can.

My priorities will continue to be education, health care, and sharing our history with young people. I've always liked the words in the freedom song "We Are Soldiers in the Army": *My mother was a soldier / She had her hands on the gospel plow / One day she got old, she couldn't fight anymore / She said, "I'll stand here and fight anyhow."*

I'm going to stand and fight as long as I can.

In December 2001, I went to another funeral, for Miss Daisy Young, who lived to be seventy-five. Her service was held two days after Christmas at Fountain Chapel AME Church in Tallahassee, where we held some of our CORE meetings in the 1960s. The seats were filled with hundreds of mourners. As John and I walked into the church, the choir was singing the hymn "There's a Sweet, Sweet Spirit," which was very befitting because there have been few spirits as sweet, or as strong, as Miss Daisy O. Young's.

I didn't know if I would be able to make it through Miss Young's funeral. I really didn't. Miss Young died on December 15, 2001, while I was writing this book. She had worked at FAMU until 1991, when she retired as the assistant admissions director after 39 years.[1] She died right before Christmas, which was already such a hard time for me, bringing back memories of the awful shock of Mother's death on Christmas morning the year before. To make matters worse, Tananarive and I had been unable to find Miss Young for some time because she had left Tallahassee, and we finally tracked her down only a couple of weeks before she died. We discovered that she was bedridden and living in Miami with a sister-in-law, Mrs. Theresa Young Brunt. I told Mrs. Brunt that I was about to leave town for a family Christmas and Kwanzaa celebration upstate, but I would drive to visit after the first of the year. I wanted to let Miss Young know I had finally finished writing this book. Every time I saw Miss Young on my visits to Tallahassee over the years, she said to me, "Pat, when are you going to finish that book?" But she died before I had the chance. I tell you, people slip away from us so quickly.

When the choir began singing "Amazing Grace," I squeezed John's hand and tried to pull my emotions away from that service. It had been a very difficult month; not only had we just passed the anniversary of Mother's death, but on December 14 I'd had to put my Great Dane, Samson, to sleep after he had been part of our family for almost nine years. I had also just been to another funeral in Miami right before

Thanksgiving. Anna Price, a dear friend of mine, had lost her mother, and I broke down during that funeral. I didn't want that to happen again, especially once John pointed out that my name was on the program to give civil rights remembrances about Miss Young. Many of the people at the service knew Miss Young from her untiring work in her community, her church, and at AME conferences. The presiding elder, Bishop A. J. Richardson of the XIX Episcopal District, was there, but I wanted to remind everyone how much she had meant to the Movement.

I guess I always want to make sure the stories are told. That gives me strength.

Henry Steele, the son of Rev. C. K. Steele, who went to jail with me in 1960 as a high school student, was also at the service. So was Mr. Edwin M. Thorpe, the registrar at FAMU who had been Miss Young's boss, warning her in the 1960s that her job was in danger.

The room was also full of ghosts, in my mind. I could imagine Rev. Steele there in his bow tie. I could also imagine Richard Haley, my music professor, who had been so close to Miss Young during the jail-in and the theater demonstrations. I guess all of us were there in spirit.

Bishop Richardson set the tone by telling the mourners how FAMU's president, Dr. Gore, called the meeting of his faculty and staff to warn them against activism in the 1960s, telling them they should either stay on the ship or get off the ship—a story I had heard many times. Dr. Gore's hands were shaking so badly during that speech, the bishop said, that his voice could barely be heard over the noise of the trembling microphone.

When it was my turn to speak, John walked with me up to the podium to give me moral support. Forty years earlier, John had proposed to me—the first time, anyway—on the porch of Miss Young's house on Pinellas Street. I wondered again: *Where does the time go?*

"You know, Miss Daisy O. Young might have been very small in stature, but she was a giant," I said, trying to keep my voice steady. "All of us are standing on her shoulders. Without people like Miss Young, Tallahassee's history might have been very different."

So I told them what I knew. About how Miss Young wore many hats, working with the NAACP, CORE, the SCLC, and the Inter-Civic Council, among other organizations. How she assumed the risk so few others in her place were willing to. How dangerous those times were.

"Miss Young told me a story," I said. "She told me how one night in the nineteen sixties she and Mr. Haley were alone in the CORE office on Floral Street when they heard a knock at the door very late. They were *very* concerned. That's just how bad it was in those times. Mr. Haley told her, 'Miss Young, you go in the back. If I don't come out in five minutes, you get out of here.' And when he went to the door, there were two white men who'd brought seven thousand dollars to get the arrested students out of jail."

As I spoke, those mourners sat up straight, their faces glowing, their eyes wide open.

They listened. They heard.

---

After The Gathering civil rights reunion we hosted some years ago, Tananarive told me that, to her, many of the activists sounded like we felt hopeless, which she could not understand. She said we tend to look at how much remains to be done rather than what has already been accomplished. Well, Tananarive is wrong about that. Just because I can see all the work that remains does not mean that I feel hopeless. I am full of hope.

First of all, I am very proud of all three of my daughters, who have grown up to be their own people. They have always tended to judge themselves against me and John, but they are unique individuals with their own special lives. I can honestly say that there are ways in which they have surpassed me. And I am glad. That's what any mother wants for her children.

This book is one thing that gives me hope, as well as other books that tell our history. I am very grateful to Tananarive for helping me document the story at last. I will always be active, but even at the age of sixty-two, there are ways in which I now believe I can discover what I really want to do with my life. That is a wonderful, wonderful feeling.

There are also some other young people who have demonstrated to me through their actions that the Movement is not dead the way so many people seem to think. People of my generation tend to say that the younger generation has a short memory, but that isn't always true. I saw that for myself in January 2000, during a sit-in outside of Florida Governor Jeb Bush's office in Tallahassee. I felt as if I had stepped back in time.

John and I heard that two young Florida legislators, Sen. Kendrick Meek from Miami and Rep. Anthony Hill of Jacksonville, had staged a sit-in at the capitol. I have known Kendrick's mother, a former state senator and U.S. congresswoman named Carrie Meek, for years; Kendrick is a few years younger than Tananarive, and I remember him when he was only a little boy. Now a Florida senator himself, Meek and another lawmaker had refused to leave Lieutenant Governor Frank Brogan's office when Governor Bush refused to meet with them on the question of affirmative action. (The two offices are in the same suite.) Under a plan called the "One Florida Initiative," Governor Bush was pushing to do away with affirmative action in university admissions and the state's hiring and contracts. Florida is only one of several states toppling affirmative action gains. Truly, the clock is turning back. I have been saying that for years.

As soon as I heard about the sit-in, I knew John and I had to be there. We dropped everything and made reservations to fly to Tallahassee from Miami. As usual, before I left, I called Tananarive in Washington to leave a detailed telephone message so she could tell the other girls where we were. Ever since my days in the Movement, I never travel anywhere without leaving word of my whereabouts. On Tananarive's voice mail, I quickly explained what had happened with the two legislators. Tananarive still had the recording of the message nearly two years later, so it was preserved: "They sat all night in the office," I said with both pride and indignation in my voice. "John and I are headed to Tallahassee on a 1:45 P.M. flight. I don't know where we're staying. I'll get back to you all later. We are in a hurry. We're on our way to Tallahassee for you, for Justin, and for all the people who need to be treated with dignity. These people are crazy. And if you watch the news, you'll see Governor Bush said, 'Get their asses out of there.' Well, we're going to take our asses *up* there."

With that, we were on our way. When we arrived, the black cabbie who drove us from the airport was very enthusiastic. "Somebody better stand up and say something," he said.

I could hardly believe the scene waiting for me and John when we arrived at the state capitol. A huge crowd had amassed in a lobby area, made up of local residents, activists, and students from Florida A&M University and local high schools. Some people were carrying picket signs, and protesters sang "We Shall Overcome." A pack of reporters was also there to document it. There were so many people, we could hardly squeeze inside. Instead of being in Tallahassee in the year 2000, I felt as if I was back in Tallahassee in 1960 or 1963. I could feel a powerful, familiar charge in the air.

When we arrived, Sen. Meek and Rep. Hill were conducting a press conference. Another black legislator from Miami, Rep. James Bush, noticed that we had come. "John Due and Mrs. Patricia Due are here!" he said, waving us to the front of the crowd. "Mrs. Due has been to jail fighting for civil rights. Mrs. Due, come say a few words."

I had not planned to make a speech, and I was tired from our sudden trip, but the crowd gave me energy. As I walked forward, people began to clap. I looked at their young, encouraging faces—so many of them looked like children—and I could hardly believe I had been their age when I took part in my first sit-in, when my life changed forever.

"I'm so happy to be here," I said, "because I'm proud to see Senator Meek and Representative Hill carry on the second generation. I spent forty-nine days in jail in 1960 for sitting-in at a Woolworth lunch counter. You see I'm wearing these dark glasses. Well, it's because a police officer hit me in the face with tear gas while I was taking part in a peaceful march from FAMU's campus. As I look at you all today, I am so proud, and at the same time I can hardly believe we're still here trying to fight for the same things. We're still trying to fight for dignity as black people."

Soon afterward, I was invited by U.S. Rep. Carrie Meek, who was also in Tallahassee, to speak again at a meeting in a nearby upstairs conference room, which was also packed. Again, I told my story. I didn't notice it at the time, but I was told later that Sen. Kendrick Meek was visibly emotionally affected and that Rep. Tony Hill was in tears as they heard me speak. I was nearly in tears myself, but not from sadness. Not from hopelessness. As I stood in that hot, crowded room of people of all ages who had faced arrest and discomfort for the sake of their beliefs and I told them about the history of our collective struggle, I felt absolutely free.

That feeling of liberation was multiplied many times over only two months later, on March 7, 2000, when Tallahassee was the site of the largest protest march in the state's history.

The march was such a success because of the efforts of people throughout the state. John did his part, too. Weeks after the sit-in, John helped build a coalition between Monica Russo, president of the Service Employees International Union 1199 of Florida, and Miami-Dade NAACP chairman Leroy Thompson to sponsor a "Jobs with Justice" Task Force, supporting low-income workers to achieve a living wage and exercise their right to organize. Sen. Meek and Rep. Hill then asked Jobs with Justice to help them mobilize a statewide march on Tallahassee, in conjunction with the Florida State Conference of NAACP branches. John asked Dorothy Thompson of the American Federation of State,

County, and Municipal Employees (AFSCME) to organize the twenty-three buses of marchers from Miami, and other leaders statewide worked to bring people to the state capital.

John and I drove to Tallahassee, spending the night in Tallahassee at Mary Lee Blount's house with her and her mother, Mrs. Dorothy Jones, who had a cross burned in her yard in the 1960s after she gave me shelter in Quincy. Tuesday morning, John and I set out for a restaurant to meet our host for the march, Jeanette D. Wynn, the Florida president of AFSCME, AFL-CIO. Then, we joined the masses assembling on Apalachee Parkway for the uphill march to the state capitol building.

At any march, I'd learned from experience that you never know until the day of the event exactly how many people will turn out, but it was obvious to me right away that this march would be one to remember. The people came, and they kept coming. Some people had driven all night to get to Tallahassee by the time the march began. Buses came from Atlanta and all over the state. Lined up, the buses stretched for a mile. The streets were crowded with men, women, and families, and many people were wearing "March on Florida" T-shirts from vendors or carrying picket signs that read JEB CROW, or ONE FLORIDA—ONE TERM, or ONE FLORIDA CHEATS MY GRANDKIDS.[2] Spurred by a sit-in started by only two young state legislators, protesters came in unprecedented thousands to march on the state capitol.

As is usually the case with large-scale demonstrations, there were conflicting reports on how many people attended the march; the NAACP estimated that there were 50,000 people, while the city's estimate ranged between 9,000 and 11,000. But official numbers didn't matter to me. All I know is that there were marchers everywhere I looked, in every direction. I felt as if I had been completely swallowed inside a sea of people in a way I had not been since the March on Washington in 1963. "This is like the Million Man March," John said, excited. All of us had our different reasons for wanting to be there—and different histories that had brought us to that day—but we were all marching together.

John and I met up with Mrs. Vivian Kelly, who walked the entire march, despite being eighty years old. It was March, but it was warm, so I was worried about Mrs. Kelly. But she is still a real soldier, just like she was when she did voter registration in Quincy in the 1960s and had to outrun a farmer's dogs. "I'm all right, Pat," Mrs. Kelly kept saying when I asked how she was doing under the Tallahassee sun.

Rev. Jesse Jackson was there, as were SCLC president Martin Luther

King III, national NAACP president Kweisi Mfume, activist Dick Gregory, U.S. congressmen, and many others. I also saw James Orange, another of the longtime SCLC activists, who had helped me carry Lydia during Florida's Poor People's March, when she took her first steps. I know there were many people in that crowd I had probably been arrested with in the 1960s, but whom I had never met.

That day, as we marched up Apalachee Parkway, I was literally surrounded by history. Jesse Jackson led his familiar chant: "I am somebody!" And just as I had thought as I basked in the fellowship of activists during the March on Washington, as John and I marched in Tallahassee that day, I thought to myself, "A job well done!"

"This is not about the swift," Sen. Kendrick Meek said in his speech. "It's about those willing to endure, to hold on for their children and their unborn children."[3]

He was right. When we risked our lives in the 1960s to register blacks to vote, we did it because we believed—and I still believe—that voting can make a difference. Nothing happens overnight, but I believe leadership can emerge to create a brighter tomorrow for everyone. I have seen it happen time and again.

Rep. Anthony Hill and Sen. Kendrick Meek, for instance, did not stop trying to get their message heard with their sit-in or the march. They crossed back and forth across the entire state of Florida in eight months to help register more than 30,000 new voters, encouraging each person to bring five people with them to the polls. It was the most successful voter registration drive in state history.[4]

The whole world saw the result of their efforts.

In November 2000, as a result of Florida's newly registered voters, the presidential election between Al Gore and George W. Bush was so close in Florida that a winner could not be determined right away. In a history-making moment, the world had to wait while lawyers argued about how to count the ballots in Florida. Although the United States Supreme Court stopped the recounts, our message had been heard loud and clear.

*We are somebody.*

We did not win our battle against One Florida. Governor Bush dismantled most aspects of affirmative action in Florida soon after the sit-in and the historic march on Tallahassee in 2000, but none of us had been there in vain. In our willingness to stand up for what we honestly believed was right, and to demand our right to be heard, we had won something no one could take from us: We gave each other the strength to fight another day.

Yes, the fight will go on.

To me, that's what history is all about. Once you know what others have done, it helps you understand what you can do.

I originally wanted to call this book *Ordinary People, Extraordinary Things,* because that is the key. Experience has taught me a great secret I have spent most of my life trying to share with my children and anyone who will listen: History happens one person at a time.

# Acknowledgments

## PATRICIA STEPHENS DUE

*I would like to thank the people who opened up their hearts and shared their memories, pain, and hope for the future with us to make certain our history is not forgotten. A special thank-you to the families of all the deceased foot soldiers whose everlasting spirits will always protect and inspire us. I have always said that my parents, Mother and Daddy Marion, are responsible for the person I am, and for this I am forever indebted to them.*

*I thank John, my husband, for his endless support as I struggled over the years to start and to finish this book. He never once complained as I took over room after room in our home, spreading my papers and books everywhere. He smiled and said that this was my job, a job I must do, and that I had his unwavering support.*

*To my sister, Priscilla, who was at my side in the 1960s during some of the most traumatic events either of us has experienced. I know how difficult it was to relive that part of our history that she has tried so hard to forget. My special thanks to her for going back in spite of her pain so that these events would be known.*

*The most heartfelt thanks and love to my oldest daughter, Tananarive, who put her career on hold and helped turn my dream into reality. We pushed and helped each other to face and articulate some painful and overwhelming memories so that they no longer were obstacles to our writing this book, but springboards from which my words—and the words of the other foot soldiers—could fly, and our stories could be told. I would like to thank my dear daughters Johnita and Lydia, who early on told their classmates and teachers and inspired me to tell the full history, as only I could know it, and to include the many people who have contributed to it. Special thanks to Johnita for her relentless support in making certain that this history would be told, and for her many suggestions, ideas, and editorial comments over the years. Thanks to Lydia for providing much-needed audiovisual equipment. Without the love and support of all of you, this book would not have been possible. And last but not least, to my Great Dane, Samson, who traveled across the state with me for almost nine years as I documented these stories.*

*My thanks to those writers upon whose shoulders I stood as I traveled this long and difficult journey. Glenda Rabby, thank you for* The Pain and the Promise; *August Meier and Elliot Rudwick for* CORE: A Study in the Civil Rights Movement 1942–1968; *Charles U. Smith, for* The Civil Rights Movement in Florida and in the United States; *James Max Fendrich, for*

Ideal Citizens: The Legacy of the Civil Rights Movement; *Leedell W. Neyland, for* Florida Agricultural and Mechanical University: A Centennial History, 1887–1987. *I also thank Keith Miles, Eddie Jackson, and Dr. Dhyana Ziegler (from the FAMU School of Journalism) for producing the videotape* Southern Tales, *and for their assistance in preserving portions of the history. Thanks to Jane Carnegie Tolliver, with Flair Enterprise, for videotaping The Gathering. Thanks to Janell Walden Agyeman, for having so much faith in us. And to Heidi Sullivan and E. F. Ambassadors, for providing a video camera to help me document this book. Thanks also to the many newspaper reporters over the years who have supported our efforts and helped us preserve these events, special thanks to Garth Reeves of* The Miami Times; *and Dave Lawrence and Margaria Fichtner of* The Miami Herald. *To Anita Diggs, for recognizing that this story needed to be told. And to John Hawkins of John Hawkins & Associates for his role in bringing this book to life.*

*Thanks to the Florida State Archives, which has a collection of photographs from the civil rights movement; and to the Florida State University and Leon County libraries, which have extensive collections of newspaper clippings from the era. Thanks to Professor James N. Eaton and Dr. Muriel Dawson, from the Black Archives Research Center and Museum at Florida A&M University, for making their collection available to me. And to former FAMU student Duane Filey, who wrote an excellent paper about the history of activism at his university. Special thanks to Mrs. Vivan Kelly, Mrs. Dorothy C. Jones, and Mary Lee Blount, for always having their hearts and homes open to me. Special thanks to Bob Thompson, for being such a good neighbor and an important part of our extended family. Special thanks to my good friend Dan Harmeling, for being an example of the ideals of fairness and compassion he has long fought for. And to the late Roberta Hunter, Nancy Adams, and Judy Benninger Brown, three good friends who always believed I could do anything and whom I miss.*

*I also thank this community for being part of our extended family.*

*This book honors those unsung heroes and heroines who gave so much to make this country live up to its promise of equality and justice for all of us. There were so many people I worked with that it would be impossible to name everyone, but all of you are part of this story, and each of you has a story of your own to tell.*

# Acknowledgments

## TANANARIVE DUE

*First, to the heroes and heroines of the civil rights movement, for dreaming a better world.*

*To John Hawkins, agent extraordinaire, for envisioning the mother–daughter telling of this story that enabled us to find a home for our book. To E. Lynn Harris, who caught John's ear by telling him about our civil rights project. To Janell Walden Agyeman, who gave us invaluable support and her deep belief in this project. To Anita Diggs, our first editor at One World/Ballantine, for giving us a wonderful home and making the book better than it was when she first read it. And to Betsy Mitchell, editor-in-chief at Ballantine/Del Rey Books, for shepherding us through to the end.*

*Many thanks to Boston-based transcriber Johanna Kovitz, who is prompt and professional. Thanks to the Martin Luther King Jr. Papers Project at Stanford University, for its assistance transcribing Henry Steele's interview. Thanks to Yolanda Everette-Brunelle for her transcription assistance. And thanks to the members of the SNCC online mailing list, at www.honors.olemiss.edu/mailman/listinfo/sncc, for their ongoing commitment to human dignity. And many thanks to Jeanne Killebrew, founder of the Lyles Station Historic Preservation Association.*

*In remembering my childhood, names occurred to me that are much worthy of mention, including many of my teachers: Ms. Harris, Ms. Abramowitz, Ms. Willig, Mr. Hallberg, and Ms. Jack from elementary and junior high school, and Mitchell Kaplan, Susan Estaver, Lynn Shenkman, Tom McClary, and Ann Hayward from Miami Southridge High School, as well as guidance counselor Barbara A. Anders. Thanks to Heath Meriwether and Joe Oglesby, who hired me at the Miami Herald when I was fifteen. And thanks to the late Susan Burnside, formerly of the Herald, for her guidance as my editor both while I was still in high school and again when I came to work full-time. Also, many thanks to my childhood friends: Chip Davis, Michelle Ricciardi, Craig Bell, Ivan Yaeger, Nancy McElrath, Juan Strickland, Lisa Stockham, and Andy Enriquez. Thanks to my college friends: Susan "Charlie" Jordan, Kathryn Larrabee, Rob Vamosi, Rob Sidney, Craig Shemin, Mary Dickman, Donna Washington, D. J. Wells, and Albert Mensah. And thanks to Larry Hildes and Roger Gorham, for their example in commitment. I also mustn't forget Nadine, Sharmila, Nigel, Berhanu, and Kofi. Your friendship was invaluable.*

*Thanks to the community members who enriched my life beyond measure while I was young: Thelma Gibson and the Theodore R. Gibson Foundation; Nancy Dawkins of the Theodore R. Gibson Oratorical Contest; Cornelia "Corky" Dozier of the Coconut Grove Children's Theater; former state Rep. Gwendolyn Cherry; former state Sen. Carrie Meek; Dr. William Perry, former president of the Greater Miami Branch of the NAACP; Doris Hart, Miami-Dade's county-wide coordinator for the NAACP's ACT-SO program; and Vernon Jarrett, who breathed national ACT-SO to life. Thanks also to perennial Miami-Dade County ACT-SO volunteers Lee Harris and Pat Daniels. And to the late Rotarian Jim Lee.*

*Thanks to Big Brothers/Big Sisters of Greater Miami, and especially to Penny Darien, for allowing me to share her childhood with her.*

*Thanks to my sisters, Johnita and Lydia, for their constant support.*

*Thanks to my wonderful husband, Steven Barnes, and my stepdaughter, Nicki.*

*But mostly, thanks to my parents, for more than I can say.*

# Notes

## Three: Patricia Stephens Due

1. Lorraine Nelson Spritzer and Jean B. Bermark, *Grace Towns Hamilton.* Athens: University of Georgia Press, 1997, pp. 70, 161.
2. Interview with Walter Stephens, November 29, 2001.
3. Dr. Gilbert L. Porter and Dr. Leedell W. Neyland, *History of the Florida State Teachers Association.* Washington, DC: National Education Association, 1977, pp. 173–88. Based on the study by Dr. Everett Abney, "A Survey of Black Public School Principals Employed in Florida During the 1964–65 School Term."

## Four: Tananarive Due

1. Marvin Dunn, *Black Miami in the Twentieth Century.* Gainesville: University Press of Florida, 1997, pp. 221–22.

## Five: Patricia Stephens Due

1. Interview with Dr. John O. Brown and Marie Brown, August 20, 2001.
2. Charles U. Smith, ed., *The Civil Rights Movement in Florida and in the United States.* (Chapter Two, "The Tallahassee Bus Boycott in Historical Perspective: Changes and Trends," by Leedell W. Neyland.) Tallahassee: Father and Son Publishing, Inc., 1989, p. 42.
3. "Four Youths Get Life Terms in Rape Case," *St. Petersburg Times,* June 23, 1959.
4. Stephen Birmingham, *Certain People: America's Black Elite.* Little Brown & Co., 1977, pp. 184–85; and Lorraine Nelson Spritzer and Jean B. Bergmark, *Grace Towns Hamilton and the Politics of Southern Change,* Athens: University of Georgia Press, 1997, p. 57.
5. Glenda Rabby, *The Pain and the Promise: The Struggle for Civil Rights in Tallahassee, Florida.* Athens: University of Georgia Press, 1999, p. 85.
6. Interview with Daisy Young, January 26, 1993.
7. *The Civil Rights Movement in Florida and the United States,* p. 31.
8. James Max Fendrich, *Ideal Citizens: The Legacy of the Civil Rights Movement.* Albany: State University of New York Press, 1993, p. 10.
9. Miles Wolff, *Lunch at the 5&10.* Elephant Paperbacks, 1990, pp. 11–12.
10. *The Pain and the Promise,* p. 88.
11. James Peck, *Freedom Ride* (Chapter 6: "Tallahassee: Through Jail to Freedom," by Patricia Stephens). New York: Simon & Schuster, 1962, pp. 73–75.
12. Interview with Mary Ola Gaines, June 23, 1990.
13. *Freedom Ride* (Chapter 6: "Tallahassee: Through Jail to Freedom," by Patricia Stephens), p. 76.
14. *The Pain and the Promise,* p. 92.
15. Emanuel Perlmutter, "Sit-ins Backed by Rallies Here," *New York Times,* March 6, 1960.
16. *The Pain and the Promise,* p. 93.
17. *The Pain and the Promise,* p. 95.

18. Virginia Delavan, "Editor and Friends Land in Jail for Talking to Negroes," *Florida Flambeau* (Florida State University), March 15, 1960.

## SIX: TANANARIVE DUE

1. Mark Silva and Karen Branch, "State Approves $500,000 for Pitts and Lee," *Miami Herald*, May 23, 1998.
2. Edna Buchanan, *The Corpse Had a Familiar Face.* New York: Charter Books, 1989, pp. 300–302.
3. Donna Gehrke, "Ex-Chief of Schools Jones Dies," *Miami Herald*, December 1, 1993.

## SEVEN: PATRICIA STEPHENS DUE

1. *The Pain and the Promise*, p. 104.
2. Mary Ola Gaines, June 23, 1990.
3. *The Pain and the Promise*, p. 105.
4. Jailhouse notes from Barbara Broxton, March 21, 1960, from the archives of Patricia Stephens Due.
5. Interview with Clifton Lewis, August 7, 1996.
6. Jailhouse notes from Barbara Broxton, March 21, 1960, from the archives of Patricia Stephens Due.
7. *The Pain and the Promise*, p. 3.
8. *The Pain and the Promise*, p. 106.
9. *The Pain and the Promise*, p. 107.
10. *The Pain and the Promise*, p. 110.
11. Interview with Daisy Young, January 26, 1993.
12. "Vandals Attack Freedom Fighters' Property," *Pittsburgh Courier*, April 9, 1960.

## EIGHT: TANANARIVE DUE

1. Patrice Gaines, *Laughing in the Dark: From Colored Girl to Woman of Color—A Journey from Prison to Power.* New York: Anchor Books, 1995, p. 210; and Edna Buchanan, *The Corpse Had a Familiar Face.* New York: Charter Books, 1989, p. 284–90.
2. *The Corpse Had a Familiar Face*, pp. 284–93.
3. *Laughing in the Dark*, p. 209–210.
4. Edna Buchanan, "Ex-Officer Who Testified, Charles Veverka, 'Numb' at Verdict," *Miami Herald*, May 18, 1980, page 3-A.
5. Gene Miller and Joe Oglesby, "Jury Out in Less than 3 Hours," *Miami Herald*, May 18, 1980, page 1A.
6. Fred Grimm and Ellen Bartlett, "McDuffie Decision Brings Dismay, Disbelief, Anger," *Miami Herald*, May 18, 1980.
7. Gene Miller and Joe Oglesby, "Jury Out in Less than 3 Hours," *Miami Herald*, May 18, 1980, page 1A.
8. Kwame Anthony Appiah and Henry Louis Gates Jr., editors, *Encyclopedia Africana.* New York: Basic Civitas Books, 1999, p. 1,277.

## NINE: PATRICIA STEPHENS DUE

1. *The Pain and the Promise*, p. 117.
2. *Jet* magazine, March 19, 1960, p. 20.
3. *Pittsburgh Courier*, May 14, 1960.

4 David Halberstam, *The Children*. New York: Random House, 1998, pp. 215–19.
5. *Time*, "Problems of Integration," May 30, 1960.
6. *The Pain and the Promise*, p. 119.
7. *Washington Post*, "Girls Jailed in Sit-Down Talk Here on Campaign," June 1, 1960.
8. Open letter from Eleanor Roosevelt to CORE supporters, May 31, 1960.
9. Press release from the personal files of Patricia Stephens Due, June 29, 1960.
10. Jim Reed, *Pittsburgh Courier*, April 23, 1960.
11. Gordon R. Carey, *CORE-lator* newsletter, "An Intensive Three Weeks," September 1960.
12. *Ibid.*
13. Interview with Priscilla Stephens Kruize, July 16, 1996.
14. Interview with Walter Stephens, November 29, 2001.
15. Leedell W. Neyland, *Florida Agricultural and Mechanical University: A Centennial History, 1887–1987*. Tallahassee: The Florida A&M University Foundation, Inc., 1987, p. 424.
16. CORE "Sit-Down Newsletter," Number 5, June 7, 1960.
17. August Meier and Elliott Rudwick, *CORE: A Study in the Civil Rights Movement*. Urbana: University of Illinois Press, 1975, p. 153.
18. Interview with Daisy Young, January 26, 1993.
19. *The Pain and the Promise*, p. 121.
20. Press release from the personal files of Patricia Stephens Due, June 1, 1960.
21. *CORE: A Study in the Civil Rights Movement*, p. 112.
22. Lorraine Calhoun, *Florida Information Exchange* newsletter, December 1960.

## TEN: TANANARIVE DUE

1. Interview with Susan "Charlie" Jordan, July 19, 2001.
2. Interview with Harry J. Lennix, August 30, 2001.
3. R. Bruce Dold, *Chicago Tribune*, "95 Students Arrested at Apartheid Sit-In," May 10, 1985.
4. Kathryn Larrabee, *An Everyday Savior*. New York: Four Walls/Eight Windows, 2002.

## ELEVEN: PATRICIA STEPHENS DUE

1. *The Pain and the Promise*, p. 62.
2. David J. Garrow, *Bearing the Cross*. New York: Vintage Books, 1988, p. 96.
3. *The Pain and the Promise*, pp. 122–24.
4. "Court Rejects Appeal by 'Sit-In' Students," UPI/*St. Augustine Record*, March 6, 1961.

## THIRTEEN: PATRICIA STEPHENS DUE

1. Interview with Ben Cowins, April 3, 1997.
2. *The Pain and the Promise*, p. 130.
3. Interview with Ben Cowins, April 3, 1997.
4. *The Pain and the Promise*, pp. 131–32.
5. "The Core of the Matter," Tallahassee CORE newsletter, May 25, 1961.
6. *CORE: A Study in the Civil Rights Movement*, pp. 135–40.

7. *Ft. Lauderdale News,* "10 'Riders' Fined in Tallahassee," June 23, 1961.
8. *The Pain and the Promise,* pp. 138–39.
9. *The Pain and the Promise,* p. 140.
10. Tallahassee CORE affidavit from the personal files of Patricia Stephens Due.
11. *The Pain and the Promise,* p. 141.
12. Interview with Rev. Henry Steele, July 22, 1996.
13. *The Pain and the Promise,* p. 50.
14. Jan Pudlow, "From Crack's Grasp to God's Glory," *Tallahassee Democrat,* p. 1D. 1998.
15. *The Pain and the Promise,* p. 142.
16. Information on the Baha'i faith from www.bahai.org.

## FOURTEEN: TANANARIVE DUE

1. Letter from John Due to Mrs. Lydia Graham, postmarked June 19, 1956.
2. FBI report cover sheet, Jacksonville, Florida, November 14, 1968.

## FIFTEEN: PATRICIA STEPHENS DUE

1. "Tallahassee Desegregates Lunch Counters," *Miami Times,* January 26, 1963.
2. *The Pain and the Promise,* pp. 144–45.
3. "Tension in Tallahassee," *Tallahassee Democrat,* May 30, 1963.
4. "Hearing Set on Picketing of 2 Theaters," *Tallahassee Democrat,* May 30, 1963.
5. *The Pain and the Promise,* p. 146.
6. *The Pain and the Promise,* p. 147.
7. "Pushing On for Civil Rights," *Miami Herald,* June 2, 1963.
8. Rick Tuttle, "Negroes Free, Picketing OK in Tallahassee," *Miami Herald,* June 1, 1963.
9. "Court Upholds Right of Group to Protest, Picket Theatres in Tallahassee Peacefully," *Florida Times-Union* (Jacksonville), June 1, 1963.
10. "Arrested at Negro Pool," [newspaper unknown], May 31, 1963.
11. Interview with Priscilla Stephens Kruize, July 16, 1996.
12. *The Pain and the Promise,* p. 148.
13. *The Pain and the Promise,* p. 185.
14. Taylor Branch, *Parting the Waters: America in the King Years, 1954–63.* New York: Simon & Schuster, 1988, p. 764.
15. Clayborne Carson, David J. Garrow, Vincent Harding, Darlene Clark Hine, editors, *Eyes on the Prize: America's Civil Rights Years, A Reader and Guide.* New York: Penguin Books, 1991, p. 160.
16. Mrs. Medgar Evers, *For Us, The Living.* Garden City, NY: Doubleday & Co., 1967, p. 302.
17. Interview with Zev Aelony, May 4, 2001.
18. Interview with Bettie Wright, December 3, 2001.
19. Don Pride, "Ocala Judge Sentences Negro Leader to Jail," *St. Petersburg Times,* January 8, 1964.
20. *Parting the Waters,* pp. 865–66.
21. Today, Zev lives in Minneapolis, where he and his wife run a small business representing manufacturers of electronic security equipment. They are parents to four adult sons, and Zev has told his children about his civil rights involvement.
22. Blanche Calloway, "Freedom Train Ride from Miami Was Most Memorable Experience," *Miami Times,* September 7, 1963.

23. *Parting the Waters*, pp. 890–91.
24. Interview with Rubin Kenon, April 18, 1997.
25. Interview with Cherrye Bess, October 24, 1996.

## SEVENTEEN: PATRICIA STEPHENS DUE

1. Interview with Doris Rutledge Hart, "The Gathering," August 23, 1997.
2. "100 More Jailed; Total Now 348," *Tallahassee Democrat*, Sept. 15, 1963.
3. Douglas Star, "156 Students Fined for Race Wrangle: Tallahassee Judge Calls It Contempt," *Bradenton Herald*, October 4, 1963.
4. *The Pain and the Promise*, pp. 231–35.
5. Interview with Judy Benninger Brown, May 26, 1990.
6. Interview with Dan Harmeling, April 17, 1997.
7. Ibid.
8. Interview with Ernestine Benninger, April 24, 1997.
9. *The Pain and the Promise*, p. 158.
10. William Bradford Huie, *Ruby McCollum: Woman in the Suwannee Jail*. New York: E.P. Dutton & Co. [This reference summarizes large portions of the book's text.]
11. " 'Time Wasted' Gore Says," *Tallahassee Democrat*, Sept. 17, 1963.
12. Letter from Rutledge Pearson to Dr. George W. Gore, October 24, 1963.
13. Interview with James Robinson, September 28, 2001.
14. John Due, "Klan Politics Prevent the Killing of a Prominent Civil Rights Leader," *Miami Times*, p. 8B. September 11, 1997.
15. Interview with Dr. Robert Hayling, May 13, 1998.
16. *Bearing the Cross*, pp. 326–27.
17. Fred W. Friendly and Walter Cronkite, *I Can Hear It Now: The Sixties*, New York: Sony Music Entertainment, 1970.

## NINETEEN: PATRICIA STEPHENS DUE

1. Interview with Dorothy C. Jones, July 24, 1989.
2. Interview with Mary Lee (Jones) Blount, January 25, 1993.
3. *The Pain and the Promise*, pp. 165–66.
4. CORE press release, "News Flash!!!" from the archives of Patricia Stephens Due, April 1964.
5. *The Pain and the Promise*, p. 165.
6. Judy Benninger letter to Senator Hubert Humphrey, April 26, 1964.
7. "Quincy Police Arrest Coed," *Florida Flambeau*, January 28, 1964.
8. *The Pain and the Promise*, p. 177.
9. Joe Rice, "Registration in Gadsden County Booming—One Way or the Other," *St. Petersburg Times*, February 1, 1964.
10. "Negroes Meet Subtle Antipathy in Quincy, Fla., Voter Campaign," *New York Times*, May 14, 1964.
11. Judy Benninger letter to Carey McWilliams, editor of *The Nation*, May 14, 1964.
12. Robert Sherrill, "CORE's dilemma: Where to from Here?" *Miami Herald*, February 9, 1964.
13. "NEWS FLASH!!!" CORE publication, April 1964, from the archives of Patricia Stephens Due.
14. Interview with Doris Rutledge Hart, April 29, 1997.

15. Summary written by John Due, "Leon County Harassment, Intimidation and Defamation of Character," April 28, 1964.
16. Robert S. Boyd, "Planned Stall-In Runs Out of Gas," *Miami Herald*, April 23, 1964.
17. Fred Powledge, [headline unknown], *New York Times*, April 23, 1964.
18. Robert S. Boyd, "Planned Stall-In Runs Out of Gas," *Miami Herald*, April 23, 1964.
19. Letter from Marion M. Hamilton, March 7, 1964.

## TWENTY-ONE: PATRICIA STEPHENS DUE

1. "Negroes Meet Subtle Apathy in Quincy, Fla., Voter Campaign," *New York Times*, May 18, 1964.
2. *CORE: A Study in the Civil Rights Movement*, p. 277.
3. Seth Cagin and Phillip Dray, *We Are Not Afraid*. New York: MacMillan Publishing Co., 1988, p. 36.
4. Interview with Marvin Rich, October 4, 2001.
5. *Bearing the Cross*, p. 317.
6. *Bearing the Cross*, p. 329.
7. *Bearing the Cross*, p. 325.
8. Taylor Branch, *Pillar of Fire: America in the King Years, 1963–65*. New York: Simon & Schuster, pp. 380–82.
9. Interview with Vivian Kelly, October 22, 1996.
10. Judy Benninger Brown essay, dated Winter 1964.
11. Robert Sherill, "Quincy Hits Back at Charges of Voter Bias," *Miami Herald*, July 19, 1964.
12. *The Pain and the Promise*, pp. 176–77.
13. "350 Negroes Sign to Vote in Gadsden County," *St. Petersburg Times*, July 28, 1964; CORE press release, July 30, 1964; and "Gadsden County Free Press" newsletter, August 1, 1964.

## TWENTY-TWO: TANANARIVE DUE

1. Interview with Witt Campbell and James Palmer, July 24, 1989. Also, interview with Vivian Kelly, January 1, 2002.

## TWENTY-THREE: PATRICIA STEPHENS DUE

1. "Seven Registration Workers Arrested," Gadsden County Citizenship Project newsletter, August 9, 1964.
2. *The Pain and the Promise*, p. 187.
3. "Terror in Havana," *Florida Free Press*, December 11, 1964.
4. *The Pain and the Promise*, p. 178.
5. "Negro Votes Record in Gadsden County," *St. Petersburg Times*, Nov. 4, 1964.
6. "Woman, 109, Votes First Time; She Hopes It Was for Johnson," UPI, Nov. 4, 1964.
7. *The Pain and the Promise*, p. 178.
8. *Florida Free Press*, published by North Florida Citizen Education Project, November 6, 1964.

## TWENTY-FOUR: TANANARIVE DUE

1. Curtis Morgan, "They Shared a Dream," *Miami Herald*, April 4, 1998, p. 1A.
2. Diana Jean Schemo, "U.S. Schools Turn More Segregated, a Study Finds," *New York Times*, July 20, 2001.

## TWENTY-FIVE: PATRICIA STEPHENS DUE

1. Interview with Dan Harmeling, April 17, 1997.
2. Letter from Judy Benninger Brown to Patricia Stephens Due, February 9, 1970.
3. Letter from Marvin Rich to John and Patricia Due, March 10, 1967. [Marvin and Evie Rich would lose their own adult son, Gordon, in 2000.]

## TWENTY-SIX: TANANARIVE DUE

1. Interview with George Calvin Bess, October 24, 1996.
2. Interview with Cherrye Bess, October 24, 1996.
3. Interview with Kwame Turé, November 5, 1996.

## TWENTY-SEVEN: PATRICIA STEPHENS DUE

1. Memo from Patricia Stephens Due to NAACP Legal Defense and Educational Fund, Inc., "Report on Educational Situation in Leon County, Florida. April 15–May 4, 1967."
2. *CORE: A Study in the Civil Rights Movement*, pp. 406–10.
3. Ibid., p. 424.
4. *Bearing the Cross*, pp. 548–50.
5. *Bearing the Cross*, p. 575.
6. Charles Johnson and Bob Adelman, *King: The Photobiography of Martin Luther King, Jr.* New York: Viking Studio, 2000, p. 268.
7. *Bearing the Cross*, p. 622.
8. *Bearing the Cross*, pp. 604–608.
9. Song lyrics from personal archives of Patricia Stephens Due, author unknown.

## TWENTY-EIGHT: TANANARIVE DUE

1. "Just Not Fair," *Miami Herald*, October 29, 1997, page 18A.

## TWENTY-NINE: PATRICIA STEPHENS DUE

1. From FBI memo to the Director's office from SAC, Tampa, October 30, 1968.
2. From FBI reports, reported December 23, 1970.
3. Ralph David Abernathy, *And the Walls Came Tumbling Down.* New York: Harper & Row Publishers, pp. 500–39.
4. Ibid., p. 498.

## THIRTY: TANANARIVE DUE

1. *CORE*, p. 114, 166.

## THIRTY-ONE: PATRICIA STEPHENS DUE

1. E. A. Torriero, "Take Moton Off School Hit List, Supporters Plead," *Miami Herald*, April 20, 1978.
2. Susan Murphy, "Moton PTA Upset Over Staffing Cuts," *South Dade News Leader*, October 24, 1977, page 1A.
3. Ibid.
4. E. L. Torriero and Christopher Cubbison, "War of Words: Perrine School Debate Divides Moton Parents," *Miami Herald*, July 9, 1978, page 1D.

## THIRTY-THREE: PATRICIA STEPHENS DUE

1. Melanie Yeager, "Local Civil Rights Activist Dies," *Tallahassee Democrat*, December 21, 2001, page 1B.
2. Bill Cottrell and Juana Jordan, "Thousands Jam Capitol," *Tallahassee Democrat*, March 8, 2000. Also, Rev. Abraham Thomas, *Tallahassee: March 7, 2000*, Miami: Historical Preservation Co. Inc., 2000, cover photograph.
3. Bob Shaw and Melanie Yeager, "Protest Leaves Marks, but No Trash," *Tallahassee Democrat*, March 8, 2000.
4. Andrea Robinson, "Meek Emerges as His Own Man," *Miami Herald*, February 25, 2001, p. 1B.

# Index